Foundations of Argumentative Text Processing

Foundations of Argumentative Text Processing

Edited by
Jerry Andriessen and
Pierre Coirier

AMSTERDAM UNIVERSITY PRESS

Studies in Writing

General editors: Gert Rijlaarsdam and Eric Espéret

Effective Teaching and Learning of Writing
Current Trends in Research
Edited by Gert Rijlaarsdam, Huub van den Bergh and Michel Couzijn

Theories, Models and Methodology in Writing Research
Edited by Gert Rijlaarsdam, Huub van den Bergh and Michel Couzijn

Knowing What to Write
Conceptual Processes in Text Production
Edited by Mark Torrance and David Galbraith

The Cognitive Demands of Writing
Processing Capacity and Working Effects in Text Production
Edited by Mark Torrance and Gaynor Jeffery

According to the Publication Manual of the American Psychological Association (4th Edition), one should refer to this work as to chapters in a volume series: [Authors of the chapter]. [1999]. [Title of the chapter]. In G. Rijlaarsdam & E. Espéret (Series Eds.) & Jerry Andriessen and Pierre Coirier (Vol. Eds.) *Studies in Writing: Vol. 5. Foundations of Argumentative Text Processing* [pages]. Amsterdam: Amsterdam University Press

Cover design: NAP-ontwerpers, Amsterdam
Typesetting: beeldvorm, Leidschendam

ISBN 90 5256 340 7

©Amsterdam University Press, Amsterdam, 1999

All rights reserved. Without limiting the rights under copyright reserved above, no part of this book may be reproduced, stored in or introduced into a retrieval system, or transmitted, in any form or by any means (electronic, mechanical, photocopying, recording, or otherwise), without the written permission of both the copyright owner and the author of this book.

Preface

Argumentative text processing is concerned with the psychology of the production and comprehension of argumentative texts. Argumentative texts are pieces of discourse in which an attempt is made to settle issues concerning a controversial topic, with the purpose of modifying another person's representation concerning the issue. Text is defined here as a written or oral piece of discourse, containing a minimal number of linked statements, which form an overall structure. Although the focus of this book, and indeed of this series, is on written text production, the book contains research on oral argumentation as well. Foundations of argumentation are to be found in oral dialogues, and the importance of negotiation with (potential) addressees seems to be more important than in many other types of discourse.

Already at the age of three or four, children interacting in particular situations have been found to use relatively complex argumentative strategies. They are able, under specific circumstances, to justify and negotiate, implying the ability to consider their audience. While young children can only do this when the audience is present, and the negotiation process is often inconsistent, older children also learn to negotiate systematically when the audience is absent. Negotiating with a virtual audience is crucial for written communication. When considering writing, it has been observed that elaborated argumentative discourse – that is, discourse containing at least a claim, and some arguments related by restriction, specification, counterargumentation – is mastered relatively late. The difficulties that arise may be related specifically to the argumentative process of negotiation.

Writing argumentative texts presents specific difficulties, for adults as well as for children. Some of these problems are related to difficulties with writing in general, others are specifically due to the production of arguments. We will focus here on the second type of problems. Each chapter in this book provides a survey of the latest research on argumentative text processing. The rationale behind the choice of topics is the focus on the fundamental components of the argumentative process. To this end, the chapters discuss the topics of reasoning, argumentative theory, social context, interaction, development, knowledge, planning and translating, education, collaboration and electronic argumentation. It is the first book that has assembled some of the world's leading scholars on argumentation from different disciplines (psychology, linguistics, educational science, and computer science) to discuss these issues. It should serve as a basic overview of the field for many years to come.

OVERVIEW

The first chapter, by Coirier, Andriessen, and Chanquoy, discusses the specificity of argumentative text writing. Their main hypothesis concerns the idea that problems that specifically characterize written argumentative text production concern the articulation between planning and writing. This not only requires the ability to linearize a complex conceptual representation, but also specific linguistic expertise.

A foundation of argumentative text processing is reasoning. The chapter by Voss, Wiley and Sandak discusses the relation between human reasoning and argumentation. Psychological research on argumentation has generally neglected this relationship. A model is proposed, which assumes that reasoning and inference making can be approximated by a Toulmin-like argument structure. This claim is supported by examples from the domain of legal discourse. Another foundation is argumentative theory. Van Eemeren and Grootendorst discuss developments in the analysis, production, and evaluation of argumentation. They approach these topics from a descriptive point of view as well as from the perspective of the validity of argumentative reasoning. After a discussion of the dominant approaches of the last decades, they conclude their chapter by distinguishing some important trends that characterize current theory.

Two chapters discuss the pragmatic foundations of argumentation. The chapter by C. Santos and S. Santos provides an overview of findings related to the effects of content and context on conflict talks and resolution strategies used in argumentation. These authors argue that the understanding of any argumentation requires specification of its contextual dimension, instead of relying solely on underlying logic. This contextual dimension comprises variables such as the individual's position on a certain topic, their commitment to that position, and its relationship to socially shared beliefs.

Stein and Bernas address the relevance of social dimensions for the understanding of argumentation. In their chapter, they discuss a model that focuses on similarities and differences in thinking across different domains and situations. In particular, they claim that the ability to understand an argument emerges very early in development, and they discuss the situations in which young children enter an argument. One consequence of this early emergence of argumentative literacy is a bias for supporting a particular stance, thereby largely ignoring the opposite point of view. This raises the issue of conceptual change: under which circumstances are arguers willing to change their point of view? Finally, these authors discuss the intrinsic importance of arguing as a vehicle for learning.

The next three chapters discuss the development of argumentative writing from a psycholinguistic perspective. The chapter by Piolat, Roussey, and Gombert focuses on the role of the argumentative schema in young children's writing. These authors provide an overview of a number of studies that employ the notion of argumentative schema, and conclude that there are important differences between the ways in which these studies conceptualize the notion of schema, in relation to the types of tasks and the observations that are analyzed.

The chapter by Golder and Pouit provides a survey of research about the situational and cognitive factors implied in the production of elaborated argumentative discourse. This type of argumentative text contains systematic justifications, plausible and well-organized arguments, and takes into account of the opposite point of view, which requires the use of restriction, specification, and counterargumentation. Within this perspective, the authors focus on the debatability of a discourse, that is, the acceptability of the argumentation according to social values, which is clearly apparent when the difference between oral and written situations is considered.

This book does not consider pedagogy directly, but it contains a chapter that proposes a theoretically based approach to writing argumentative texts. The strategies outlined in the second chapter by van Eemeren and Grootendorst provide a bridge between their theoretical concepts and the practical application of these ideas.

The final three chapters concern collaboration. Collaboration is, on the one hand, a method to externalize thought by verbalization, allowing the on-line analysis of argumentative text production. On the other hand, collaboration is a problem space in itself, comprising a domain gaining importance as a result of current educational ideas and technological possibilities.

The chapter by Giroud focuses on the study of the process of collaborative argumentative text production. The author provides a detailed overview of the procedures and methods involved in such assignments, and discusses several research questions that may guide this type of approach. The reflection on the polyphonic aspect of argumentation shows that enunciative strategies are inextricably linked to argumentative strategies.

The chapter by Baker shows a different approach to collaborative argumentation. First, his research is on oral dialogues, analyzing in detail the relationship between communication and problem resolution during collaborative interaction. Second, his approach is computational, aiming at modeling of such interactions. Third, it focuses on learning, that is, on the complex links between argumentation, problem solving, and learning processes. After a discussion of all these issues, a crucial question is raised: how should collaborative learning situations be designed to encourage the spontaneous generation of productive argumentation dialogue?

This question is taken up in the final chapter of the volume. Veerman and Treasure-Jones review the possibilities of new media to investigate and support argumentative text production. Again, electronic text production provides the means to externalize and study thought processes, and it comprises a new context presenting its own problems. The authors tackle these issues by considering a number of electronic environments suitable for collaborative argumentative text production.

After reading these chapters, the reader will get a good idea of what today constitutes the main critical issues for research on argumentative text processing: What are the pragmatic and cognitive requirements for an elaborated argumentation to emerge? Does an argumentative cognitive schema exist, what are its constituents, function? What is the role of language, of reasoning? What characterizes a good argument, and why and when is it acceptable? However, at the same time, the reader will be able to notice that, despite the numerous and sometimes important differences between theoretical and empirical approaches, some well-established points emerge concerning the main requirements of elaborated argumentative writing. We mention here the role of the addressee and that of topoi, the clear constraints on argumentative situations, and the complexity of the corresponding type of text in relation to its multiple components: reasoning, generating and evaluating relevant and acceptable arguments, elaborating the appropriate text organization, *etc.*

Much has yet to be done in this interdisciplinary field. However, researchers do not need to start from zero. Indeed, it was not possible to include in this book all the research on argumentation and argumentative text writing. Our goal will be achieved if, as we hope, the book is able to give a clear idea of what in this field has been established, and which are the main issues still to be explored.

Gert Rijlaarsdam
University of Amsterdam
The Netherlands

Eric Espéret
University of Poitiers
France

Contents

Pierre Coirier, Jerry Andriessen and Lucile Chanquoy
From Planning to Translating: The Specificity of   *1*
Argumentative Writing

James F. Voss, Jennifer Wiley and Rebecca Sandak
Reasoning in the Construction of Argumentative Texts   *29*

Frans H. van Eemeren and Rob Grootendorst
Developments in Argumentation Theory   *43*

Frans H. van Eemeren and Rob Grootendorst
From Analysis to Presentation: A Pragma-dialectical   *59*
Approach to Writing Argumentative Texts

Clara Maria M. Santos and Selma Leitão Santos
Good Argument, Content and Contextual Dimensions   *75*

Nancy L. Stein and Ronan Bernas
The Early Emergence of Argumentative Knowledge and Skill   *97*

Annie Piolat, Jean-Yves Roussey and Anne Gombert
The Development of Argumentative Schema in Writing   *117*

Caroline Golder and Delphine Pouit
For a Debate to take place the Topic must be Debatable.   *137*
Developmental Evolution of the Negotiation and Debatability
of Arguments.

Anick Giroud
Studying Argumentative Text Processing through   *149*
Collaborative Writing

Michael Baker
Argumentation and Constructive Interaction   *179*

Arja L. Veerman and Tamsin Treasure-Jones
Software for Problem Solving through Collaborative   *203*
Argumentation

References   *231*

Registers   *254*

From Planning to Translating:
The Specificity of Argumentative Writing

Pierre Coirier
CNRS-University of Poitiers
Jerry Andriessen
University of Utrecht
Lucile Chanquoy
University of Montpellier III

ABSTRACT

Even very young children can produce elaborated argumentation when the constraints of the situation are clearly defined: if the topic and the addressee are familiar and the goal is relevant. Conversely, adolescents and adults do not frequently produce elaborated argumentative texts. In order to describe the specificity of argumentative writing in relation to other types of texts, we rely on a 'functional approach'. Essentially this approach consists in (1) analyzing the strong interrelationships between the characteristics of the discursive situation, the corresponding communicative goal, and the linguistic devices required to produce a text which adequately realizes the goal; and (2) assigning a central role to the goal of the discourse or text. We describe research on argumentative writing, from this perspective, in three sections. The first section defines the functional constraints of argumentative situations. In the second section, we specify the main characteristics of argumentation in relation to the different processes classically included in written composition. The third section consists of an experimental simulation, based upon the conclusions of the preceding sections. By means of the simulation we aim to experimentally analyze the potential conflict between the conceptual structure of argumentation and the different requirements of linearization.

In our conclusion we underline two main points. First, we state the need for a more precise definition of the processes and subprocesses implied in argumentative writing, insisting particularly on the interdependency of these processes. Second, we argue that in argumentation, knowledge of and access to language is fundamental to the translating process, as well as to idea generation and organization.

1 INTRODUCTION

Nearly twenty years ago, Hayes and Flower (1980) proposed a general model of the nature and architecture of processes and representations underlying text writing activity. Since the publication of this initial model, other relevant models have been elaborated (for example: van Dijk & Kintsch, 1983; Bereiter &

Scardamalia, 1987; Levelt, 1989; Hayes, 1996; Kellogg, 1996; Galbraith, 1999). All of them are built up in the form of a global architecture, and aim at the description of the complete course of the text production activity. Three major processes are usually distinguished: planning, translating, and revising. These processes are supposed to operate in a sequence, with possible recursion. Most models include the following components (see Alamargot & Chanquoy, in press, for a critical review):

1. *Conceptual or referential planning.* This process comprises the three subprocesses of (1) idea generation, that is, retrieval of ideas from memory and/or from external sources; (2) selection and evaluation of the retrieved ideas, and (3) organization of ideas, that is, relating these ideas to each other in accordance with goals, instructions, addressee, type of text, *etc.* There is much discussion about the nature of the output of the planning process. Proposals involve, for example, pre-textual structures (such as an outline), or mental networks of relationships (such as a diagram). Such proposals also touch upon the nature of the next writing process, translating (Hayes & Nash, 1996; Kellogg, 1993).
2. *Translating.* This process comprises sequential ordering of the information (linearizing) and linguistic coding of the resulting sequence: the plan is being translated into a grammatically correct and pragmatically adequate linear text.
3. *Revising.* During this process the writer may modify his/her text, evaluate its adequacy to the assignments (addressee, goal, *etc.*), and possibly re-organize the initial mental structure. This process most probably does not only intervene at the end of the writing phase, but during the whole composing process. We will not develop this last writing component in the present chapter, but for a review, see Fayol (1992) and Rijlaarsdam & Van den Bergh (1996).

In this chapter, we will discuss the specific problems for the production of argumentative texts within this general framework. Composing argumentative texts presents specific problems for writers with respect to content, structure, textual organization, as well as linguistic coding (Applebee, Langer, Jenkins, Mullis & Foerscht, 1990; Hays, Brandt & Chantry, 1988; Marchand, Coirier & Dellerman, 1996). Research about argumentation is numerous and various, but also divergent with regard to theoretical backgrounds, methods, results, explanations and conclusions. Argumentative text processing is clearly a field which extends beyond the writing process. Writing research on argumentation requires input from many disciplines. In the other chapters of this volume, different approaches are found to the most important topics in this field.

In this chapter, we provide an overview of research on argumentation within the writing process. We focus on psycholinguistic research, but we often need to borrow from linguistics and social studies. We will discuss the main issues by developing the following points:
1. What is argumentation and what are its main requirements?
2. What are the specific problems for argumentation in writing?
3. What are the main problems linked to the transition from conceptualization to effectively written text: an experimental simulation.

In our conclusion we underline the functional interdependency of the different cognitive processes in argumentative writing, the need for a more detailed specification of the components of the planning process for argumentative writing, and the decisive role of language in argumentation.

2 ARGUMENTATION: DEFINITIONS AND REQUIREMENTS

The study of argumentation pertains to various theoretical dimensions: formal or natural logic, dialectics, pragmatics, rhetoric and persuasion, social interaction, *etc.* (see the chapters by Baker, and van Eemeren & Grootendorst, in this volume). Champaud (1994) characterizes argumentation as a continuum ranging between two poles. The first pole involves providing evidence to support a conclusion, which is exemplified as the claim-backing structure by Toulmin (1958). Logic and sound reasoning are here considered to be important requirements. The second pole regards argumentation as an action aimed at modifying the beliefs or the behavior of a given audience. This is preferably to be characterized in terms of the psychosocial aspects of the communicative situation, especially by the participants' goals.

The perspective adopted by Grize (1982, 1990) combines the two poles: argumentation is the construction of a 'logico-discursive schematization', aimed at changing the addressee's representation on a given topic. In Grize's theory, argumentation is defined as a natural, or informal, reasoning process (quite similar definitions can be found in the chapters by Baker, van Eemeren & Grootendorst, or Voss *et al.*); examples, analogies, or arguments of authority can support a point of view as firmly as pure deductive rules (Apotheloz & Mieville, 1989; also the 1992 and 1995 issues of the review 'Travaux du Centre de Recherches Sémiologiques de Neuchâtel'). Furthermore, the aim of argumentation is not merely to act upon representations of objective knowledge, but mainly on judgments, opinions, beliefs, desires, and subjective preferences (Perkins, Farady & Bushey, 1991). This requires a deliberate use of specific linguistic forms and structures, as we will see later.

2.1 A functional approach

Current models of writing do not deal adequately with the interactions between situations, communicative goals, and their realization in writing. Above all, most writing models underestimate the functional relationship which relates communicative goals and assignments to the conceptual and textual means specifically required for the realization of these goals: textual superstructures, schemas, particular semantic constituents, and linguistic means (see Alamargot & Chanquoy, in press).

It is particularly interesting to explore the types of cognitive activities required by the characteristics of pragmatic constraints and the referential domain associated with a given type of text. Within this perspective Brewer (1980) proposed interesting ideas. Descriptions could be associated with veracity of information, argumentation with plausibility or acceptability, narration with interest, instructional texts with efficiency, *etc*. In each case, there is a difference in the mental representations, memory retrieving procedures, and attentional strategies (if not in kind, then in degree).

Within a perspective similar to that of Brewer (1980), concerning the processing of different types of texts, Coirier (1999) proposes a 'functional' approach to explain how writers or speakers establish specific relationships between the goal of the text and the parameters of the situation where this goal can be appropriate, and between the goal of the text and the conceptual and linguistic devices which

are necessary to its realization. Concerning argumentation, the following schema can express the functional approach:
Argumentative situation ⇒
desire to convince the opponent ⇒
supporting one's point of view but taking into account the opponent's arguments ⇒
use of justifications and also refutation of counter arguments ⇒
necessity to coordinate pro and contra-arguments ⇒
use of complex syntax, concessive devices, enunciative markers, etc.

Thus, within the functional perspective, the production of argumentative text relies on cognitive processing of the situation involving 'choices' about constraints such as:
- Is *the situation* polemic or cooperative, what knowledge is shared by interlocutors, and is the topic familiar?
- Is *the goal* of participants to convince or to compromise?
- Does the content bear upon *factual* issues, or does it concern an *ideological* debate?
- Is this content already *organized* in the cognitive representation of the writer? If not, can it be organized from more general knowledge and logical schemas?
- Does the debate bear upon the *veracity* of facts, *acceptability* of reasons, *reliability* of information, and *coherence* of the reasoning?
- Is there a perspective of *gain*?

Once these parameters of the situation have been processed (Bronckart, 1985) there remains the question of the cognitive tools that writers have at their disposal to compose their argumentation. These tools pertain to varied domains, for example:
- Can they use specific *textual models (e.g.* the Toulmin's schema, van Dijk and Kintsch's superstructure, Hayes & Flower 'stored writing plans')?
- Are different *rhetorical strategies* available, concerning the 'dispositio' [order] of arguments?
- Do writers master some important *linguistic devices*, such as setting a proposition in assertive, conditional, ironic, or prescriptive form? Can they easily use the different enunciative modalities, *etc.*?

Any given text-type requires the use of specific knowledge, appropriate schemas, and attentional strategies. In addition, some linguistic devices are specific to some types of texts (De Weck & Schneuwly, 1993). For the comprehension of narratives, for example, the reader's interest constitutes a critical issue ('Stories are to entertain' is the title of Brewer & Lichtenstein's 1982 paper). Narrative constituents inducing motivation and suspense are more important than veracity or even strict causality (Hidi & Baird, 1988; José, 1988; José & Brewer, 1984; Stein & Glenn, 1979). Conversely, in an event report, the veracity of information should be the main point. In argumentative texts, coherence of reasoning, veracity or plausibility of the proposed reasons, addressee's opinions, 'debatability' of the topic, knowledge of the domain, *etc.*, appear as the critical factors. This, in turn, should have consequences for the writing process.

The functional approach, linking communicative goals and textual organization, offers a basis for the study of processing of different types of text. However, it is quite neglected in current models of writing, where rhetorical and pragmatic components are given a 'purely theoretical' role. The corresponding characteristics of the task environment, and the processes associated with the consideration of the audience, are defined in a very general way and are not supposed to induce *specific* processing. In Bereiter and Scardamalia (1987) for instance, the importance of rhetorical and pragmatic components is acknowledged, but their functioning is not elaborated.

In the next two sections, we discuss research concerning the requirements for an argumentative text to be developed. After that, we propose a functional definition of 'elaborated argumentative text' (called EAT) based on these requirements.

2.2 Prerequisites of argumentation

According to many authors (Antaki & Leudar, 1990; Stein & Miller, 1993b; van Eemeren & Grootendorst, 1984), the first prerequisite for an argumentation to be developed is the existence of a *recognized* disagreement about a given issue. There is no reason to argue if there is no disagreement. This point has been formalized by Charolles (1980) as a set of implicit criteria (analogous to the conversational implicatures by Grice, 1975). Considering a speaker A, debating with B, about an opinion O, at a moment T, Charolles defined 'appropriativity' [French: appropriativité] rules that have to be implicitly adhered to in effective argumentative communication:
- A believes (B does not believe O at Tx < T0): there is a supposed disagreement;
- A believes (it is possible (B believes O at T1 > T0)); B can change his/her point of view;
- A believes (it is possible (B believes O at T1 (rightly))); B is supposed rational;
- It is probable (B believes (A believes O)); sincerity postulate.

Such rules are actually set to work when understanding short argumentative dialogues (Golder & Coirier, 1994). For example, readers rightly verify the following inference: when debating with Paul and sustaining the point of view that smoking is dangerous, John cannot at the same time offer Paul cigarettes at his birthday, which would violate the second appropriativity rule. Charolles' proposed rules are related to the most obvious pragmatic constraints of argumentation. Moreover, they underline the importance of the representation the writer has about his/her audience.

2.3 Pragmatic constraints

Recent experiments allow us to specify the most important pragmatic features in argumentation and in argumentative writing (see Golder & Pouit, Santos & Santos, Stein & Bernas, in this volume). It must be noted that argumentation is initially practiced and learned in dialogues about familiar topics. Children are used to arguing about questions in which they are subjectively involved and where the issue of argument is most often an issue of material or moral gain (Chanquoy, 1996; De Bernardi, 1996; Stein & Miller, 1993a & b). The next sections examine some of the corresponding constraints.

2.4 Familiarity, knowledge, involvement

In dialogues, and with familiar topics, children from age three to four can use minimal argumentative operations such as justifying a claim and taking into account the addressee (Eisenberg & Garvey, 1981; Genishi & Di Paolo, 1982), but the use of these operations strongly depends on the addressee's familiarity (Clark & Delia, 1976; Beaudichon, 1982). The addressee's familiarity provides a 'common ground' between interlocutors (Clark & Haviland, 1977). The familiarity effect is consistent through ages (Pouit & Golder, 1996). As underlined by Stein and Bernas (this volume), one of the real difficulties arguers have is understanding the beliefs and assumptions of people who have goals that are different from their own. Successful conflict intervention forces opponents to understand what the other person values or fears, and perceive the positive and negative impact of a proposed position.

From the age of five (Weiss & Sachs, 1991), or later (Knudson, 1994), argumentative texts try to systematically take into account the addressee's interests (*'If you give me that toy, I will clean my room'*). Stein and Trabasso (1982) observed complex moral justifications from age five. They showed that children were able to produce logical and sound reasons very similar to those of adults.

More recently, Stein and Miller (1990, 1993a & b) showed that the emergence of complex reasoning in young children was linked to three cognitive and contextual requirements: (1) the familiarity of the topic and the situation, (2) a minimal level of subjective involvement and some perspective of gain, and (3) the data of the problem must be understandable and memorable. When such requirements are met, from eight years old onwards, children can produce sound reasons in favor of their standpoint. In this respect their reasoning is similar to that of adults, and equally biased by congruency effects. In addition, and this is a capital point as regards elaborated argumentation, these children can imagine and attribute good reasons in favor of the opposite standpoint.

An important consequence of these observations is that the difficulties of argumentative writing observed in children cannot be attributed to a deficiency in reasoning ability, nor to obstacles in retrieving arguments in familiar situations and for well known topics. Maybe the most critical problem is not to produce complex argumentation, but to write it.

2.5 The type of cooperation between interlocutors

Taking into account the addressee depends on many parameters. Some dialogues produced by children as well as by adults are no more than parallel monologues, without any cooperativity except for very formal rules of dialogues. Conversely, some monologues can be characterized as internalized dialogues (Bakhtine, 1981), where varied positions are exposed and compared (Giroud, this volume; Golder, 1992a).

Research on cooperative writing may provide insights into the roles and effects of addressees. Even when cooperation is invited (*e.g.* by instructions or by the experimental situation) it can be more or less efficient. Roussey and Gombert (1996) observe that cooperative writing leads to argumentative texts of a better quality, but only by experts. A related study by Erkens and Andriessen (1994) deals with the strategies used in cooperative problem solving. They formulate the following conclusion:'Cooperation requires that the cooperating subjects acquire a common frame of reference in order to be able to negotiate and communicate their individual viewpoints and inferences' (p. 124).

2.6 Debatability of the topic

We already noted that disagreement was a prerequisite for an argumentation to develop. But there are topics for which the community does not allow disagreement: racism, revisionism, or pedophilia. There are also topics which are either unquestionable, or at least difficult to be envisaged within smaller social areas; for example, within a given social group, a religious group, or the family. Debatability is related in part to cognitive and social development. It also depends on context: argumentation presupposes that participants are inclined to solve their conflicts (Stein & Miller, 1993a), but to solve them by the means of discussion (Stein, Bernas, Calicchia & Wright, 1995; Voss, Fincher-Kieffer, Wiley & Silfies, 1993). Golder & Pouit (this volume) analyze this point clearly, so we will not develop it here.

2.7 Instructions

Coirier (1992) contrasted explaining and argumentative instructions for two groups of children who had to discuss exactly the same question: giving pocket money allowance to children or not. The explanation instruction was: 'There is no question, specialists of the matter, such as psychologists and doctors all agree: pocket money allowance should not be given before age....., *explain why*' (the age varied according to the children's level). In the argumentative instruction it was indicated:'not all specialists agree as to the age to which one can give pocket money allowance. *What is your opinion?*'. In the first case, there is no initial disagreement, only explanation is necessary. In the second case, the disagreement is clearly stated, so argumentation is invited. This difference between the two instructions induced different processing of the same problem-content: with the explaining instruction there was a lack of enunciative involvement markers (*e.g., In my opinion, I think that*) or more generally of argumentative markers. In addition, counterarguments were mainly found in the case of argumentative instruction. In other words, at the level of reasoning, the structure of the problem to solve is the same, but the explaining instruction leads the writer to limit his/her composing to that aspect of the task. Conversely, the argumentative instruction leads the writer to envisage the problem as a conflict, and to process it accordingly by using typical argumentative operations.

In summary, considering pragmatic constraints, argumentation is more likely to develop in certain situations. It requires disagreement on a topic, and the desire to solve – or at least to manage – this disagreement by using reasons. This results in three requirements: (1) the familiarity of the topic, the addressee, and the whole situation, which allows generating understandable and acceptable reasons; (2) the intention to cooperate, which depends on the polemicity of the issue, but also on strategies induced by a given situation; and (3) the importance of a common frame of reference: common knowledge, general beliefs, and opinions. This explains why experimental situations most efficient at inducing elaborated argumentation are those where the conflicting opinions are clearly exposed from the start (Coirier, Andriessen, Chanquoy & De Bernardi, 1997; De Bernardi & Antolini, 1996), and where cooperation is strongly invited (Golder, 1992b; Stein, Bernas, Calicchia & Wright, 1995).

3 FROM ARGUMENTATIVE REQUIREMENTS TO THE DEFINITION OF ELABORATED ARGUMENTATIVE TEXT

By now, it may be quite obvious that composing an argumentation supposes adherence to many requirements. Minimal argumentation (a claim and some reasons) can already be observed in very young children. But composing an argumentation complying with all of the requirements implies writing an 'extended text' (McCutchen, 1987) that is, a text comprising several sentences, organized into a coherent structure. Articles in reviews, political discourses, or social debates provide varied examples.

For the purpose of this chapter, we define elaborated argumentative text (EAT) as a type of text that complies simultaneously with eight crucial argumentative constraints, derived from research and theory on argumentation, most of which have been discussed above and which we will try to synthesize now (see Coirier, 1996, for a review). The first four constraints constitute preconditions to be realized by the individual in a situation for an argumentation to develop. Four additional constraints are typical for the argumentation itself, as they correspond to genre specific constituents of elaborated argumentative texts (partly akin to schematic approaches such as that of Toulmin, 1958).

1. To recognize the existence of a conflict between two different positions on the same topic (Stein & Miller, 1993b; van Eemeren & Grootendorst, 1984).
2. To recognize the topic as 'debatable' socially, ideologically, and contextually (Charolles, 1980; Golder, 1996).
3. To be inclined to solve the conflict (Stein & Miller, 1993b), which presupposes a favorable negotiation context (Stein, Bernas, Calicchia, & Wright, 1995; Stein & Miller, 1993a; Voss, Fincher-Kiefer, Wiley & Silfies, 1993).
4. To be inclined to try to solve the conflict by means of language (Charolles, 1980; Perelman & Olbrechts-Tyteca, 1988).
5. To claim a position (Stein & Miller, 1993b; van Eemeren & Grootendorst, 1984; Coirier & Golder, 1993; Golder & Coirier, 1994).
6. To support that claim with reasons (claimbacking) (Adam, 1992; Antaki & Leudar, 1990; Apotheloz & Mieville, 1989; Coirier & Golder, 1993; Grize, 1982; Stein & Miller, 1990).
7. To assign a minimal value to the opposite claim and reasons (Grize, 1982; Brassart, 1992; Stein & Miller, 1993b).
8. To restrict or modulate the opposing claims, by using counterargumentation (Adam, 1992; Crammond, 1998; Gombert, 1997; Moeschler, 1985; Perkins *et al.*, 1991).

With these constraints in mind, we may start to examine how an EAT can be constructed, and what processes should be specified in an adequate writing model. Our purpose is to move somewhat closer to an answer to the question: what is specific to composing argumentative texts?

4 ARGUMENTATION AND THE WRITING PROCESS

In this section, we will discuss experimental evidence pertaining to the written composition of argumentative texts. We will not evoke questions that are still open in the study of writing in general, but focus on the questions that are specific to argumentation. As our starting point, we take the main processes distinguished in the Hayes and Flower model, presented in the introduction of the chapter.

4.1 Idea generation and retrieval

Bearing upon desires, opinions, and/or beliefs, argumentation belongs to the domain of malleable definitions and discursive negotiation (Grize, 1982). In argumentation, finding the appropriate words and establishing the right connections between words and clauses can be crucial for understanding. At the level of retrieval, getting one precise idea will thus often involve getting the precise words to specify this idea. This imposes a number of strong requirements on language.

The retrieval process may follow different lines according to the specific characteristics of the knowledge to-be-retrieved (Galbraith, 1996, 1999). For example, if the goal is to compile arguments about a topic, then an automatic retrieval from some probes in long-term memory can be sufficient. Conversely, in a juridical conflict, in which a specific position has to be systematically defended against an opponent, specific strategies and rules must be used; for example, constructing a negative argument out of a corresponding positive one (Stratman, 1994). It is thus possible that some variables particular for argumentation can function as determinants or probes to idea retrieval from long-term memory.

Automatic or strategic recovery of ideas from memory for argumentative purposes has not been systematically investigated. Some results are available on the use of topic knowledge for argumentation. On the basis of rather different studies, evidence has been collected which suggests that topic expertise (Kuhn, 1991) or topic elaboration (Andriessen, Coirier, Roos, Passerault & Bert-Erboul, 1996) are not systematically linked to improved argumentative reasoning, particularly with respect to the generation of more and stronger arguments, and better text organization. Specific properties of the retrieved information may be important: argumentative orientation, topic familiarity, social acceptability, *etc.*. Some results are available, but it is unclear whether these observations pertain to an automatic recovery of ideas or to a strategic selection of information during planning and other phases of writing. Furthermore, divergent or even contradictory data may result from the difficulty to define and operationalize variables such as interest, desire, motivation, value, and familiarity (Hayes, 1996, formulates new proposals concerning these variables).

Voss, Perkins, and Segal (1991) have shown that reasons that are supposed to provide a stronger support to the chosen thesis are activated faster. Stein *et al.* (1995), for their part, indicate that in domains involving moral values, most reasons produced in favor of a thesis are values and beliefs about the benefits and costs for holding a particular point of view. In addition, De Bernardi and Antolini (1996) found that protocols written about an uninteresting but well-known topic have a better argumentative structure than protocols on an interesting but unfamiliar topic. Finally, Gombert (1997) found that it is much more difficult to argue on a highly polemic topic than on a non-polemic one. Each in its own way, these data suppose strategic control of the idea generation process: retrieval of arguments is strongly linked to the values of the functional constraints outlined above. Much more research is needed in this domain. Santos and Santos (this volume) elaborate this topic extensively.

To conclude this short section on idea generation in writing, argumentation presents two specific characteristics: (1) the quantity of knowledge seems to be less important than specific qualities of this knowledge; (2) the domain of argumentation mainly consists of negotiable information, beliefs, and opinions, rather than facts. Expressing such information adequately requires proficiency in language to use the appropriate words and connections between them.

4.2 Idea evaluation and selection

Idea evaluation and selection are important components of any writing task, and are described in most models. Idea selection and evaluation in argumentation essentially involve using the appropriate criteria to select and evaluate relevant arguments, considering the goals of the task. Therefore, these criteria should be available and related to the communicative situation. It is not easy to elaborate a unique definition of concepts such as appropriateness, usefulness and relevance. An argument can be relevant for a particular topic, but not appropriate in every context, and argumentation is specifically dependent on context (as was shown in the first section). Furthermore, it is difficult to completely separate the retrieving process from evaluating. Selection can be considered as a first step after idea retrieval. There are lots of reasons to reject retrieved ideas for inclusion in a text, and many ideas are often left implicit, for the sake of economy (according to Grice's implicatures), or for rhetorical reasons. For example, texts differ according to the type of instructions: instruction to win or to compromise can make a great difference in the selection-evaluation process (Golder, 1992c; Stein & Miller, 1990; Veerman & Treasure-Jones, this volume).

In any writing task it is necessary to select ideas and to evaluate them. In argumentation evaluation plays a central role and includes many aspects, such as the orientation of arguments, their importance in the reasoning process, their general acceptability, *etc*. Moreover, the writer's knowledge about the addressee is viewed as an important constraint in the idea evaluation process. The question is not only that of sharing knowledge or understanding as such (as in other types of texts), but also of computing which reasons will be more easily accepted, or at least considered relevant by the addressee (Golder, 1996; Gombert, 1998).

4.3 Sound reasoning

According to Blair and Johnston (1987a), a sound argumentative chain of reasoning from premises to a conclusion should respect the three following criteria: (1) *relevance*: there exists an adequate relation between the premises and the conclusion; (2) *sufficiency*: the premises provide enough evidence for the conclusion; (3) *acceptability*: premises should be true, probable, and/or reliable.

However, Blair and Johnson do not explain how it is possible to consider a premise as relevant, sufficient or acceptable, according to what criteria, and for what audience.

On the basis of what they consider 'good reasoning' (justification and counter argumentation, also elements of EAT), Voss, Perkins and Segal (1991) propose two different approaches for selecting arguments:
- *'makes sense epistemology'*: trying to satisfy the criteria of truth and congruence with the most important beliefs; which, in our mind, means adapting to socially accepted ideas, but also to scientific rules;
- *'critical epistemology'*: looking for possible incoherence, counter-examples, and multiple perspectives; this second point then insists on logic, in relation to the possibility of conflicting opinions in a given domain.

The authors distinguish formal reasoning, based on critical evaluation, and informal reasoning (see Voss *et al.*, this volume). Informal arguments can be evaluated on the basis of soundness (or acceptability of reasons), the relevance and strength of the support from the reason to the claim, and the degree to which counter arguments are taken into account. Again, it is not clearly specified with what precise norms or rules (social, legal, religious, scientific) it is possible to define acceptable reasons.

4.4 Acceptable reasons

Another proposal for criteria to select ideas comes from Apotheloz and Mieville (1989). They propose a definition of a 'good' support (p. 72): 'A supporting discourse segment is a segment which lends credit to, makes more plausible, strengthens, *etc.* the asserted content of another discourse segment, *whatever the nature of this support may be* [italics added]'. This anti-normative definition of the minimal argumentative structure must be emphasised: natural argumentation can not be reduced to logical reasoning, not even to predetermined pragmatic schemes. Hence, supporting relations can be quite diverse: logical, analogical, teleological, based on knowledge, beliefs, authority, or example. Thus the supporting relations can be defined neither a priori nor out of context. Evaluation of arguments relies primarily on the representation of the audience, 'a good argument is an argument that is accepted or at least taken into account by the addressee'. In other words, a good argument must be defined considering the particular audience to which it is addressed (see below for the notion of topoi).

Bereiter, Burtis and Scardamalia (1988) discussed how main points are established during the writing process. A main point becomes the goal of a piece of discourse, when it is related to a critical issue relevant for the content problem. In their approach, a content goal is also a goal for rhetorical problem solving. This leaves room for a contextually defined search for the information to be used, according to the task assignment and the audience. Highly rated main points can generate a variety of problem solving activities, such as elaborating, focusing, evaluating, and linking information. Accordingly, good reasoning relies on efficiency in the situation. Thus, if the debate confronts, for instance, scientists, on a scientific topic and in a scientific context, it is reasonable to suppose that the evaluation and selection of arguments has to obey the (institutionally defined) rules of the scientific community. An important idea is developed here: good reasoning refers to a specific audience, sharing the same rules and opinions.

Topoi
The degree of acceptability of a reason is generally based on 'topoi'. Topoi refer to relationships implicitly accepted in a community which authorize an argumentative move (Ducrot, 1980). For instance, the topos: 'the more the temperature rises, the nicer it is to take a walk' authorizes the argumentative move: 'it's 65F or maybe even 68F, so a walk would be nice'. But there is always the possibility of superior topos. So the previous reason could be opposed by the equally acceptable topos: 'the hotter it gets, the more one feels the need to refresh oneself, so going to the pool would be a better idea'.

Miller (1986) and Klein (1985) have studied the issue of argument acceptability in children's disputes concerning moral dilemmas. They observed three developmental stages. The first stage (around age three) is characterized by a simple counterposition with no arguments and without rational reasoning. The emergence of arguments based on shared values defines the second stage. Finally, around age fourteen, the use of logical rules and norms characterizes the last stage. Klein insists on the lack of the absolute validity of arguments. For argumentation it is not sufficient to take into account a universal addressee, a specified interlocutor is needed. This is illustrated by the transition, between ages eight and eighteen, from egocentric forms ('School on Saturday would be good because it would allow *me*...') to more collective forms ('...it would allow *us*') and later on, around age 18, to more specified forms ('...it would allow *us*..., because *I*...') (Coirier & Marchand, 1994; Golder, 1992c). Hence, empirical rules are needed which ensure the development of reasonable argumentation, at least if the social community that is susceptible to adopt them is clearly defined. Such rules can be assimilated to the functional requirements of argumentation.

Pragma-dialectics
The purpose of van Eemeren and Grootendorst (1992b; see also Lapintie, 1998) is to provide a social model for 'efficient' argumentation. Their pragma-dialectic theory of argumentation combines empirical and normative rules. Arguments in different fields may substantially differ, but rules for critical discussion can be given as norms of argumentation in any field. Relying largely on Grice's implicatures (1975), van Eemeren and Grootendorst propose, for instance (pp. 202-209), that: (1) parties must not prevent each other from advancing standpoints or casting doubts on standpoints; (2) when attacked, a standpoint must be defended; (3) something must not be presented as a premise, if the other party does not express it as such; (4) a party may only use arguments that are logically valid or validated by explicating one or more unexpressed premises.

These rules are close to the constraints we defined for the minimal structure of an elaborated argumentation (EAT): justify your claims with 'acceptable' reasons, and do not deny the value of opposite claims and arguments. Developmental research has confirmed that, with age, children progressively apply such rules (Coirier & Golder, 1993; Golder & Coirier, 1994).

Concerning the specificity of argumentation for idea selection and evaluation, the following three conclusions can be drawn:
1. The *evaluation and selection* process in EAT writing cannot be dissociated from the idea generation process. The former can strongly control and constrain the latter, with respect to individual strategies and pragmatic requirements.

2. Selection of *main points in argumentation* does not only depend on the writer, but should be based on a representation of the audience and the nature of the conflict. Much more than any other type of text, elaborated argumentation is a 'potential dialogue': the issue is not, primarily, shared knowledge, but shared opinions and values; providing, not information as such, but acceptable reasons.
3. There is no strict *definition of a good argument:* in natural argumentation, quality of argument is primarily based on shared beliefs (topoi). It seems possible to propose some empirical rules concerning the validity of an argumentation, or the soundness of reasons, as in van Eemeren and Grootendorst's theory: provided that soundness is related to a definite situation (topic, audience, *etc.*). One of the main consequences is the role of 'discursive negotiation' in argumentative writing (Coirier *et al.*, 1990; Golder & Pouit, this volume), the frequent need for reformulation, modalization, and restriction, to ensure the sharing of minimal common rules.

Organization and coherence
Organizing processes have a fundamental status in the writing process models (Bereiter & Scardamalia, 1987; Hayes & Flower, 1980; van Dijk & Kintsch, 1983). These operations relate ideas to each other in a hierarchical structure as a basis for a coherent text structure. Organization processes rely on different sources. The first source is an efficient topic structure in long-term memory, which is characteristic of expert knowledge (Voss, Vesonder & Spilich, 1979). When the topic is not well organized, a second source is playing a role: the application of mental schemas (logical, spatial, temporal) (see, for example, Trabasso & van den Broek's 1985 model about the role of causal thinking in narratives; Black & Bower (1982) about plans and goals in understanding stories). In addition, the organization can be realized during the translating process.

These sources of organization are not necessarily incompatible, particularly in complex referential domains. In addition, particular pragmatic constraints can lead to competition between them. This leads us to emphasize that the knowledge transforming process described by Bereiter and Scardamalia (1987) is not restricted to the interaction between the content space and the rhetorical space. Knowledge transformation may also be applied to content restructuring when a topic is organized from different perspectives, goals, or points of view, and this frequently occurs in argumentation, as we will see now.

Sources for organization
According to van Dijk and Kintsch (1983), the organization of ideas retrieved from long term memory provides both the macro- and the microstructure of the text. Two principles would guide the idea organization in a text. The first consists of exploiting the constraints inherent to ideas, for instance their logical relationships, or their chronological order. As for any text, this could be an important characteristic of coherent argumentation. The second principle is the use of rhetorical strategies (Meyer, 1975) to impose a structure to the retrieved ideas. An example in argumentation is the organization based on the orientation of arguments: pro or contra the thesis. Bromberg and Dorna (1985), for example, have observed three main types of argument organization: (1) grouping the *pro*-arguments on one side, and the *contra*-arguments on the other side, (2) linking directly each *pro*-argument with the corresponding *contra*-argument, and (3) the

in-depth development of one main line of arguments, integrating (subordinating) *contra*-arguments to this main line.

The role assigned to the second principle postulated by van Dijk and Kintsch (1983) can be assimilated to the use of organizing strategies, such as making drafts, outlines, or diagrams. In a recent study about argumentative writing, Isnard and Piolat (1994) experimentally manipulated these strategies. Text composition was preceded by three conditions: (1) free-association of ideas, (2) outlined organization, and (3) diagrammatic organization. The authors observed that:

> Writers who are not forced to organize their ideas in a given fashion do not perform in-depth reorganization, and pass directly from the jotting down of a few and disorganized and undeveloped ideas to the writing of an elaborated final text. Mandatory structuring, on the other hand, allows writers to discover new ideas. *It remains to be seen whether these 'discoveries' enhance the quality of the final text as a whole* [italics added] (p. 463).

The last sentence underlines that the quality of an argumentative text cannot only be measured by counting the number of arguments. The way in which arguments are connected, their textual structure, constitutes by itself a large part of argumentation, as can be observed in the role of rhetorical figures, but also in the fact that textual structure is one way of determining main points in a text.

Another source for organizing operations is the use of schemas (see Piolat *et al.* in this volume). Toulmin (1958) has proposed a prototypical schema of argumentation[1], which includes five components (the different examples are taken from Espéret, Coirier, Coquin-Viennot, and Passerault (1987)): (1) *Claim*: taking a stance in a discussion (*Children should be given pocket money as soon as they reach the age of twelve years*); (2) *Evidence*, data: reason, proof, and facts (*it would allow them to buy what they want*); (3) *Warrant*: inference (linking) rules (*it's quite natural that children be allowed to choose what they buy*); (4) *Backing*: support of the warrant (*it teaches them to deal with money*); (5) *Rebuttal*: restrictions or specifications (*especially if they don't spend it inconsiderately*) and counter-arguments (*even though they may be given quite a lot*).

Even adults do not systematically use all these components in all argumentation. In addition, the components are not easily and unambiguously identified in actual discourse. Warrants, for instance, are frequently implicit and considered to be shared beliefs (topoi). Despite these practical drawbacks, Toulmin's model is based upon characteristic operations in argumentation. The products of these operations are very likely to be found in argumentative texts, whether written or oral, in monologues, as well as in dialogues. Crammond (1998) has recently specified some components of the model, such as the role and specification of counterarguments and modulations (qualifiers, rebuttals). Moreover, she has proposed complex text analysis procedures (referring to the framework of Frederiksen, 1975; 1987), which allow a precise description of written argumentative texts.

Gombert (1997) has used a quite different approach, based on the interplay of pro- and contra-arguments (Adam, 1992; Charolles, 1980, 1986; Moeschler, 1980; Perkins, Farady & Bushey, 1991). She has distinguished two components in the argumentative process: a justification process, similar to Toulmin's claim-backing, where arguers mainly provide reasons defending their point of view, and an argumentative process, where arguers also take into account the opposite information, integrating the point of view of their (potential) opponents. The study of the interrelationships among pro-arguments and contra-arguments, by taking into account the text structure, allows Gombert to operationalize a typology of argumentative strategies. These strategies range from a pure justification to a 'true' argumentation, the latter being more or less complex as a function of the realized interplay between the pros and contras.

One possible criticism to Gombert's framework lies in the fact that the difference between 'justification' and 'argumentation' is a question of degree in cognitive development, and may be dependent on task assignments. It was observed in many developmental experiments that justification (claim-backing) always precedes the use of counterargumentation. More particularly, from twelve years onwards, the claim-backing structure constitutes an important (and sufficient) condition for a text to be judged as argumentative. However, the use of counterarguments, or even modulations (restrictions or specifications), leads students to consider such a text as argumentative only from the ages of fifteen to seventeen (Golder & Coirier, 1994). The argumentative schema, which seems to constitute the basis of the judgments, may evolve quite gradually from justification to argumentation.

Gombert and Crammond's frameworks help to pay attention to an important requirement of elaborated argumentation: the mastery of linguistic relationships in order to express the complex structures implied in elaborated argumentation (subordination, concession, embedding). This is also implied by Bakhtine's (1981) conception, according to which monologal argumentation can be conceived as an internalized dialogue. In this line of reasoning, Roussey and Gombert (1996) have analyzed differences between individual composition and a collaborative situation in which two participants compose a text together. The individual writer, who respects the dialogic character of the argumentative text, must thus 'write for two'. The authors further distinguished in each situation expert and non-expert writers. They showed that the collaborative writing condition leads to texts of higher quality in terms of appropriate use of a schema, but only for experts (adult writing serving as reference). Conversely, collaborative writing does not help (nor hinder) the non-expert writers. For non-experts, collaborative argumentative reasoning results in higher cognitive load, because a dialog plus an argumentation have to be simultaneously managed. This load is greatly reduced for textual experts who are able to use the required linguistic means (concerning cooperative writing, see Giroud, and Veerman & Treasure-Jones, this volume).

Reasoning, problem solving, and argumentation
The organizing process in elaborated argumentative texts, and particularly the processing of relationships implied in complex reasoning, is a real problem for writers. Therefore argumentation can be seen as a problem solving task. Voss, Green, Post and Penner (1983) have analyzed the production of texts from documents concerning the solution to sociopolitical difficulties in the former USSR. Problem solving in the social sciences is characterized by the lack of an agreed upon solution, and writers must provide arguments to justify the solutions they propose. This is a typical argumentative situation: there is an initial disagreement and a claim-backing. Moreover, the evaluation of the proposed solutions relies on unclear constraints. Voss and his colleagues have revealed the double component of these texts; they are organized both from a problem solving perspective (goals, sub-goals, prerequisites, *etc.*), and from an argumentation perspective (identifying conflicts, evaluating, justifying, *etc.*). Experts and novices in social sciences use different strategies for the organization of their texts. For example, top-down strat-

egies are more frequent with experts, who, in addition, assign a more important role to argumentation (the Voss, Wiley & Sandak's chapter in this volume illustrates the same framework in the field of legal controversies).

Different studies undertaken by Perfetti *et al.* (Britt, Rouet, Perfetti & Georgi, 1994; Perfetti, Britt, Rouet, Georgi & Mason, 1994), refer to the problem of historical document processing. A writer involved in the synthesis of historical documents, most often polemic, must deal with two types of information. First there is a 'situation model' which expresses the chronological and causal structure of events (Trabasso & van den Broek, 1985). Secondly, there is an 'argument model' which, in reference to Toulmin (1958), integrates argumentative components such as evaluations, restrictions, counterarguments, and the explicitation of enunciative sources. These authors observe the effects of expertise, as in argumentative writing, particularly with regard to domain knowledge. In addition, procedural knowledge (about processing the historical controversies) appears to be a crucial factor. Experts give more importance to the evaluation of the enunciative sources (Rouet, Favart, Gaonac'h & Lacroix, 1996), and it is obvious that this last component pertains to argumentation.

So, most often in argumentation, two perspectives are playing a role: a problem solving/topic structure, and an argumentation structure. Experts can solve the dissonance between these perspectives: they can rely on expert knowledge about the two dimensions. Non-experts rely mostly on the topic structure.

In an approach more specific to problem solving studies, Brandt (1989) has asked children to play a game, the 'Nim game', where two children had to play cooperatively against the experimenter. This game implies a succession of turns, both players (both: the two children, then the experimenter, then the children, *etc.*) alternatively making a move and to justifying it. During the whole game, the conversations between the two children were audiotaped. Such a paradigm allows us to clearly differentiate two components: (1) the reasoning steps implied in the solving process (for example: goals, sub-goals, preconditions, *etc.*), and (2) the argumentative component; that is, the way in which the children justify each move in the game. Their verbal exchanges were analyzed according to argumentative categories such as the use of an example or an analogy, the degree of certainty about the issue, the contrast (another move would lead to a loss), the legality of the move according to the game rules, the uncertainty because the reply of the adversary cannot be predicted, *etc.* Brandt's main results show that the quality of the argumentation strongly depends on complexity of the problem at a given step in the solution process. The more complex the problem, the more complex is the argumentation. In other words, argumentation relates to the organization and the complexity of the referential field: the execution of a complex move implies that the player must be an expert. A triangular relationship can thus be formulated: the complexity of the organization process is related to the complexity of the topic, and a more complex organization requires more justifications and refutations.

In the section on definitions and requirements we already referred to the study by Erkens and Andriessen (1994) about the strategies used in cooperative problem solving. These authors conclude that fruitful cooperation requires participants to negotiate a common frame of reference. Their conclusion can be related to Brandt's results, and it corresponds to the main goal of argumentation: the building up of common frames of reference which allows us to elaborate the common representations required by solutions to the problems of everyday life.

This resembles the rules formulated by van Eemeren and Grootendorst (1992b), at least for complying with a civilized way of ruling conflicts.

We defined organizing as the process by which writers relate ideas; the relationships may be varied (logical, causal, *etc.*) and lead to the formation of complex structures. Organizing constitutes an important process in 'EAT' writing, and reasoning - informal or not - is a strong basis of argumentation. The above mentioned results support the following two conclusions:

1. It is necessary to differentiate (1) the processes associated with the organization or re-organization of the referential domain, and (2) the more specifically argumentative processes: identifying the main conflicts, taking into account the counterarguments, appreciating the other's reasons, *etc.* The organization process clearly relies on reasoning and cannot be entirely dissociated from either the idea generation process, or from the selection and evaluation process.
2. The same topic can be organized in several ways, according to goals, pragmatic assignment, *etc.* In addition, any argumentation can include explanation, reasoning, problem solving, and rhetoric 'dispositio'[2]. Any writing model of argumentation should include these sub-components. Besides, their interrelationships constitute a major source of difficulty for the organizing process. Precisely identifying the many constraints implied in such a complex task, and their role in argumentative writing, requires specific indicators or operators. These are currently not available, even if some proposals of artificial intelligence research (see Baker, this volume) may shed some light on the question.

4.5 Translating: Linearization and linguistic coding

From conceptualizing to linearizing
Linearization can be defined as the process of expressing a cognitive representation into a linear sequence of information. When composing an elaborated argumentation, the writer must carefully order the presentation of information in the text. This information can be linked by a great variety of relationships: logical chaining for causality (exemplified by a connective such as *then*), coordination of arguments with the same orientation (*e.g., and*), opposition of orientations (*e.g., but*), restrictions (*e.g., only if*), *etc*. At the same time, structuring the information has to be done in such a way that the text converges towards the main communicative goal: to make the addressee accept the proposed standpoint.

According to many researchers (*e.g.*, Levelt, 1981; Bock, 1982), the linearization process is a major problem in discourse production. We illustrate this problem here with an example taken from Marchand (1993). She asked participants to write a text where they had to combine eight predetermined arguments to make a coherent text, with the following instruction: '*Convince your addressee that It's good to practice sport regularly*'. The text had to end with this italicized sentence (9). The participants were required to put these arguments in a coherent order, and were allowed to add text (especially connectives) if necessary. The eight imposed arguments were:
1. sport ensures better work at school
2. sport takes up time
3. practicing sport ensures good health
4. some sports are dangerous

5. sport is a good way to relax
6. sport is a pleasant leisure activity
7. sport may interfere with schoolwork
8. too much endurance sport is a risk for the heart

In terms of their relationships, these eight arguments can be organized as is shown in Figure 1.

Figure 1 Possible organization of arguments in the sport example

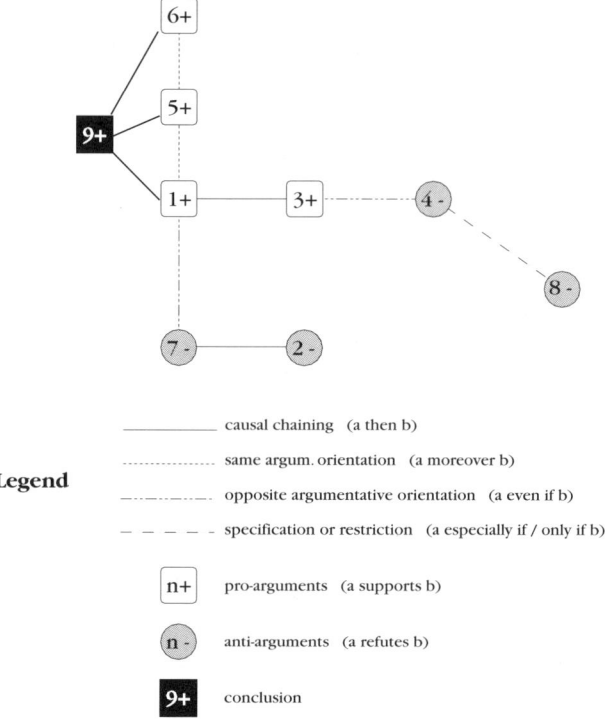

This hierarchical organization can be seen as a 'conceptualization' expressing the output of the organization phase in writing. The task for the writer is now to linearize the arguments, to put them in the order as they would appear in the actual text, and then to linguistically code the resulting sequence, by specifying the relationships between arguments in order to form a coherent structure of sentences. One actually observed textualization was:

> (7) Sport may interfere with schoolwork, because (2) it takes up time. However, even if (4) some sports are dangerous (especially (8) endurance sports), (3) practicing sports regularly ensures good health. Thus (1) it allows for better work at school. Moreover, (5) sport is a good way to relax and (6) a pleasant leisure activity. Thus (9) you should practice sports regularly.

This example allows us to differentiate four typical processes in argumentative writing:

1. the *reasoning* process – that is, the computation of logical relations between pieces of information; for example, (7) and (2) are in a causal relation, (8) constitutes a specification of (4), and (1) is incompatible with (7);
2. the *argumentative* process, consisting of choosing the best hierarchical organization of argumentative information, taking into account the orientation (for or against the main position) of arguments;
3. the *linearization* process, to combine pro- and counterarguments in a sequence;
4. the *linguistic coding* process to express, with means of linguistic tools (connectives, embedding), the structure which has been built up;

These four types of problems are very much interrelated, and they can only be observed separately in constructed experimental conditions. In the next main section, we will discuss such an attempt to study more specifically the linearization process. Before that, we will address the issue of linguistic coding.

Linguistic coding
In most models of writing, linguistic coding is underestimated. It is generally restricted to lexicalization and sentence generation. For example, Kellogg (1996) wrote: 'The outputs of planning may be propositional representations that are *readily handled* by the process of linguistic translation [italics added]' (p. 60). Indeed, as noted by Fayol (1991), the problem of linearization is often characterized by the translation of a multidimensional structure (from long-term memory) into a unidimensional structure (in the text surface). However, the problem does not only concern ordering: the writer also has to define the structure of the sequence, and to preserve markers of the mental organization (Coirier, 1996). The group of successive sentences must express complex relationships between these sentences: subordination, coordination, specification or concession relationships, and this has to be expressed especially by means of syntax, punctuation, connectives, and the anaphoric system. These *textualizing operations* (Apotheloz, 1990; Bronckart *et al.*, 1985; Fayol & Schneuwly, 1987; Schneuwly, 1988), or *organization devices* (Boscolo, 1995), are crucial for the linguistic realization of the text plan, at least if the text has to express the structure of the information. It raises the question of the textual devices, and the specific linguistic skills required by the text structuring. In an ideal situation, the specification of relationships between elements by use of syntax, connectives, and textual organizers should allow the reader to exactly reconstruct the original structure in the mind of the writer. But that supposes high linguistic expertise.

Indeed, many textual devices are mastered late in the course of development: this can be observed for punctuation (Chanquoy, 1998; Fayol, 1989; Favart & Passerault, 1996; Chanquoy & Fayol, 1991, 1995; Fayol & Abdi, 1988), anaphorae (De Weck, 1991), thematic elaboration (Apotheloz, 1990; Coirier, Broggio & De Bernardi, 1996; Marchand, 1993; Marchand, Coirier, & Dellerman, 1996; Scinto, 1984), connectives (Chanquoy, 1998; Chanquoy & Costeplane, 1995; Fayol, 1986; Schneuwly, 1986; Schneuwly, Rosat & Dolz, 1989), and complex syntax (Feilke, 1996). However, the issue is not restricted to the mastery of linguistic devices as such. These linguistic tools must often be managed simultaneously when writing a text: lexical choices are associated with grammatical constraints, introducing a concession implies managing the thematic structure adequately, and restricting or specifying is generally linked to subordination. In addition, linguistic devices are partly interdependent: syntactic choices will set constraints on connectives,

connectives on punctuation, punctuation on anaphora, *etc*. The different textual devices are not entirely interrelated, but they nevertheless constitute what can be defined as an integrated textual system. From a psychological perspective, managing this whole system constitutes a critical issue. Different types of empirical data can be considered here, mainly: (1) the strong need for explicitness (hence cohesion devices) when the relationships between ideas are not easily inferable, which is the case in argumentative essays (McCutchen, 1987); (2) the interference between insufficient automatization of the linguistic processes and the organization of content (Bourdin & Fayol, 1994; Glynn, Britton, Muth & Dogan, 1982; Jeffery & Underwood, 1996; McCutchen, 1984; 1988; McCutchen, Covill, Hoyne et Mildes, 1994); (3) the interdependence of conceptualization and linguistic skills (Dellerman, Coirier & Marchand, 1996; Gombert & Roussey, 1994).

Linguistic expertise thus appears as an important constraint on the emergency of elaborated argumentative texts, and this till the age of twelve to thirteen. In a revision task, Akiguet (1992; Akiguet & Piolat, 1996) observed that before the age of ten, children are not able to select the correct connectives needed to compose a coherent sequence with arguments and counterarguments. Even ten to eleven year olds did not find many optimal solutions.

Besides the difficulties resulting from an insufficient linguistic expertise, the problem raised by the need to manage the different devices simultaneously can be illustrated in a study led by Marchand, Coirier, and Dellerman (1996), where twelve to eighteen year old students were asked to write several argumentative essays. The results obtained showed that between eleven to eigtheen there is an increased mastery of textual devices (anaphora, connectives, complex syntax, thematic continuity, *etc*.), which is commonplace. However, in the younger children, a factorial analysis showed the main differences to be associated with the degree of linguistic expertise, opposing low to high degrees of mastery. With older children, no such factorial opposition was observed. The analysis showed two main axes. The first one opposed a focus on cohesion and thematization on the one hand, to the use of enunciative markers, on the other. The second opposition was between intrasentential organization (syntax), and intersentential organization (connectives).

Mastery of linguistic devices on the one hand, and of their interdependency and simultaneous managing on the other, could well appear as the main obstacle to the production of EAT, where complex relationships have to be expressed precisely. This differentiates argumentation from narration or, more generally, from all types of text where the translating can rely on simple structures: causality, chronology, and space organization. In addition, it must also be noted that one essential aspect of argumentation is that translating relies solely on the writer's mental organization, and most often, the corresponding referential domain (main ideas are opinions and beliefs) is not strongly structured (Voss *et al*., 1983). Thus it is no surprise that EATs are rarely observed in young children.

Finally, considering the characteristics of argumentation and the important role of language in that domain, it seems doubtful that linguistic coding could be located at such low levels as it is in some models. Defining ideas and their interrelationships, and organizing the argumentative structure, probably requires sophisticated linguistic skills from the very start of composing. Moreover, the linguistic specification of the relationships between ideas may constitute an argumentative operation by itself: it is not the same to use 'however', 'even though', or 'but', when expressing the opposition between two arguments.

To conclude, concerning the translating process in argumentative text writing, we would like to underline the following points:
1. Linearization, at least for elaborated texts (EATs for example), cannot be restricted to sentence formulation, nor to lexical and semantic choices. The expression of the main structural relations in the organized content relies on higher linguistic levels, 'textual' levels: thematic continuity, structuring by punctuation, intersentential organization, *etc*. Although this is not specific to argumentative texts, the above considerations lead us to assume that the dependency is much more critical in this case.
2. Writing models are not precise enough as regards the exact level where linearizing can be distinguished from linguistic coding (Berninger & Swanson, 1994), mainly because they do not take into account (or underestimate) the level of the linguistic structure of the text.

In the preceding sections we discussed a theoretical definition of elaborated argumentative texts, and the specific difficulties associated with their compositions, and we found problems in all components of the writing process. In the next section we will present an experimental simulation of argumentative writing. This simulation aims primarily at distinguishing what exactly characterizes the difficulties of argumentative writing: the conceptual or global level – that of the choice of arguments – or the more local level – that of the linear organization of the chosen arguments.

5 AN EXPERIMENTAL SIMULATION

In the process of composing a text, two main groups of processes can be distinguished: the processes of conceptual planning, including idea generation, evaluation, and organization; and the translation of the constructed conceptualization into a linear sequence of sentences. The translation process can again be divided into two subprocesses, linearization and linguistic coding. The main assumption put forward in this chapter is that the transition from conceptualization to effectively written texts presents specific difficulties for argumentative writing. More precisely, as the 'sport example' has shown (see above), this problem can be envisaged as that of ordering the ideas included in a multidimensional conceptual structure, as a linguistic sequence, which represents the initial conceptual structure as effectively as possible. It seems that a writer must comply with contradictory requirements, both respecting the hierarchical organization of reasons, and respecting textual constraints such as topic continuity and thematic organization. The requirements of conceptualization would be much better described as a diagram of relationships than as a linear sequence.

The goal of the present section is to simulate this conflict by experimentally isolating argumentative and thematic constraints in a sentence selection paradigm. In the first part of this chapter we defined a number of requirements for the composition of an elaborated argumentative text (EAT). These requirements are operationalized as argumentative and thematic constraints that have to be met by the children (ten to fourteen years old) in our experiment. In this chapter we only present the most relevant results, more details of the experiment are reported elsewhere (Andriessen, Coirier, Roos, Passerault & Bert-Erboul, 1996; Coirier & Andriessen, in preparation).

5.1 The alpha-omega paradigm

The alpha-omega paradigm (Brassart, 1992) involves composing an argumentative text on the basis of an imposed starting claim, Alpha (*e.g., speeding is advantageous*), and an imposed contradictory or opposing conclusion, Omega (*e.g., speeding is dangerous*). The participants' task is to produce a text between Alpha and Omega, and still generate a coherent argumentation. The argumentative and thematic constraints that are supposed to compete during linearization and formulation are illustrated in Table 1. The first type (argumentative) involves grouping arguments according to their argumentative orientation, which implies starting with arguments *in favor* of Alpha (α+ and ω+), to be followed by an explicit shift to arguments *in favor* of Omega (α- and ω+). The other type (thematic) involves starting with arguments *about* Alpha (α+ and α-), to be followed by an explicit shift to arguments *about* Omega (α- and ω+).

We used this paradigm in a series of experiments in which we not only imposed the first and the last sentences, but also the options for the sentences that could come in between. For example, Andriessen *et al.* (1996) asked the participants to select six sentences from a list of twenty-four. These sentences comprised equal amounts of the four following types of arguments:
1. pro-alpha (α+): arguments justifying alpha;
2. anti-alpha (α-): arguments refuting alpha;
3. pro-omega (ω+): arguments justifying omega;
4. anti-omega (ω-): arguments refuting omega.

Table 1   Argumentative and thematic constraints during an argumentative text production.

Textual organization Argumentative orientation	Theme Alpha (Arguments related to Alpha)	Theme Omega (Arguments related to Omega)
Arguments pro-Alpha	α+, α+, α+...	ω-, ω-, ω-...
Arguments pro-Omega	α-, α-, α-...	ω+, ω+, ω+...

Different constraints for selection and types of presenting the instructions were systematically used (Coirier & Andriessen, in preparation). For our current purpose, we collapse the data of 578 individual protocols. The goal of this presentation is to provide information about the extent to which thematic and argumentative constraints are dealt with in a task to which they are explicitly addressed. Because, in this paradigm, content generation and sentence formulation problems (and advantages) are artificially removed, it becomes possible to focus on evaluation and selection, as well as on organization and linearization. A focus on evaluation, for example, could involve a comparison of preferences for arguments in terms of differing strength and relevance. A focus on organization could be the analysis of different types of sentence re-ordering, as in a diagram. A focus on linearization could involve the analysis of the consecutive selection of argumentative sentences. This last task also implies selection and evaluation.

In this chapter we use the results to analyze the types of selected arguments in terms of their argumentative orientation and the ways in which these arguments were put into a sequential order. As this concerns an experimental task, and not a writing assignment, it seems precarious to generalize the obtained results to actual writing situations. We can only suppose that important overlap exists with the above mentioned writing processes. The results must to some extent be comparable to more natural writing situations, while at the same time addressing specific issues that cannot be obtained in those situations. In our opinion, analyzing how the constraints we formulated for argumentative writing are met in the alpha-omega paradigm, should be considered as an important step towards greater insight into the selection and linearization problems in argumentative text production.

Argumentative and textual constraints in alpha-omega
For this task, we re-defined the argumentative *constraints* provided earlier in the chapter in the following way:
1. Recognizing the existence of a conflict between two different positions on the same topic: ω arguments (+ or -) and α arguments (+ or -) should be present in the text.
2. Recognizing the topic as debatable is presupposed by the instructions.
3. To be inclined to solve the conflict is a default supposition for participants in this study.
4. To be inclined to try to solve the conflict by means of language follows because it is a task that uses language.
5. Taking a stance, in this case it is imposed that Ω is superior to A, thus arguments in favor of Ω should be more important than arguments favoring A.
6. Supporting the claim with reasons (claim backing): Ω should have more support, so (ω+ and α-) should be more important than (ω- and α+).
7. Assigning a minimal value to the opposite claim and reasons: α+ and ω- should be included in the text.
8. Restricting or modulating the opposing claims, by using counterargumen-tation (Ω, but ω-; A, but α-), implying that both α- and ω- should be included into the text.

If all provided arguments are considered to have the same strength (which is not a decision that can be made for every participant), we would generally predict for all protocols that ω+ arguments would be selected most often, followed by α- arguments, which would be more frequently selected than α+, and that the selection of ω- would be the least frequent. From the examination of our 578 protocols we observed the following frequencies: ω+: 52.4%, α-: 25.5%, α+: 10.7% and ω-: 11.4%. This is quite in line with the predictions. The predominance of the arguments favorable to Omega (77.9%) is probably due to the fact that Omega is the assigned goal. In addition, participants also used many counterarguments (22.1%).

In this artificial situation, *textual requirements* mainly concern local coherence and thematization (do not go from alpha to omega, back and forth, *etc.*). They can be defined in the following way:
- to ensure local coherence in the textual sequence:
  - co-orientation of arguments, requiring linguistic coordination (*and* or equivalents):
    α+ *and* α+; α+ *and* ω-; ω+ *and* ω+; ω- *and* α+;

- anti-orientation of arguments, requiring opposition or concession (*but, even if,* etc.):

  α+ *but* α-; ω+ *even if* ω-; α+ *but* ω+; etc.
- to ensure thematic continuity:
  - if starting with alpha, maintain theme A:A $\Rightarrow$ α (+ or -), α (+ or -), α(+ or -);
  - if ending with omega, develop theme Ω: ω (+ or -), ω (+ or -), ω (+ or -) $\Rightarrow$ Ω.

Complying with both argumentative and textual requirements could lead to this textual structure:

ALPHA

/because/ [α+, α+...]

/but/ [α-, α-...] /moreover/ [ω+, ω+...]

/then/ {/even if/ [ω-, ω-...] /however/ [ω+, ω+...]}

/so/

OMEGA

Rules operationalizing the main constraints

In order to analyze the extent to which the participants meet the constraints, we formulated a series of rules that may be considered a possible operationalization of these constraints:

- Rule 1: Alpha thematization is respected if there are at least 2 alpha (+ or -) in the first half of the text.
- Rule 2: Omega thematization is respected if there are at least 2 omega (+ or -) in the second half of the text.
- Rule 3: Thematization constraints are fully respected if rules 1 and 2 are jointly respected (*i.e.*, are present in the same protocol).
- Rule 4: Alpha orientation is respected if there are at least 2 pro-alpha (alpha+ or omega-) in the first half of the text.
- Rule 5: Omega-orientation is respected if there are at least 2 pro-omega (omega+ or alpha-) in the second half of the text.
- Rule 6: Orientation constraints are fully respected if rules 4 and 5 are jointly respected.
- Rule 7: Textual organization is optimally realized if rules 3 and 6 are jointly respected. This is what could be called textual expertise.

Table 2 shows the percentages of participants that respect each of these rules, based on the analyses of texts produced by 578 writers, between ten and fourteen years old.

The first point worth noting is that the obtained results are neither incoherent, nor opposed to results established by other researchers in more natural situations (*e.g.*, Brassart, 1992; De Bernardi & Antolini, 1996). Most of the participants respect the alpha-thematization constraint, *or* the omega-thematization constraint. Some children respect the alpha-orientation constraint and, as expected, most of the graders comply with the goal they are ascribed to, which is to defend omega (85.3%). With 24% of the writers omega is never simply asserted, as they also produce restrictions on omega. Moreover, there are more participants who respect omega-thematization (70.2%) than alpha-thematization (40.1%). However, and this is a main point, only 22% of the writers manage both alpha- and omega-thematization (R3). The same problem is observed with the orientations, as 24% of the participants respect alpha-orientation, 85.3% omega-orientation, but the combined alpha- and omega-orientation (R6) is only respected by 16.3% of the writers. Finally, no more than 6.4% of the participants were able to simultaneously respect thematization and argumentative requirements (R7), and, consequently, to follow all the rules.

Table 2   *Proportions of subjects respecting the rules of argumentative writing*

Respect of Alpha ⇒ Omega requirements	
Rule 1: Thematization alpha: 2 alpha (α+ or α-) in 1st half	40.1
Rule 2: Thematization omega: 2 omega (ω+ or ω-) in 2nd half	70.2
Rule 3: Rule 1 + Rule 2	22.0
Rule 4: Orientation alpha: 2 pro alpha (α+ or α-) in 1st half	24.0
Rule 5: Orientation omega: 2 pro omega (ω+ or α-) in 2nd half	85.3
Rule 6: Rule 4 + Rule 5	16.3
Rule 7: (Experts): Rule 3 + Rule 6	6.4

In conclusion, it appears that simultaneously complying with the complex requirements of written elaborated argumentation can be considered as a difficult task. This can be attributed to a multiplicity of factors, among them the difficulty to combine a non-linear argumentative structure (or a random list of arguments) with the necessary linear structure of a text. This problem can be explained in terms of cognitive overload, or yet in terms of inefficient processing strategies. This question remains largely open to more specific investigation.

Some more light can be thrown on this issue by looking at the experimental assignments used in this simulation. As previously mentioned, there were many different conditions. For example, we compared situations in which participants were required start with alpha and to end with omega, with a situation in which only omega was imposed at the end, and also with a situation in which it was possible to freely choose alpha or omega as the conclusion to be supported. It is interesting to note that in this last condition, the percentage of experts (*i.e.*, writers who respect all the rules) sensibly increases: 21.4% vs. 6.4% averaged over all conditions.

In summary, simultaneously managing the (more or less contradictory) constraints of textual thematization and argumentative orientation constitutes a critical difficulty when writing elaborated argumentative texts. De Bernardi and Antolini (1996) have shown that this difficulty can be reduced if both conflicting points of view are presented from the start, and if the task allows a clear separation between the conceptualization process and the linearization process (see also: Andriessen *et al.*, 1996). It would be interesting to experimentally dissociate the various processes (despite their interrelationships) which intervene during the production of elaborated argumentative texts. This would be particularly useful in clarifying the difficulties encountered in such complex tasks.

6 CONCLUSION

A functional approach to define the characteristics of argumentative text writing entails establishing specific relationships (1) between the goal of the text and the parameters of the situation in which this goal can be appropriate, and (2) between the goal of the text and the different pragmatic, conceptual, and linguistic devices necessary for its realization.

The goal of argumentation is to persuade other persons to modify their opinions or beliefs about a controversial topic. This presupposes a situation in which a conflict is identified as such, it has to be a conflict on debatable topics, and participants have to be inclined to solve the conflict by means of discussion, hence the use of language. Once these constraints are satisfied, the goal to convince the addressee requires the application of a number of relevant operations: supporting one's claim with acceptable reasons, and recognizing the strength and relevance of the opposite position. The discursive goal and the ensuing operations impose specific constraints on the various processes involved in text composition. Satisfying the argumentative constraints usually implies the use of complex linguistic devices, 'textual' tools such as complex syntax, connectives, punctuation, anaphorae, and thematization. These tools are mandatory for translating an initially multidimensional mental structure into a linguistic sequence of sentences, while preserving at the same time the markers of the mental organization. Such tools are far from being mastered, but are unconsciously applied by young children, which could explain the developmental lag between early complex argumentation and later argumentative textual elaboration.

Looking more closely at the different processes implied in writing, we can point out four characteristics that stand out in argumentative writing.

1. Most of the time the main points to be generated in argumentation (for example, warrants) consist of opinions and beliefs. The meaning of such abstract objects is generally malleable, negotiable, so there is a strong need to be clear and explicit. At the level of content organizing, idea relationships also must clearly defined, especially by precise lexical choices, textual organizers, and connectives.
2. Convincing another person supposes generating the appropriate reasons for supporting one's point of view. It also supposes taking into account other's reasons and interests. This has two consequences: first, the generation of ideas in argumentation strongly relies on the search for 'debatable', and acceptable, reasons for this precise addressee, in this precise context; second, the linguistic formulation of reasons (*e.g.* modulation, modalization) and their textual presentation constitute important argumentative (rhetorical) means.
3. An elaborated argumentation will have to integrate in the same text both supporting reasons and the refutation of opposite claims, thus coherently managing conflicting arguments in the same linguistic sequence. Again, this requires linguistic expertise. In addition, argumentation usually includes at least two different types of organization: reasoning and arguing. This double organization has to be expressed in a coherent sequence by, again, the use of specific linguistic structural operators (syntax, connectives, *etc.*).
4. Taking into account the previous characteristics and their processing consequences lead us to attribute a decisive role to the final stages of writing: linearization and linguistic coding. All the difficulties encountered in the other processes converge at this level. Perhaps one of the most striking difficulties is

managing the conflicting requirements ensuing from the other processes; trying to comply simultaneously with a coherent presentation of the argumentative structure and the linguistic requirement of thematic continuity in a linear sequence.

Considering the requirements of elaborated argumentative writing, it is necessary to ask to what extent the current writing models are appropriate to describe the implied processes. It is obvious that idea generation, evaluation, and organization are to be considered distinct, but interdependent, processes. For example, idea organization may lead to the research and generation of new ideas (Galbraith, 1996; 1999). Similarly, argumentative strategies simultaneously intervene in the selection of ideas, in their recovery, but also in their organization. It is thus not possible to conceive the three processes as strictly ordered in time. Some complex system of interdependencies must be envisaged.

The idea generation process raises the question of knowledge. Finding or elaborating arguments presupposes that the corresponding information is available in the long-term memory. However, this problem probably concerns the nature more specifically than the quantity of available knowledge. For example, opinions and beliefs play a very central role, and access to memory may be controlled by standpoints, or by particular strategies. Moreover, opinions, beliefs, and desires are socio-cultural objects, with a malleable meaning. Consequently, the discursive negotiation appears as a fundamental process, which relies strongly on linguistic skills.

Concerning evaluation and selection, the use of appropriate strategies is also considered as fundamental. In this respect, soundness and acceptability of reasons are crucial factors. However, there are no strict rules (except in formal domains such as scientific or legal debates) to define what is a good reason, because it depends on socio-cultural factors. Acceptability seems a better concept as it leads to the definition sound reasons in relation to a given audience, hence to shared opinions (*i.e.*, topoi). Within this perspective, soundness should be defined in relation to a given community - a community sharing opinions and beliefs in a given domain. In other words, soundness could be reformulated as 'acceptable in this context and for these people'.

The organization process manifests complex characteristics. As with the other writing processes, it depends on long-term memory, the organization of information, the presence of an eventual argumentative schema, and so on. The Toulmin schema offers here a good basis, but it minimizes the role of counterarguments. Conversely, the schema proposed by Gombert emphasizes the interplay of pro- and contra-arguments, but its structure as a schema can be discussed. Indeed, this schema could be conceived as a means of structuring the text; that is, connecting the different arguments in a coherent way.

While writing an argumentative text, the linearization process involves constructing a linear sequence out of a multidimensional structure. This activity appears to depend on at least two constraints: (1) the idea organization must allow building of coherent sequences, rightly reflecting the mental organization, and (2) the linguistic or textual devices must play a fundamental role ensuring text cohesion, and expressing the precise structure of the information. These devices enable the writer to determine what must be clustered, opposed, or embedded, which lines are parallel, *etc*. This last point leads to the main difficulties associated with EAT writing. More particularly, it is now well established that young children do not master many of the required corresponding linguistic devices, and neither do all adults. In addition, writing an elaborated text raises the problem of managing different constraints at the same time. Without appropriate strategies, this can lead to a cognitive overload, and it could explain the positive effects of assignments allowing the separate management of the different sub-processes, such as a preplanning strategy.

Recent writing research has revealed that the processes described in most models are too general and insufficiently specified. This is particularly the case for the pragmatic component (Alamargot & Chanquoy, in press). Despite the importance attributed to the functional control of the main components of argumentative writing, the definition and the roles of this process are still not clear. Proposals by Bronckart (1996; Bronckart *et al.*, 1985) are interesting steps in this direction. Finally, it is possible to make the same remarks concerning the lack of clear specifications about the concepts of evaluation, selection, relevance, and appropriateness. However, the main criticism about available writing models, when envisaging elaborated argumentative texts, concerns the role of language. This role is clearly underestimated in the process of linearizing-translating, and it is probably one of the most interesting issues in future research about argumentative writing.

NOTES

1   This schema, of course, is not only helpful for organizing texts, but also for idea generation, selection, and evaluation: *'Do I have enough ideas? No, I forgot the rebuttal...'*.
2   Rhetoric dispositio: the way, the style, the order in which ideas are related, or presented: irony, false interrogation, degree of implicitness... (Brewer, 1980).

Reasoning in the Construction of Argumentative Texts

James F. Voss
University of Pittsburgh
Jennifer Wiley
University at Vancouver
Rebecca Sandak
University at Vancouver

ABSTRACT

This chapter is concerned with the relation between reasoning and argumentation. The position taken is that reasoning generally takes place in one of two task contexts, a formal logic-based context and/or an informal context. After contrasting reasoning in these two contexts, argumentation is considered, followed by an examination of the relation between argumentation and reasoning, emphasizing reasoning in informal tasks and argumentation. The results of a protocol study are presented, addressing the question of how reasoning occurs in the construction of an argumentative text. The chapter concludes with a discussion of how argumentative texts may be evaluated.

1 PRELIMINARY COMMENTS

The purpose of this chapter is to examine the relationship between reasoning and argumentation, and more specifically, to examine reasoning and its relation to the production and evaluation of argumentative text. The relationship between the concepts of reasoning and argumentation is neither resolved nor frequently discussed (Govier, 1989; Walton, 1992), but it is hoped that the present considerations will help to bring the issues involved into focus. In the first section of this chapter, the concept of reasoning is considered, and there is a discussion of reasoning as found in formal logic-based tasks and informal tasks. The second section presents a discussion of argumentation while the third presents data related to reasoning concerning the processing of argumentative texts. The final section considers the evaluation of argumentative texts.

2 COMMENTS ON REASONING

Definitional Issues
In this chapter we approach reasoning from a psychological perspective. Within this context, Halpern (1996) has provided an acceptable definition of reasoning, namely:

Colloquially, reasoning tells us 'what leads to what'. When we reason, we use our knowledge about one or more related statements that we can reasonably believe are true to determine if another statement, the conclusion, is true. (p. 119).

This definition points to particular characteristics. First, reasoning is a process. Second, in reasoning, an individual moves from a given state to a new or another state via an inference. Thus, if you have the given information, 'He placed the cigarette in his mouth and he lit it with a match', you may infer that 'he began to smoke'. Or, you may know 'He placed the cigarette in his mouth and he began to smoke', from which you may infer that he lit the cigarette. Third, to explain the reasoning process, it is necessary to determine what enables the individual to go from the given state to the new state. Fourth, an aspect of reasoning not mentioned in the provided definition is that reasoning is usually goal-related, as when solving a problem or making a decision.

Reasoning, of course, can be more extensive and complex than considered in the above definition given that the reasoning process may involve going through a series of steps; as in the solving of a problem in mathematics, physics, social science, or when solving a puzzle problem. Reasoning also increases in complexity when a group of people become involved. In such cases, individuals make inferences, perhaps based upon what other people say, and they may criticize and modify statements made by others. In such relatively complex situations, reasoning may be analyzed in steps. For example, when reasoning through a problem, a series of operators may be defined, including an operator consisting of the means by which the reasoner moves from one state of the problem to the next. The use of operators in this manner is an important part of the information processing model of problem solving (Newell & Simon, 1972; Voss, Greene, Post & Penner, 1983). We return to this point later.

Reasoning in logic-based tasks
Reasoning has been studied typically in one of two types of task situations. One of these, the formal task situation, has involved the use of formalized structures such as those found in mathematics and in formal logic. The second type of task situation, termed informal because of the lack of a better word, involves structures that are not part of logical systems. Deciding whether a syllogism is valid is an example of the former, whereas saying political candidates should not be elected because you disagree with their position on a number of issues, is an example of the informal context. Going back to the Greek period, the distinction is approximately that made by Aristotle in his dialectic and rhetoric (see van Eemeren, Grootendorst & Henkemans, 1996).

A large number of studies of reasoning involve deductive reasoning. Tasks used in such studies, for example, may involve asking an individual to generate a syllogism's conclusion after being given the premises (Johnson-Laird, 1983), to evaluate a syllogism for validity (Wilkins, 1928; Woodworth & Sells, 1935), or to perform a Wason and Johnson-Laird four-card task (Cf. Garnham & Oakhill, 1994). Generally, the goal of such tasks is to study whether performance is in agreement with the logical model. The question is usually, 'Did the person perform the task correctly, and if not, why?' Models of correct or error performance may also be developed (*e.g.*, Johnson-Laird, 1983). Indeed, some authors have advocated that individuals have an intrinsic rule-based mental logic that enables them to think logically when confronted with reasoning tasks such as modus ponens (Braine & Rumain, 1983; Henle, 1962; Rips, 1994).

Until the last few decades, psychological research on reasoning focused almost exclusively on formal logic-based tasks, especially the logic of deductive reasoning. There are a number of reasons why researchers have been preoccupied with such tasks. The tasks are more tractable than informal tasks; that is, the solution usually consists of a single correct answer, the materials and/or the solution process are logically constructed, and computer simulation of such tasks is more feasible than that found in informal reasoning tasks. But two other factors may also be of importance. One is that psychology, in its often positivistic outlook and in its concern about its status as a science, has frequently involved the study of issues that are quantifiable and deterministic rather than probabilistic and 'soft'. Certainly, deductive reasoning has deterministic characteristics to a greater extent than the less-structured everyday reasoning. Also, in the twentieth century, there has been a carryover from the post-evolutionary thinking of the nineteenth century which made humans feel a need to demonstrate their mental superiority to nonhumans via the ability to reason or, in other words, to show rationality. Indeed, Halpern (1996), in a widely cited text, states, 'Reasoning is often taken to be the hallmark of the human species'. (p. 119). Interestingly, a researcher working in argumentation theory, Fisher (1987), has argued that it is the ability to create narratives that characterizes humans.

The following are characteristics that distinguish logic-based tasks from informal tasks. First, deductive reasoning tasks can be typically represented by symbols, such as converting a sentence to 'All A are B.' Converting the propositions into logical form, thus makes the statements content-free. The specific contents of the sentences are not taken into account; the only important issue is the logical form. Second, there is typically one correct answer. A conclusion does or does not follow from the premises. Because of this, there are typically no counterarguments. Third, evaluation occurs via an application of the rules of the logic, as the categorical syllogism or propositional logic.

Three other points concerning tasks of formal logic are noted. One example of a type of rationality ascribed to humans involves a person performing a Bayesian task, or generating the conclusion to a syllogism, which is judged 'rational' if the person's performance conforms to the particular model under study – for example, providing the answer predicted by Bayesian theory. Thus the model is a standard, and 'rational' performance constitutes being in agreement with the standard, as mentioned above. This is an interesting view of rationality because humans developed the mathematical or logical system and if some other human conforms to the human-based system, then 'rationality' is demonstrated; that is, when the person is performing in a way like other humans, in this case human system-makers, say he should.

A second point is that the structure of logic-based tasks is an argument. The type of argument may vary, as in a categorical syllogism or in a propositional structure of 'modus ponens' or 'modus tollens'. Nonetheless, the structure is that of an argument. However, there is little argumentation in the sense of social disagreement and interchange. As noted above, there are not usually two sides, and persuasion is a relatively minor matter or virtually non-existent.

The third point about logic-based arguments is when they are used. What is the goal in using logic-based tasks? Apart from the use of such tasks in research and mathematics, logic-based arguments seem to be used infrequently in everyday life, occurring in cases such as, 'There are three ways in which this could have happened. It could not be the first or second, so it must be the third'. From this example, it is apparent that the goal of reasoning in using formal logic structures is generally to arrive at a conclusion that is the one and only correct answer. The structure is usually deterministic, and, as is the case with analytic arguments, the conclusion provides no information that is not in the premises. Correspondingly, if a person evaluates a logic-based argument, the evaluation involves going through the steps to determine whether the correct conclusion was reached.

Reasoning in informal reasoning tasks

Informal reasoning tasks typically involve the use of a different argument structure than that found in logic-based tasks. The structure is the enthymeme, as found in Aristotle's Rhetoric (1960), and consists of a claim supported by a reason. Combining arguments may readily develop a more extensive argument structure.

Informal reasoning – that is, reasoning in informal task situations – takes place in many contexts. These include decision making, in which a person may generate pro and contra reasons for a claim (Perkins, Allen & Hafner, 1983), and tasks calling for justification (Kuhn, 1991; Means & Voss, 1996; Voss, Perkins & Segal, 1991). For example, Kuhn (1991), studying evidential statements, asked people of various ages and educational backgrounds questions such as why so many prisoners, after being released, committed crimes and re-entered prison. Similarly, Stein and Miller (1991) studied children's perceptions of breaking promises, and the justifications thereof.

In informal reasoning tasks, contents are important because evaluation is based upon the contents. There is no 'right' answer, only an argument that may be stated and considered to range in strength from relatively strong to relatively weak. Counterarguments may be offered; that is, an argument in which the claim is a contradiction of the claim of the original argument.

With respect to the evaluation of arguments in informal reasoning, two factors are important. First, in an argument consisting of a claim and a supporting reason, the supporting reason needs to be plausible or acceptable. Moreover, the plausibility or acceptability of the reason may be judged or rated on a scale from 0 = not acceptable to 10 = highly acceptable, with the numbers 1 to 9 ranging between the extremes. Thus, in the argument 'Capital punishment should be outlawed because it is inhumane', the supporting reason 'it is inhumane' may be rated by some people with a '9' or '10', while other individuals may think capital punishment is not inhumane and may provide a relatively low rating.

The second factor is that the reason needs to support the claim, a factor sometimes called relevance (*Cf.* Angell, 1964). Again, the perceived extent of support may vary from person to person. In some unpublished work, we found a relationship between the two factors, such that if the reason was relatively unacceptable, the perceived support for the claim was relatively low. This result is not surprising, as a substantial perceived strength of the supporting reason should be a necessary, but not sufficient, condition to perceive the argument as being relatively strong.

A third factor of evaluation sometimes indicated is that of taking counter-arguments into account (Angell, 1964). This factor is included when the strength of an argument cannot be appropriately judged unless arguments against the position are taken into account. This criterion, however, is infrequently found.

An important question reasoning in informal situations is the goal of such reasoning. A primary goal is persuasion, broadly conceived to include self-persuasion. Informal reasoning can also take place in the context of goals such as solving a problem, considering choices and making a decision, and other probabilistic situations.

In sum, reasoning takes place when a given situation evokes it. To avoid the circularity implicit in this statement, such situations typically arise when the individual seeks a particular goal and is required to think about what steps are needed to reach that goal. The process of taking those steps, which usually involves explicitly or implicitly stated language or other symbols, constitutes reasoning. The situational context may consist of the premises, and the goal may be to generate a conclusion, as in the case of a syllogism. Or, the context may consist of a probabilistic situation in which a person is deciding what to do. The logic-based and informal tasks are different, however, in the ways previously described, and everyday situations typically involve informal rather than formal reasoning. The above portrayal explicitly assumes that the type of reasoning that takes place is a function of the circumstances or situations, including the goal of the reasoner. Having considered the issues involving reasoning, we turn to the topic of argumentation.

3 ARGUMENTATION: SOME COMMENTS

Definitional considerations

Argumentation has been defined by Zarefsky (1995) as 'the practice of justifying decisions under conditions of uncertainty' (p. 43). This definition seems reasonable, although our preference would be to change 'decisions' to 'claims'. Van Eemeren, Grootendorst, and Snoeck Henkemans (1996) define argumentation as 'a verbal and social activity of reason aimed at increasing (or decreasing) the acceptability of a controversial standpoint for the listener or reader, by putting forward a constellation of propositions intended to justify (or refute) the standpoint before a rational judge' (p. 5). This definition, compared to Zarefsky's, explicitly makes argumentation a social phenomenon. However, we feel that 'of reason' and 'before a rational judge' could be deleted because it is not clear what 'of reason' could mean (is it opposed to 'of emotion'?), and the concept of a 'rational judge' seems to connote an abstract fiction. The term argumentation is thus taken to refer to the attempt to persuade another party or parties of one's own position about a controversial issue.

Because argumentation, as described in the latter definition, is a social process, it is important to consider the term 'argument' in relation to argumentation. Argument refers to a language structure having a particular form: this usage says nothing about social processes any more than any statement about language. A second usage is that argument constitutes a disagreement in which two or more people disagree regarding a particular proposition: this usage is directly related to argumentation as a social process (see also O'Keefe, 1977).

Characteristics of argumentation

When does argumentation occur? If there is agreement about an issue, there is no argumentation (ignoring a devil's advocate role). When there is disagreement and positions are known to be firm and will remain that way, there is no argumentation. Argumentation occurs when individuals are attempting to defend their own position, attack another position, and/or persuade those holding the opposing position. It is important in this context to note that frequently the goal is to persuade and not to resolve. It is to win and not compromise. On the other hand, in a conflict situation such as negotiation, the goal may be to resolve (*Cf.* Stein, Bernas, Calicchia & Wright, 1996).

Argumentation may also be used cooperatively. In a study of mathematics learning Vye, Goldman, Voss, Hmelo, Williams & the Cognition and Technology Group at Vanderbilt (1997) found that when working in pairs, one child, in disagreeing with the other child of the pair, was most frequently serving a monitoring function. It examined the correctness of the statements, suggesting a change if there was disagreement. Corrective steps were then sometimes taken. While this is a cooperative effort to reach the appropriate answer, persuasion is nevertheless a component.

Argumentation may also occur within an individual. Often, when an individual makes a decision, the costs and benefits of each side are considered. And, as Gross (1990) commented about scientists, 'Rhetorically, the creation of knowledge is a task beginning with self-persuasion and ending with the persuasion of others.' (p. 3). Similarly, costs and benefits or pro and contra reasons may be generated when an individual is considering a choice or decision (Cf. Toulmin, 1958; Zammuner, 1987).

Argumentation is generally public. When two people or more are involved, argumentation is a public process. It may also take place in classroom settings (*e.g.*, Pontecorvo & Girardet, 1993), with students attempting to reach a final answer, as in mathematics, or attempting to provide supportive and opposing arguments to a given claim about history.

In sum, argumentation, as outlined in this chapter, denotes a particular type of social interaction involving disagreement. The language structure employed is the argument, and arguments are presented for persuasion, or sometimes for resolution. Interestingly, psychological investigation on argumentation has not been extensive. Social psychologists have employed argumentation in their concern with attitude change. Moreover, each of the two theoretical notions of attitude change (Chaiken, 1980; Petty & Cacioppo, 1986) has delineated a more central, deeper means of attitude change, and a more peripheral means – not unlike the distinction of 'convince' and 'persuade' that has been made in argumentation theory literature (*e.g.*, Perelman & Olbrechts-Tyteca, 1958). In general, the central means is via a 'deeper' processing in which an individual's beliefs are activated and related to the new information, while in the peripheral case, attitude change may result from more superficial processing as via the use of heuristics.

Persuasion may also take place because of the context in which an argument is presented. As noted in Aristotle's Rhetoric, persuasion occurs not only via logos, the substance of the argument, but via ethos and pathos, the appeal to the speaker and to the audience, respectively. Argumentation, however, is primarily concerned with logos. Thus far we have considered reasoning and argumentation. We now turn to the relation between the two concepts.

4 THE REASONING UNDERLYING ARGUMENTATION

In this section we consider the nature of reasoning when it is used in the development of argumentative texts. The assumption is that in the development of argumentative text, reasoning takes place, typically informal reasoning, in which an individual considers aspects of the issues under consideration, ultimately producing a text consistent with the choices and justifications occurring in the reasoning process. However, the text does not summarize the process itself, but provides the primary conclusions that are the product of the reasoning process.

In a study by Voss, Greene, Post and Penner (1983), the solving of ill-structured problems was studied – the problems being about the Soviet Union. Protocols were collected from experts and novices about how to increase Soviet crop productivity. The protocols were analyzed, with the problem solving process divided into problem representation and problem solution phases.

The authors made a distinction between a problem solving structure and a reasoning structure. The problem solving structure contained representation and solution phases, with the reasoning structure involving the breakdown of the representation and solution phases. The reasoning structure was thus at a lower-level, and involved the step-by-step reasoning that occurred in the reasoning's subordinate relation to the problem solving structure.

It is of importance is that the problem solving and reasoning structures each contained a set of operators. Operators vary with the task, and in this case the reasoning operators were: state argument, state assertion, state fact, present specific case, state reason, state outcome, compare and/or contrast, elaborate and/or clarify, state conclusion, and state qualifier. These operators were sufficient to describe the protocol contents of the reasoning structure. The problem solving structure operators were: state constraint, state subproblem, state solution, interpret problem statement, provide support, evaluate, and summarize. These are relatively high level problem solving operators, while the reasoning structure served to unpack and develop the problem solving structure.

Given the nature of the operator concept, it seems reasonable to hypothesize that when an individual is generating an argumentative text, a process similar occurs to that which occurred during protocol generation in the solving of an ill-structured problem. The individual is attempting to generate a text that is persuasive, and reasoning takes place in order to construct such a text. Furthermore, while the goal is to construct an appropriate and quality text, it is during the construction that various factors can influence the reasoning process. These factors are the writer or speaker's perception of the audience, the beliefs and attitudes of the writer, the knowledge of the writer, perhaps the writer's personality and emotionality, and particular stylistic characteristics. In other words, these factors can influence the reasoning process that feeds into the text construction.

Given that the individual has a goal – that is, the writing of the argumentative text to produce some type of effect – and given that reasoning takes place when trying to reach this goal, it would be reasonable to hypothesize that a finite number of operators will describe the steps that take place in the writing of this text. These operators will tell us something about the reasoning process occurring in this context. More specifically, if 'think aloud' protocols are collected while the individual is generating the text, it should be possible to define the operators, and thereby try to provide an accurate analysis of the reasoning process that fed into the writing of the text. The results of such a protocol analysis are examined in the next section to provide a sense of the reasoning processes which occur when generating an argumentative text.

Some data
Since the operators employed are a function of the task, the question is what operators are used when a person constructs an argumentative text. The following operators can be expected to be present: state a claim for one side of an issue, state a claim for the other side of an issue, provide a fact or other statement in support of a given side, provide a fact or statement in opposition to a given side, refute a statement, and elaborate or clarify. Other operators could include state interpretation, state strategy, and state conclusion.

We conducted a brief study in which two undergraduates and one faculty member, an attorney, were provided with two fictional legal cases. Each involved a murder and each consisted of the presentation by testimony of a number of witnesses in a courtroom trial situation. While reading each case, each participant was asked to say anything that came to mind. In the case discussed in this chapter, an individual driving home from work struck a small girl as she ran out into the street from behind a car. The driver got out and checked the girl, finding she was not seriously hurt, but a group of teenagers attacked the driver, one of whom was the older brother of the girl. One of the teenagers hit the driver with a baseball bat and the driver was killed. A witness from across the street could not identify who had the bat. The police came and found a bat in the back seat of the car of the girl's older brother, the bat having the victim's blood and hair on it as well as the fingerprints of the brother. The brother said he had used the bat earlier in the day for playing baseball, and pointed out that someone wearing batting gloves (to hold the bat) could have also handled the bat but did not leave any fingerprints.

The participant read the testimony of 'witnesses', which provided the basic description of the events, and then was asked to think out loud and decide whether he would want to defend the accused – that is, the older brother – or be the prosecuting attorney. After deciding which side he would take, he was asked to type a summary statement of his case from his side's perspective. He was also to think out loud when typing. After completing the summary, each participant was asked to type the summary he would present if he had chosen the other side of the case. The procedure was then repeated for the second text, which concerned three men deer hunting, with one man shooting one of the other two. The question was whether it was an accident or murder. Only the first case is discussed in this chapter.

Taking the expert first, during the reading of the 'witness' statements, the following comments were made. The operators employed by the expert were presented in Table 1.

Table 1 Operators used by the expert.

Operator	Operator's Purpose
State recapitulation (Recap.)	Review information
State observation (Obser.)	Comment not directly related to case
State interpretation (Inter.)	Comment interpreting aspect of case
State need for search (Search)	Look for information or outcome
State strategy (Strat.)	Statement of case-related strategy
State claim for defense (Cl-def.)	Statement of claim for defense
State reason support defense	Statement of reason supporting

claim (Re-def.)	defense claim
State fact (may be neutral, favoring defense side, or favoring prosecution side) F neu, F defs, or F pros, respectively	Statement of fact
State claim for prosecution (Cl-pro)	Statement of claim supporting prosecution position
State reason supporting claim for prosecution (Re-pro)	Statement of reason support defense position
State evidence for prosecution (Ev-pro)	Statement of evidence for the prosecution
State evidence for defense (Ev-def.)	Statement of evidence for the defense
State disagreement (Disag.)	Statement of disagreement

> I want to see who we are talking about here. Richard Martin is the victim. His is the one who approached with the car. Mary Hawkins is the five year old. He gets out. The defendant is Anthony Hawkins, but we have not met him yet. But we know from witnesses he was there. (Recap. for all statements in the paragraph).
> The defendant is the older brother of the girl. The bat was found in his car. (Recap.)
> The defendant's testifying, huh? (Obser.)

When making the choice of whether to prosecute or defend, the following statements were made.

> I am thinking about what kind of argument I could make on behalf of the defense. (Search). I would focus on a lack of connection between Anthony Hawkins and the person who struck the victim with the bat. (Strat). Richard Martin was killed by this bat but we do not have anybody who actually saw Anthony Hawkins striking the victim with the bat. (Cl-def, Re-def). It is his bat. (F pros). And presumably we also would have a motive because he would have been angered because Martin hit his sister. (Cl-pro, Re-pro). But no witness saw him strike the blow. (Cl-def (implied), Re-def). There were other people around, the bat was there, somebody else could have struck the blow and put the bat in the car. (Cl-def, Re-def). Why would somebody else strike the blow? (Search). A neighborhood crowd was there and somebody wanted to do what Anthony Hawkins wanted him to do. (Cl-def). But then why would they take the bat and put it in the car? (Search). There is the question about the lack of anyone else's fingerprints on the bat. (Search, ev-pro). And his explanation of why there are no other fingerprints on the bat involves batting gloves. (Search, ev-pro). And that strikes me as unplausable. (Disag). I think this is not a good situation for the defendant. (Inter). And the best think going for him is that nobody saw him with the bat. (Cl-def (implied), Re-def). But his explanation regarding fingerprints is weak. (Cl-pro).
> I would take the defense side since it is a strong case against the defense side since it is a strong case against the defense and that makes it more interesting.

The listing of the operators used by this expert as found in Table 1 provides a sentence level analysis of the reasoning operators used. Further study of this type would no doubt require some additions, and perhaps deletions, of operators, and certainly some fine tuning. But at a more general level, expert performance embraces the following characteristics. First, the expert reviewed the evidence and made sure that he understood what the events and who the people were. Second, there is a virtual on-going examination of the evidence. The expert asked questions about the evidence and about what more might be needed. He searched for inconsistencies in the evidence, and he thought about what evidence made sense and what did not. Third, the overall schema he employed was to develop his representation of the case by considering the case from both sides, and examining the evidence for each side. This procedure is in all likelihood a practice acquired in training and refined through experience. Yet, to use this general approach effectively also requires that the person takes the appropriate steps in the lower level reasoning process.

The case summary that the expert wrote was:

No one saw Anthony Hawkins strike Richard Martin with the bat. Yes, it was Anthony Hawkins' bat, it was found in Anthony Hawkins' car, but in a crowded situation, no one saw Anthony Hawkins strike. In the emotional melee that followed the accident in which Richard Martin struck Anthony Hawkins' sister, any one of the seven men, all of whom were Anthony Hawkins' age, might have picked up the bat out of the unlocked car, struck Martin and returned the bat to its place. Odd: the bat is returned to the car.

Seven males were walking in the neighborhood after the ballgame. Hawkins' bat was put in his car. He might have been seen by others putting it into the car. The accident occurs. He recalls the bat and grabs, strikes Martin, and replaces the bat in a panic. But it could have been any of them. It is true, no fingerprints were on the bat other than Hawkins', but he was playing with the bat. But the other people coming home from the game may have been wearing batting gloves. Standard is beyond reasonable doubt.

When subsequently responding on the prosecutor's side, the expert stated:

We have a weapon; Anthony Hawkins' bat. We have a motive: Anthony Hawkins witnesses Richard Martin's striking his little sister. The bat is readily at hand in Hawkins' car. It has the blood of the victim on it. It has Hawkins' fingerprints on it. No one else's fingerprints are on the bat. Witnesses saw someone swing a bat and hit Richard Martin. They may not have seen Anthony Hawkins swing the bat, but they saw Anthony Hawkins in the group. Significantly, only Anthony Hawkins' fingerprints are on the bat. There is no plausible explanation for how someone else swinging the bat would not have left fingerprints on it. We do not have any testimony that anyone was wearing any gloves, as suggested by Anthony Hawkins.

The expert's reasoning, as shown in his protocol and subsequent statements, indicates that the operators employed were quite goal-oriented, isolating the strengths and weaknesses of each side of the case. He considered how to strengthen the weaknesses of his own case, which by-and-large meant weakening the strength of the opponent's case – as shown by the use of the 'state fact' and 'state interpretation' operators, with the interpretation usually occurring in relation to one side of the case. Interestingly, the case summary of the expert does not include the events perceived as inconsistencies, and presents a more straightforward summary of the defense's case. The summary which the expert wrote is a sense of the summary of the points he made in his deciding about the side he wanted to pursue, and he was actually focusing on the defense from the beginning.

The protocols of the novices are not presented in detail; instead, they are summarized and compared to that of the expert. First, the novices used many of the same operators as the expert, including the statement of interpretation, of facts that supported the side of the case they had chosen or would choose to defend, and the statement of observations. This result suggests that at the lower level, novice reasoning was similar to that of the expert. Secondly, novices did not recapitulate information as did the expert. Thirdly, novices did not examine both sides of the evidence and seek inconsistencies. They were much more likely to state that they thought a given person was guilty or not guilty and look at evidence supporting their own side.

The results of the exploratory protocol study suggests that in the preparation for writing an argumentative text – that is, the prosecutor or defending lawyer's summary – reasoning consisted primarily of four components. One is an analytic component in which the expert participant determined the strengths and weaknesses of each side of the case. The expert was more inclined than the novices to examine both sides of the case. A second is a clarification and recapitulation component which enabled the participant to be sure he understood the text contents. The third consisted of generating possible interpretations, including alternative interpretations, to those offered or implied by one interpretation of the presented information, with experts more astute in this regard. The fourth component is the elucidation of unexplained questions, facts, oddities, and inconsistencies. It was again the expert who concentrated to a greater extent on seeking and finding oddities or inconsistencies, and seeking to resolve them.

5 THE EVALUATION OF ARGUMENTATION FOUND IN NARRATIVE TEXTS

There are two aspects to an argumentative text, its generation and its evaluation. The focus of study in the present chapter has been on the former, but the issue of argumentative text evaluation requires study. Recently, we studied the question of the evaluation of arguments when the arguments are found in narratives (Voss, Wiley & Sandak, in press). Such arguments occur in history, for example, or in a courtroom. With regard to the courtroom context we considered earlier, a prosecuting attorney in his or her summary statement could make the claim that the defendant was guilty, with the summary narrative that is presented supporting the claim. As noted by Voss, Wiley and Sandak, the narrative may be viewed as having two components. The first component is the set of 'facts' of the case – that is, the statements of the witnesses and the exhibits – while the second component is the narrative as it weaves together the 'facts' into a coherent 'story' which, for the prosecutor, points to the accused as guilty.

The two-component concept leads to the hypothesis that the 'facts' of a case may be kept constant across different narratives, while the narrative structure is varied. Under such conditions, the characteristics or quality of the narratives may be judged, as well as the contents. In the present case, for example, a judgment about contents would involve the possible guilt or innocence of the accused.

But judgments about the narrative and the contents may not be independent. Specifically, it may be hypothesized that if the narrative is deficient in some way, not only may judgments of narrative quality be lower than those made for a standard narrative, but the judgments of guilt would also be lower: that is, opposed to the prosecutor's case which constituted the narrative.

In such a study, narratives need to be constructed that are deficient in narrativity. In a study by Leinhardt, Stainton, Virji and Odoroff (1994), historians were asked what were the characteristics of a good narrative, indicated that of importance were coherence, chronology, completeness (in the sense of using available information), causation, and colligation (placing the narrative in the appropriate time and place). Moreover, in their work on jury decision making, Pennington and Hastie (1993) stated similar characteristics.

In the study we conducted, there were four narrative conditions: a standard narrative, a narrative deficient in chronology/coherence, a narrative deficient in causality, and a narrative deficient in completeness. It was found that if a standard narrative were modified to decrease its coherence/chronology or its causative components, judgments of narrative quality were lower than for the standard narrative. In addition, judgments of the accused's guilt in these two conditions were also less than those found in the standard condition.

The results of the above study suggest that in the evaluation of an argumentative narrative, the argument may be evaluated based upon the previously mentioned criteria. However, the quality of the narrative, as defined in relation to the characteristics of good narrativity, is also important. One may argue, of course, that an argumentative text is often expository, but in history, narrativity is relatively common, and whenever a 'story' is used to support a claim, issues of narrativity are important. Indeed, Aristotle pointed out that narrative is used rhetorically to persuade, being used as a form of support for a claim. Thus, while the reasoning that is involved in the generation of argumentative text may be studied via the use of reasoning operators, the evaluation of argumentative text leads us to the need to consider not only the contents of the argument stated in the text, but also the quality of the text's structure. Our work applied to the narrative genre, but the same idea would likely hold for other text structures, such as expository ones. Further work is needed, however, to understand more clearly the relation between judgments made about narrativity and text structure in general, and judgments made about the contents of a given text.

Our conclusion about the relation between reasoning and argumentation is that one aspect consists of examining the use of particular reasoning operators to develop a better understanding of the reasoning that goes into the generation of an argumentative text. Furthermore, a study on the evaluation of argumentative text suggested that for an argumentative text to be effective, both the contents of the argument and the quality of the text structure are of importance. Consequently, this conclusion is relevant to argumentative text construction.

Our conclusion does not imply that the issues discussed are the only ways in which reasoning and argumentation are related. From a psychological viewpoint, for example, we would argue that inferences, by the nature of the case, are generally arguments (see Pinto, 1995). But that is a matter outside the scope of this study.

6 CONCLUSIONS

The study of reasoning, as viewed by a psychological perspective, requires the separation of logic-based deductive reasoning tasks from informal and everyday tasks. While the former is concerned with logical thinking and the validity of conclusions, as based upon the rules of logic, informal reasoning is related to dialectic and rhetoric, and bears a close relation to argumentation. In the present chapter we presented some data and a summary of results of another study suggesting two things. First, the nature of the reasoning that occurs when constructing an argumentative text may be studied by the use of reasoning operators involved in the reasoning taking place. Second, the quality of argumentative text must refer not only to the argumentative text contents, but also to the quality of the text – as for example, the quality of a narrative stating the argumentation. Furthermore, the reasoning operators obtained in the present study – that is, those found in Table 1 – would likely generalize to other courtroom situations and, for the most part, also to decision situations. This possibility suggests that in generating argumentative text, individuals employ operators selected from a group that are relevant to the existing context; that is, type of issue or problem in its total context. Moreover, the argumentative text development involves informal reasoning that consists of making claims and examining their viability by considering support and opposition to the claims.

Developments in Argumentation Theory

Frans H. van Eemeren
University of Amsterdam &
New York University
Rob Grootendorst
University of Amsterdam

ABSTRACT

In Developments in argumentation theory, we provide a survey of the state of the art in the discipline that studies the production, analysis, and evaluation of argumentation with a view to developing adequate criteria for determining the validity of the point of departure and presentational layout of argumentative discourse. Argumentation theory has a descriptive as well as a normative dimension: it investigates the practice of argumentative discourse empirically, and reflects critically on the reasonableness of that discourse. After discussing the dominant approaches of the last two decades (Toulmin's model, New Rhetoric, Informal Logic, Communication and Rhetoric, Formal Approach to the Fallacies, Formal Dialectics, Pragma-dialectics, Radical Argumentativism), we note several important tendencies: (1) A growing interest in developing a fully fledged theory of argumentation among scholars from a variety of disciplines, manifesting itself internationally in publications by philosophers and logicians, rhetoric and communication scholars, linguists and discourse analysts, lawyers, psychologists, and other social scientists; (2) A keen interest in the prospects that recent developments in formal logic, especially in dialogue logic, have to offer to the study of argumentation; (3) A spectacular revaluation of the importance of rhetoric for the study of argumentation; (4) An increased empirical interest in how argumentative discourse is conducted in various kinds of argumentative practices or fields; (5) A renewed interest in 'old' theoretical concepts such as 'relevance' and the 'fallacies', which are crucial to the development of an adequate theory of argumentation.

1 INTRODUCTION

Argumentation is a speech act complex aimed at resolving a difference of opinion. According to a prominent handbook definition, it is a verbal and social activity of reason carried out by a speaker or writer concerned with increasing (or decreasing) the acceptability of a controversial standpoint to a listener or reader; the constellation of propositions brought to bear in this endeavor is intended to justify (or refute) the standpoint before a rational judge (van Eemeren *et al.*, 1996). *Argumentation theory* is the name given to the (systematic results of the) study of this discourse phenomenon. Argumentation theory studies the production, analysis, and evaluation of argumentation with a view to developing adequate criteria for determining the validity of the point of departure and presentational layout of argumentative discourse.

The constellation of propositions advanced in argumentation is often referred to by the term *argument*, particularly by logicians and philosophers. This may lead to confusion because – in English – the word 'argument' has various meanings. Apart from (a) a reason and (b) a logical inference of a conclusion from one or more premises, 'argument' can also denote (c) a discussion, and (d) a quarrel. In order to avoid ambiguity, O'Keefe (1977) distinguishes between arguments in sense (a), (c), and (d), but for the purposes of argumentation theory it is the obscuring of (a) and (b) that causes most confusion. It blurs the distinction between the logical and the pragmatic aspects of argumentative discourse[1].

Argumentation theory has a descriptive as well as a normative dimension. It is descriptive because it investigates the practice of argumentative discourse empirically; it is normative because it reflects critically on the reasonableness of that discourse. Normative theorists, such as those inspired by logic and philosophy, concentrate on the criteria that need to be satisfied in reasonable argumentation. Descriptive theorists, who often have a background in discourse analysis or social psychology, examine how argumentation is used to convince or persuade the interlocutors or readers. It is the divergence of normative and descriptive approaches to argumentative discourse – and the ensuing controversies[2] – that creates another source of confusion in argumentation theory. For the purposes of argumentation theory, both descriptive and normative insights are indispensable. A fully-fledged argumentation theory therefore requires a comprehensive research program that integrates the descriptive dimension and the normative dimension. For a research program that encompasses both the descriptive and the normative dimension of argumentation theory, see van Eemeren & Grootendorst (1992a) and van Eemeren, Grootendorst, Jackson & Jacobs (1993).

This chapter provides a survey of the state of the art in argumentation theory by describing some of the major developments that have taken place in the past two decades (see for a more comprehensive survey van Eemeren *et al.*, 1996). The survey is based not only on books, but also on papers published in professional journals or included in conference proceedings. Starting in the late seventies, argumentation has become a subject of interest to scholars in a growing number of disciplines, and the number of publications on argumentation has risen accordingly. There has also been a considerable increase in professional journals, argumentation conferences, and organizations devoted to the study of argumentation (see the Annex for institutional information concerning the discipline).

2 TOULMIN'S MODEL AND PERELMAN'S NEW RHETORIC

The study of argumentation was for a long time dominated by the – still influential – contributions of Toulmin and Perelman. Their approaches are in both cases characterized by the attempt to provide an alternative to formal logic that is more suitable for dealing with everyday argumentation in ordinary language. Toulmin (1958) presents a model of the various elements constituting an argumentation. His central thesis is that rationality can, in principle, be claimed for every sort of argumentation, and that its soundness criteria depend on the nature of the problems at issue. He rejects the view that there are universal norms for the evaluation of argumentation and that these norms are supplied by formal logic. Sound argumentation – *i.e.* argumentation containing arguments which may be called valid in a broader sense – is for Toulmin argumentation conducted in accordance with a formally valid *procedure* and in conformance with the specific soundness conditions of the *field* (or subject) concerned.

According to Toulmin, a procedural interpretation of 'form' can lead to a more adequate model of argumentation, in which the characteristic differences between sorts of argumentation in the wide range of fields to which argumentation may refer are taken into account. There are ('field-invariant') elements which remain the same in all fields of argumentation, and ('field-dependent') elements which differ from field to field. In all fields of argumentation, certain steps can be distinguished, and in this respect the procedural form of argumentation is field-invariant.

The model Toulmin introduces to represent the layout of arguments is a procedural one – *i.e.* one in which the various functions of the steps that are successively taken are given due consideration. The first step is the expressing of a standpoint or, in Toulmin's terminology, a *claim* (C). One way of defending a claim, the second step, is to point to certain facts on which the claim is based, the *data* (D). Even if the data produced are accepted as accurate, the challenger may require an account of how the data lead to the claim in question. The third step in the argumentation consists in providing the justification or *warrant* (W) for using the data concerned as support for the claim. In principle, the warrant has a hypothetical form ('if [*data*] then [*claim*]') and functions as a bridge between the data and the claim.

By reference to an example used by Toulmin, we shall draft his first, simple model of argumentation, and introduce the questions he asks to indicate the function of *data* and *warrant*:

Claim   Harry is a British subject
(C)   What have you got to go on?
Datum   Harry was born in Bermuda
(D)   How do you get there?
Warrant A man born in Bermuda will
(W)   be a British subject

In this example, it is assumed that the warrant is a rule without any exceptions, and that the accuracy of the warrant itself is not at issue. The force of the warrant would be weakened if there were exceptions to the rule, in which case a *rebuttal* (R) would have to be inserted. The claim must then be weakened by means of a *qualifier* (Q). A *backing* (B) is required if the authority of the warrant is not accepted straight away. Toulmin's extended model of argumentation therefore contains six elements:[3]

Claim   Harry is a British subject
(C)   What have you got to go on?
Datum   Harry was born in Bermuda
(D)   How do you get there?
Warrant A man born in Bermuda will
(W)   generally be a British subject
                                                     Is that always the case?
Rebuttal No, but it generally is. If
(R)   his parents are foreigners or
           if he has become a naturalized
           American, then the rule doesn't
           apply

Qualifier True: it is only *presumably* so
(Q)

Then you can't be so definite in your claim, can you?

Come to think of it, what makes you think people are generally British just because they were born in Bermuda?

Backing It's embodied in the following
(B) legislation: ...

Perelman and Olbrechts-Tyteca (1958/1969) provide an inventory of argumentation schemes that can be instrumental in employing effective argumentation techniques: 'quasi-logical argumentation', 'argumentation based on the structure of reality', 'argumentation establishing the structure of reality', and 'dissociation'. In *quasi-logical argumentation* the illusion is created that there is a relation between the argumentation and the posited opinion just as compelling as between the premises and the conclusion of a logical argument form that resembles it. This suggestion is misleading: the similarity between argumentation and a formal argument is never sufficient to justify the validity claim, hence the prefix *quasi*:

> The sanctity of all human life has always been a foremost principle of our party. It would be to go against that principle if we now went along with the proposal before us to legalize abortion. The members of my party in this House will therefore vote against the proposal.

In this example, the sanctity of all human life and the legalization of abortion are presented as *contradictory*; the implication is that to defend *both* things would be a logical inconsistency. The suggestion is that, logically speaking, maintaining both points of view is untenable and that, therefore, at least one of the two must be dropped. Although this form of argumentation may appear compelling to some, others may not be convinced.

In *argumentation based on the structure of reality*, there is an appeal to the way in which reality is constructed to bring about a transfer between opinions that the audience already adheres to, and the thesis being defended. This type of argumentation draws on the view that the audience has formed of reality:

> That Bloggs fellow must be a pretty unreliable person – he's been a member of the Socialist Party for years.

In *argumentation establishing the structure of reality*, elements of reality are linked with one another in such a way that an order is created that is *new* to the audience. The plausibility of the new order then invests the elements adduced in defense of a thesis with a certain plausibility of their own:

> Women make better interviewers than men because you only have to look at the interviews by such renowned female interviewers as Oriana Fallacci or Barbara Walters to see that they can get much more out of their subjects than their male colleagues.

Alongside these types of argumentation, which are based on the principle of association, Perelman and Olbrechts-Tyteca distinguish *argumentation based on the dissociation of elements*. The process of dissociation entails the introduction of a division into a concept that the audience previously regarded as constituting a single entity. In practice, this means that a concept is differentiated from the concept that it was originally a part of. In cases in which this renouncement serves the justification of an opinion, the dissociation is a technique of argumentation:

> Christian Democrat politician: 'There is a great need for genuinely Christian political policies.'
> Opponent: 'You wouldn't think so, with all the figures showing dechristianization: the churches are getting emptier.'
> Christian Democrat politician: 'Ha, but that's where you make your mistake: that people go to church less is a sign of secularization, and that is not to be confused with them being less Christian.'

Originally, the elements divorced from one another by dissociation constituted – at least, that was the arguer's impression – a unity in the opinion of the audience; they were part of a single concept ('dechristianization'). Dissociation changes this and introduces a differentiation within the original concept. Since maintaining the original concept would lead to incompatibilities, the dissociation is presented as unavoidable. The arguer establishes the dissociation terminologically, by placing a new term alongside the old one.[4]

In Toulmin's model as well as in Perelman's new rhetoric, the rational procedures of judicial reasoning are taken as the starting point. In neither case, however, has the aim the author sets out to tackle been truly achieved. This may, at least partly, be due to Toulmin and Perelman's limited views of logic. They conveniently identify logic with traditional syllogistic logic. Modern developments are largely ignored, or – as in the case of dialogue logic – could not yet be taken into account. Another inadequacy is that no justice is done to the fact that argumentation is primarily a discourse phenomenon, which is always embedded in a specific contextual and social environment. In order to study argumentation adequately, it must be viewed as a form of linguistic action that is to be approached pragmatically. The neglect of insights from both (dialogue) logic and (pragma-)linguistics has been an impediment to the development of a sound theory of argumentation. It may explain why neither Toulmin's model nor Perelman's new rhetoric offers a satisfactory alternative to formal logic, however inspiring these contributions to the study of argumentation may be.

3 INFORMAL LOGIC

'Informal logic' is a movement, originating in North America in the early seventies, which grew out of a dissatisfaction with the usual treatment of argumentation in introductory logic textbooks. It is inspired by the works of Toulmin and Perelman and by the ideas of some other dissenting philosophers. Since 1978, the voice of this movement has been the journal *Informal Logic*, edited by Blair and Johnson.[5]

Although the name suggests otherwise, informal logic is not a new kind of logic. It is rather a normative approach to argumentation in everyday language which is broader than formal logic. According to the informal logicians, the validity and cogency of argumentation is not identical to formal validity in deductive logic. Blair and Johnson (1987a) argue that the premises for a conclusion must satisfy three criteria: (1) 'relevance', (2) 'sufficiency', and (3) 'acceptability'.[6] With relevance, the question is whether the contents of the premises and the conclusion are adequately related; with sufficiency, whether the premises provide enough evidence for the conclusion; and with acceptability, whether the premises are true, probable or otherwise reliable.

The informal logicians' objective is to develop norms, criteria and procedures for the interpretation, evaluation and construction of argumentation. The problems for which solutions are sought are largely the same as in other approaches: how to analyze argumentation structures, how to classify argumentation schemes, how to assess argumentation, how to identify fallacies, how to conduct a discussion, *etc*. In its present state, informal logic is a comprehensive research program rather than an elaborated theory of argumentation.

There is a striking overlap between the aims and scope of informal logic and those of pragma-dialectics. An important difference is that informal logic concentrates primarily on the relation between premises and conclusions, while pragma-dialectics pretends to cover all aspects and stages of a critical discussion. Another difference is that informal logic studies all kinds of reasoning whereas pragma-dialectics, as will be explained (p. 59), focuses on reasoning that is directed at resolving differences of opinion. A third difference stems from the distinct theoretical backgrounds: in analyzing argumentation, informal logic is geared to disclosing the logical qualities of argumentative discourse, and pragma-dialectics to examining the pragma-linguistic properties that can be taken into account in its reconstruction.

4 FORMAL THEORY OF FALLACIES

The Canadian logicians Woods and Walton (1989) have made a substantial contribution to the study of argumentation, concentrating on the fallacies. Their formal approach is exhibited in a series of jointly and independently authored articles and books. Many of their co-authored papers are collected in Woods and Walton (1989). The basic principles of their approach of the fallacies are explained in their textbook Woods and Walton (1982).[7]

The Woods-Walton approach of the fallacies is *pluralistic*: in their opinion, it makes no sense to suppose that all fallacies must be given the same kind of analysis. Their general methodological view is that fallacies are usefully analyzed with the help of the structures and the theoretical vocabulary of various logical systems, including systems of dialectical logic. This does not mean that they take a fixed position on whether fallacies are inherently logical. In Woods and Walton's view, this will vary depending on the fallacy in question. It is their claim that a great many fallacies can best be analyzed in a way that can in some sense be qualified as *formal*.

Woods and Walton's analysis of fallacies, which draws upon Hamblin's dialectical concepts of 'commitment set' and 'retraction' as methodological tools, is formally oriented, but also dialectical. Woods and Walton tend to organize the many fallacies they have recognized in their writings into three grades of 'formality'. First, there are those fallacies (such as the fallacy of four terms) which are formal in the strict sense. At the next grade of formality come those fallacies (such as the fallacies of ambiguity) that are not formal in the strict sense, but whose commission is at least partly made explicable by reference to logical forms. Much more prominently realized in Woods and Walton's work is a third grade of formality that applies to theories whose key concepts are analyzable using the vocabulary and concepts of a system of logic or some other formal system.

Woods and Walton (1982) emphasize the theoretical importance of characterizing fallacies as features of arguments in actual use. A pragmatic feature of their approach is that it admits many different contexts or frameworks in which argumentation could be used. In theory, all of these contexts or frameworks should be definable under the general rubric of a structure of dialogue where the participants, moves, locations, commitments, and other factors that define the dialogue exchange, are clearly and precisely defined.

5 FORMAL DIALECTICS

Formal logic was given an important dialectical turn in Barth and Krabbe (1982). Building upon Lorenzen's dialogue logic, they described a formal procedure to check whether a given thesis can be logically maintained in light of certain assumptions. This dialectical interpretation of logic is known as 'formal dialectics'.[8]

In formal dialectics, reasoning is viewed as a dialogue between a proponent and an opponent of a certain thesis. Together, the proponent and the opponent attempt to find out whether this thesis can be successfully defended against critical attacks. In his defense, the proponent of the thesis can make use of the opponent's 'concessions': statements that the opponent is prepared to take responsibility for. The proponent must parry any attack on one of his own statements. In this endeavor, the proponent can either give a direct defense or undertake a counterattack on a concession by the opponent.

The opponent is obliged to defend any concession that comes under attack. If this should result in him being unable to do anything other than assert something that he had attacked earlier in the dialogue, this would benefit the proponent. Therefore, the proponent attempts to maneuver the opponent into this position by cleverly using the opponent's concessions. If he is able to do so, according to the rules of the game, the proponent has successfully defended his position – thanks to the opponent's concessions, hence *ex concessis*.

The discussion envisioned in formal dialectics differs fundamentally from ordinary argumentative practice. The assumed starting-point can only occur after a party in a discussion has already presented his argumentation in defense of a standpoint. It arises if he and the other party decide to discover whether this standpoint can be maintained in the light of the argumentation. The parties then initiate a procedure to check whether the standpoint can be logically concluded from the premises that have been presented in the argumentation. If the other party is indeed prepared to take on the role of opponent, he needs to add the proponent's argumentation as a set of concessions to his own commitments.

6 PRAGMA-DIALECTICS

There are a number of direct links between formal dialectics and 'pragma-dialectics', the theory of argumentation developed by van Eemeren and Grootendorst

(1984, 1992a). As indicated by the joint use of the term *dialectic*, the general objective is in both cases the same. The theoretical orientation of pragma-dialectics, however, is different from that of formal dialectics. This difference is clearly expressed in the choice of the prefix *pragma(tic)* rather than *formal*. Pragma-dialectics is primarily a theory of argumentative discourse, not a theory of logic.[9]

Unlike the formal dialectical rules for generating rational arguments, the pragma-dialectical rules for resolving a difference of opinion are envisaged as representing necessary conditions for carrying out a critical discussion in argumentative discourse. In van Eemeren and Grootendorst (1984), a code of conduct was introduced for resolving differences of opinion in a reasonable way. This discussion procedure was summarized in van Eemeren and Grootendorst (1992a: 208-209) in ten basic rules, the 'Ten Commandments' of a critical discussion:

1. Parties must not prevent each other from advancing standpoints or from casting doubt on standpoints.
2. A party that advances a standpoint is obliged to defend it if asked by the other party to do so.
3. A party's attack on a standpoint must relate to the standpoint that has indeed been advanced by the other party.
4. A party may defend a standpoint only by advancing argumentation relating to that standpoint.
5. A party may not deny a premise that has been left implicit by that party or falsely present something as a premise that has been left unexpressed by the other party.
6. A party may not falsely present a premise as an accepted starting point nor deny a premise representing an accepted starting point.
7. A party may not regard a standpoint as conclusively defended if the defense does not take place by means of an appropriate argumentation scheme that is correctly applied.
8. In the argumentation, a party may only use arguments that are logically valid or capable of being validated by making explicit one or more unexpressed premises.
9. A failed defense of a standpoint must result in the party that put forward the standpoint retracting it, and a conclusive defense of the standpoint must result in the other party retracting its doubt about the standpoint.
10. A party must not use formulations that are insufficiently clear or confusingly ambiguous, and a party must interpret the other party's formulations as carefully and accurately as possible.

A precondition for resolving a difference by means of a critical discussion is that the appropriate 'higher order' conditions have already been met (see van Eemeren and Grootendorst, 1988: 287-288 and van Eemeren *et al.*, 1993: 30-34).

In a critical discussion, one language user (the 'protagonist') expresses a standpoint and another language user (the 'antagonist') expresses doubt with respect to this standpoint, or advances a contradictory standpoint. The protagonist defends his standpoint by putting forward argumentation, and if confronted with critical reactions, further argumentation to support his prior argumentation. The difference of opinion is resolved when either the antagonist is convinced by the protagonist's argumentation and accepts the defended standpoint, or the protagonist withdraws his standpoint as a result of the antagonist's critical reactions.

Based on a reconstruction of the resolution process, four stages are analytically distinguished in the conduct of a critical discussion. These are: defining the difference of opinion ('confrontation' stage), establishing the starting point of the discussion ('opening' stage), exchanging arguments and critical reactions in order to resolve the difference ('argumentation' stage), and determining the result of the discussion ('concluding' stage).[10] At every stage of a discourse aimed at bringing about a critical discussion, specific obstacles may arise that can impede the resolution of the difference of opinion. The pragma-dialectical rules are designed to prevent such obstacles from arising; they provide a definition of the general principles of constructive argumentative discourse. Supposedly, obeying all the rules obviates the obstacles, which are traditionally known as 'fallacies'. This is why the rules are purported to be 'problem-valid' (see Barth & Krabbe, 1982: 21-22). Van Eemeren and Grootendorst (1992a: 102-107) explain the fallacies as violations of pragma-dialectical discussion rules. A well-known example of a fallacy, 'Some dogs have fuzzy ears, my dog has fuzzy ears; therefore my dog is some dog', for instance, involves a violation of rule 10.

A crucial difference between the pragma-dialectical rules and the rules of formal dialectics is that the former are linked to ordinary discussions in everyday language. Their scope extends over all aspects of a critical discussion, inclusive of the logical inference relations between premises and conclusions. The rules cover all speech acts performed in all stages of a discourse aimed at resolving a difference of opinion. In van Eemeren *et al.* (1993), it is shown how the model of a critical discussion can be applied to the analysis of argumentative discourse as it occurs in various kinds of practices. In this endeavor, van Eemeren *et al.* explain which transformations need to be performed in order to deal with digressions and repetitions, to do justice to implicit and indirect speech acts, *etc.* Jackson and Jacobs have also made an important contribution to the study of conversational argument in its own right (*e.g.*, Jackson & Jacobs, 1980, 1989).

7 RADICAL ARGUMENTATIVISM

In the seventies, the French linguists Ducrot and Anscombre started to develop a linguistically oriented approach to argumentative discourse. They label this approach 'radical argumentativism' because in their view every form of language use has an argumentative aspect (Anscombre & Ducrot, 1986). The outlines of radical argumentativism have been presented in Ducrot (1980), Anscombre and Ducrot (1983), and Ducrot (1984, 1996).[11]

Ducrot and Anscombre's basic idea is that every piece of discourse contains an explicit or implicit dialogue. They describe how 'argumentative connectors' (such as *but*, *even*, and *at least*) and 'argumentative operators' (such as *only*, *no less than*, and *very*) give specific 'argumentative power' and 'argumentative direction' to the discourse by activating a certain *topos*.[12] According to Ducrot and Anscombre's theory of 'many-voicedness' or 'polyphony', argumentative connectors such as *but* can be responsible for a conflicting argumentative direction since they create a silent second voice which reveals the structural presence of two incompatible conclusions.

In 'That book is fantastic, but it is hard to understand', for example, the listener may conclude on the basis of the first part of the sentence that it would be wise to read the book. On the basis of the second part, he or she might conclude that this is not so wise. The opposing conclusions suggest different 'argumentative principles' or *topoi*: 'The more fantastic a book is, the more reason there is to read it' and 'The less understandable a book is, the more reason there is not to read it'. The use of argumentative operators can have the same effect. Compare the sentence 'The ring costs only one hundred dollars' with the sentence 'The ring costs no less than one hundred dollars'. In a certain context, the first sentence can point to the conclusion 'Buy the ring', the second to the conclusion 'Do not buy the ring'. In the first sentence, the argumentative operator *only* activates the *topos* 'The cheaper the ring is, the more reason there is to buy it'. In the second sentence, the argumentative operator *no less than* activates the *topos* 'The more expensive a ring is, the more reason there is not to buy it.'. Recently, Bruxelles, Ducrot and Raccah (1995) have presented a method of marking the emergence of the topoi used in utterances. They describe the lexical items with argumentative 'ingredients' – topical fields. The topoi used in each utterance containing these lexical items are constructed on the basis of these topical fields and the situation in general.

In the field of argumentation theory, Ducrot and Anscombre's view that 'argumentativity' is a feature of all language use is not generally accepted: argumentation is usually seen as a special form of discourse with a specific communicative and interactional function. Another distinctive feature of Ducrot and Anscombre's radical argumentativity is that it is not aimed at developing norms and criteria for the evaluation of argumentation. Its aim is exclusively descriptive: providing a description of the syntactic and semantic elements that play a role in the argumentative interpretation of sentences.[13]

8 MODERN REVIVAL OF RHETORIC

Over the past few years, a powerful revaluation of classical rhetoric has been in progress. It has become accepted in the professional literature that the a-rational (sometimes anti-rational) image of rhetoric must be revised. As a consequence, the sharp opposition to dialectics should be moderated too. A number of authors claim that rhetoric as the study of effective techniques of persuasion is not incompatible with the critical ideal of reasonableness upheld in dialectics. Others maintain that there are fundamental differences between a rhetorical and a dialectical conception of reasonableness, but see no reason to regard the rhetorical conception as inferior to the dialectical conception.

The rehabilitation of rhetoric goes together with a general acknowledgement that the non-rhetorically oriented theories of argumentation are saturated with insights from classical rhetoric. It is striking that the rise of rhetoric has progressed almost simultaneously in different countries.[14] The survey by Foss, Foss and Trapp (1985) discusses most of the works that have contributed significantly to the resurgence of rhetoric in the United States. Farrell (1977) and McKerrow (1977/1992) in particular, have defended the rational qualities of rhetoric. Rhetoric is also given its due by Wenzel (1980/1992), but emphatically in relation to logic, and primarily dialectics.

In France, it is first of all Reboul who is responsible for giving rhetoric a fully-fledged position in the study of argumentation. In 'Can there be non-rhetorical argumentation?' (1988) he discusses the rhetorical characteristics of argumentation: its formulation in ordinary language, its orientation to an audience, the probability (at best) of its premises, and the lack of logical necessity in the connection between its premises and its conclusion. Although Reboul (1990) regards rhetoric and dialectic as two different disciplines, they do exhibit some common traits. Rhetoric is dialectic applied to discussions of social issues; at the same time, dialectic is part of rhetoric, because it provides rhetoric with its intellectual instruments.

In Germany, Kopperschmidt goes a step further. In a sequel to an exploratory article on the relation between rhetoric and argumentation theory (1977), he contends that rhetoric is the subject of research in argumentation theory. This agrees with the historical view of rhetoric (ed., 1990). The Austrian Kienpointner (1991b) offers an even more radical revaluation of rhetoric: he defends a relativistic conception of reasonableness and contends that rhetoric constitutes the most productive instrument for resolving social dissension.

In the Netherlands, Braet has been active in stimulating rhetoric. Braet (1984) emphasizes the importance of the classical theory of status for modern argumentation studies. He illustrates his point by comparing this classical theory with the theory of stock issues in American academic debate.

9 OTHER SIGNIFICANT APPROACHES

Each of the approaches to argumentation discussed up to this point has been explored in a comprehensive research program. Other recent contributions to the study of argumentation may be equally interesting, but they are less focused on developing a general theory of argumentation, more limited in scope, less elaborated, or not accessible in English. To conclude our survey, we shall mention a few.

First, there are the Swiss logician Grize and his colleagues (Borel, 1989; Borel, Grize and Miéville, 1983; Grize, 1982, 1996; Maier, 1989), who have been developing a theory of 'natural logic' at the Centre de Recherches Sémiologiques of the University of Neuchâtel.[15] Their main motive has been dissatisfaction with formal logic. Natural logic is designed for everyday discourse as it manifests itself in advertisements, political addresses, etc. Although in these two respects it corresponds with informal logic, in its theoretical approach natural logic is much different. Without assuming any *a priori* normative concepts of 'truth' and 'validity', natural logic aims to expose the 'logic' of such argumentative texts. The term *logic* here refers to the commonplaces (*topoi*) and rules used in everyday argumentation and reasoning, not to the formal logical systems for deductively valid reasoning. Relying on abstract 'schematizations' of persuasive forms of presentation and on discursive logical operations instrumental in the creation or elimination of contradiction or inconsistency, natural logic gives a description of argumentative language use.

Second, there is the Unité de Linguistique Française at the University of Geneva, a research group of Francophone Swiss pragma-linguists (*e.g.* Luscher, 1989; Moeschler, 1982, 1989a, 1989b; A. Reboul, 1988; Roulet, Auchlin, Moeschler, Rubattel & Schelling, 1985). Since the beginning of the eighties they have devoted themselves to giving pragmatic descriptions of French markers (pragmatic connectives, modal adverbs, illocutionary verbs) within a general model of discourse structure. Speech act theory, Ducrot and Anscombre's radical argumentativism, and Goffman's symbolic interactionism influence their pragmatic studies. An essential characteristic of their approach is that speech acts are not examined in isolation, but in relation with other speech acts in a discourse. Making use of Sperber and Wilson's theory of relevance, they have recently added a cognitive component to the 'Geneva model', which distinguishes between different levels of the discourse, describes the relations between these levels, and indicates which linguistic markers may be indicative of the various relations.[16] From a somewhat different angle, Vignaux (1992) gives an analysis of denial as a verbal and cognitive operation, and with the help of Aristotelian logic he attempts to account for the role of negations in argumentative strategies.

Third, there is the theory of 'problematology', developed in the early eighties by the Belgian philosopher Meyer, both in order to solve philosophical problems and as a model for argumentation (1982a, 1982b/1986a, 1986b).[17] In his skeptical attitude towards formal logic, Meyer shows himself a true disciple of Perelman, his teacher at Brussels Free University. According to Meyer, the function of argumentative discourse is, on the one hand, to provide an answer to a specific problem in a specific context. On the other hand, argumentation can also be seen as the 'problematizing' of an answer; that is, as the recognition of the question contained in a given answer. In non-formal reasoning there is no guarantee that a posed question will not remain an open question, and final answers are not to be expected: they can only be given in the formal language of a logic in which there is no room for doubt or contradictory propositions. In problematology, there is only room for a non-formal logic governing 'nonconstraining reasoning' (1986a: 130-131).

Fourth, there is the German argumentation tradition.[18] Its most prominent representative is Kopperschmidt (1978, 1980, 1989), whose normative approach to argumentation combines insights from classical rhetoric with insights from speech act theory, text linguistics, and Habermas's theory of communicative rationality (1981).[19] Habermas's influence is equally apparent in the work of the linguistically and descriptively oriented German theorists who attempt to apply speech act theory and conversation analysis to spoken and written argumentative discourse.[20] Their work has been strongly influenced by Toulmin too.[21] Another German contribution to the development of argumentation theory is the dialogue logic of the Erlangen School of Lorenzen et al. (e.g. Lorenzen and Lorenz, 1978), which is fundamental to Barth and Krabbe's formal dialectics and has already been mentioned.[22]

Fifth, there is the richly varied American tradition in the field of speech communication, with prominent scholars such as Willard, Zarefsky, and Goodnight. Willard (1979a, 1979b, 1983, 1989) has developed a social-epistemological approach to argumentation based on insights from phenomenology, symbolic interaction, and constructivism. In his view, argumentation is a form of conversation ensuing from differences of opinion; the interaction between arguments is a source of human knowledge.[23] Other American rhetoric and communication scholars approach argumentation with divergent interests. A useful survey of the main contributions to the various areas is offered by Benoit, Hample and Benoit (eds., 1992). This collection includes classical articles by (Pamela) Benoit, (William) Benoit, Brockriede, Burleson, Ehninger, Gouran, Gronbeck, Hample, Jackson, Jacobs, Kneupper, McKerrow, (Daniel) O'Keefe, Rowland, Trapp, Wallace, Wenzel, Willard, and Zarefsky. Some of these names have already appeared in earlier sections of this survey.

Last but not least, there are numerous authors who, from various theoretical starting points, have given special attention to specific topics: validity, unexpressed (or implicit) premises, argumentation schemes, argumentation structures, fallacies, relevance, cognitive processing of argumentative discourse, acquisition of argumentative skills, teaching of argumentative skills, conversational argument, field-dependent argumentation, and intercultural argumentation. On most of these topics, vast numbers of publications have appeared.

10 COMMONALITIES, DIFFERENCES, AND TRENDS

Without making any claim to being exhaustive, we think that the following commonalities, differences, and trends are worth noting in the study of argumentation during the last two decades:

1. A growing interest in developing a fully-fledged theory of argumentation among scholars from a variety of disciplines. This interest manifests itself internationally in publications by philosophers and logicians, rhetoric and communication scholars, linguists and discourse analysts, lawyers, psychologists, and other social scientists. It is accompanied by an increased awareness of the need for multidisciplinary and interdisciplinary collaboration.
2. A keen interest in the prospects that recent developments in formal logic, especially in dialogue logic, may have to offer for the study of argumentation. This interest is usually coupled with a realistic appreciation of the limitations of a formal approach when dealing with the peculiarities of genuine argumentative discourse. It expresses itself in various kinds of dialectical approaches to argumentation that have resulted in several models for analyzing argumentative discourse.
3. A spectacular revaluation of the importance of rhetoric for the study of argumentation. This revaluation has led to the realization that a dialectical approach to argumentation, even if it is primarily normative, and a rhetorical approach, even if it is primarily seen as descriptive, need not necessarily be at loggerheads. Since it has become clearer to many that rhetoric is not by definition related to effective, though often irrational, persuasion techniques, the idea has gained ground that studying rhetoric may lead to beneficial insights concerning the reasonableness of argumentation.
4. An increased empirical interest in how argumentative discourse is conducted in various kinds of argumentative practices or fields. Such practices can be highly institutionalized, as in the case of most judicial argumentation, but they can also be more or less informal. Paying special attention to the linguistic means that are brought to bear in the execution of specific argumentative practices, detailed studies have been undertaken or are being undertaken into the characteristic features of academic discussions, mediation talks, policy making, and negotiation. Besides field-dependent argumentative conventions, the intercultural differences in argumentation styles seem to have become another focus of attention.
5. A renewed interest in 'old' theoretical concepts such as 'relevance' and the 'fallacies', which are crucial to the development of an adequate theory of argumentation. Argumentation theory can only live up to its practical ambitions if a satisfactory treatment can be given of these concepts. After Hamblin's devastating critique of the logical Standard Treatment of the fallacies, various new approaches have evolved. These approaches tend to be much broader in scope than the logical Standard Treatment and they are usually in a dialectical vein.

ANNEX

Institutional information concerning the discipline
The most important argumentation journals published in English are *Argumentation* (since 1987), the *Journal of the American Forensic Association* (since 1954), since 1988 continued as *Argumentation and Advocacy*, and *Informal Logic* (since 1978). Argumentation conferences are generally held under the auspices of the International Society for the Study of Argumentation (ISSA), the Association for Informal Logic and Critical Thinking (AILACT), the Ontario Society for the Study of Argumentation (OSSA), and the American Forensic Association (AFA), which is part of the National Communication Association (NCA). Conferences are also often organized by specific universities or included in broader conferences on philosophy, linguistics, speech communication, law, or some other discipline.

AUTHORS' NOTE

This chapter is based on a paper presented at the Colloquium 'Logic and Argumentation' of the Royal Netherlands Academy of Arts and Sciences (1994) and is in its earlier version included in the Proceedings.

NOTES

1. This distinction plays a vital part in the reconstruction of unexpressed premises, the classification of argumentation schemes and the analysis of argumentation structures. See van Eemeren and Grootendorst (1992: 60-62).
2. Extreme normativists (*e.g.* Siegel, 1987; Biro and Siegel, 1992) frequently combine their position with a rejection of a relativist stand, whereas extreme descriptivists (*e.g.* Willard, 1989) defend it.
3. For an elaborate discussion of Toulmin's model, see van Eemeren *et al.* (1996: 129-160). See also Hample (1977) and Healy (1987). Less critical are Burleson (1979) and Reinard (1984).
4. For an elaborate discussion of Perelman and Olbrechts-Tyteca's new rhetoric, see van Eemeren *et al.* (1996: 93-128). See also Ray (1978), JAFA's special issue edited by Dearin (1985), Golden and Pilotta (1986), and Corgan (1987).
5. For the object and research program of informal logic, see Blair and Johnson (1987b). A brief historical survey is provided in Johnson and Blair (1980). See also van Eemeren *et al.* (1996: 163-188).
6. These criteria were first discussed in Johnson and Blair (1977). Although the labels are not always the same, the three criteria have been adopted by Govier (1985), Damer (1987), Freeman (1988), and others.
7. See also Walton (1982). For a more elaborate discussion of Woods and Walton's theoretical position, see van Eemeren *et al.* (1996: 213-245).
8. For an explanation of Lorenzen's dialogue logic and Barth and Krabbe's formal dialectics, see van Eemeren *et al.* (1996: 246-273).
9. As for its dialectical starting point, pragma-dialectics has been inspired by insights from Crawshay-Williams (1957), Popper (1972, 1974) and Barth and

Krabbe (1982); its pragmatic theoretical orientation is based on insights from Austin (1962), Searle (1969, 1979) and Grice (1975). For a more elaborate discussion of pragma-dialectics, see van Eemeren *et al.* (1996: 274-311).
10 See van Eemeren and Grootendorst (1992: 35).
11 Only lately Ducrot and Anscombre's theory has become somewhat better known outside the French-speaking world, due to articles in English such as Lundquist (1987), Verbiest (1991) and Nølke (1992). For a more elaborate discussion of radical argumentativism, see van Eemeren *et al.* (1996: 312-321).
12 For a brief explanation of the meaning of the term topos in classical dialectic and rhetoric, see van Eemeren *et al.* (1996: 37-50).
13 In Ducrot (1995) the question of argumentative force is studied, addressing it from the perspective of the description of the lexicon, and in the light of the influence of certain modifiers on the modified 'predicates' (noun phrase or verb phrase). Ducrot and Anscombre's theory has also been the basis for carrying out empirical research regarding the interpretation of sentences. See, for example, Bassano (1991) and Bassano and Champaud (1987a, 1987b, 1987c).
14 For a more elaborate discussion of recent developments in the rhetorical approach to argumentation, see van Eemeren *et al.* (1996: 189-212, 345-349).
15 For a more elaborate discussion of natural logic, see van Eemeren et al. (1996: 322-328).
16 See van Eemeren *et al.* (1996: 35-351).
17 See van Eemeren *et al.* (1996: 343-344).
18 For a survey, see Kienpointner (1991a). See also van Eemeren *et al.* (1996: 341-343, 347-348, 350, 354-355).
19 For a brief discussion in English of Kopperschmidt's ideas, see Kopperschmidt (1985, 1987) and van Eemeren *et al.* (1996: 342-343).
20 For the remarkable influence of Habermas on speech communication in the United States, see the special issue of the Journal of the American Forensic Association (1979), with contributions from Burleson, Farrell, and Wenzel. See also Doxtader (1991).
21 For Habermas's influence, see, for example, Berk (1979); for Toulmin's influence, Göttert (1978), Quasthoff (1978), Völzing (1979), Öhlschläger (1979), and Kienpointner (1983).
22 See van Eemeren *et al.* (1996: 253-262).
23 See van Eemeren *et al.* (1996: 197-198).

From Analysis to Presentation:
A Pragma-dialectical Approach to Writing Argumentative Texts

Frans H. van Eemeren
University of Amsterdam &
New York University
Rob Grootendorst
University of Amsterdam

ABSTRACT

In this chapter, we outline a theoretical framework for developing strategies for writing argumentative texts. In much of the literature on writing more is said about the preconditions for writing and the principles for pedagogy than about the ways in which writing problems can be solved. Authors who do pay attention to writing problems usually do so in an unmethodical way, and their recommendations are based on common sense rather than theoretical considerations. We attempt to offer an alternative that is based on our pragma-dialectical theory of argumentation. The strategies we propose can be used by a writer in order to transform an analytic overview of the argumentation to be conveyed into a comprehensible and acceptable argumentative text. First is explained what one should imagine the various presentation transformations to be, then is shown, by way of concrete examples, exactly how the strategies involved are put into practice. Thus, it is made clear that the pragma-dialectical approach provides an opportunity to develop a methodical perspective which, so far, is lacking in the practical literature on writing.

1 INTRODUCTION

In much of the literature on writing, more is said about the preconditions for writing and the principles for pedagogy than about the ways in which writing problems can be solved. Authors who do pay attention to writing problems often do not do so in a very systematic way; they mainly try to be practical, and their recommendations are based on common sense rather than theoretical considerations (Elbow, 1981; Stewart, Kowler & Bullock, 1987). Recently, there has been a growing interest in the theory of writing, which is primarily focused on the writing process (see Witte & Cherry, 1986, and also Rijlaarsdam, van den Berg & Couzijn, 1996a, 1996b). Most prominent in this endeavor is the model of Flower and Hayes (1977, 1981), in which the writing process is schematically represented (see also Hayes & Flower, 1980). In her useful textbook, Flower (1981) presents a number of strategic heuristics for improving the writing process, but - as a matter of course - the theoretical problems involved in writing a text are hardly dealt with.[1]

Some authors try to provide directions on how to write or rewrite a text by starting from some theoretical conception of the general outline of the kind of text which has to be written. In such an approach, a concept of the desired structure of the text is the basis for text construction.[2]

We think that the writing of argumentative texts can benefit from using the ideal model of 'critical discussion' developed in the pragma-dialectical theory of argumentation (van Eemeren & Grootendorst 1984, 1992).[3] In this chapter, we outline a theoretical framework for carrying out research aimed at developing strategies for presenting argumentative texts. These strategies can be used by a writer in order to transform an 'analytic overview' of the argumentation into a comprehensible and acceptable text. We first explain in an abstract way what one should imagine the various 'presentation transformations' to be, and show by way of concrete examples exactly how such strategies are put into practice. In this chapter, it is indicated where the transformation of 'deletion' would lead us if presentation transformations were systematically linked with 'analytic transformations'. Thus it is made clear that the pragma-dialectical approach provides an opportunity to develop a methodical perspective which, so far, is lacking in the practical literature on writing. It is intrinsic to the educational pedagogy of this approach that any methodical perspective can only be put into practice if first a reflection-minded attitude is stimulated among would-be writers that enables them to discover the rationale of the proposed procedure (see van Eemeren & Grootendorst, 1992: 8-9; also Couzijn, 1995; Couzijn & Rijlaarsdam 1996; Couzijn, 1999).

2 THE ANALYSIS OF ARGUMENTATIVE TEXTS

In the pragma-dialectical model we have developed for resolving differences of opinion, argumentative texts are regarded as crucial components of a (partially implicit) critical discussion (see section 6 of our chapter on 'Developments in argumentation theory' in this volume, and also van Eemeren & Grootendorst, 1984). When dealing with an argumentative text, a careful analysis is required in which the text, with the help of the ideal model, is reconstructed as a critical discussion. In this way, one gets an analytic overview of the argumentative text in which only those elements which are relevant for resolving a difference of opinion are included. An analytic overview of an argumentative text mentions exactly which difference of opinion is to be resolved in the text, how the various stages of a critical discussion are represented, and what the structure of the argumentation is.

In order to get an adequate analytic overview of an argumentative text, one or more transformations, whether or not in combination, have to be applied to the text. These transformations are aimed at bringing together the elements that are dialectically relevant (van Eemeren, 1986; van Eemeren, Grootendorst, Jackson & Jacobs, 1993; van Eemeren *et al.*, 1996: 288-298).

The first *analytic transformation* that must be carried out in making an analytic overview is *deletion*. It consists in leaving out all elements which are not immediately relevant to resolving the difference of opinion, such as repetitions, digressions, asides, clarifications, and anecdotes.

The second analytic transformation is *addition*. Elements are added which were left implicit but which are immediately relevant to the resolution of the difference of opinion, such as unexpressed arguments, standpoints, or any other unexpressed elements.

The third analytic transformation is *permutation*. It amounts to a (re)arrangement of elements that reveals which steps are taken in the resolution process. The various steps are clearly distinguished, overlapping steps are separated, and anticipatory or retrogradatory steps are reordered.

The fourth analytic transformation is *substitution*. It consists in replacing formulations which do not make sufficiently clear what the function of an element is in resolving the difference of opinion, by means of formulations which indicate this function unequivocally. Elements which have the same function are formulated in the same manner: a rhetorical question which serves as an argument is represented in exactly the same way as an argument which was formulated immediately as an argument.

An analytic overview based on these four transformations contains relevant information – and nothing but relevant information – in its most relevant place, and formulated in a way which explicitly expresses its relevance.

3 THE PRESENTATION OF ARGUMENTATIVE TEXTS

While argumentation theorists have carried out a lot of research regarding the analysis and evaluation of argumentative texts, the problems of writing an argumentative text have not yet been properly investigated (for a survey in the study of argumentation, van Eemeren *et al.*, 1996). From the literature on argumentative writing skills one gets the impression that advice that is based on common sense is usually thought to suffice. In practice, however, this proves to be a false assumption.

In our opinion, the pragma-dialectical approach to argumentation enables us to develop more adequate insights concerning the construction of argumentative texts. These insights are, to some extent, analogous to those concerning the analysis of argumentative texts. In both cases, *the ideal model of a critical discussion* serves as a methodical starting point. It provides a systematic framework for determining which is the relevant information presented, or to be presented, in the argumentative text. The main problem in writing or rewriting the argumentative text is therefore how this information can be presented as comprehensibly and acceptably as possible.

So, a pragma-dialectical approach to writing starts from an analytic overview which contains all of the information that is regarded to be dialectically, relevant and which is based on an analysis of an existing text or on a plan for such a text. On the basis of this analytic overview, an argumentative text is to be written in which this information is presented in such a way that optimal comprehensibility and acceptability are ensured.

As a text is never either absolutely incomprehensible and unacceptable or absolutely comprehensible and acceptable for everybody, but always more or less comprehensible and acceptable for certain readers, the notions of comprehensibility and acceptability are both gradual as well as relative.[4] We consider the presentation of an argumentative text to be sufficiently comprehensible and acceptable if it enables the intended readership to carry out a normative reconstruction that leads to an accurate analytic overview of the critical discussion the text is dealing with.

Generally, the comprehensibility and acceptability of argumentative texts can be diminished in four ways: first, by redundancy; second, by implicitness; third, by disarrangement; and, fourth, by lack of clarity. Therefore, in order to aim systematically for comprehensibility and acceptability, four kinds of dialectical presentation transformations must be distinguished. These presentation transformations refer to the step from the analytic overview of an existing or planned text, to the eventual argumentative text. They mirror, as it were, the analytic transformations, which refer to the step from the text to the analytic overview.

A simple approach to rewriting
For the sake of clarity, when dealing with presentation transformations we shall concentrate on the situation in which there is a provisional version of an argumentative text that requires rewriting due to a lack of comprehensibility and acceptability. In order to characterize our point of departure more clearly, we shall make use of the following terminology. The text that requires revision is called the *primary text* (T0*), the text that results from the revision, the *revised text* (TR*). A *normative reconstruction* (NR) of the *primary text* (T0*) leads to an *analytic overview* (AO). The *analytic transformations* (AT) that are carried out in creating an analytic overview are part of the *analytic transformation route* (—>). *Systematic rewriting* (SR) of the analytic overview (AO) into a revised text (TR*) leads to an *adequate presentation* (AP). The *presentation transformations* (PT) that are carried out in creating an *adequate presentation* (AP) are part of the *presentation transformation route* (===>).

The simplest characterization of the rewriting procedure is as follows:

$$(1) \quad T_0 \xrightarrow{SR} T_r$$

In most writing methods, this is taken to be an adequate description of the situation we start from. Without a particular perspective of the rewriting procedure, all kinds of factors are – in random order or simultaneously – dragged into the process of rewriting. Of course, this approach is unsystematic and *ad hoc*.

A more sophisticated approach to rewriting
A more sophisticated approach to rewriting, in which textual analysis is taken into account, is the following:

$$(2) \quad T_0 \xrightarrow{NR} AO \xrightarrow{AP} T_0$$
$$\underset{SR}{=\!=\!=\!=\!=\!=\!=\!=\!=\!=\!>}$$

First, an analytic overview is made of the text which requires improvement. Then, on the basis of this analytic overview, the revised text is written. One important advantage of this approach is that it starts from the relevant information. There is a risk, however, that the revised text does not actually relate anymore to the primary text. As it is this primary text which requires revision, in the rewriting procedure all pointers provided by the primary text should be duly taken into account. By doing this, the rewriting process can also be considerably facilitated. Evidently, the primary text is not altogether adequate, but that does not automatically mean that it does not contain any elements, which, though they do not play a part in the analytic overview, can be helpful in improving the presentation.

Our approach to rewriting
If, in rewriting the analytic overview, feedback from the primary text is systematically ensured, then the presentation in the revised text can be improved in a way which can be accounted for. The analytic overview guarantees that the dialectical line remains clear, whereas a comprehensible and acceptable presentation is furthered by information from the primary text. This procedure can be represented as follows:

$$(3) \quad T_0 \xrightarrow{\begin{array}{c} SR \\ <=== \\ NR \end{array}} AO \xrightarrow{AP} T_r$$
$$========>$$
$$SR$$

Our opting for this last approach to rewriting procedures does not mean that we think it always necessary, in order to rewrite adequately, to first have a primary text which can be the basis for an analytic overview (and for the revised text). It is quite possible for the writer to start by making a text plan that contains exactly the sort of information that is otherwise included in an analytic overview. In fact, our approach is neutral with respect to the question whether it is preferable to start the writing process with writing out an elaborate draft version, which can then be improved upon, or with first developing a text plan, which can then be worked out. Thus, we do not take a stance in the 'thinking while writing' or 'think first, then write' controversy.

4 FROM ANALYTIC TRANSFORMATIONS TO PRESENTATION TRANSFORMATIONS

In our approach, rewriting an argumentative text entails applying presentation transformations to an analytic overview of the text which needs improvement. These presentation transformations are aimed at increasing the comprehensibility and the acceptability of the text. In pursuing this objective, we have to make sure that the presentation transformations get appropriate feedback from the primary text. We can try to achieve this by systematically checking the ways in which the analytic transformations that are applied to the primary text when making the analytic overview, though dialectically indispensable, may or may not reduce the comprehensibility and acceptability of the text.

Four ways of dealing with feedback from the primary text
There are four possibilities to be distinguished for getting feedback from the primary text. With the help of the analytic transformation of deletion, we shall clarify what we mean.
1. An analytic transformation, which is carried out in the normative reconstruction of the primary text, is maintained in transforming the analytic overview

into a rewritten text. This would, for instance, mean that an element, which is deleted in the normative reconstruction, remains deleted. Such a case may be characterized as *confirmation of deletion*.
2. An analytic transformation, which has not been carried out in the normative reconstruction, is also not carried out in transforming the analytic overview into a rewritten text. This would, for instance, mean that an element from the primary text, which is not deleted in the analytic overview, is also not deleted in the rewritten text. Such a case may be characterized as *confirmation of non-deletion*.
3. An analytic transformation, which is carried out in the normative reconstruction of the primary text, is annulled in transforming the analytic overview into a rewritten text. This would, for instance, mean that an element which was deleted in the normative reconstruction reappears unmodified in the rewritten text, or is replaced by another element which is added to the analytic overview. In both cases, a (presentation) addition replaces an (analytic) deletion. The first case may be characterized as *identical deletion compensation* and the second as *non-identical deletion compensation*.
4. An analytic transformation, which had not been carried out in the normative reconstruction, is nevertheless carried out in transforming the analytic overview into a rewritten text. This would, for instance, mean that an element from the primary text – for example, an argument – which has not been deleted in the analytic overview, *is* deleted in the rewritten text – and functions as an unexpressed premise. This case may be characterized as *deletion introduction*.

The four possibilities, which have been distinguished here, can be summarized as follows. Either a transformation which is carried out in the analysis is maintained or not maintained in the presentation (1 and 3 respectively), or a transformation which is not carried out in the analysis is or is not carried out in the presentation (4 and 2 respectively). These options can be represented schematically:

Table 1   Analytic transformations and presentation transformations.

	T_0	—>	AO	—>	T_r
		AT		PT	
1		+		+	AT-confirmation
2		−		−	Non-AT-confirmation
3		+		−	AT-compensation
4		−		+	PT-introduction

AT = analytic transformation   PT = presentation transformation

When applied to the transformation of deletion, this outline will be filled in as follows:

Table 2 Deletion transformations.

	T_0	—>	AO	—>	T_r	
		AT		PT		
1	X	DEL+	0	[DEL+]	0	DEL-confirmation
2	X	DEL-	X	[DEL-]	X	Non-DEL-confirm
3	X	DEL+	0	ADD+	X/Y	Identical/Non-identical DEL-compensation
4	X	DEL-	X	DEL+	0	DEL-introduction

DEL = deletion   ADD = addition   X, Y = element of T_0 or T_r

4.1 Four questions a rewriter has to deal with

The presentation transformations to be carried out in transforming an analytic overview while taking the primary text into account, correspond roughly to the following four questions which a rewriter has to ask and answer:
1. what can be left out of the analytic overview (presentation deletion);
2. what should be added to the analytic overview (presentation addition);
3. what should be changed in the arrangement of the analytic overview (presentation permutation); and
4. which formulations must be changed in the analytic overview (presentation substitution)?

Although the one sequential order for carrying out the presentation transformations may seem to be more logical than the other, the order is not actually definitively fixed. Sometimes it is better to begin with the deletion transformation, and sometimes the permutation transformation, the addition transformation, or the substitution transformation provides an easier point of departure. Often the one transformation can only be carried out after the other has been carried out first. In practice, as a rule, several transformations are carried out more, or less simultaneously, whether or not in a more or less fixed combination. The various transformations can be carried out several times: in principle, carrying out presentation transformations is a dynamic and cyclic process.

Naturally, the big question is exactly how the execution of each presentation transformation can be accounted for. Here, the analytic transformations can be of help. The clearer it can be explained on the basis of the primary text why certain analytic transformations are carried out, the clearer it will be at which points the primary text should be (re)considered when carrying out presentation transformations. For example, an element from the primary text is left out of the analytic overview because it is a repetition of something that has been said before. It might, on closer inspection, prove better not to maintain this deletion with a view to an adequate presentation in the rewritten text, because the comprehensibility and acceptability of the text for the intended readers would benefit from the deleted passage. In other cases, such as when an elucidation is deleted in the analytic overview, it would not even have occurred to the rewriter to carry out a certain presentation transformation of addition if it were not for the feedback from the primary text.

The analytic overview is the starting point for rewriting. A sound strategy when rewriting is to maintain the analytic transformations of the primary text unless there is a special reason not to do so. It is also recommendable not to carry out presentation transformations of the analytic overview, which do not, in any way, relate to analytic transformations – unless again, there is a special reason to do so. This does not mean, incidentally, that it will ever be not at all necessary to carry out any presentation transformation whatsoever; an analytic overview is, as such, never a presentable text.

It is not easy to answer the question: Which considerations play a part in carrying out a specific presentation transformation? It is clear, however, that each presentation transformation must, directly or indirectly, serve the dialectical goal, but it is equally clear that it can never be motivated purely and exclusively on dialectical grounds. Besides, in principle, a presentation transformation should also make it easier to analyze the revised argumentative text dialectically.

This last demand means that the final presentation of the text must be as comprehensible and as acceptable as possible to the reader. It goes without saying that, in order to achieve this, pragmatic knowledge about the rules and principles that govern verbal communication and interaction – such as the recognizability and correctness conditions for the performance of speech acts, the communicative maxims and the principles of 'face' protection and politeness – is indispensable. The same applies to empirical knowledge about how texts are processed and conversations conducted. Insights from discourse studies, notably speech act theory, psycholinguistics, sociolinguistics and conversation analysis, can be of great help here (see, to start with, Grice, 1975; Leech, 1983; Levinson, 1983; Searle, 1969, 1979; van Eemeren & Grootendorst, 1984, 1992; van Eemeren *et al.*, 1993).

5 PRESENTATION TRANSFORMATIONS CONCERNING DELETION

Transformations of the analytic overview are pragma-dialectically justified only if the presentation transformations concerned further the comprehensibility and acceptability of the argumentative text. The various kinds of considerations, which may lead to the carrying out of a presentation transformation, can be illustrated by considering the relation of presentation transformations to analytic transformations which are carried out in making an analytic overview. Again, we choose deletion as an example. With regard to analytic deletion, four possibilities can be distinguished:

1. Deletion-confirmation

If elements are deleted in the analytic overview because they have no dialectical role to play, and they fulfill no other useful function in making the text more comprehensible and acceptable to the reader, then there is enough reason to maintain their deletion in the presentation of the argumentative text.

A minimum requirement for a comprehensible and acceptable presentation of an argumentative text is that it should not violate the communicative rules which can be derived from speech act conditions and Grice's Cooperative Principle and maxims (see van Eemeren and Grootendorst 1992). In principle, a writer has to comply with all the communicative rules of the game. A writer would, for example, violate the efficiency rule if he kept repeating an argument, which had already been mentioned several times. Such a superfluous repetition, which is of course deleted in the analytic overview, must therefore also remain deleted in the rewritten text. The same applies to digressions, which are deleted in the analytic overview because they violate the rule that all contributions must be to the point.

2. *Non-deletion-confirmation*
If elements are not deleted in the analytic overview because of their dialectical function, then they will, in principle, also have to be maintained in the rewritten text. Otherwise, the comprehensibility and acceptability of the presentation are, as a rule, immediately affected. This would occur, for instance, if a standpoint which is being defended in the primary text, and which is therefore included in the analytic overview, were left out in the rewritten version. As a consequence, it would become difficult, if not impossible, for the reader to determine exactly what exactly the arguments which are put forward refer to. In such a case, the clarity rule is being violated.

3. *Deletion-compensation*
If the presentation should otherwise lose some of its comprehensibility or acceptability, then the deletion of elements in the analytic overview should be undone in the transformation of the analytic overview into a rewritten version of the argumentative text. Compensation of the analytic deletion can take place by having the deleted elements reappear in the revised version or by adding other elements instead (identical and non-identical deletion-compensation, respectively).

Identical deletion-compensation is, for instance, called for when a clear explanation, elucidation, clarification, illumination, exemplification, or illustration is required in order to make the text easily and fully comprehensible. Non-identical deletion-compensation is called for when an unclear, or in any other sense inappropriate explanation is required and cannot be missed. If the deleted explanation were not, in some way or other, compensated for in the rewritten text, then the communicative rule of clarity would be violated.

Because of the clarity rule, it also may be necessary to add some organizational comment to the rewritten version, in order to explain the structure of the text, as in 'First, I shall clarify my point of view and then I shall put forward three arguments to support it'. Such organizational comments are, as a rule, omitted in the analytic overview. In longer and more complex texts, however, it would be helpful to give the reader something to grasp when trying to discover the structure of the text.

4. *Deletion-introduction*
When transforming an analytic overview into an argumentative text, it is sometimes necessary to delete elements that occur in the primary text and that are maintained in the analytic overview. This procedure deviates from the rule mentioned under (2) that something which is not deleted in the analytic overview should also not be deleted in the rewritten version.

There is a sound reason to deviate from this rule if applying the rule leads to violating one or more of the communicative rules. This is the case, for example, when a point of departure is explicitly mentioned in the primary text, which is already completely obvious to the reader because it is understood in the way he is used to dealing with things. Mentioning this starting point, all the same, in the rewritten version would amount to 'stressing the obvious' and therefore to a violation of the efficiency rule.

OTHER PRESENTATION TRANSFORMATIONS

Similar considerations apply to the question of whether or not corresponding presentation transformations are required in order to deal adequately with the analytic transformations of addition, permutation, and substitution which are carried out, or not carried out, in drawing up the analytic overview. What the outcome of these considerations will be, depends, among other things, on the context in which the argumentative text is to function (its institutional surroundings, degree of conventionalization, usage procedures, *etc.*), and on its intended readers (their language skills, motivation, interests, background knowledge, *etc.*). At any rate, each presentation transformation, whether it applies to smaller or to larger text units, to the communicative force of speech acts or to their propositional content, should always be instrumental in furthering the dialectical goal of the text, and in increasing its comprehensibility and acceptability to the readers in view of the communicative rules.

The presentation transformation of addition
The reasons that apply to the question of whether or not a presentation transformation of *addition* should be carried out, are analogous to those which have been discussed with regard to deletion. In fact, the reasons for maintaining an analytic addition in the revised text are basically the same as those for undoing an analytic deletion, and those for undoing an analytic addition are basically the same as those for maintaining an analytic deletion.

The presentation transformation of permutation
As far as the presentation transformation of *permutation* is concerned, a choice must always be made between the arrangement in the ideal model and some other ordering. Of decisive importance here is what the reader already knows: the writer can link up with this. Sometimes, it may therefore be advisable to have the opening stage precede the confrontation stage, or to have the argumentation stage wholly or partially precede the opening stage. This would, for example, result in mentioning the arguments first and only then indicating which common argumentation principles ensure the soundness of these arguments, or in establishing the principles first and only then indicating what exactly the difference of opinion is. Eventually, the predominant requisite is that the structure should be transparent to the reader, and that the presentation should be geared to achieving this effect.

The presentation transformation of substitution
As far as the presentation transformation of *substitution* is concerned, the first question is always to what extent the formulations in the rewritten text must agree with the standard phrases in the analytic overview. Exaggerating explicitness can easily be at odds with the efficiency rule and carrying through the standardization too far can lead to a text which is deadly dull.

The real art is to achieve stylistic variation, which combines clarity with avoiding too much formalization. It would do no harm, once in a while, to phrase a standpoint as a rhetorical question instead of in the form of an assertion. Some arguments may even come across better if they are not officially announced as arguments, but presented as expressions of personal feelings.

Incidentally, there is not one clear dimension of style at stake here, but a great number of diverse stylistic dimensions which must be taken into account, such as formality, specificity, and concision. These dimensions can be characterized by pairs of notions which indicate the extremes on a scale (formal/informal, general/specific, lengthy/concise). The appropriateness of a certain stylistic choice always depends on the specific characteristics of the context and the readers. The list of pairs which make up the various stylistic dimensions, include, for instance: formal/informal, abstract/concrete, general/specific, vague/precise, indirect/direct, unfamiliar/familiar, difficult/easy, complex/simple, lengthy/concise, obscure/lucid, unclear/clear, unattractive/attractive, incorrect/correct, dull/vivid, ugly/beautiful. All these dimensions should be subject to systematic research (see, for an introduction, Rowan, 1988, who discusses the problem of explaining difficult concepts to lay audiences).

6 AN EXAMPLE OF PRAGMA-DIALECTICAL PRESENTATION STRATEGIES

Primary text
In the following text – a pamphlet distributed door-to-door in the neighborhood – we have indicated some of the analytic transformations which have to be carried out in order to produce an analytic overview.

Hello everybody!
1   If you've got children you'll know me or my wife, Judy, she's the one who works at the library. Because for some time now we've been engaged in a campaign for a safe crossing point for the little ones. You may have heard of it even if you haven't got children.
2   Now it's about something else, or rather it's the same thing really. This time the initiative hasn't come from Judy and me but from a whole club of people, parents that is. The action group 'Ververstraat Play Street'. We want Ververstraat to be a play street and we need your help for it.
3   Together, we should be able to do it. 'Unity is strength', they say, and it's true. Others have realized that quicker than we did and now they've got a full-scale play park complete with climbing frames and all the rest of it. And even there they still say 'if only we'd done it earlier'. It is important that Ververstraat should be a play street. The kids are confined to the park on the corner of Zwanenburgwal, but that's one great pool of mud and a muddy place is no suitable playground. Besides, because of all the dogs, it's full of you know what I mean. It's terrible. Friends, it's obvious. Closing off Ververstraat is in the best interests of the whole neighborhood. It ought to have been done long ago. If we succeed, you'll never be troubled again. The people of Zwanenburgwal and Groenburgwal will be able to take a chair out in the summer and sit in the road together, with a barbecue maybe, in Ververstraat, while the kids are happily playing. Can't you imagine it? Wouldn't that be great?
4   I would say, Ververstraat is not wide enough for traffic. Then the kids can't play there at all and if there's a fire nothing can get through because of all the parked cars. And the stink! Besides, where are you supposed to go if there is a fire?
5   If Ververstraat could be turned into a play street the parents won't have to sit and worry all the time. We won't have to wonder where they've got to all the

time. They can romp around as much as they like, they won't have to keep looking out for cars. Not to mention bikes. We'll be able to put out nice plant boxes.

John

Analytic overview of the primary text

An analytic overview (AO) of this primary text (T0) runs as follows:

(Non-mixed and single) difference of opinion
John and Judy: protagonist of the standpoint that Ververstraat should be a play street.
Neighbors: (potential) antagonist of the standpoint that Ververstraat should be a play street.

Dialectical stages
- *Confrontation*: In paragraph 2, John acknowledges that his neighbors have to be convinced of the standpoint that Ververstraat should be a play street.
- *Opening*: In paragraph 2, John expresses his intention to defend this standpoint by means of argumentation.
- *Argumentation*: In paragraphs 3-5, John puts forward argumentation to support his standpoint.
- *Concluding*: In paragraph 3, John assumes that he has convinced his neighbors of his standpoint.

Argumentation structure

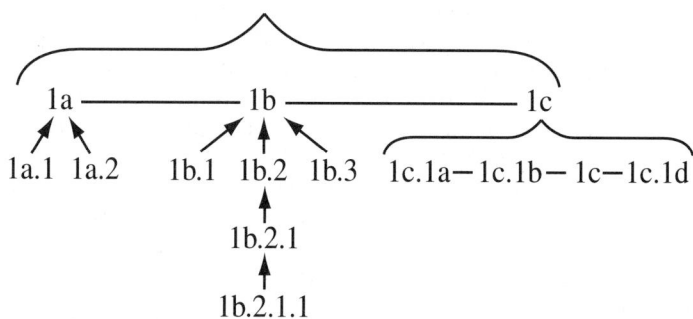

SP   Ververstraat should be a play street
1a   The park on the corner of Zwanenburgwal is not a suitable play ground
    1a.1 The park is a pool of mud and a muddy place is no suitable play ground
    1a.2 The park is full of dog shit
1b   Traffic in Ververstraat is not desirable

      1b.1   Ververstraat is too narrow for a smooth flow of traffic
      1b.2   Traffic in Ververstraat is dangerous in case of fire
                1b.2.1 The fire brigade cannot get through
                     1b.2.1.1 There are always too many parked cars
      1b.3   Traffic in Ververstraat causes stink
1c   It would be nice if Ververstraat were a play street
      1c.1a The children can romp about as much as they like
      1c.1b The parents won't have to worry about the children
      1c.1c The neighbors from Zwanenburgwal and Groenburgwal can take a chair out and join the people from Ververstraat for a barbecue
      1c.1d It would be possible to decorate the street by putting out nice plants

Unexpressed premises

1(a-c)'	If there is no other choice and Ververstraat does not serve other purposes and would be nice as a play street, then Ververstraat should be a play street
1a.2'	A place full of dog excrement is no suitable playground
1b.1'	A traffic road must be wide enough to allow the traffic to flow smoothly
1b.2'	The traffic situation must not be such that it hinders the fire brigade from extinguishing a fire
1b.2.1'	It is dangerous if the fire brigade cannot reach the fire
1b.2.1.1'	Too many parked cars prevent the fire brigade from getting through
1b.3'	A stinking street is undesirable
1c.1(a-d)'	It is nice if children can play in the street without their parents having to worry, while the whole neighborhood socializes and the street is nicely decorated

Revised text

Starting from this analytic overview, the text can be rewritten into the following revised text (T_r):5

    Dear neighbors,
1   If you have children, you'll know me and my wife, Judy, because we've been campaigning for a safe crossing point for the little ones. Now, Judy and I, together with a whole club of other parents, have formed the action group 'Ververstraat Play Street'. By way of this letter, we are trying to get your support.
2   'Why is it so important that Ververstraat should be a play street?', you may ask. 'The kids can go into the park on the corner of Zwanenburgwal, can't they?!' But then, we would say: 'Just go and have a look!' It's one great pool of mud. And it's full of dog shit. We can't let our kids play there!

3 Ververstraat is too narrow for traffic anyway. More importantly, it's dangerous in case of fire: The fire brigade can't get through because of all the parked cars. And the stink all this traffic causes! Imagine having to live there!
4 It would be so nice if Ververstraat could be turned into a play street. Then, the children don't have to look out for cars all the time, so that they can romp around as much as they like. We parents won't have to worry about them. Instead, the Zwanenburgwal and Groenburgwal residents will be able to take a chair out in the summer and join us for a barbecue. We'll be able to put out nice plants, so that the surroundings will be perfect.
5 We're sure that everybody will support us because it must be obvious by now to all concerned that closing off Ververstraat and turning it into a play street is in the best interests of everyone. So support our campaign, 'Ververstraat Play Street'.

John de Wit,
on behalf of 'Ververstraat Play Street'

Some presentation transformations carried out in writing the revised text
Among the presentation transformations, which have been carried out in writing this revised text, are:
1. Deletion confirmation: the first three sentences of paragraph 3 of the primary text remain deleted (superfluous);
2. Deletion introduction: in paragraph 3 of T_0 the unexpressed premise which goes with the mud argument is deleted (obvious);
3. Addition confirmation: the subordinate argument which supports the argument (1b.2) that Ververstraat is dangerous in case of fire – which is left unexpressed in T_0, and which is supported in paragraph 4 of T_0 by the argument (1b.2.1.1) that there are always too many parked cars – is added in paragraph 3 of T_r (clarity);
4. Addition compensation: in the analytic overview, the argument (1b) that traffic in Ververstraat is not desirable is added to paragraph 4 of T_0, but this argument is left out in paragraph 3 of T_r (obvious);
5. Permutation confirmation: the last part of paragraph 3 of T_0, which, in the analytic overview, has been moved to the concluding stage, remains at its new place in T_r: paragraph 5 (appropriate order);
6. Substitution confirmation: the phrase 'you know what I mean' in paragraph 3 of T_0, which has been replaced by 'dog shit' in the analytic overview, remains 'dog shit' in paragraph 2 of T_r (clarity).

7 CONCLUSION

In this chapter we outlined of a theoretical framework for carrying out research aimed at developing pragma-dialectical presentation strategies. To be able to formulate the precise strategies a writer can use to transform an analytic overview into a comprehensible and acceptable argumentative text, more detailed research has to be undertaken. We have tried to indicate what one should imagine the various presentation transformations to be, but it goes without saying that it should be shown by way of concrete examples how such strategies are to be put into practice.[6]

NOTES

1. Also process-oriented is the textbook by Murray (1987).
2. Although some authors with empirical pretensions seem to suggest that the structure that is the basis for text construction is directly derived from reality, such structural outlines fulfill the function of an ideal model. In several studies it has been shown convincingly that structural outlines of, for example, a literary review or a policy document can be useful for improving the presentation of texts. See Hillocks Jr. (1986).
3. We agree with Beale (1986) that argumentation is fundamental to all writing, but this is, of course, not to say that all writing problems can be dealt with by concentrating on argumentative texts. The advantage of developing a method for (re)writing argumentative texts is that we have an ideal model available that can serve as a starting-point. To develop methods for (re)writing the various types of non-argumentative (parts of) texts, other models are needed.
4. As Naess (1975: 48-51) observes, writing for different purposes and for different audiences can involve a difference in 'Intentionstiefe' (depth of intention).
5. For the sake of simplicity, we assume here that the analytic overview represents an adequate defense of the writer's case, and refrain from going into the problems of dialectical evaluation and detection of fallacies treated in van Eemeren and Grootendorst (1992: 93-217).
6. To validate the writing strategies, empirical research will be needed, for example, making use of a pre-test/post-test design.

Good Argument, Content and Contextual Dimensions

Clara Maria M. Santos & Selma Leitão Santos
Universidade Federal de Pernambuco, Recife, Brazil

ABSTRACT

Despite the contribution that research from various perspectives has made towards a better understanding of reasoning as argument, two issues still call for further clarification. First, the impact of content and contextual dimensions on argumentation. Secondly, how to describe, in a useful, testable, and psychologically valid way, what typifies good argument. Without ignoring the specificity of each, we believe that the time has come to bring together these two streams of investigation. This chapter represents a first step towards this goal. As such, it is necessarily tentative in nature. To examine the possible ways in which the above issues can be reconciled, we first look at some findings in the literature that demonstrate how content and contextual dimensions affect resolution strategies used in argumentation. Following this, an attempt is made to highlight some concepts of good argument that appear to underlie those categories from which people's arguments are generally analyzed in empirical research. In conclusion, we will suggest that the content and contextual dimensions of argument (as shown by descriptive approaches) determine the constraints upon which psychologically valid models of good argument can be built (normative approach).

1 CONTENT AND CONTEXTUAL DIMENSIONS OF ARGUMENTATION

Despite the contribution that research from various perspectives has made towards a better understanding of reasoning as argument, two issues, which are recurring problems in the literature on argumentation, still call for further clarification. First, the impact of content and contextual dimensions on argumentation. Secondly, how to describe, in a useful, testable, and psychologically valid way, what typifies good argument. Over recent years, the situation-based nature of argumentation has increasingly attracted the attention of scholars from a variety of research traditions. The result of such research is reflected in the ever-increasing number of studies in which the situation-based nature of argumentation is investigated and theory connecting social context and argumentation is advocated (Stein, Bernas, Calicchia & Wright, 1995; Stein & Miller, 1993a; Voss, Fincher-Kiefer, Wiley & Silfies, 1993). In contrast, the issues related to the criteria for good argument have not yet been properly addressed by research that takes a more empirical stance on argumentation. Researchers' assumptions in this respect tend to remain unspoken and implicit in current empirical studies.

Without ignoring the specificity of each of these two points, which will be apparent throughout the following sections, we believe that the time has come to bring together these two streams of investigation. By saying this, of course, we are not ignoring earlier discussions which call attention to the impact of contextual variations on the definition of what a good argument should look like (see Toulmin, 1958, 1976, for instance). The point to be stressed here is that, even though this sort of discussion does exist, it has not yet been carried out in the light of current situation-based theories of argumentation.

This chapter represents a first step towards this goal. As such, it is necessarily tentative in nature. To examine the possible ways in which the above issues can be reconciled, we first look at some findings reported in the literature, which show different ways in which content and contextual dimensions affect conflict talks and resolution strategies used in argumentation. A review of the many existing findings would be voluminous and is beyond the scope of this chapter. In order to put forward our view, we examine well-known empirical works, as well as some pieces of our recent work, selected to illustrate the various perspectives from which content and contextual dimensions of argument have been addressed in current research programs. Although it would seem premature to extract generalizations from these studies, a number of content and context related variables which have often been investigated in empirical studies deserve mention in the following sections. Following this, an effort is made to make explicit some concepts of good argument that appear to underlie those categories from which people's arguments are generally analyzed in empirical research. In conclusion, we will suggest that a better understanding of the effects of contextual dimensions on argumentative discourse may contribute to the establishment of criteria to determine what counts as good argument.

Before turning to these points, we first need to take up matters of definition, and attempt to clarify the notions of argument or argumentation adopted in this chapter.[1] We recognize as argumentative those texts, whether oral or written, in which two fundamental operations are verbally carried out with the aim of changing someone's position on a polemical topic. These operations are the justification of viewpoints and the recognition of opposing arguments. A second point should be made clear by now. Even though we do not assume parity to exist among the various terms by which matters concerning argumentation are referred to in the literature (*e.g.*, informal, practical, and everyday reasoning, and critical reasoning/thinking), these expressions are not assigned any different significance in this chapter. Accordingly, we will regard as an empirical study of argumentation, in the following sections, any study that examines text, in which the two above-mentioned defining operations can be identified.

2   CONTEXT AND CONTENT

Contrary to what happens in formal reasoning, where the focus is on the underlying logical relations, argumentative reasoning is characterized by the way in which particular factors of the situation enter into the reasoning. In this sense, the 'extralogical' dimensions cannot be isolated from, but are an integral part of the nature of argumentation (Miller-Jones, 1991). More recently, scholars have approached this issue by suggesting that thinking as argument is inevitably involved in the beliefs we hold, the judgments we make, and always arises when we are about to make an important decision (Billig, 1987; Kuhn, 1991). These remarks point to the fact that, by definition, social or contextual dimensions have to be taken into account in the investigation of argumentation.

When we talk about contextual variables of argumentation we refer both to the aspects of the situation in which the argumentation takes place, and to the specific features of the task the subjects are asked to perform. They include variables such as task features, type of setting, and type of interaction. When referring to the content dimension of argumentation, we understand the content or topic under discussion, but also the possible relationship between the topic of argumentation and the subjects' position, prior knowledge, and beliefs/values associated with the issue in question. These are the context and content related variables tackled in this section.

2.1 Contextual dimensions of argumentation

Most of the work on argumentative reasoning occurs in laboratory conditions. Therefore, if we are to speak of *contextual dimensions* it seems natural to begin with variables that are directly associated with the laboratory situation in which argumentation research occurs. We will start by focusing on features of argumentative tasks that may influence a subject's performance and, consequently, the conclusions about argumentative competence that can be drawn from studies on argumentation. One of these features is task instruction.

Type of instruction

When looking at the type of instruction used in studies on argumentative reasoning we could start with the use – or not as the case may be – of the so-called *scaffolding technique*. As the expression is used in psychological and educational studies (Rogoff, 1990, for instance), scaffolding technique refers to the numerous ways by which a person who is more experienced in the handling of a particular task can make it easier for a less experienced person to improve their performance of that task. In argumentation research, the scaffolding technique is used to to observe how much further subjects can develop their initial arguments. This procedure suggests an emphasis on subjects' argumentative competence, and a possible way for contrasting subjects' performance in a specific situation, with their potential ability at developing argumentative discourse. We can observe the use of the scaffolding technique in studies such as those by Perkins, Farady & Bushey (1991)[2], Kuhn (1991), and C. M. Santos (1996).

Perkins and his collaborators used a three-part experimental procedure that was aimed at examining subjects' performance and competence. In the first part of the experiment, subjects were asked to give their immediate opinion on the issue they were presented with. In the following stage, subjects were asked to take their time thinking about the issue, to reach a position if they could, and to write down their reasons. Guidance was still minimal in this second phase. In the third and last part of the experiment, the scaffolding technique was used and the subjects were provided with some prompts that were assumed to help them seek and evaluate reasons that supported alternative positions on the issue under discussion.

When looking at the specific gains that metacognitive prompts – such as the scaffolding technique – could bring to people's thinking, Perkins and his colleagues found that subjects improved their initial performance in terms of both completeness and bias. Perkins refers to completeness as the consideration of as many arguments as possible on an issue. Bias means the tendency to consider arguments mainly – or exclusively – from one side of an issue, the arguer's. With the use of the scaffolding technique, my-side arguments increased by 109%, whereas other-side arguments increased by 700%. Perkins interprets this result as suggesting that the subjects' initial argumentative performances were not as good as they could have been because even though, in principle, subjects can scaffold themselves, they in fact do not know how to do this. Perkins' results clearly demonstrate how the type of instruction affects subjects' performance on argumentative tasks and, consequently, the conclusions that can be drawn about people's ability to develop argumentative discourses.

Kuhn (1991) carried out a comprehensive empirical study of informal reasoning as argument involving the use of metacognitive prompts similar to the scaffolding technique. This author investigated people's argumentative skills by analyzing the causal and correlational theories that subjects hold with respect to real urban social problems. Subjects were first asked to describe their views on the selected topics. After subjects offered their theory regarding the cause of the social problem in question, they were asked to provide supporting evidence for their theories, and, in addition, encouraged to consider alternative theories, and generate counterexamples and rebuttals. In the final part of the interview, a series of questions was addressed to subjects' reflections on their own thinking. Contrary to Perkins, in her analysis Kuhn did not focus on the effect that the interviewer's prompts had on subjects' initial views about the issues in question. Nevertheless, the design of her research interview indicates that her main interest was in investigating how far subjects were able to set out their – probably underelaborated – initial views or theories, as she names them. It also points out a preference for investigating subjects' competence; therefore, establishing an implicit difference between what they were capable of doing, and their initial spontaneous performance.

The overall picture of a person's ability to reason as argument, drawn from Kuhn's study, shows that people could easily give an explanation for the issue under discussion, and they were highly confident of the correctness of their theories. Subjects performed poorly when trying to consider alternative theories for the problem in question, or to think about evidence that went against their viewpoint, even after they had been prompted to do so. The presence/absence of alternative theories and counterarguments was one of the criteria used by Kuhn in order to evaluate a subject's ability to develop causal arguments.

Following a procedure similar to that used by Kuhn (1991), in the first of a series of experiments, the 'Four topics experiment', C. M. Santos (1996) investigated the effect of the scaffolding technique. Subjects were asked to present their views on four controversial issues: capital punishment, animal experimentation, euthanasia, and the resurrection of Christ. The participants were first asked to talk freely about a particular issue, and subsequently prompted to give additional supports to their arguments, counterarguments, and rebuttals that they could give to those counterarguments. An effect of the scaffolding technique was observed in the production of both supports and counterarguments. Subjects produced a significant number of additional reasons that could support their viewpoint, and an even greater increase in the production of counterarguments was observed as the result of the use of the scaffolding technique. The effect of the scaffolding procedure regarding the production of supports and counterarguments also varied with topic. In a subsequent experiment, the 'Make-believe experiment', C. M. Santos (1996) observed that the presence and frequency of counterarguments in subjects' discourse could undergo a further improvement when a role-play instruction was used. In this experiment, subjects were asked to make-believe they were somebody else who held a position that directly opposed theirs. The fact that subjects are able to think of more counterarguments as a result of a more elaborate metacognitive repertoire is an interesting finding. This finding may raise some doubts about the generalization of the hypothesis that a biased argument may be a direct consequence of the individual's prior knowledge on a particular topic (*e.g.*, Stein, Bernas & Calicchia, 1996). We will return to this discussion later on in this chapter.

Another example of effects that task features may have on the conclusions that are drawn about people's argumentative ability can be observed in the comparison between the results of Baron (1995) and C. M. Santos' (1998) studies. In one of his experiments, Baron (1995) asked university students to evaluate lists of arguments produced by hypothetical students as if they were notes for a class discussion about the morality of early abortion. The lists contained either reasons that supported only one side of the question or supported both sides of the debate. Subjects tended to give higher scores to one-sided lists, which strengthens Baron's myside bias hypothesis (Baron, 1991; 1995). This hypothesis assumes that people tend to think essentially about reasons that support their side of the question, and that they do this because this 'unbalanced' way of thinking corresponds to their idea of good thinking. C. M. Santos (1998) found the same result when Baron's procedure was used. However, when subjects were asked to evaluate the same sets of arguments written as short essays referring to students' *reflections* on early abortion, and not as lists of notes for a class *discussion*, the tendency to favor one-sided argument was no longer observed. Regardless of questioning Baron's hypothesis that people's ideas of what counts as good thinking must influence their own evaluation and production of argument, it seems that he did not take into account the effects that subjects' pragmatic interpretations of the task could have on their performance. Once more, these results point to the relevance of taking into account the situation-based nature of argumentation if a comprehensive understanding of this phenomenon is to be achieved.

The findings presented in this subsection point to the fact that task instructions affect the presence as well as the frequency of indicators of good quality argument, when, for instance, such evaluation criteria refer to completeness and balance, or to the presence/absence of myside bias.

Comments about subjects' pragmatic interpretations of the task and the situation-based nature of argumentation can also be associated with the effects that another variable may have on argumentative reasoning, namely, type of setting.

Type of setting
The emphasis on the situation-based nature of argumentation implies looking at specific features of the situations in which argumentation occurs, be it an experimental or a more or less naturalistic setting. In most of the studies on argumentative discourse, the locus of argumentation has been seen more as the situation in which argumentative reasoning may be developed, and there has been little interest in observing the effects that some specific aspects of these various situations may have on argumentation. An exception to this tendency has been the work

developed by S. L. Santos (1993, 1995, 1997). In her work, she analyzes the differences between the purposes of the interactions in experimental and in naturalistic settings, and the effects that these differences may have on argumentative reasoning.

S. L. Santos (1993, 1995) compared the strategies that university students used when constructing arguments in experimental and naturalistic situations. In the experimental setting subjects were asked to give their opinion on capital punishment, and guidance was kept to a minimum. The naturalistic setting corresponded to planned and spontaneous discussions that occur in the classroom. She found that, regardless of the type of setting, most of the time, argumentation was organized as what she refers to as a sort of match between supporting versus undermining ideas. However, her findings also showed some differences in the ways in which subjects conducted this pro-con comparison in different settings. One of the most interesting findings regards the nature and frequency of counterarguments in the two settings. Different kinds of counterarguments were prevalent in each setting investigated. Whilst a counterargument which challenges the speaker's own position appeared in most of the subjects' speeches in the experimental setting, it was virtually absent in the naturalistic setting. Instead, a counterargument here was mostly used to challenge somebody else's position.

S. L. Santos (1993, 1995) claims that the above-mentioned difference might be explained in terms of the specific constraints governing the settings in which the argumentation took place. First, she contrasts the spontaneous interpersonal interactions of the naturalistic situations – in which opponents provided the subject with immediate counterargument – with the artificiality of the experimental setting, in which no opposition was provided by the experimenter. Secondly, she suggests that the ways in which the subjects' persuasive purposes operate in the two settings should also be taken into account. In this respect, quite different purposes seem to rule the subjects' argumentation in these settings, namely: making their viewpoint prevail over opposing ideas (in the naturalistic situation), and making their own position known (in the experimental setting). A question that remained unanswered in this study, however, was whether variations in the subjects' argumentation should primarily be associated with either of the two hypotheses.

This point has been addressed in a more recent study by the author. S. L. Santos (1997) asked subjects to talk about two topics: a general, socially relevant issue and one concerning each subject's specific daily activities. Subjects were randomly assigned either to a symmetrical condition (a counterargu-ment was presented by the experimenter) or an asymmetrical condition (no intervention was made). The main hypothesis predicted that if facing opposition lead subject to refrain from generating counterarguments to their own position, such an effect should be observed in a condition like the symmetrical one described above. This prediction, however, did not turn prove true: no difference was found between groups regarding the number of counterarguments generated.

According to S. L. Santos (1997), this result strengthens her initial contention concerning the influence of the purpose of argumentation on the argumentative strategies people adopt in naturalistic and experimental contexts. It is arguable that in situations in which arguers actually need their view to prevail over their opponent's, the purpose of winning may have a decisive impact on the strategies an individual adopts. Such situations can be sharply contrasted to those in which different purposes hold. For instance, those in which subjects are induced by experimental instructions to *fight to win*. Although, in such cases, subjects *pretend* they are fighting to win, actually, they are not. Their main purpose is to comply with previously agreed experimental arrangements. By saying this, of course, we are not neglecting the well known benefits of laboratory studies, but rather stressing the risk of overemphasizing the similarities of subjects' performances in naturalistic and experimental settings. The need to take both differences and commonalties into account is what is at stake here. In our view, it is a necessary implication of any situation-based theory of argumentation. The cost of ignoring common aspects as well as dissimilarities in the two settings may be the drawing of inaccurate conclusions about the quality of people's argumentative discourse.

The above paragraph introduces yet another variable which is also considered a relevant contextual aspect, namely, the type of interaction people are engaged in when developing an argumentative discourse.

Type of interaction

Overall, this variable refers to the presence or absence of an audience – which may mean at least one opponent – when arguers are putting forward their views on a polemical issue. This rather simple definition, however, overlooks some less explicit aspects associated with the type of interaction established during the production of an argument. These less explicit aspects include, for instance, the purposes of the participants engaged in a particular argumentative interaction (S. L. Santos, 1997; Stein & Miller, 1993a). Another more refined analysis of the interactional effects on people's argumentation focuses on the specific characteristics of the opponents. It emphasizes *who* the opponent is – or what this opponent represents – for a particular group of subjects, and not only the opponent's presence.

The fact that specific characteristics of the opponent influence an individual argumentative behavior could be observed in C. M. Santos' 'Devil's advocate experiment' (1996, 1997). In this experiment, Christian and non-Christian subjects were engaged in a discussion about capital punishment with an opponent who was himself a Christian and had been previously trained to act as the 'devil's advocate'. Contrary to what was expected, the analysis of subjects' production of counterarguments showed that they did not mention fewer counterarguments in their speech than the participants in the first part of the Four topics experiment, when asked to talk freely about the death penalty. It was interesting to notice, however, that Christian subjects nearly always did the anticipation of counterarguments in the dialogue situation. This result might be related to the fact that all of these subjects but one found out that the opponent was also a Christian. The knowledge of the beliefs they had in common might have led the Christian subjects to anticipate some of the counterarguments that the opponent could use in order to challenge their point of view. Also, sharing some basic beliefs with the opponent might have led the Christians to represent him as less of an opponent than if they did not have such common beliefs.

The findings indicate that the representations that people constructed of their opponents in an argumentative situation, affect the use, frequency, and type of counterarguments they mention in their argumentation.

2.2 Content related variables

In the previous subsection we tried to demonstrate how elements of the contexts in which argumentation occurs may influence the subjects' argumentative behavior and the conclusions that can be drawn about a person's ability to produce and evaluate arguments. Hereafter, the focus of our discussion will change to aspects of argumentation related to the content – topic – a person argues about. These aspects refer to matters of knowledge and beliefs/values. Despite this shift in focus, it will be noticed that the effects of contextual and content variables are often intertwined.

As with the contexts of argumentation, scholars vary in the way they treat the topic of argumentation in their studies. They may use topic either as a necessary element to allow argumentation to occur, or as a variable to be manipulated and have its effects investigated. When used as a variable, the focus of the investigation may be either on the common argumentative strategies subjects show across topics, or on variations in the subjects' performance. A question that is directly related to this theme is whether the subjects' performance simply reflects their knowledge of the issue.

Prior-knowledge

In investigating the role of knowledge in informal reasoning, Perkins, Farady & Bushey (1991) suggested that 'the knowledge most relevant would be prior experience in thinking about the issue' (p. 94). Using the amount of *prior-thought* as synonym for prior-knowledge, Perkins and his colleagues did not find any significant correlation between prior familiarity with the topic, and the subjects' performance in terms of completeness and bias. The authors explain these results as being partially an artifact of experimental design, insofar that the issues in question were not ones in which subjects were likely to have high expertise; they suggest that had it been so, the subjects' performance would have been affected. Another finding that points to the relatively minor role of prior knowledge in everyday/argumentative reasoning was the fact observed by Perkins and his collaborators that the scaffolding technique improved the subjects' performance independently of one prior thought. However the question – well put by Johnson & Blair (1991) – remains as to 'whether prior thought is the only variable that should be considered in testing for the influence of knowledge on the quality of argumentative reasoning' (p.146). Other scholars use different measures.

In her work, Kuhn (1991) used two ways to examine the influence of prior knowledge on argumentative skills. The first one was similar to Perkins' 'prior-thought'. She found that overall, subjects tended to present the most complex form of argumentative reasoning for the topic on which they were more likely to have personal knowledge and the reverse pattern for the topic with which they were least familiar. Despite this general difference, when analyzing each of the argumentative abilities examined in her work, Kuhn concludes that they show some degree of generality, even though the number of subjects displaying a particular ability for only some topics is larger than the number of those who always or never exhibit it.

Kuhn (1991) also investigated the influence of prior-knowledge by examining the relationship between expertise in a particular field and argumentation. For this purpose, she included in her study a group of experts from three different fields related to the three topics she used. The author also included in her sample a group of philosophers whom, she claims, are regarded as having expertise in reasoning itself. Based on her findings, Kuhn concluded that expertise on a particular topic could expand the amount of knowledge that was available, but that this did not mean the use of better forms of reasoning, on the contrary. She suggests that experience regarding a particular topic could make it more difficult to think about opposing views. As yet another support for the author's hypothesis regarding the generality of argumentative ability, she found that philosophers showed the best performance across topics, showing perfect ability to generate genuine evidence for their theories, alternative theories, counterarguments, and rebuttals. Based on these results, Kuhn (1991) claims that 'it is possible to attain expertise in the reasoning process itself, independent of any particular content to which this reasoning is applied' (p. 262).

A third way to assess prior-knowledge and its effect on students' argumentative skills was used by Means & Voss (1996). These authors designed a knowledge test consisting of multiple choice questions to assess participants' knowledge of the topic area used in their experiment. The findings of Means & Voss (1996) seem to corroborate Kuhn and Perkins' suggestion regarding the minor role of prior-knowledge in argumentative reasoning. These authors found that knowledge was positively related to the number of reasons generated, and to the number of qualifiers generated, but not to the final quality of the arguments subjects produced.

The influence of knowledge on argumentation has also been looked at in the studies carried out by Stein and her collaborators (Stein, Bernas & Calicchia 1996; Stein *et al.*, 1995; Stein & Miller, 1993a; Stein & Miller, 1993b). Stein & Miller (1993b) posed the question whether the way of developing an argument would be related to subjects' amount of knowledge about their own and their opponents' position. In order to answer this question they asked elementary school children and adults to generate reasons to different types of argument knowledge: reasons for supporting a favored position, reasons for opposing a favored position, reasons for supporting an opponent's position, and reasons for opposing an opponent's position. Stein & Miller (1993a) found that both children and adults could generate supports for their own position and at least one supporting reason for their opponent's position. Subjects could also talk about problems related to their opponent's position, but had great difficulty generating reasons that would weaken or negate their own position. Stein & Miller (1993a) concluded that arguers initially support one side of a particular issue over the other because they have more knowledge about the advantages of holding their own position than their opponent's. These authors also provide an alternative hypothesis about the causal relationship between biases in decision making and knowledge. They suggest a two-way influence between desire/bias and knowledge, and are inclined to give more weight to the knowledge – bias/desire direction.

Stein and her colleagues' ideas introduce other aspects involved in argumentation, such as bias and desires, and we could add values and beliefs. They also point out that these aspects often appear intertwined in the argumentation process. Our comments in the following subsection will concentrate on these matters.

Beliefs, values, and desires
We tend to agree with the bi-directionality of the regulatory forces existing between knowledge, and bias and desire. However, findings from studies in which metacognitive prompts are used (C. M. Santos, 1996; Perkins, Allen, & Hafner 1991) suggest that the type of knowledge people bring into their argumentation ap-

pears more as a result of subjects' desires, biases, beliefs, intention, and purposes than the other way round. The fact that subjects increase their production of counterarguments after the use of the scaffolding technique and make-believe instruction, for instance, suggests that arguers know more about the opposing position than a first analysis of their initial performance would suggest. These might be examples in which *excluding* does not mean *denying* or *not knowing*.

This comment is directly associated with a person's involvement with the topic in question. Stein and her colleagues (Stein *et al*. 1995) claim that in most arguments, and especially those in the sociomoral domain, reasons given in support of a position are closely associated with the arguer's values and beliefs about the benefits and cost of holding a particular view. An implication of this association is that different weights are given to different supporting reasons. This may mean that occasionally, a single *strong* reason may appear sufficient for defending a particular position. This seems to have happened when subjects defended their position against capital punishment with an opponent in C. M. Santos' 'Devil's advocate experiment' mentioned earlier in this section (C. M. Santos, 1996; 1997). Although all subjects gave more than one reason to support their views, they often emphasized one basic reason for being against the death penalty. In the great majority of the cases, this reason was the first one mentioned by the subjects, and was strongly associated with their moral or religious values. The finding that strong reasons are put forward first in subjects' argumentation seems to be in line with the findings of Voss *et al*. (1993). They observed that the subjects activated the reasons judged as providing strong support more rapidly. Those reasons also activated a value more rapidly than the others. C. M. Santos' (1996) findings reinforce Voss *et al*. (1993), and both studies point to the fact that one cannot isolate people's argumentation processes from their beliefs and values.

Other aspects can be commented on here regarding the fact that only one supporting reason may suffice for defending a particular view. C. M. Santos (1996) noticed that Christian subjects often mentioned religious reasons when justifying their positions. Sometimes, a single religious reason was the only support that subjects gave as justification for their position, while, at the same time, they could easily think of reasons of a different nature that could support an opposing view. Their religious reasons, however, seemed to be sufficient for them to justify their position. Could those cases be generally taken as biased arguments? We would not tend to make this generalization. In these cases, it seems that the kind of links that the speakers are building between their position and the supports they are giving to it are more relevant than the content or the strategy that subjects use. Say, for example, somebody believes that to kill is wrong under any circumstances and this same person believes that switching off a life support machine, *i.e.* committing euthanasia, is killing. Then, the necessary conclusion that follows is that euthanasia is wrong and no counterargument – or counterexample – would have any major effect on such reasoning. This example seems to indicate that psychological variables may influence not only one's argumentative behavior, but also the criteria used to evaluate the quality of one's argument.

Personal opinions and favored social discourses
A final comment remains to be made on the link between values/beliefs and argumentation, which appears to integrate contextual and content-related variables. This comment is based on C. M. Santos' (1996) results, which showed that sub-

jects' personal opinions on a particular issue seemed to influence the kind of argumentative strategies they used to present their viewpoints.

An individual's beliefs and values develop within a social context. One does not hold an opinion in a sterile environment, but in some kind of society or group where its members share common principles, values, and ideas about all kinds of subject matter. We suggest that the match between justifying and criticizing views in one's argumentative discourse may be affected by the relationship between the opinion that people hold on a particular topics and the social meaning of their views. If a person's position is assumed to violate some shared group principle, their argumentation will most likely focus on defending or supporting that position. If, on the other hand, it is the view that people disagree with that is supposed to violate a social – moral, ethical, religious, *etc.* – principle, then their argumentation will probably focus on attacking the opposing position. So, this process could be said to depend not only on a subject's position and individual abilities, but also on the social context where this argumentation happens. In other words, it is not only the immediate situational context, with its meanings and pragmatic demands, but also the broader social which context has to be taken into account in the investigation of argumentative reasoning. The fact that either one or the other type of argumentative strategy is used is taken as an indicator of the quality of the arguments and that this choice is affected by context and content variables.

When defining argumentative text at the beginning of this chapter we stated that we recognized as argumentative those texts in which justification of viewpoints and recognition of opposing arguments were carried out in order to change a person's position on a polemical topic. Throughout the first part of this chapter, we have tried to demonstrate how context and content variables influence people's use of these two fundamental operations. The relevance of such analysis lies in the fact that these variables affect aspects of the argumentation process, which are used as criteria to evaluate the quality of an argument. Even though there seems to be a consensus about some of these criteria – the presence of counterarguments, for instance – they are often left implicit in empirical studies. In the following part of this chapter we discuss standards of quality by setting out explicit criteria for good argument, which underlie current empirical research on argumentative discussion.

3 GOOD ARGUMENT

Traditionally, research on argumentation has focused on describing and explaining the actual practices by which individuals produce and evaluate argument in various contexts, without entering into the discussion of how individuals should and should not argue. This may sound like a paradox, if one accepts the view developed by van Eemeren *et al.* (1993), according to whom 'many so-called questions of empirical description already have a normative component implicitly built into them (*e.g.*, questions of competence)' (p. 23). The authors make a strong point against what they see as an unacceptable dichotomy between normative and descriptive approaches in the study of argumentation. They argue that making such normative components explicit is a desirable and theoretically necessary enterprise if 'the risk of allowing superficial, peripheral, or incidental characteristics of argumentation to dominate the argument analysis' is to be avoided (p. 23).

In this section, we take a first step in that direction. Our purpose is to characterize the perspectives, recurrent in the literature, which cast some light on the standards of good argument that appear to underlie current empirical research on argument. Five perspectives are examined in this section. These are the views of good argument as: (1) argument in which elements that support as well as oppose a defended position are considered, (2) argument in which the quality of the inferential chain leading from premise to conclusion is seen as appropriate, (3) being the result of a set of personal individual dispositions, (4) argument suitable for achieving the goal of argumentation, and (5) being acceptable to the addressee.

Following the procedure adopted in the previous section, we will concentrate on examining some pieces of well-known empirical work (mainly those quoted above) selected to illustrate each perspective. It is important to note that our focus in this section is not on researchers' descriptions of people's ideas of good argument (Baron, 1991; 1995; C. M. Santos, 1997; Golder & Coirier, 1994) but on what the researchers themselves focus on as they judge the virtue of an argument. It should also be noted that the perspectives discussed here are not mutually exclusive. Instead, they seem to combine in the various works examined (even though the emphasis on each perspective may vary).

3.1 The arguer's recognition of opposing views

It appears to be a matter of consensus that part of what predicts good reasoning is the extent to which arguers are able not only to justify their own positions, but also to take real or virtual opposition (counterargument) into account.

The emphasis on justification and counterargumentation as useful and testable measures of good reasoning is particularly clear in the notions of *completeness* and *bias* (Perkins et al., 1991). The findings from a series of experiments, mentioned earlier in this chapter, showed that subjects tended to present a significantly higher number of supporting elements for their own viewpoints than for any other side of the question. The authors interpret these findings as reflective of faulty *situation modeling* (Perkins, 1989). According to Perkins et al. (1991), a 'situation model typically involves one or more imagined scenarios and invokes a variety of common sense, causal, and intentional principles both to construct and to weigh the plausibility of alternative scenarios' (p. 85). People might reason the way they do because they are using 'a competing standard for good situation modeling' (p. 98). This competing model is suggested as one that satisfies people's criterion of truth and appears to be congruent with their most prominent prior beliefs. It reflects what the authors call a *makes-sense epistemology*. The authors contrast this notion with a *critical epistemology*, in which the reasoners' criteria for good situation modeling go beyond *making-sense* and include, for instance, checking their data base of information for the existence of possible inconsistency, constructing counterexamples, and taking multiple perspectives. It should be noted that Perkins and his colleagues do not propose a dichotomy between these two types of epistemology, but rather an *epistemological continuum* in which different levels of makes-sense and critical epistemologies can be found. Despite this fact, the superiority of the former over the latter is beyond any doubt: it is the critical epistemology that gives us a model of an idealized skilled thinker.

The work of Voss, Perkins and Segal (1991) provides us with another example of an approach and regards counterargumentation as a necessary attribute to a definition of good argument. In the introduction to the above work, the authors attempt to clarify the nature of so-called informal reasoning (of which argumentation is a part), by contrasting it with the well defined notion of formal reasoning. Although they propose several dimensions from which formal and informal reasoning can be distinguished, a single one warrants special mention here. In their view, a crucial distinction between the two kinds of reasoning as regards the nature of the standards against which the quality of formal and informal reasoning is evaluated. Whilst in the former, formal validity is the principle from which a critical evaluation of an argument is made possible, the basic principle underlying informal reasoning is soundness. Soundness refers to '(a) whether the reason providing support is acceptable or true, (b) the extent to which the reason supports the conclusion, and (c) the extent to which an individual takes into account reasons that support the contradiction of the conclusion' (p. xiii). This latter aspect is particularly worthy of note here. As in Perkins *et al.* (1991), the ability to reflect on instances that undermine one's position is regarded here as an unavoidable aspect of any reasoning that is to be defined as sound argument.

Similarly, Kuhn (1991) brings the handling of supporting elements, alternative views, and counterevidence to the core of what she presents as a model of competent argumentative reasoning. To develop good (causal) argument, one must be able to understand what counts as genuine evidence (which bears upon the correctness of the causal theory they defend) and distinguish it from pseudoevidence (a scenario that depicts how a phenomenon might occur, without ensuring one that it follows from a given precedent). Moreover, one should be able to think of alternative theories and to identify what counts as evidence that refutes one's espoused theory (counterargument). Finally, one should envision those conditions in which the counterargument does not hold. The author found that subjects could easily give an explanation for the issue under discussion, and they were highly confident of the correctness of their theories. However, subjects performed poorly when trying to consider alternative theories or to think about evidence that ran against their viewpoint. In Kuhn's view, their failure to envision conditions that falsify the theories they hold is a main obstacle to developing critical reasoning (Kuhn, 1991).

Finally, the view of good argument as a text in which opposing sides of a case are taken into account has also been found in current developmental approaches to argumentative writing. In Coirier and Golder's account (Coirier & Golder, 1993; Golder & Coirier, 1994; Golder & Coirier, 1996), the mastery of argumentative text writing implies moving from a pre-argumentation level (where either no stance is taken, or a stance is taken without being supported) through a minimal argumentation level (where a stance is taken and supported by a single reason) to an elaborated argumentation level in which multiple and related elements are presented to support a stance. Besides the improvement of the quality of the argument supporting structure, however, the production of elaborated argumentative writing also requires the writers to leave room for negotiation (generally conceived as taking the audience's opposing views into account) as they take and defend a position. Although reflecting on the quality of the argumentative reasoning does not appear to be the focus of these studies, an ideal of good reasoning seems to underlie the very notion of elaborated argumentative text. To be defined as elaborated argumentative writing, a text must satisfy at least two conditions: first, present a set of ideas to support the writer's point of view; second, include explicit negotiation marks. Such a view of elaborated argumentation has been taken as a starting point for recent studies on argumentative writing (Akiguet & Piolat, 1996; De Bernardi & Antolini, 1996; Dolz, 1996; Roussey & Gombert, 1996; Santos & Vasconcelos, 1998; Schneuwly, 1996).

However, in the light of the empirical findings mentioned earlier in this chapter, this view of good (elaborated) argumentation as a necessarily counter-argumentative discourse, seems open to criticism. To the extent that arguers consider opposition to be sensitive to contextual and thematic variations, the status of counterargument as a defining characteristic of a model of good argument should perhaps be reexamined. On the other hand, it is a quasi-consensual view among argumentation researchers and theorists, that argumentation integrates multiple 'voices' (the polyphonic dimension). So the problem of how to reconcile a view of argumentation as polyphonic discourse and data that emerge from situated approaches to argumentation is far from trivial. We come back to this question in the concluding section.

3.2 Appropriacy of reasons with a conclusion

The second perspective on good argument we would like to mention here emphasizes the strength of the link between a premise and the conclusion it is supposed to justify. In contrast with the previous approach, from this perspective, the mere presence of pros and cons is not altogether sufficient to define one's argument as good argument. Rather, the quality of what one considers to be a supporting (or an opposing) element plays the most crucial role here. Good argument is that in which a set of given premises succeed warranting the conclusion. It is the notion of relevance that appears to be the crucial defining attribute here.

The perspective defined above can be identified in several works mentioned throughout this chapter, such as the work by Perkins, Allen and Hafner (1983). In their view, shortcomings in everyday argument are mainly dominated by an underelaboration of situation modeling (see above). Despite such emphasis, their description of the various errors people make when arguing leaves room for two more criteria to be viewed as part of their general conception of good argument. First, good argument must not contain formal errors (*e.g.*, affirming the consequent). Secondly, it should avoid informal fallacies. Unfortunately, Perkins *et al*. (1983) do not tell us how they define the concept of fallacy, how formal standards of validity should enter into a conception of good argument, and how the various attributes that characterize good argument interrelate. Despite such a gap, the reader is left with no doubts regarding the nature of the demands of a critical epistemology. In addition to those attributes mentioned earlier in this section, it requires a 'formal repertoire' which is described in terms of the knowledge of logical and heuristic forms that can be applied to practical reasoning (p. 188).

Contrary to the work of Perkins *et al.*, in which the risk of making faulty inferential moves is not expected to be the main sort of difficulty that people face in argumentation, the strength of the link between premises and conclusion of an argument is at the heart of Kuhn's (1991) model of good argument. In her work, pitfalls occur not only because subjects fail to generate evidence or counterevidence to their espoused theories, but also because of the poor quality of the evidence and counterevidence they generate. In most cases examined, people fail to recognize evidence that can refute their views. Pseudo, rather than genuine, evidence is the favored kind of support for their theories. Likewise, when it comes to the reflection of evidence that runs against their views, subjects tend to concentrate on weaker forms of counterargument – those which are not altogether satisfactory in refuting the subject's defended theory.

3.3 Arguers' dispositions

The third major approach to good argument we now turn to comes from works which define good argument in terms of an individual's attributes and personal dispositions. Such seems to be the perspective taken by Baron's (1995) work in which he proposes what he labels an *active open-mindedness* as the ideal standard for 'good thinking'. This means engaging in an active process of seeking evidence that runs counter to one's own claim – beliefs, opinions, conclusion, *etc.* – before accepting it as true. It means trying to see a situation from alternative perspectives. In an ideal model, this should be the attitude behind the *search* and *inference* processes that, according to Baron (1991), may account for all kinds of thinking. Like authors such as Perkins *et al.* (1983) and Kuhn (1991), Baron (1991) points out that individuals usually fail to adopt this attitude. He proposes that they might fail because an individual's standard of good or critical thinking may be different from the normative model. Baron has observed that one of these differences is that individuals seem to judge the quality of an argument by focusing predominantly on the consistency between the conclusion and the evidence that is given in support of it, and pay less attention to the search for alternative evidence or views, a disposition which generalizes across different settings.

Emphasis on attitudes and dispositions may also be identified in Kuhn's already extensively mentioned work (Kuhn, 1991). In the description of her results, she notes that subjects tended to incorporate contrary evidence into their own theory as if they were one and the same thing. Kuhn interprets this finding to be a result of the fact that subjects were not really separating their theories from the evidence they used to support them. As she puts it, in these cases, subjects were not reasoning *about* their theories, but reasoning *with* them instead. Rather than looking at their theories as an object of analysis (to think in a metacognitive framework) or evaluation, they tended to view them as a given 'truth' (Kuhn, 1991). From such results she concludes that good argument depends not only on specific skills, but also on *epistemological understanding* which allows to examine the thruth of one's beliefs, as opposed to simply accepting them to be true.

Kuhn's notion of epistemological understanding calls attention to the role played by people's attitudes toward knowledge and argument as one more element of constraining the quality of the argument they produce. Without the disposition to see knowledge as a never-ending source, and argument as the means which one construes and changes knowledge, there is no reason for one to engage in the examining of positions. Consequently, there is no opportunity for good argument to arise.

3.4 Procedural and goal-oriented standards

As far as the present literature review is concerned, the three perspectives discussed above seem to be the most frequently adopted in current empirical research. But before moving to the concluding section of this chapter, two important views can be added to the discussion on the criteria for good argument. The first comes from studies developed within the framework of the pragma-dialectical approach to argumentation (van Eemeren, 1994; van Eemeren *et al.*, 1993; van Eemeren & Grootendorst, 1994). Pragma-dialecticians regard argument as part of a critical discussion aimed at resolving a difference of opinion between two (or more) parties. Normative rules are then prescribed which are claimed to be powerful in shaping those attitudes and behaviors necessary for the goal of argumentation to be achieved. As a consequence, the main criterion for reasonableness in argument is 'whether an argumentative procedure is instrumental in achieving this goal' (Van Eemeren & Grootendorst, 1994, p. 4). Thereby, pragma-dialecticians relate the concept of good argument to normative procedures in discussion. Thus, the structure of the context (a method for organizing disputation that requires the arguer to comply both with logical and pragmatic principles) in which argument takes place is the crucial element which allows good argument to emerge.

3.5 Audience acceptability

Research supporting this final view of good argument couples the quality of an argument not only with issues related to argument structure or arguers' dispositions and procedures, but also with its acceptability by an audience. Matters of acceptability are found, for instance, in the core of Miller's (1987) developmental approach to argumentation. In exploring the potential of collective argumentation as a mechanism that leads to advances in individuals' knowledge, the author starts by defining collective argumentation as a 'method for jointly solving problems of interpersonal co-ordination' (p. 231). As such, it 'only succeeds if the participants manage to develop a joint argument which is collectively accepted as an answer to the "quaestio" (the one that elicited the ongoing argumentation) (p. 232). Crucial to this process is that participants are be able to co-ordinate their contributions in such a way that they can find and agree on a *set of collective valid statements*. By valid statement Miller means a statement accepted by all the participants at a given stage of the argumentation. In Miller's approach, however, the acceptability of a statement by an audience is not only a defining attribute of successful argumentation. It is also the crucial criterion that defines whether or not a statement has been justified in the course of argumentation, and a central parameter against which individuals' development can be assessed. The development of argumentation skills in children is here envisaged as a move from an early egocentric and undifferentiated perspective, to a stage in which they rely on collective valid statements to justify their positions.

Although not extensively explored, the notion of acceptability is also part of the general background against which the development of argumentative writing has been explored. Links between the addressee's acceptability and argument validity are found, for instance, in Dellerman, Coirier and Marchand (1996) and Coirier (1996). A recent and more systematic attempt to examine this issue in the context of the empirical research on argumentative writing is made by Golder and Pouit (in this volume).

What should be noted in the view examined here is that the move from argument structure to audience acceptability clearly pushes the standards of sound argumentation in the direction of the situation-based approaches to argumentation mentioned earlier in this chapter. To use Govier's (1987) words, arguments 'to be acceptable, must be acceptable to some persons and these persons will deem them acceptable only on the basis of some other beliefs they hold' (p. 281). And, we would add, on the basis of the circumstances they face and purposes they pursue in specific contexts.

4 CONCLUSION

In previous sections, issues related to both the contextual dimensions of argument and the notions of good argument underlying empirical studies were examined separately. In this concluding section, we would like to bring such issues together by reflecting on the extent to which findings discussed in the first section may contribute to the issues addressed in the second one.

At the broadest level, we believe that the research findings examined in the first part of this chapter can shed light on those criteria examined in the second, at least in two interrelated ways. First, they provide an important basis for *evaluating the adequacy of some criteria* for good argument, which are commonly adopted in current empirical research. Secondly, they help to *unveil the limits* of the area to which those standards may be applied. At a more specific level, the crucial issue that should be addressed is: how can empirically based descriptions of people's performance in argumentation serve the (more theoretical) purpose of defining what should count as good argument? Whatever answer may be given to this question, we believe it should take the three following directions.

Direction one.
First, and most important, the extent to which people contemplate opposition during argumentation should be assigned a primary role in argument evaluation.

In the first of the perspectives on good argument discussed in this chapter, a good argument is defined in terms of the extent to which both sides of a polemical issue are countered. Among all the perspectives examined, this one appears to benefit most from studies that show, beyond any doubt, the impact that the content and context of argument exert on the breadth and depth of the reasoning which subjects develop. These studies show, for instance, that the extent to which subjects examine different lines of reasoning that support a position varies as a function of the metacognitive prompts they are faced with, and the relative importance given by the arguers to the content of the premises they present. Regarding the extent individuals consider data that runs contrary to the positions they defend, similar results are found. The presence of counterargument in discourse, the frequency of its occurrence as well as its nature – all such variables have been shown to be sensitive to content and context-related factors. These are: specific knowledge, know-how in argument strategies (metacognitive knowledge), the type of audience a speaker addresses, the purposes of participants in specific argumentation events, arguers' attitudes and beliefs towards a topic discussed, and commitment to favored or disfavored positions in society. Findings have also been reported showing that subjects' opinions about whether or not the presence of *data against* is a defining attribute of good argument, vary as a function of their pragmatic interpretations of the instructions they are faced with.

In our view, results such as these introduce important limits for a psychologically valid definition of good argument in terms of a more thorough and less biased examination of evidence and counterevidence. The profile that emerges from empirical studies is not of subjects as even-handed souls, who take a balanced view of whatever issue they decide to reflect upon. Rather, it is of an arguer who responds to specific demands coming from particular contexts in which an argument develops. If such is the case, to think of *unbiased argument* (in Perkins *et al.* (1991) terms) as a sort of invariant criterion of good reasoning may not be altogether satisfactory.

Despite the limits stressed by the preceding paragraph, two things are certain. First, that the emphasis on the fact that contextual dimensions constrain the way people contemplate opposing sides in argumentation *should not* lead to counterargument being assigned a secondary (or even unnecessary) role in argumentative text. Rather, the view of argumentation as discourse that only emerges where both dilemmatic issues (Billig, Condor, Edwards, Gane, Middleton & Radley, 1989) and persuasive purposes are at stake, makes the need for counterargumentative thinking self-evident. How can differences be overcome unless arguers allow themselves to contemplate them? Besides, the value of counterargument to reasoning is hardly to be overestimated. It calls a speaker's point into question and gives people grounds for examining their own views. In any case, dealing with counterargument is a central demand of rational thinking. Secondly, it is certain that however crucial the search for counterarguments may be for the assessment of quality of an argument, one cannot rely solely on such a criterion for distinguishing between good arguments and bad ones. A critical comment that can be made on the limitations of such a criterion, is that it does not allow the quality of the reasons generated in the argumentation process to be evaluated. In other words, the questions it cannot answer are whether a supporting reason really justifies a claim, and to what extent a counterargument really undermines one's own reasons. The second perspective on good argument examined in the previous section appears to operate precisely at this level of analysis. Rather than focusing on the mere presence and frequency of supporting and opposing elements in discourse, it concentrates on evaluating the weakness or strength of a reason to warrant a given claim. This is the view we will comment on subsequently.

Direction two.
In evaluating the quality of arguments, one cannot avoid taking a critical stance on the appropriateness of a reason presented with the conclusion it is supposed to support. Similarly, it is essential to consider how crucial a counterargument is in revealing the weaknesses of the argument in question.

The above seems to be a less frequent level of analysis as far as the studies mentioned in the first part of this chapter are concerned. Among these, Kuhn's (1991) work seems to be most representative of the perspective being discussed here. Instead of concentrating on describing whether or not subjects were able to generate the elements they were required to produce, it is the quality of what they produce, that she focuses on. When analyzing arguments, the nature of the causal link her subjects establish stands behind the judgements she makes on the quality of the arguments produced. Necessity and sufficiency are the two logical criteria against which she evaluates the relation between the reason the subjects state and the conclusion they derive from that reason.

Two points in Kuhn's findings are particularly relevant to what we have being discussing in this section. The first is that the participants in Kuhn's study differ as to what they consider to be evidence for a causal claim. Apart from necessity and sufficiency, they also acknowledge plausible narratives as an adequate means of establishing the correctness of a causal theory. It is also to note that sometimes even those participants from the highest educational backgrounds (university graduates), who proved to be familiar with logical principles implied in causal arguments (philosophers), also recognized plausible narratives as an adequate means of establishing the correctness of a causal theory. A plausible narrative describes how a causal sequence might evolve. The crucial distinction between the former and logical criteria (necessity and sufficiency) is that, while the logical criteria are capable of establishing the correctness of a causal link, a narrative one can only show its plausibility.

The second relevant point in Kuhn's findings it that the extent to which participants use each of the above criteria in their arguments is sensitive to variations in the topic of an argument. As Kuhn acknowledges, 'Certain content is apparently more conducive to certain forms of argument' (p. 90). The question that remains to be answered is why this should be so.

The interpretation Kuhn offers of her findings places special emphasis on the presence or lack of some kinds of competence that can be generalized across contents and contexts. We contend, however, that the occurrence and type of what a speaker elects as evidence in an argument might be constrained by factors other than the presence/absence of cognitive competence. The hypothesis that such choices can also be explained pragmatically based on the content and contextual constraints of specific argumentation settings should not be underestimated. This might account, for example, for why sometimes the speakers investigated relied upon logical criteria to support their views, but not always. This is even more interesting if one considers that the speakers knew they were talking about mundane subjects on which one can never achieve certainty. Plausible accounts of causal effects seem to be all the speakers are left with.

Direction three.
In evaluating the quality of arguments, a distinction should be made between the characteristics of an argument and those of the individual who produces it. The third perspective on good argument we commented on in this chapter emphasizes the dispositions and attributes arguers must show in order to generate a good argument. The studies we reviewed seemed to indicate that what is described as a consequence of individual attributes may be influenced by the context and content in which people are involved. For instance, the degree of engagement in searching for counterevidence may vary as a function of the purposes of the situation in which arguments emerge. We have no disagreement concerning the relevance of readiness to examine one's own positions. What we emphasize, however, is the fact that such a notion for evaluating the quality of argument appears to shift the focus from the argumentative text to the arguers themselves. This perspective does not seem to be satisfactory, since it does not state what good argument is. Instead, it limits itself to proposing the pre-conditions for the production of such an ideal of good argument.

After considering these three dominant directions, two more factors should be addressed: the specific purposes served by the context in which argumentation occurs and matters of acceptability. These bring us to the remaining perspectives on good argument mentioned throughout this chapter.

Despite variations in the specific questions addressed in the studies mentioned in the first part of this chapter, they seem to converge towards a common point. We learn from all of them that the complexity of argumentative thinking is regulated by the particular demands of an argumentative situation, rather than by general ability factors that control complexity of thinking. The specific purpose with which individuals enter an argument is certainly one of these situational demands.

It is reasonable, for instance, to think of individuals as engaged in the examination of the greatest possible number of pros and cons for a position, if we know they are about to make a very important decision. But the question to ask is: why should they do the same if mentioning just a few reasons proves sufficient to make their point in a dispute, to convince an audience, or to make a decision under different conditions?

Taking this line of reasoning, S. L. Santos (1997) suggests that the investment in winning a dispute might lead speakers to invest strongly in revealing the weaknesses of their opponents' arguments, rather than reflecting on the limits of their own. This strategy results in a wide range of counterargument being produced against the opponent's position, but not on the speaker's own views. A different argument structure may emerge, however, if it is only the interlocutor's ignorance of the speaker's reasons for holding a particular position that serves as the starting point for the speaker to put forward an argument. Different goals in argumentation would certainly make the structure of the argument vary. Similarly, C. M. Santos (1998) has shown how individuals assign different degrees of persuasiveness to the same argument as a function of what they believe such an argument was produced for.

Similarly to what has been said concerning most of the directions examined above, recognizing that taking matters of acceptability into account is a necessary implication of pragmatically oriented approaches to argumentation should not lead to the view of audience acceptability as the defining criterion of good argument. By saying this, of course, we are not discarding such a perspective as irrelevant in a discussion about acceptable standards of argumentation; we simply do not consider it as a sufficient criterion on its own.

A final remark. We think that the increasingly detailed description of what people *actually do* when they engage in argumentation, which emerges from empirical research, should not preclude us from thinking about what they *should do*. In other words, the emphasis on variations, which undoubtedly encompasses a certain relativity, does not exclude reference to norms, if norms are themselves seen as conventional and socially defined products. Such a comment clearly brings us back to van Eemeren *et al.* (1993) contention that the issue of normativity should be taken seriously both in theoretical and empirical approaches to argumentation. In this sense, we think that the content and contextual dimensions of argument (as shown by descriptive approaches) determine the constraints upon which psychologically valid models of good argument can be built (normative approach).

AUTHORS' NOTE

The authors' studies mentioned in this chapter were supported by CNPq (Brazilian National Research Council).

NOTES

1. Although argument and argumentation are not always used as synonyms in the literature, these terms are not assigned any relevant difference in this work.
2. The summary presented here is based mainly on Perkins, Farady & Bushey (1991), in which the authors summarize their studies over the last ten years.

The Early Emergence of Argumentative Knowledge and Skill

Nancy L. Stein
University of Chicago
Ronan Bernas
Eastern Illinois University

ABSTRACT

We discuss a model of argument understanding that focuses on the reasoning, thinking, and learning that occurs when two people argue in both social and academic situations. We argue that the mental structures used to understand arguments are linked directly to those that are used to understand social and goal-directed action. The ability to understand an argument emerges very early in development. By the age of three years, children are able to understand and generate all components of argumentative discourse. We present different types of empirical evidence in support of our hypothesis, and we compare our early emergence hypothesis to the claim that argumentative skill emerges late in childhood and early adolescence. In support of this 'early emergence' hypothesis, we focus on situations that are personally meaningful to young children and those that impact directly on their goals, beliefs, and well being. We show that even the youngest children entering into an argument are able to generate and think about positive and negative reasons for pursuing different courses of action or for holding specific sets of beliefs. We also show, however, that argumentative thinking has an inherent bias that can be seen in adults' thinking as well as in young children's thinking. Arguers generally have more supporting knowledge for their own position than they do for their opponent's position. They also have more knowledge about the problematic aspects of their opponent's position than they do about their own position. Thus, they support a particular stance because they perceive more benefits accruing from their own position versus another. We discuss the learning strategies that ameliorate this bias, both in social and in academic settings. We argue that current instructional strategies are often aimed at the wrong level of knowledge acquisition, as regards teaching students how to write good arguments. Further, the rhetorical concept of argument is often insensitive to the ways in which argument knowledge is stored psychologically, and the mental structures that regulate the use of argumentative knowledge. Most arguers, even adults, lack accurate knowledge about another's position. The focus for us, in terms of instruction and learning, has more to do with the values and beliefs underlying a position, the necessity to put each position on an equal footing, and the willingness to consider the legitimacy of different goals.

1 INTRODUCTION

Our goal in this chapter is to describe a model of argument understanding and reasoning that illustrates how children and adults represent, evaluate, and resolve arguments. We also discuss training strategies that increase the accuracy and complexity of argument understanding and resolution. Our combined work (Bernas & Stein, 1995, 1996; 1997; Stein, Bernas, & Calicchia, 1997; Stein, Bernas, Calicchia, & Wright, 1995; Stein & Miller 1990, 1993a, b) focuses on both oral and written argument skills. In this chapter, however, we focus primarily on oral argument skill. Observing children and adults during interactive arguments has allowed us to describe the detailed processes of thinking, decision making, and learning that are carried out during attempts to resolve everyday arguments.

The fact that we study arguments in real world contexts and focus on everyday disputes adds a strong validity to our approach. If we are to build a psychologically valid theory of argumentation skill, we must do so in environments where both children and adults have intentionally chosen to argue about an issue. When people voluntarily enter into an argument, they have at least enough knowledge to believe that their stance is better than their opponent's stance. In many current argument studies, participants are not given the choice of voluntarily supporting a position. As a consequence, both children and adults often appear illogical because they lack the prerequisite knowledge to take a stance and defend it in a coherent manner. Further, they are often required to use rhetorical and organizational structures that directly interfere with their ability to express the types of reasoning and thinking they have actually carried out about an issue. Toulmin's (1958) analysis of argument structure serves as an excellent example of a rhetorical theory that is widely used, especially in school situations. Little evidence exists, however, as to its psychological validity or to the comprehensibility of arguments that are generated following the scheme proposed by Toulmin.

The theory we present is different from Toulmin's theory in both form and content. We begin with assumptions about the importance of human goals in regulating the structure and content of an argument. Just as in our theory of narrative understanding (Stein & Glenn, 1979; Stein & Trabasso, 1982; Stein & Trabasso, 1989; Trabasso & Stein, 1994, 1997), we believe that argument knowledge is acquired in the process of coping with challenges to the attainment of personally meaningful goals.

Arguments differ from narrative accounts, however, in the following ways. First, arguments focus on *two* (or more) people's conflicting views about the worth of accomplishing a particular goal. Second, a primary aim of arguing is to persuade another person of the validity and beneficial nature of a favored stance. Third, the evaluation and control of social relationships is an ever-present goal in most arguments. If an arguer concludes that his or her stance is more important than continuing an interchange with an opponent, the arguer may decide to dissolve the relationship with the other rather than continue the argument (Fisher & Brown, 1988; Fisher & Ury, 1981; Stein, Bernas & Calicchia, 1997; Stein, Bernas, Calicchia & Wright, 1995; Stein & Miller, 1990, 1993a, b; Ury, 1991). Two people may also argue to determine who will be the more dominant person in a relationship (Maynard, 1985).

The importance of interpersonal relationships between two arguers has been shown to be a significant predictor of the content and coherence in argumentative interchanges in all of our studies (Albro & Stein, 1999; Sandhya & Stein, 1998;

Bernas & Stein, 1997, 1998a, b; Stein & Ross, 1996) and across the life span (see Gottman, 1994). Albro & Stein (1999) have shown that the impact of arguing on interpersonal relationships is just as important to four-year-old children as it is to adults. In the Albro and Stein (1999) study, the degree to which children liked each other was significant in determining the frequency of expressing concern about the impact of the negotiation on the relationship. The outcomes of arguments were also a function of the desire to maintain the relationship. Upon being asked to negotiate with a best friend over the division of three dinosaurs, one of which was huge (and preferred) and two of which were very small (and not preferred), several four-year-old children would not willingly begin a negotiation with their best friend. They believed that the negotiation would harm their friendship. A boy who was finally coerced into beginning an attempt at negotiation, said to his friend, after the seventh conversational turn, 'Josh, there's no way to divide the dinosaurs. You take them because if you don't get to have them, you won't be my friend no more.' The little boy continued by telling Josh, 'Just remember the next time we have a fight about something, I win'.

These children's spontaneous comments underscore the important role that relationship goals play in all types of argument negotiations pertaining to children, adolescents, and adults. To divorce the development of argumentation skill from the achievement of personally significant goals is to omit the most critical parts of a theory of argumentation. We have been swayed far too long by theories of rationality (Rescher, 1988) and formal logic in formulating models of argumentation. As a consequence, argumentation skill is studied most often by using topics that are unfamiliar and not very stimulating (Rest, 1983). The unfamiliarity of a topic often requires a good teacher to provide students with an enormous amount of background knowledge before students can even begin to formulate a point of view. Further, even when teachers succeed in conveying enough background knowledge about a topic, no guarantee exists that students will care enough to engage in and write an argument about the topic. They may decide that the issue is not worth their energy and effort.

When people engage in arguments in every day interaction, however, they are highly motivated because the outcomes are critical to their well being. Similarly, international conflicts and negotiations among countries involve life and death issues. The outcomes of these negotiations affect millions of people, and almost every person has an opinion about the appropriate stance their country should adopt, whether or nor they are accurately or well informed.

Later in the chapter, we discuss the ways in which oral argumentative skill is similar to and different from situations in which written arguments must be generated. Our hypothesis concerning the ease of arguing in oral communicative contexts versus the 'difficulty' of producing written arguments has little to do with the development of knowledge about the form and logic of arguments. We contend that the primary difficulty in writing an argument has to do with a lack of knowledge about the specific topic at hand (Rest, 1983; Rottenberg, 1985), and/or a lack of knowledge about the organization of an argument according to the teacher's viewpoint.

Many teachers blindly teach rhetorical argument structures based on principles of philosophy and rhetoric (*e.g.*, Kneupper, 1978; Ramage & Bean, 1992; Rottenberg, 1994), not on principles of psychological meaning, coherence, and comprehension. Thus, students are often asked to familiarize themselves with various types of argument forms (*e.g.*, argument types from Aristotle, syllogisms, and

Venn diagrams). Teachers often warn students about inappropriate conclusions and logical errors that might be made during argument construction (Nickerson, 1986; Rottenberg, 1985), but rarely do they provide students with an explanation as to why these errors might be made. Kneupper (1978), for example, suggests that students take a hierarchical approach to writing an argument by first presenting the claim, then presenting a warrant, followed by the presentation of the evidence or backing. This structure basically reflects Toulmin's analytical model of argument.

Fulkerson (1996), however, raises several criticisms regarding the use of Toulmin's model for argument generation. He contends that the model is primarily an analytic tool (*i.e.*, a framework for analyzing argumentative texts). Even when the model is used for analysis, argument scholars themselves have difficulty identifying warrants in a text. Further, the only empirical study that tested the effectiveness of Toulmin's model does not present positive results (McCleary, 1979). Thus, although philosophical principles of argumentation are interesting, they often have little bearing on the ways in which arguments are organized, understood, and produced in everyday settings.

The prototypic claim, evidence, warrant, qualification, and counterargument sequence of Toulmin's model, although possessing certain types of logical coherence, does not include several key dimensions for an argument to have validity and credibility in a psychological sense. Consequently, the rhetorical structures that children are often required to learn in school settings often hinder their understanding and resolution of arguments that occur on an everyday basis. Indeed, training in formal argumentative analysis may make it more difficult for students to become good negotiators in social contexts, where the goal is not to win but to compromise. One reason that compromise becomes difficult is that it requires the integration of goals and the formulation of an entirely new plan. We discuss further the differences between our approach and the more traditional approaches after we present theory and data on the nature and organization of interactive argumentation skill.

2 A THEORY OF ARGUMENT UNDERSTANDING

Knowledge about arguing develops very early. Even three- to five-year-old children have acquired a rich array of knowledge about the form, content, and function of arguments, especially in oral contexts. Young children use their argument skill during all types of interactions, and by the age of five, many have become sophisticated negotiators, especially with their parents and peers (Boggs, 1978; Chittenden, 1942; Eckerman & Stein, 1982; Eisenberg & Garvey, 1981; Maynard, 1985; O'Keefe & Benoit, 1982; Shantz & Shantz, 1985; Stein & Trabasso, 1982).

The traditional belief about the development of argumentation skill, however, is that its development occurs late in childhood, during the beginning of adolescence. Traditional theorists have claimed that even adults have difficulty mastering the knowledge and skills needed to become good arguers, especially when written arguments are required. Kuhn (1995, 1996) and Nickerson (1986) are two investigators who have focused on the difficulties adults experience in constructing coherent arguments. Gilbert (1997), in his book, *Coalescent Argumentation*, is a third investigator who partially adopts this position, except that Gilbert asserts that we should simply accept the inadequacies of argument skills so that we can teach people how to be more constructive when they do engage in arguments.

Our theoretical position (Stein & Miller, 1990, 1993b) has been that argumentation skill emerges very early in development and that neither children nor adults have intellectual difficulties understanding the basic components of an argument. Knowledge about argument, in terms of its function, form, and content, emerges out of a desire to ensure that personally meaningful goals are attained. Focusing on the attainment of personal goals regulates the ways in which arguments are understood throughout the lifespan, and seeking to achieve personally meaningful goals does not predispose people to be illogical, irrational, or to function with illusions, as many philosophers and psychologists would have us believe. The missing component in almost all philosophical and rhetorical theories of argumentation is a fundamental understanding of how people function and understand each other in everyday emotional contexts. Few, if any, approaches to argumentation incorporate ways in which people think and reason in emotionally relevant situations. The only thing said about emotion in argument contexts is that highly charged emotional interactions serve to make people irrational, especially during the resolution of disputes.

However, our studies and those of others (*e.g.*, Jacobson & Gottman, 1998) have demonstrated that emotional interactions are not irrational, in the sense of arguers carrying out unintended actions that are not well formulated. Although the aftermath of an emotionally violent conflict often includes recantations of insanity or lack of reason by perpetrators of violence, access to the perpetrators' thinking and planning before the violence is carried out almost always shows them to be in full command of their actions and able to acknowledge the harms that they will inflict on other people. Perpetrators of violent action not only acknowledge the damage they will cause; they often acknowledge the pleasure they will experience if they are successful in harming other people. To think that violent or emotionally charged action is not planned or rational is a serious error in understanding the nature of thinking and action in conflictual interactions.

Thus, our theory begins with the assumption that four components underlie decision making, reasoning, and negotiation during an argument. These are the desire to achieve personally meaningful goals, knowledge about the positive and negative consequences of action, that are associated with the attainment of these goals, knowledge about the obstacles that stand in the path of goal attainment, and beliefs about the consequences of not attaining these goals. To describe the nature, content, and function of personal goals during social interaction we use a theory of emotional understanding, in conjunction with a theory of argument knowledge, that describes the beliefs, desires, and actions people use to monitor success or failure at attaining personally significant goals.

Our theory of emotional understanding gives a robustness to our theory of argument understanding because understanding the nature of personal goals allows us to predict the thinking, reasoning, and actions that are carried out during attempts to resolve conflicts. Thus, we define an argument as a specific type of interpersonal interaction where two people recognize that they have goals opposing, and both believe they should be allowed to maintain these goals (Stein, Bernas & Calicchia, 1997; Stein, Bernas, Calicchia & Wright, 1995; Stein & Miller, 1990, 1993a, b). For example, when two young children engage their parents in a discussion about which movie the family should see, the parents soon discover that one child wants to see the Lion King and the other wants to see Aladdin. No possibility exists for both outcomes to be realized simultaneously, especially when the family outing involves the entire family seeing a movie together.

When these two children recognize that they have conflicting views, both willingly engage in an argument, and both initially believe that their stance is more legitimate and more viable than the other's stance. They also believe that their stance should be maintained over the other's stance and that more positive benefits will result from their stance than their opponent's stance. Otherwise, neither would engage in a discussion about the conflict. The same holds for adults who willingly enter into an argumentative discussion. Many studies on children's arguments provide strong evidence that children recognize conflicting views. O'Keefe and Benoit (1982), for example, observed that children's arguments begin when opposition is displayed overtly and continue as the opposition remains manifest. Other researchers (Chittenden, 1942; Eckerman & Stein, 1982; Eisenberg & Garvey, 1981; Shantz & Shantz, 1985) also note that a dominant aspect of children's arguments involves assertion, disagreement, defense, and negotiation.

Further, arguers, no matter what age, almost always begin a negotiation by trying to convince the other person about the greater legitimacy of their position. Persuasion is carried forward by providing justifications for supporting one position and for opposing the other. In the give and take of conflict talk, even children of preschool age provide reasons for supporting their side of the issue (Dunn, 1988; Eisenberg & Garvey, 1981; Goodwin, 1990; Stein & Liwag, 1997; Tesla & Dunn, 1992) and for opposing that of their opponent (Albro & Stein, 1999). Eisenberg and Garvey (1981) remark that children know they are expected to provide reasons, and that they do not accept a simple 'no' from a peer. Our studies (Stein & Trabasso, 1982) attest to the complexity of children's reasoning during argumentation. When children were asked to evaluate a moral dilemma about attaining a goal (*e.g.*, obtaining a medicine to help a sick person) but having to fulfill the goal at the expense of hurting another (*e.g.*, pulling whiskers from a tiger to obtain the medicine and thus harming the tiger), children supported their decisions with moral or social codes.

Analysis of reasons given in support of a position are critical because they demonstrate an effort to justify the *positive benefits* of adhering to personal goals that underlie a particular stance. Miller, Bernas, Ross, and Stein (Stein, Bernas & Calicchia, 1997; Stein & Miller, 1990, 1993a, b; Stein & Ross, 1996) have shown that across the life span, arguments are almost always goal driven. Over 90 percent of the reasons arguers give in favor of or against a position function to illuminate the *consequences* of adhering to one goal (position) versus another. The quality and specific content of reasons given in support of or in opposition to a position are critical in determining whether or not another person will believe and accept statements of the positive or negative outcomes associated with a particular stance. Thus, justifying a favored position is inherent in the definition of an argument, even for very young children. The goal of justification is to persuade the other person about the benefits of the favored position and the problems inherent in the opposing position.

3 THE ASYMMETRICAL ORGANIZATION OF ARGUMENT KNOWLEDGE

According to our theory of argument understanding (Stein, Bernas & Calicchia, 1997; Stein, Bernas, Calicchia & Wright, 1995; Stein & Miller, 1990, 1993a, b), arguers initially support one side of an issue over the other because they have more knowledge about the positive benefits of their position than the positive benefits of their opponent's position. They also have more knowledge about problems with their opponent's position than they do about problems with their own position. Thus, the content and structure of argument knowledge for the two positions is asymmetrical.

Figure 1 Mean number of reasons given in support of and against a favored versus an opposed position (summarized across three different studies).

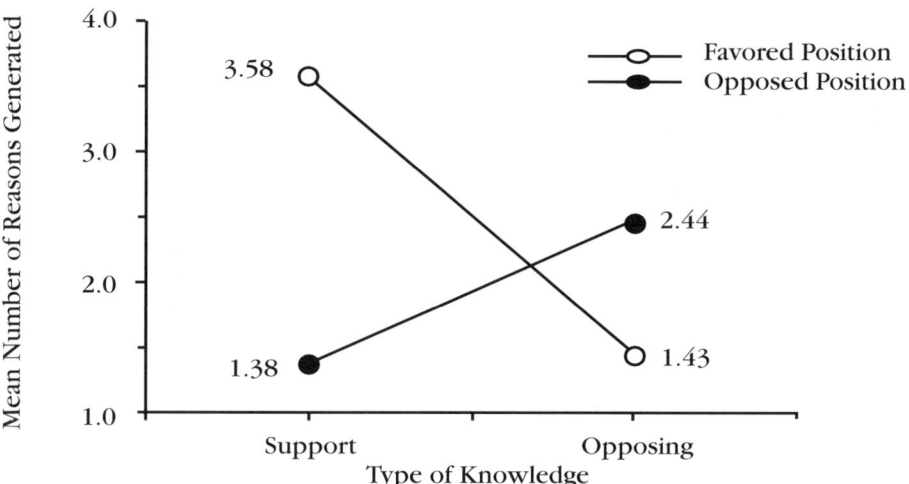

Figure 1 shows the nature of this asymmetrical knowledge at the beginning of an argument. These data are taken from three different studies. We collapsed the data across three age groups: (1) four-year-old children arguing with a peer about how a conflict should be resolved; (2) adolescents arguing about their stances on an argument; and (3) married couples recalling and discussing a past argument they have had. Knowledge about both positions in an argument is measured before arguers engage in face-to-face interaction with one another.

Figure 1 illustrates two findings. First, all arguers have approximately twice as many reasons for supporting their own position as they do for supporting the opposing position. So, even though arguers can list at least one supporting reason for the opposing position, they generate twice as many reasons for their own position. Second, arguers generate almost twice as many problems with their opponents' position as they do with their own.

We contend that this asymmetry holds until an arguer decides to switch stances or create a new stance. Thus, even though we can train people to understand the opposing position in a more accurate and complex fashion, arguers will still be able to list more reasons for supporting their own position until they begin to change their stance. If knowledge and beliefs about the goodness of a position change, such that an arguer can now generate as many reasons to support the opposition as the favored point of view, then two types of changes occur. Either the arguer will switch positions and support the opposition, or the arguer will formulate a new position that incorporates some of the benefits of both positions. The latter solution is known as a compromise.

The important point that we wish to make is that the asymmetrical organization of knowledge about two positions at the beginning of an argument *defines* what an argument is. This assertion goes against many philosophical theories of argumentation, especially the theory advanced by Toulmin (1958). Although Toulmin would like us to believe that the core purpose for arguing is to establish the validity of each of two positions, using the assumptions of formal logic, this is not the primary goal in human arguing, whether the argument is social, academic, or legal. Putting forth an argument *always* carries a persuasive thrust, and the support of any position is always contingent upon human evaluation as to which position results in more benefits to the arguer.

Further, the outcomes of arguing are always contingent upon the values that arguers hold, in terms of which goals are considered to be more worthwhile. Although philosophers and rhetoricians focus on the logical reasoning that people use to support their conclusions, they have failed to understand the role that value judgments play in the organization and promotion of reasons for supporting a particular position. Value, at its core, cannot be reduced to right or wrong. Value is synonymous with liking, goodness, and preference. And in the end, all reasons for goals and assertions in arguments include appraisals about what is good and valuable. Who wins an argument has more to do with convincing the other that less harm and more good will come from the support of one position over another. Given that we hold these assumptions about the nature of argumentation, even in written contexts, we now address the issues of the nature and organization of an oral argument.

4 MEMORY AND UNDERSTANDING OF INTERACTIVE ARGUMENTS

Given that we focus on oral argumentation and conflict resolution, our goal is to describe the schematic organization of the knowledge arguers use to report and present arguments in both private and interactive contexts. The private context is important for those researchers who study the written form of argument, because private oral reflection is similar to private written reflection about an argument. In a study of married couples carried out by Ross and Holmberg (1990) at the University of Waterloo, married couples were asked to talk about a recent argument. All of the couples had agreed upon which argument they were going to report, and then half of the couples recounted the argument in private, and half recounted the argument in a face-to-face interaction with each other. Ross and Holmberg (1990) analyzed the data for different types of phenomena regarding salience of argument memory. Later, Stein and Ross (1996) carried out data analyses on other aspects. These were the content of arguments, the types of appraisals that husbands and wives make about each other, the reasons given in favor of and in opposition to both positions, the types of outcomes that resulted from the arguments, and the rate of agreement between husbands and wives in both private and face-to-face interactions.

Table 1 Percentage of adult spouses who recalled each argument category (Stein & Ross, 1996).

Argument Category	Separately	Together
Topic	100*	87*
Recognition of Conflict	94*	96*
Reasons for Supporting or Opposing a Position	92*	91*
Who Initiated the Event that Led to the Conflict	94*	91*
Who Brought Up the Discussion of the Conflict	78*	61
Verbal Interchange in Resolving the Conflict	82*	87*
Outcomes	92*	96*
Repercussions	78*	78*

*significant at $p < .05$, unless otherwise stated

Table 1 contains the eight types of content information that were generated in both private and face-to-face reports of an argument. The eight types are: Topic, Recognition of the Conflict, Reasons for Supporting or Opposing Each Point of View, Who Initiated the Event that Led to the Argument, Who Brought Up the Discussion of the Conflict, The Specific Verbal Interchange in Resolving the Conflict, The Outcome of the Conflict, and the Repercussions of the Argument. The analysis of the content is exhaustive in that every clause in every argument was classified into one of these eight content categories. The frequency of including information in each of the eight content categories was significantly above chance for all of the couples narrating privately and in face-to-face interaction. The only content category that was not highly represented was the category that focused on who brought up the topic of the argument for discussion. Omission of this piece of information occurred more frequently in face-to-face than in private reports of arguments.

Topic of the argument. The topic was mentioned by virtually all of the husbands and wives either narrating separately or in face-to-face interaction because of the constraints of the experimental design. Each couple was required to agree upon which argument was to be privately or jointly reported. Each spouse narrating privately stated the topic as the very first sentence of their report. Interestingly, 87 percent of partners in face-to-face interaction also stated the topic, indicating the importance of the topic in reporting an argument.

Recognition of conflict. This category included explicit statements of the two spousal positions, with or without explicit reference to the fact that the positions were incompatible. A spousal position statement could be expressed by reference to a goal, a preference, a prescriptive belief, or an action. Mention of the two positions often occurred in close proximity to one another and was accompanied frequently by the admission that the conflicting goals caused an argument. Examples of recognition of conflict are:

> And I remember that he wanted to go back and I didn't, so we had a fight.
> I wanted to have a home that was older, and a home that was more traditional, a home that had some character. My husband on the other hand, was more practical, and he wanted to have a newer home.

Recognition of conflict was also identified by the explicit mention of one spouse's position and the other's emotional reaction to the position. Examples are:

> She would like to refurbish the house with all new furniture. This would mean selling our furniture and buying new stuff. Well, being that the furniture is in good condition, I was not very happy with this idea.
>
> He could be so callous about it, I mean just so nonchalant, that yes, let's throw the plans for the vacation out the window because work has called [...]. This gets on my nerves.

Table 2 Recognizing conflict during individual and face-to-face interaction (Stein & Ross, 1996). Percentages

Narrative condition		Both positions	Wife's position only	Husband's position only	No position
Together					
	Husband	70	4	22	4
	Wife	70	26	4	0
Separate					
	Husband	88	4	8	0
	Wife	100	0	0	0

Table 2 contains a breakdown of the percentage of spouses who verbalized their knowledge of their conflicting goals. In private narration, all of the wives acknowledged both goals and the conflict between them, and 88 percent of the husbands acknowledged both goals. In the face-to-face condition, however, only 70 percent of both spouses acknowledged both goals. A clear bias existed for each spouse to state his or her goal at the beginning of the face-to-face discussion, without stating the spouse's goal. This omission, however, may not be due to the lack of knowledge about the other's position. Rather, the omission may be due to an unspoken agreement between the spouses that when discussing a conflict, each spouse has the responsibility to state exactly what their goal was during the argument. Rules of politeness may imply that each spouse knows their own goal better than the other spouse. Thus, the burden of responsibility for stating spousal goals accurately lies with the spouse whose goal is being discussed. Not withstanding the use of a politeness rule, however, the majority of spouses in both conditions found a way to state the initial conflict of positions and to acknowledge the mutual opposition that motivated the argument.

Reasons for supporting and refuting a position. Explanations given for advocating or challenging a particular position were identified. Explanations focused on future outcomes, adherence to agreed upon moral principles, preferred states, and existing conditions as reasons for supporting their own point of view. Examples of reasons in support of a position were:

I figured *it was my TV* (Supporting Reason, Principle of Ownership) and I could do whatever I wanted with it (Supporting Reason, Principle of Ownership). She had no say in the matter, it was my possession (Supporting Reason).

I thought *it would be very interesting* (Supporting Reason, Preference), why not do it?

Opposing Reasons were stated frequently in conjunction with a refutation of the other spouse's position or goal. Examples are:

She would like to refurbish the house with all new furniture. Well, *being that the furniture is in good condition* (Opposing Reason, Existing Condition), I was not very happy with this idea, and I opposed it (Refutation of Wife's Position).

I wanted to raise the barbecue up. She didn't like the idea too much (Preference) and disagreed (Refutation of Husband's Position) *because she felt it would be too high for her* (Opposing Reason, Negative Personal Consequence).

I wasn't too pleased with his trip (Refutation of Husband's Position) because he was coming home the very day of our third anniversary (Opposing Reason) and I knew he would be jet-lagged (Opposing Reason) and we would never celebrate our anniversary (Opposing Reason).

Figure 2   Number of reasons given in support of or opposing each position (Stein & Ross, 1996)

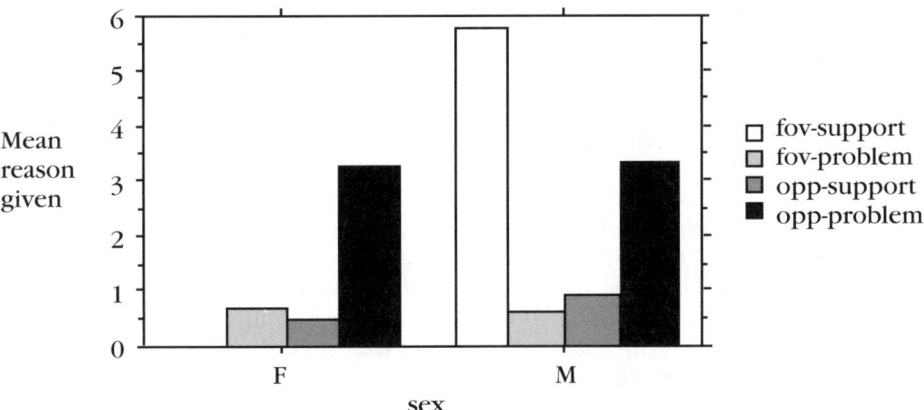

Figure 2 presents the number of reasons that each spouse gave in support of or in opposition to their own and their partner's positions. We present this graph to illustrate the asymmetrical nature of reasons for and against the favored and opposed position. The data are similar to the data presented for children and adolescents. The conditions under which spouses reported their explanations (privately or in a face-to-face interaction) did not affect the pattern of reasoning. Spouse's always gave more reasons in support of their own position than their partner's position, and they always gave more opposing reasons for their partner's position than for their own.

Who initiated the argument. We defined the person who carried out the action that led to the argument as the initiator of the argument. Two scores were calculated for the identity of the argument initiator. One score was derived from each spouse's report; the second was derived from an integrated representation of both reports. The second score was labeled as a collective representation score and used the couple as the unit of analysis.

Table 3 Who initiated the argument (Stein & Ross, 1996). Percentages

Narrative condition	Number of couples	Who Initiated			
		Wife	Husband	Unknown	Disagreement
Together	23	43	48	9	0
Separate	25	32	40	16	12

In the face-to-face condition, 9 percent of the couples did not mention the initiator of the argument; 16 percent did not mention the initiator in the private narration condition. Disagreements about the initiator occurred 12 percent of the time, but only in the private narration condition. Table 3 illustrates these data. In both narration conditions, husbands were perceived to be the initiator of arguments slightly more often than wives. These differences, however, were not significant.

Who brought up the disagreement for discussion. This dimension focused on who initiated the discussion of the disagreement. Two scores were again calculated for this category: one based on private reports and the other based upon a constructed collective report. Because of a failure to report any information about this category, 12 percent of the couples in the private narration condition and 39 percent in the face-to-face narration condition were eliminated from this analysis. Of the remaining couples, 8 percent of those in the private narration condition failed to agree on who brought up the topic for discussion, and these couples were also eliminated from the analysis.

Figure 3   Who raised the topic of the argument during individual or joint reports of a married couple's argument (Stein & Ross, 1996).

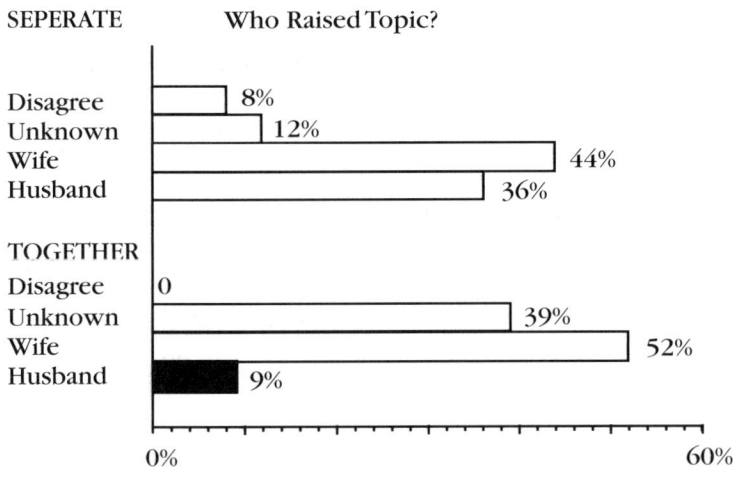

Figure 3 describes the frequency with which husbands and wives were identified as bringing up the disagreement for discussion. 52 Percent of the couples narrating together, and 44 percent of the couples narrating separately agreed that the wife brought up the topic for discussion. Husbands were identified as initiators of the discussion 9 percent of the time when couples were in face-to-face interaction, and 36 percent of the time when couples narrated separately. A chi-square analysis revealed that the initiator of discussion is more likely to be the wife when couples narrate in face-to-face interaction, but the initiator is equally likely to be either spouse when arguments are reported in private narration.

Report of verbal resolution of differences: outcomes and evaluations. This category included references to the actual verbal interchange that took place between the two spouses, the outcome of the negotiation, and appraisals of the impact of the conflict. In almost all instances, the reports of the actual conversation that took place was identified by the use of communicative verbs – *e.g.* she said, he yelled, he asked, *etc.* – in combination with a paraphrase of the actual conversation that occurred between the two spouses. Examples of these reports are:

> I said that we'd just try it for a while to see if it was really easier for me to use. I ranted and raved that he shouldn't have the car and he should be more reasonable.

The outcome of each argument was categorized as a *win-loss*, a *compromise*, or a *stand-off*, according to the criteria described below.

A WIN-LOSS was defined as an outcome in which one of the spouses ended up maintaining his/her goal, while the other one capitulated and switched to sup-

porting the other spouse's position. An example of explicit mention of the goals at the beginning and end of the argument narrative that signifies a WIN-LOSS:
Initial statement of goals:

> H: She would like to refurbish the house with all new furniture. This would mean selling our furniture and buying new stuff. Well, being that the furniture is in good condition, I was not very happy with this idea.

End statement of goals that defined a win-loss:

> H: But we did come to an agreement that it can be sold, that she'd get new living-room furniture. As usual I gave in. I think that overall she is right in this situation.

A STAND-OFF resulted when both participants maintained their goals throughout the argument and refused to accommodate their spouse's goal. An example of standoff outcomes is:
Initial statement of goals:

> W: Our daughter [was] crying in the back seat of the car. I said I should bring her in the front seat and he said 'no,' and we started getting a little bit hostile towards each other.

End statement of goals that defined a stand-off:

> W: I don't think we came to an agreement over it, so we get home and by the time we stop the car and get out and go into the house we kind of dropped the situation.

A COMPROMISE was defined as the spouses reaching a mutually satisfactory conclusion, typically by taking one of the spouse's original goals and adding conditions to it that made it acceptable to the other spouse or by substituting a new goal for the two original ones.
Examples of a compromise solution are:
Compromise Example 1:
Initial statement of goals:

> H: I felt we should buy a newer type of house in a newer area. On the other hand, my wife felt that she would prefer a house in an older section of the city which meant it would be an older house.

End statement of goals that defined a compromise:

> H: And she finally agreed with it [buying a newer house]. And I also agreed with her that we would probably feel better if the house was situated in a more established area.

Compromise Example 2:
Initial statement of goals:

H: But I felt [...] I was bumping into the couch all the time. Yeah, well because you wanted it, you wanted it over there. I didn't want to move it over there.

End statement of goals that defined a compromise:

H: and how did we resolve it? We didn't move the couch after all. What did we do?
W: Oh, we shortened the table.
H: We made the table short. So we did come to a compromise on that.
W: but I think we resolved it by compromising.

Table 4   Collective representations for the outcomes of argument (Stein & Ross, 1996). Percentages

Narrative condition	Win/Loss	Compromise	Stand-Off	Disagreement
Together	70	4	22	4
Separate	52	4	20	24

As Table 4 indicates, 96 percent of the couples narrating together and 76 percent of couples narrating separately agreed on the type of outcome that ended the conflict. The two primary ways in which couples ended their arguments were with a win-loss or a stand-off. For this particular sample of couples, compromise was not a frequent solution.

The appraisals that spouses made during their argument report were indicative of the emotion states that had been experienced by them and their spouses, the beliefs that were held by and about each of them, appraisals of the personal dispositions of each other, appraisals of the worth of the relationship, appraisals of a spouse's future behavior, and appraisals about the repercussions the argument had on their relationship. It is important to remember that these types of appraisals are the most important in determining the satisfaction that two people feel regarding the quality of a relationship. These evaluations are also directly related to the long term stability of a relationship, to the use of coercion and violence with a spouse, and to whether the two can abide each other and establish a positive relationship. Further, these appraisals are equally important in assessing the mental health (e.g., depressive mood and positive well-being, Stein and Broaders, in press) of individuals recounting a conflict.

Table 5 contains a breakdown of the three primary types of statements that were made during the recall of an argument: factual statement about the events and actions that took place; appraisals of the self, the spouse, and the relationship; and statements about the accuracy of memory retrieval. As Table 5 indicates, the majority of statements were appraisals about the self, the spouse, and the relationship.

Table 5 Types of appraisals occurring during the resolution of conflict (Stein & Ross, 1996). Percentages

FACTUAL APPRAISALS	32
What happened?	
It all started when you told me we could not go on vacation.	
SUBJECTIVE APPRAISALS	63
A. Emotional Reactions	
I was really angry.	
I was never as upset as I was then.	
B. Personality Attributions	
Liar. You know it's not true.	
It was your fault.	
You always do something stupid.	
C. Valenced Belief Statements	
We're never going to get this thing solved.	
MEMORY RETRIEVAL	5
Did that really happen?	
Okay, let's see if we got everything out.	

Table 6 contains the different types of appraisals made by each spouse. Part A shows that more than twice as many appraisals were made in the face-to-face condition than in the individual narration condition. Further, in the face-to-face condition, more than twice as many appraisals were made about the spouse as about the self. Although more appraisals were made about the spouse than the self in the individual narration condition, the difference between self-spouse appraisals was not significant. The difference was significant, however, in the face-to-face condition. The reason for the sharp increase in spousal appraisals in the face-to-face condition was that couples often got into another argument by discussing what had happened in a previous argument. When another argument ensued, both partners were on the defensive and most appraisals were directed toward the other partner's negative qualities.

Part B of Table 6 shows that although both husbands and wives appraised their partners more than they did themselves, wives made almost three times as many appraisals of their husbands as they did of themselves. This was not true for husbands.

Part C shows the distribution of positive and negative appraisals made about the self and spouse. Again, negative appraisals of both the self and spouse far outweighed positive appraisals, and again, appraisals of the spouse were more frequent than appraisals of the self. Finally, Part D shows that the number of negative appraisals made during the recall of the resolution of the argument was significantly related to the outcome of the negotiation. Three times as many negative appraisals were made when the negotiation ends in a stand-off than when the negotiation ended in a win-loss strategy.

Table 6   Types of appraisals made in individual versus face-to-face discussion (Stein & Ross, 1996).

A. Mean number of appraisals	Individual	Face-to-Face
Total	5.0	13.0
Self	4.1	7.7
Spouse	5.9	16.4
B. Appraisals made by each partner	Self	Spouse
Husbands	6.6	9.7
Wives	5.4	14.2
C. Positive and negative appraisals	Self	Spouse
Positive appraisals	9	18
Negative appraisals	27	46
D. Mean number of negative appraisals by type of outcome		
Stand-off		16.3
Win-Loss		5.4

5 SIMILARITIES IN ARGUMENT REPRESENTATION OVER DEVELOPMENT

We have spent most of this chapter discussing adult memory and understanding of arguments, first to illustrate what the adult form of argument knowledge looks like in real world interaction, and then to compare the adult form to that which occurs in early childhood and adolescence. Space does not permit the presentation of all the developmental data that we have collected. However, we present some of the most important findings from the studies that we and our colleagues have carried out.

Table 7 contains the same *Argument Representation* analysis of preschool children and adolescents' recall of arguments they had with either a peer or a parent. It does not really matter who is involved in the argument, nor does the age of the narrator matter. Seven of the eight categories found in adult recall are included in over 90 percent of all recalls of past arguments by both adolescents and preschool children. The only category not included at a 90 percent level was one that focused on who brought up the discussion of the conflict. Only 63 percent of four-year-old children and 77 percent of adolescents mentioned this category. However, all other categories were included in the recall of their arguments. It is important to note the striking similarities in the argument representation of adolescents and children compared to the argument representation of adults (see Table 1).

In terms of young children's fluency in providing reasons for and against their own and their opponent's position, their data were identical to those provided by adolescents and adults. From studies carried out by Stein and Albro (1997), by H.

Ross (1997), and by Eisenberg (1992), we know that even four-year-old children can produce every part of an argument that an adult can produce. That is, preschool children can generate reasons for the support of their own position, they can generate problems with their opponent's position, and they can even generate supports for their opponent's position and a few problems with their own position.

Table 7   Percentage of adolescents and children who recalled each argument category.

Argument Category	Stein, Bernas, & Calicchia Adolescent Study (1997)	Stein & Albro Preschool Study (1997)
Topic	100*	100*
Recognition of conflict	100*	100*
Reasons for supporting or opposing a position	94*	92*
Who initiated the event that led to the conflict	98*	92*
Who brought up the discussion of the conflict	77	63
Verbal interchange in resolving the conflict	94*	90*
Outcomes	100*	98*
Repercussions	92*	90*

*significant at p < .05, unless otherwise stated

As children move from preschool to elementary school they are able to generate longer arguments in the sense that they give more reasons for supporting their own position than a younger child, and give more problems with their opponents' position than a younger child. Older children also become more adept at winning their arguments than younger children. What older children do not evidence, however, is an increase in their knowledge about the positive aspects of another's position, or an increase in their knowledge about problems with their own position. The way in which children become better arguers is by increasing the causal complexity of the reasons that support their own position in light of the problems with the opposing position. Our results on thirteen- to seventeen-year-old adolescents are similar to those on young preschool children.

We have further shown in our studies on adolescents that individual differences in the prior knowledge that arguers have about both positions before an argument, predicts the types of outcomes that will result as a function of negotiation. Those arguers who are able to effect a compromise have more prior knowledge about both positions than either winners or losers. Winners have high knowledge regarding their own position but low knowledge of the other's position, and losers have the lowest relative prior knowledge of both positions.

Figure 4 Memory for a negotiation as a function of the outcome of the argument.

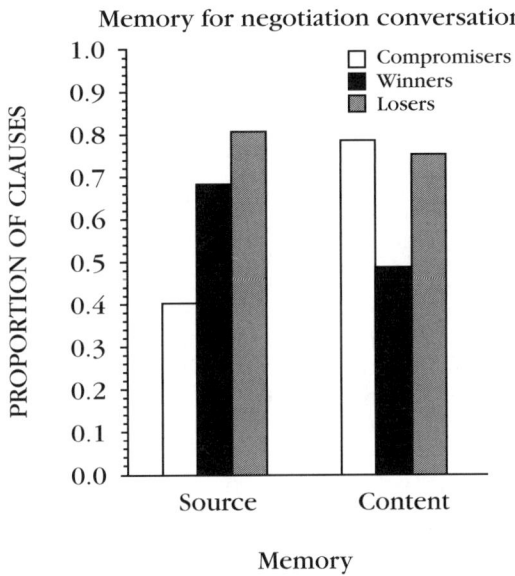

Figure 4 illustrates the types of memory that compromisers, winners, and losers show after a negotiation has occurred. Two types of memory were assessed: source memory and memory for the content of what was said. Source memory refers to the accuracy of recalling who uttered a particular statement in the argument. Content memory refers to what was said. Figure 4 shows that losers evidenced the best memory for who said something, and they tied with compromisers for remembering accurately what was said. Remember that losers have the lowest prior knowledge about their own position and another person's position (Stein, Bernas & Calicchia, 1997). Thus, during a negotiation, losers acquire substantial knowledge about the problems with their own position and the strengths of their opponent's position. Most of this information comes from the winner, and losers are very good at remembering this information. Further, it is not very difficult for a loser to be accurate in monitoring the source, because most of the rebuttals and challenges originate from the winner.

Winners are also good at accurately remembering the source, because they do most of the challenging and presentation of qualifications. However, they make many errors in remembering exactly what their opponent said either against their position or in favor of the opponent's position. Further, winners almost always misrepresent a loser's initial reasons for adhering to a particular position. Winners are relatively good at recalling some of the beliefs a loser has about the benefits of the opposing side. But they are notoriously poor at remembering the reasons that losers give in terms of why certain benefits are important.

Compromisers are the best at remembering what each person has said in support of a position. Their accuracy is critical because basically what compromisers are doing is constructing a new goal plan that incorporates some of the goals and beliefs of both positions. Thus, a compromiser must attend to and understand both sides of an argument. Compromisers had difficulty identifying accurately who made the suggestions for incorporating certain components of each original position into a new solution. A bias existed for compromisers to think that they made the majority of suggestions that allowed the construction of a new plan to go forth. This finding will need further exploration, however. We found that arguers who compromised successfully actually shared in devising each component of the solution. They simply could not identify exactly what they had suggested and what their partner suggested.

6 CONCLUSION

The data that we have presented in this chapter shows the importance of social conflict and the desire to achieve personally significant goals in regulating the knowledge that children and adults use during attempts to resolve interactive arguments. This type of argument knowledge is used not only to resolve everyday arguments, but also to mediate and resolve international disputes, disputes among businesses, dispute in the legal domain, and arguments in the scientific domain. Although we would like to think that science is free from the personal and emotional constraints that arguers face on a day-to-day basis, this is not the case. Scientific debates are as prone to the types of appraisals that we find in married couples' arguments.

In discussing the development of argument skill, researchers generally ignore the accuracy of the prior knowledge that an arguer has about an opposing position. It is frequently assumed that difficulty experienced in generating all parts of an argument is due to the inability to either reason in a logical fashion or to understand the rhetorical structure of an argument. We have found, however, that all arguers can generate all parts of an argument, especially those with which they have great familiarity. The core difficulty arguers have in understanding an argument are remembering accurately the beliefs and assumptions of people who hold goals different from their own. The imputing of positive value to things that are unfamiliar or disliked is one of the most difficult things for both children and adults to accomplish. This difficulty is expressed in almost every argument, especially those that occur in cross-cultural exchanges, where value systems in one country diverge significantly from the value systems in another country.

Our ongoing studies on teaching better conflict resolution skills have shown that the most successful intervention has little to do with teaching children and adults different parts of an argument. Rather, successful conflict intervention forces opponents to understand what the other person values, fears, and perceives as a positive and negative impact of a proposed position. Our futures studies are designed to describe the acquisition of argumentation skill in more detail, especially in young children as they enter elementary school.

Our hypothesis is that current theories of argumentation do not describe young children's capabilities in any realistic sense, nor do they capture the rich array of knowledge that young children use to increase their understanding of alternative positions. Understanding the nature and origins of argument skill as being intimately related to achieving personally meaningful goals provides an explanation for the organization of argument knowledge not captured in many current theories. For us, this approach has not only been productive in accounting for the majority of data on argumentation, but it has also been productive in showing how argumentation skills are intimately related to indices of mental health and psychological well-being.

The Development of Argumentative Schema in Writing

Annie Piolat, Jean-Yves Roussey & Anne Gombert
Centre de Recherche en Psychologie Cognitive - CNRS & Université de Provence

ABSTRACT

Psycholinguistic studies concerning narrative schema by speakers or writers have been numerous and fruitful. However, very few studies are available concerning the acquisition of other kinds of texts, in particular in relation to argumentative schema. It is unlikely that this is only due to an exclusive focus on activation modes, and to a lack of attempts to explicitly examine knowledge during writing. A review of psycholinguistic studies in relation to argumentation in text production will be carried out. Its aim is to bring about some explanatory elements concerning the relative theoretical and methodological lack of interest for the field. Thus, an assessment of the ways in which researchers define and operationalize argumentative schema among young writers will be proposed. Different types of tasks will be described and compared (highly constrained writing tasks such as the insertion of connectives and recomposition of text; constrained tasks such as beginning and end imposed; and unconstrained writing tasks) as well as different types of learning situations (such a cooperative writing and didactic sessions). The nature of the observation used for studying this schema will be described. Some analyses performed by psycholinguists lead to the conclusion that researchers study different phenomena in their investigations on the actualization of argumentative schema as guides for producing a coherent text. It is not surprising to find discrepancies (from ten to sixteen years) in the age in which a writer is supposed to produce a coherent argumentative text.

1 INTRODUCTION

Regarding the acquisition of written skill in argumentation, the study of the developmental cues of mastery of the argumentative schema is beginning to receive renewed interest. Nevertheless, the results of the different studies to date seem to be quite divergent. Certain researchers have shown that before thirteen to fourteen years, children are unable to produce elaborate argumentative texts and have difficulty coordinating the arguments and counterarguments concerning a thesis (*e.g.*, Brassart, 1989, 1992; Golder & Coirier, 1994). In contrast, others have shown that children from the age of eleven onwards, are capable of coordinating statements that defend opposing points of view (*e.g.* Akiguet, 1997; Akiguet & Piolat, 1996; Gombert, 1997; Roussey & Gombert, 1996; Roussey, Akiguet, Gombert & Piolat, 1995).

Such discrepancies may be explained by differences in the experimental conditions employed to study the use of the argumentative schema by young writers. In addition to the divergent linguistic models of argumentation that are used to formalize the argumentative schema, certain writing tasks seem to encourage children to structure their texts in a more elaborate and canonical fashion. The main purpose of this review is to show how the degree of elaboration of children's texts varies with the writing task and the instructions that accompany it. In other words, the chronological discrepancies in written argumentative skill can be, to a large extent, explained by the diversity of the experimental design and didactic that are employed.

2 ARGUMENTATIVE SCHEMA AND TEXT PRODUCTION

2.1 Text schema functions

In order to understand how young writers learn to structure information in different types of texts, psychologists have hypothesized the acquisition of prototypical schemas (or superstructures: Fayol, 1991). Text schemas, which are unique among the various schemas possessed by an individual (Kintsch & Van Dijk, 1978; Rumelhart & Norman, 1978; Schank & Abelson, 1977), are composed of knowledge relevant for guiding the structuring of information. This information can be extracted from a text (comprehension) or integrated into one (production; for a review see Coirier, Gaonac'h & Passerault, 1996). This conception, although it has been criticized (Brassart, 1996; Denhière & Baudet, 1992), has been fruitful in the analysis of how young writers from the age of nine onwards are able to control a narrative text (for a review, see Espéret, 1991; Fayol & Monteil, 1988).

Few investigations have focused on the organization of texts other than narrative (Fayol, 1991). Indeed, it should be noted that researchers in textual psycholinguistic have either not pursued the study of the cognitive structures useful for mastering these other types of texts, or have strongly criticized and abandoned this line of investigation. The different theoretical positions expressed by Brassart are noteworthy. In 1989, he interpreted his results in terms of the progressive mastery of 'a prototypical argumentative text schema'. In 1990, he stated that the argumentative schema proposed by Adam (1990, 1992) was impoverished and too far from argumentative reality to facilitate any text processing (*Cf.* for the same point of view: Golder, 1996). Most often, the development of argumentative capacities in children has been studied in situations of the oral production of dialogue (see Champaud, 1994, for a review; Stein & Miller, 1993a). In such conditions, analysis has centered on the local linguistic units (Coirier, 1996; Golder, 1996; Schneuwly, 1996), rather than the ways in which information is structured (Andriessen, 1991).

In a dialogue, argumentation is co-produced by the alternate speaking roles. According to researchers who have assessed the linguistic devices specific to argumentative discourse, the speaker/writer can justify (*i.e.*, back up his opinion and support his discourse by new assertions) and/or negotiate (*i.e.*, carefully organize a space of refutation in which the addressee may intervene). The specific linguistic markers that demonstrate recourse to these processes change with age and with the context of the productions under study (status of the participants, theme, *etc.*; Golder, 1996). Coherence results from the activity of dialogue itself, with the aid of the successive arguments and counterarguments produced by the speakers (Stein & Miller, 1990, 1993a). In contrast, in written productions the writer structures all information alone and must conceive of and coordinate the statements *for* and *against* the point of view being defended in order to build a coherent text. This requires, therefore, the ability to present ideas that should belong to the opposing point of view (Roussey & Gombert, 1992; Roussey, Akiguet, Gombert & Piolat, 1995). The ability to group information by argumentative orientation is considered to be a linguistic tool that allows the justification (*for*) or the refutation (*against*) of an assertion (Apothéloz & Brandt, 1992).

According to the previous position and Toulmin's model (1958), the psycholinguist can assume there is argumentation when statements (*for or against*) from the speaker or writer support the position. However, since Adam's model (1992; see next subsection), it appears more valid and heuristic to assume that an elaborated argumentation is linked not only to (a) the use of linguistic devices of justification and negotiation, and (b) the production of arguments and counterarguments regarding an assertion, but also, and above all, to (c) the integration of all elements into a coherent whole. Thus, in the study of the development of argumentative skill, the objective is to determine how and when young writers are able to coordinate a complete argumentative schema.

2.2 The argumentative text schema

As writers compose their texts, they may use justification or negotiation devices for or against a point of view (Coirier, Coquin-Viennot, Golder & Passerault, 1990; Golder, 1996). However, the use of these devices is not sufficient to ensure the coherent organization of the information contained in the written argumentative text. This type of text has supplementary requirements. In addition to the linearization of the information established by such linguistic operations as cohesion markers (*e.g.*, anaphoric references, connectives, *etc.* Champaud, 1994; Schneuwly, 1988), the argumentative text is also structured semantically and pragmatically by the use of textual connectives (Golder & Coirier, 1996). These connectives indicate the discursive orientation and, thereby, contribute to the hierarchical organization of the text. The argumentative text must, therefore, correspond to a specific structure in which the arguments and counterarguments that are put forward are coordinated. Writing a text cannot be reduced to a translation of alternate speaking turns. Instead, the elements of a text must be structured and coordinated into a standardized structure: the schema.

The argumentative structure was formalized by several authors, only two of whom will be considered here (Adam, 1990, 1992; and Toulmin, 1958). Those psycholinguists who consider that argumentation is essentially a justification will turn willingly to the model of Toulmin (1958). Two criticisms of Toulmin's model (1958) have been formulated. The first concerns the essentially justifying character of argumentative activity. Refutation, in this conception, is assigned a purely secondary role (Johnson, 1991; Plantin, 1990). The second criticism is that this model is difficult to use in the analysis of the text productions of children, whose inferences are often not explicit.

Those psycholinguists who consider argumentation to be a process of dialogue, in which opposing information must be coordinated, will refer instead to the model proposed by Adam (1992). This linguist clearly demonstrated the dialogical dimension of argumentation, and his model facilitates the description of texts written in monological situations by focusing on the structuring of information *for* and *against* a thesis within the same text. From the 'argumentative square', Adam (1992) proposed a prototypical argumentative sequence that integrates two supplementary elements: the premises and an explicit conclusion (*Cf.* Figure 1). The premises preceding the argumentative square announce the thematic framework of the argumentation. The conclusion presents the writer's point of view and may lead to new questions, or new theses.

Figure 1   Adam's prototypical argumentative sequence (1992).

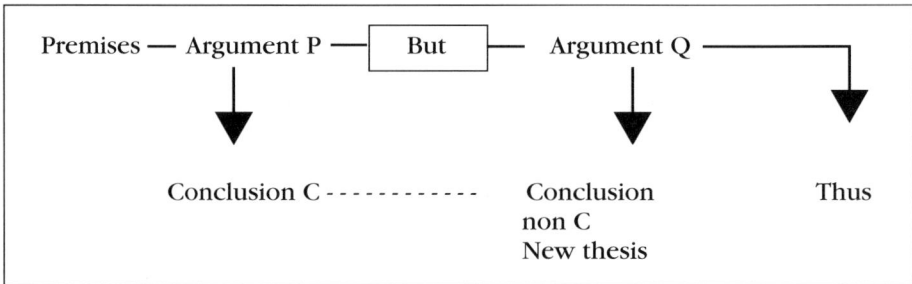

The argumentative square, which falls between the premises and the conclusion, may contain several arguments and counterarguments in chain form. Also, the statements constituting each chain should be coordinated (whatever their number) and lead to a conclusion congruent with the entire argumentative movement (for a description of the different argumentative chains, *cf.*, Gombert, 1997).

Adam (1992) preferred to abandon the concept of the prototypical superstructure (or schema) and to describe instead the formal organization of a text. He proposed that different types of sequences exist, each endowed with its own internal organization, and further suggested that a text could result from the combination of several of these sequences. He studied the following prototypical sequences: narrative, descriptive, argumentative, explanatory, and dialogical, and concluded that the text is a structure that may comprise only one sequence (narrative, argumentative, or other) or several different sequences. (N.B. the elaboration of a typology of texts raises major problems of classification, given the great heterogeneity of the texts that are produced; Adam, 1992; Fayol, 1997; Schneuwly, 1986, 1990). An argumentative text would possess at least a basic sequence that would permit the writer to coordinate the elements in such a way as to render them coherent.

3   STEPS TOWARD THE MASTERY OF ARGUMENTATIVE WRITING

The empirical studies that will be presented here are grouped according to the specific writing tasks given to children. This classification should demonstrate not only a progression in their capacity based on age, but also the fluctuations in performance within an age bracket.

Since the work of Brassart (1987), several types of tasks have been used indiscriminately to study the acquisition of skill in argumentative writing:
1. judgments concerning the structure of argumentative texts;
2. sorting sentences according to whether they are for or against a point of view;
3. writing an unconstrained text to defend a freely chosen point of view;
4. writing a text with a fixed conclusion (the point of view that must be defended) and a minimum of proposed content;
5. writing a text with both the beginning (alpha = fixed position concerning a point of view) and the end (omega = a fixed opposing position) imposed;
6. reorganization of the elements of a text;
7. insertion of connectives in an imposed text, *etc*.

These different tasks all require the mobilization of a text schema to guide the operations to be performed. But, because they all require different levels of comprehension and text production (Hayes, 1996; Kellogg, 1996; Piolat & Pélissier, 1998), the completion of these tasks is associated with diverse degrees of operational difficulty, and thus of success. Given the orientation of this chapter, only the results obtained from tasks requiring principally written production will be detailed. First, the results obtained in highly constrained, semi-constrained, and unconstrained productions will be examined. This will be followed by a review of the results obtained in learning situations (such as cooperative writing, and the performance of a series of exercises).

3.1 Highly constrained writing tasks

Highly constrained tasks (such as the insertion of connectives in a text or the recomposition of a text) are interesting because they focus children's attention only on certain operations implicated in text production (Levy, 1997; Piolat & Pélissier, 1998; Piolat & Roussey, 1996). When writers insert connectives in a fill-in-the-blank text, they are essentially required to understand the text and to propose elements (connectives) that maintain the coherence of the entire text. Similarly, when they compose a text by ordering the statements, they must manage the entire sum of information in order to organize it in a coherent fashion. Young writers do not have to search for ideas, nor do they have to translate them into language. Freed from a certain number of operations (translating, spelling, graphical production, *etc*.) that are costly because of a lack of experience (McCutchen, 1996), these writers are only expected to possess sufficient attentional resources to process the content and structure of the argumentative text that needs to be completed or reconstructed.

Insertion of connectives
Since the propositions of pragmatic semantics were first presented (Adam, 1990; Moeschler, 1989), it has become customary to define connectives as instructions that require an assessment of the type of relationship that must be marked between propositions or groups of successive propositions – or even the overall structure of a text. By studying the use of argumentative connectives in texts by young writers, it is possible to show that these markers are under the control of the argumentative schema. Indeed, certain connectives are pivotal for marking off counterargument blocks, and others, for introducing the conclusion.

In a recent study, Golder (1996) asked writers aged ten to eleven, thirteen to fourteen, and sixteen to seventeen years to fill in the blank spaces of a text with connectives. Their task was to preserve the coherence of the text, which expressed arguments both *for* and *against* a point of view. Whatever the age, the results showed that the connectives (*indeed, because, since*) that did not introduce a counterargument were mastered before the adversative connectives (*but, however, etc.*). From these results, Golder established a relationship between the knowledge of the appropriate connectives to ensure the argumentative coherence of a text, and the capacity to express in a satisfying way the information contained in an argumentation. From the ages of ten to thirteen, the capacity to justify one's point of view – a capacity considered by this author to be a minimal condition for argumentation – was acquired. The markers of causal relationships were correctly deployed in the text. Yet the marking of the overall structure of the text with adversative connectives became increasingly efficient only between the ages of thirteen and seventeen.

Akiguet and Piolat (1996) studied the use of argumentative connectives in adults and children of nine, ten, and eleven years of age. Their principal objective was to acquire a better understanding of how young writers introduce these connectives in argumentative texts constructed according to Adam's sequence (1992). In addition, the authors thought it would be interesting to vary the performance conditions of the insertion task, whose goal was 'to improve the text so that a fellow student will understand it'. In all task conditions, the children were presented with texts containing five statements on the role of television. Depending on the task condition, the activity of inserting or substituting the connectives was hypothesized to be more, or less, difficult. The tasks are presented below in order of increasing difficulty:

1. *Assisted insertion task*: Five connectives (*thus, but, indeed, as,* and *because*) were presented in random order and the locations of insertion were indicated by dotted lines. Each connective started with a specific sentence in relation with the overall structure of the text. The causal relationship, employed three times, had to be marked by *indeed, as,* or *because*. The adversative relationship was signaled by the conjunction *but*, and the consecutive relationship, by *thus*. The participants had to write these connectives in the blanks.
2. *Assisted substitution task*: The same five connectives were presented but the blank spaces were already filled in with inappropriate connectives. The participants had to spot the five inappropriate connectives (these were not signaled in the text) and substitute one of the five choices presented.
3. *Unassisted insertion task*: No connectives were given to the writers and the insertion locations were indicated by dotted lines. The writers had to write five 'words' in the blank spaces.
4. *Unassisted substitution task*: No connectives were given and the locations for substitution were already occupied by inappropriate connectives that were not signaled in any way. The participants had to spot these inappropriate connectives and substitute with the appropriate connectives.

The principal results showed that the ten- and eleven-year-olds used the connectives more correctly than the nine-year-olds. The eleven-year-olds and the adults had the best performances for the insertion tasks. Textual marking with the connectives, notably but, was better employed by the ten- and eleven-year-olds than by the nine-year-olds. For these last, the level of mastery of the argumentative connectives *but* and *thus* did not differ from that of the non-argumentative connectives *as*, *because*, and *indeed*. In contrast, the children of ten and eleven years had a greater ability to use the argumentative connectives than the non-argumentative connectives. The analysis of insertion errors (only done for the connectives *but* and *thus* and in the *assisted* tasks) showed regularity in the choices made by the children. Thus, when they made errors, the young writers integrated the connectives according to a rule, and not in random fashion. For example, the incorrect insertions of *but* were never located at the beginning or end of a text. The children thus demonstrated that they knew that this connective was used frequently more to arrange opposite orientations than to introduce or conclude a text. Lastly, the hypothesis concerning the effect of task difficulty on the level of success was partially confirmed. The two *unassisted* tasks were more difficult than the *assisted* tasks. Moreover, the *unassisted substitution* task was more difficult than the *unassisted insertion* task. The nine-year-olds performed poorly except when problem areas were indicated and solutions proposed (*assisted insertion* and *substitution*).

These results led Akiguet and Piolat (1996) to conclude that the argumentative schema acted as a guide that had been more or less mastered only from the age of ten onwards. The notion that ten years is a key age for the acquisition of written argumentative skill was supported by the results obtained in a similar computer-assisted insertion task using connectives (see next subsection). However, only approaching eleven years of age did the children possess the sufficient knowledge of the functioning of connectives and of the argumentative schema to process the overall coherence of a written text in a deliberate fashion. In comparison with the results of Golder (1996), these results indicate that it is possible to obtain good performances in ten- and eleven-year-olds – and not just in children thirteen and over – using adversative connectives, if they are given a task that reduces the number of required processes.

In view of these results, the low performances reported by Brassart (1996) for an argumentative-text recall task are quite surprising, especially regarding adults. Brassart (1996) studied eight- to ten-year-olds (both good and poor readers) and adults, and the texts were either with or without connectives. The results revealed progressive improvement in recall as a function of age and reading level. In contrast, the presence or absence of connectives had no significant effect on performance. According to Brassart (1996), the connectives that mark the argumentative schema did not facilitate the processing of an argumentative text. The children, particularly those of eight years of age, were passive readers. Yet Chanquoy (in press), who compared the spontaneous use of connectives by writers from ten to thirteen years producing a narrative text, a description, and an argumentation, observed that the argumentative text contained more connectives than the other texts, even for the ten-year-olds. According to the author, the young writers attributed a key function to these connectives in the text presentation.

Recomposition of an argumentative text
The recomposition of a text requires the writer to understand the proposed sentences and to order them in such a way that the succession of statements constitutes a coherent text. A global analysis of a reconstructed text furnishes information about the possible influence of a schema underlying the activity (Coirier & Marchand, 1994). However, the analysis of the steps by which writers reconstruct the text is far more informative (*cf.*, Piolat & Roussey, 1996), as is indicated by the results of Roussey and Gombert (1992).

The objective of these researchers was to analyze how seven- and eight-year-old writers, as well as adults, use the prototypical argumentative sequence in a computer-assisted text-reconstruction task. They postulated that from the age of eight onwards children would begin to use the argumentative schema when given a propitious writing task. Participants had to recompose a text with a fixed introduction (Example: *Children often want to watch television in the evening...*) and conclusion (Example: *Thus, it would be better not to watch television...*), by inserting statements *for* and *against* the concluding thesis (alpha-omega task). On a split screen, the incomplete text (two sentences) appeared in the top half, and the eight sentences required to complete it were on the bottom. The series of statements against the conclusion were introduced by the connective *indeed* (Example: *Indeed, evening programs are interesting...*). The series supporting the conclusion were introduced by *but* (Example: *But, watching television is tiring...*). The conclusion began with *Thus*. In all, the text comprised ten successive sentences, following the argumentative configuration proposed by Adam (1992).

The children were grouped by their teachers according to writing ability (more, or less experienced). Two conditions of text performance were examined: individual recomposition of the text or pair-work. Collaborative writing was assumed to facilitate recomposition in that the young writers who worked together had to agree before introducing a sentence into the text (Roussey, Farioli & Piolat, 1992). The quality of the final text (*e.g.*, conforming or not to an optimal order for experts) and the performance mode (*e.g.*, conforming or not to the mode of accomplished adults) were analyzed by times series methodology. This allowed the comparison of the structures representing the action sequences (Guercin, Roussey & Piolat, 1990).

The results showed that the adults correctly recomposed the text, all using the same procedure. They chose, successively and in correct order, the statements against, then for, and the concluding thesis, clearly using the argumentative structure to guide their task performance. The expectations concerning the children were only partly satisfied. Only the more experienced children working in pairs were able to group the arguments and counterarguments in such a way as to produce a text conforming to the argumentative schema. Moreover, the task was not performed using a procedure comparable to that used by accomplished adults. The young writers proceeded step-by-step, by trial and error, without necessarily starting at the beginning of the text.

Continuing with this work, Gombert and Roussey (1993) and Roussey and Gombert (1996) decided to improve the performances of eight-year-olds, both more and less experienced in written text production. To do this, they presented a task prior to the 'Television' recomposition task. This pre-task was a task of judgment, designed to provoke the young writers to consider the argumentative orientation of different statements for or against watching television. The statements to be classified were those with which the children would then recompose the text. In this pre-task, the connectives were not included in the statements, although they were in the main task. It should be noted here that Brassart (1989) observed that in a trial of sorting/classing of isolated statements, nine-year-old writers were able to group statements into argument and counterargument blocks, even though they produced justifying texts. The results of the two studies (1993, 1996) showed that after classing the sentences of the text according to an argumentative orientation, the more experienced children constructed better argumentation than the control group of children that had not performed the pre-task.

The less experienced children produced texts that did not conform to the quality expected of seven- and eight-year-olds, even though they had first performed the task designed to improve their performances. This finding indicates that they did not yet possess a well structured argumentative schema. At this age, the schema is just beginning to be mastered and cannot be used efficiently except by the most experienced children. This conclusion supports that of the earlier study (Roussey & Gombert, 1992).

The work of Akiguet (1997), in particular, has helped to determine the key age at which young writers are able to structure an argumentative text. Children of nine, ten, and eleven years reconstructed a text of five sentences about television, either with paper and pen (rewriting a text by ordering the sentences) or on computer (*cf.*, methods described in the preceding study). The text had been constructed according to Adam's prototypical schema (1992). Four performance indices were used: quality of the text (*e.g.*, conforming or not to an optimal order), grouping of the statements into argument and counterargument blocks, the mode of reconstruction, and the number of corrections performed by the children (only on computer).

The results showed that the ten- and eleven-year-olds reconstructed the text in both task conditions closer to expectations than the nine-year-olds, there being no difference between the texts of the ten- and eleven-year-olds. Accurate grouping of statements into *for* and *against* categories was accomplished approaching the ages of ten to eleven years, and few children of the age of nine were able to do this. The children of all groups used a different mode of reconstruction than that used by adults. Indeed, half the nine-year-olds reconstructed the text in linear fashion, but without producing a text conforming to the standard schema. The other half made corrections from the beginning of their text reorganization on-screen, but these corrections did not improve the final version of the text. It appeared that the nine-year-olds recognized a certain lack of coherence in the text they were preparing, but were unable to produce the expected solution, thus indicating that they had insufficient knowledge of the argumentative schema. The ten-year-olds made few corrections, and yet their final text was better than that of the younger children. This finding led Akiguet (1997) to conclude that ten years is the age at which children are able to use the standard argumentative schema in written text production correctly. Although the eleven-year-olds produced texts similar in quality to those of the ten-year-olds, they made many more corrections. But, in contrast to the nine-year-olds, the revisions were made at the end of the task and allowed the eleven-year-olds to come close to the solution. Also, at this age, the corrections seemed to result from the identification and accurate evaluation of the problem presented in the task. Elaboration of an appropriate solution led to a final text of good quality. The apparent need in these eleven-year-olds to make corrections could be explained by the amount of knowledge implied in the task of text reconstruction. This knowledge notably permits the evaluation of each step of the reconstruction with the help of an overall representation of the final product. Corrections would thus be prompted by the identification of incoherence in the text that the eleven-year-olds were finally able to resolve. These results on the efficacy of revisions agree with those obtained in the connective-insertion task on computer (Akiguet, 1997; Akiguet & Piolat, 1996).

3.2 Constrained writing tasks

'Beginning' and 'end' are imposed

Brassart (1989) clearly demonstrated the interest of constraining the written productions of children in a task that he called 'alpha-omega'. This task consists of completing a text (and not to reorganize sentences in a text) in which the first and last sentences are imposed (*e.g.*, *Cars are a practical means of transportation.... It is clear that today the best means of long-distance travel is the train*). The writers are required to keep the end in mind, even though a different beginning idea has been imposed. The argumentative and semantic contents of the 'beginning and end' statements are another constraint. These textual markers are potential counterarguments, *i.e.*, in support of the car and in support of the train. Also, in order to respect the imposed statements and produce a coherent text, the participants have to produce and coordinate *for* and *against* blocks in order to effect a change from the point of view expressed in the introductory sentence, to that expressed in the concluding sentence. This task was thus designed to elicit argumentation of the type defined by Adam (1992).

Brassart (1989) compared the performances of children from the ages of eight to twelve and those of accomplished adults in this task. The productions were classed into three categories.

1. The *failed* texts were incoherent and did not conform to the explicit instruction, which was to arrive at the final conclusion. In these texts, all arguments were developed in support of the beginning statement.
2. The *semi-successful* texts were coherent but incomplete. All arguments were in support of the conclusion (*e.g.*, against the use of the car and for the train, but never for the car).
3. The *successful* texts were the most elaborated. They contained arguments both for and against the use of the car, as well as for and against the train (*e.g.*, *The car is a practical means of transportation. Indeed, it is quite fast, but it also pollutes. The train goes more slowly, but doesn't pollute. Therefore...*).

The eight- and nine-year-olds were unable to produce an argumentation by coordinating arguments and counterarguments. Most of their texts were classed as failed. The eleven- and twelve-year-olds were more successful. However, their performances were not as good as those of the adults. Thus, based on these results, mastery of the argumentative schema begins only approaching the ages of eleven to twelve. The alpha-omega task, which was designed to facilitate the production of arguments and counterarguments, seemed, in fact, to penalize the attempts at organization of the eight- and nine-year-olds writers (although these youngest writers were able to categorize the statements according to their argumentative orientation).

A similar finding was reported by Coirier and Marchand (1994). They presented several tasks, among them the alpha-omega task, to young twelve-year-old writers. These children were asked to write an argumentative text, with the first sentence (*Speed is dangerous*) and the last (*Speed is useful*) being imposed. Only 60 percent of the writers elaborated texts containing counterargu-mentation, thus demonstrating their considerable difficulty in producing an argumentative text in this situation, and this despite the fact that, according to Brassart (1989), the character of the task was favorable to success.

The 'beginning-end' task: is it helpful?
In a recent study, Gombert (1997) analyzed the effect of contextual factors on the structuring of an argumentative text when the beginning and concluding sentences are both imposed and opposing. Factors were familiarity with the activity that is the subject of the writing task, positive opinion about the activity or point of view to be defended in the text, and so on. The crossing of these three factors permitted eight contexts of production. Four of these contexts led the writers to defend a point of view held by the majority of children of that age group. The four other contexts, in contrast, required them to defend points of view that they would not have chosen spontaneously. The children of ten, eleven, twelve and thirteen years had to write an argumentative letter to their parents to convince them to let them (or not) do one of the four following activities: *homework, travel in a foreign country, eat candy,* and *drink alcoholic beverages.* To ensure that the children integrated a minimum of statements into their texts, four arguments *for* and four *against* were supplied (for details, see Gombert, 1998). The analysis focused on the contents of the arguments integrated into the texts (either supplied or new), and the text structuration in terms of the coordination between the *for* and *against* elements and the marking of relationships between successive statements.

More precisely, in order to determine whether the use of the argumentative schema is dependent on context, a tool for textual analysis was established from the basic argumentative sequence proposed by Adam (1992). Three types of argumentative structures were defined: (a) well organized texts of opposing arguments, (b) fairly well organized texts of locally opposing arguments, and (c) poorly organized, unstructured texts with opposing arguments. In the first case, appropriate markers (connectives, coreference markers, thematisation, and negotiating markers), linked the arguments for and against the thesis. Two structures in particular characterized this type of text. In texts with dual structures, the arguments and counterarguments were grouped into distinctly separate blocks. In the embedded texts, arguments and counterarguments alternated and formed an 'argumentative chain'. In the second case, the markers of argument and counterargument were only sometimes established, and thus there were interruptions in the 'argumentative chain'. In the last case, counterargu-ments were never coordinated with opposite markers. From these definitions, the children's texts could be classified by degree of structuration.

The results showed that the writers adjusted to the context of production, with certain contexts facilitating the expression of argumentative skill more than others. The most favorable was the context in which the children expressed arguments to defend an activity that they personally approved of (*e.g., Eating candy is a good idea*). In this case, even the youngest children coordinated the statements *for* and *against* using the argumentative schema in its embedded form. Thus, from the age of ten on, children were capable of writing notably elaborate argumentation, similar to that of the thirteen-year-olds. But this performance was not observed in the other contexts, whatever the age.

Other researchers have also tried to determine whether the alpha-omega task, in comparison with others, helps young writers to produce coherent argumentative texts. De Bernardi and Antolini (1996) analyzed the impact of three writing tasks on the structural and thematic quality of argumentative texts written by children of nine, eleven, thirteen and seventeen years of age. The children produced only one text in one of three conditions. In the open task (unconstrained writing), the participants wrote an argumentative text to defend their point of view on the *utility of driving to work*. In the *opposing-opinion* task, the children wrote a text knowing that *some people think it's best to take the bus to work; others think it's better to take a car*. In the context of this unconstrained task, the writers were informed that the proposed theme was controversial. They were not, however, required to take into account the two contradictory points of view. Lastly, in the constrained alpha-omega task, the writers had to take into account the imposed first and last sentences: *It's useful to drive to work... Thus, I think it's better to take public transportation*.

De Bernardi and Antolini (1996) used Toulmin's model (1958) to define the six types of steps -all considered as argumentative by the authors- corresponding to different levels of formal and thematic structuration. De Bernardi and Antolini (1996) noted an improvement in the quality of the written texts as a function of age and type of task. The texts of the nine-year-olds were essentially justifying. From the ages of eleven to thirteen, the writers produced opposing statements in blocks, but the statements were not coordinated. Only at the age of seventeen did the writers produce veritable argumentative texts. Moreover, the performances of the writers were better when they produced the *opposing-opinion* task. This task invited the youngest children to produce oppositions, led the eleven to thirteen-year-olds to coordinate them, and helped improve the quality of the seventeen-year-olds' texts.

In sum, these two studies indicate that the 'beginning-end' task can help children to structure their argumentation in conformity with the standard schema, but that this beneficial effect is not always assured. In contrast to the expectations of the researchers, and in agreement with Brassart's findings (1989), the alpha-omega task did not notably improve the performances of the youngest children.

A variant of the imposed 'beginning-end' task consists of specifying the point of view to be defended (that which is affirmed in the concluding sentence), without, however, fixing the textual markers. In Golder and Coirier's work (1994), the eleven- to sixteen-year-old writers had to produce an argumentative text on 'Pollution'. The instructions asked them to take into account a point of view opposite to their own. This last type of task is closer to the production of a text without a formal constraint explicitly imposed, since only the theme and the point of view are fixed. The results of Golder and Coirier (1994) should thus be supported by those obtained in an unconstrained situation.

3.3 Unconstrained writing tasks

The unconstrained writing task appears to be relatively 'ecological' and allows one to make an inventory of the linguistic tools spontaneously used by children, depending on their age, to structure an argumentative text.
One of the first to study how children deal with the formal characteristics of argumentation in written production was Brassart (1989, 1990, 1991, 1992). He analyzed how children of different ages manage the argument and counter-argument blocks within the same text and defined three steps:

Step 1: Children of ages eight and nine produce non-argumentative texts. In these texts, which are frequently explanatory or justifying, the writers, for example, indicate how smokers could stop smoking, or tell them not to smoke.

Step 2: Children of ages nine and ten take a position and back it up with justification. At these ages, different degrees of textual elaboration can be observed. Texts that announce the argument contain arguments for the conclusion. These arguments are presented in an unorganized fashion, and the children simply list the produced statements (*e.g., it's important to stop smoking; it's bad for your health; it could start a fire; you could die from it*). In more elaborated texts there is *indirect argumentation*, containing *for* and *against* blocks that are not directly employed but simply attributed to others and written in the form of dialogues.

Step 3: Children of ages eleven and twelve compose elaborated argumentation. The texts include coordinated opposing sequences that lead to a conclusion.

Brassart (1990) concluded that children begin to master the argumentative schema approaching the ages of nine to ten, as this is the age in which they are capable of managing opposing points of view within the same production. At the ages of eleven to twelve, writers master the schema since they are able to coordinate the opposing points of view within the same text.

Schneuwly (1988), on the other hand, found that the capacity to structure an argumentative text was acquired late, approaching the age of fourteen. He studied the age of the writers and the use of textualisation indices (punctuation, connectives, anaphoric reprises, and modalisations) according to the type of text to be produced (explanatory or argumentative). Briefly, he presented the following point of view to children of ten, twelve and fourteen years of age: 'Children of school age should not be given personal spending money'. He then asked them to express in writing their own opinions. To help them, a few arguments *for* and *against* were presented *(e.g., Children waste money; They get used to having money; Children know how to save; They buy useful things)*.

Three levels of structuration were noted. For level one, which was characteristic of the ten-year-olds, the temporal connective *also* (a weak marker to connect facts) allowed the children to generate a series of argumentative statements in the service of a general goal, which was to express a point of view. For level two, which was characteristic of the twelve-year-olds, the arguments were written in sequential order, and use of the connective *also* diminished. Lastly, for level three, which was characteristic of the fourteen-year-olds, the structuration of the text was guided by terms permitting the children to announce an argument for a given opinion (*in my opinion, as to...*). An explicit introduction of opposition was marked by the use of *but* or by connectives of concession. The linear or temporal marking of the arguments disappeared. From all of these observations, Schneuwly (1988) concluded that the acquisition of argumentative text-writing skill occurs later (at the age of fourteen) than explanatory text-writing skill (at the ages of ten to twelve).

Coirier and Golder (1993) observed results comparable to those of Schneuwly (1988). Using an unconstrained writing task, they observed that children of the age of twelve produced principally arguments *for* the point of view they were defending. Only from the ages of thirteen to fourteen did they begin to take into account the dialogical dimension of argumentation. The marks of negotiation were more numerous, and the coordination of arguments and counterarguments was made in conformity to the argumentative procedures of connection.

The results of Feilke (1996) confirm, in part, some of these results. The writers, aged ten, thirteen, sixteen, nineteen and twenty-two, produced an argumentation on the theme of *homework*. They had to convince a teacher who was *against* homework that it was a good thing. The texts were analyzed according to (a) syntactic parameters (length of text, number of nominalisations, coordinations, subordinations, causal conjunctions, *etc.*) and (b) parameters of textual coherence (thematic compatibility between statements, and between statements and conclusion; coordination between statements, and between statements and conclusion achieved with the use of connectives, *etc.*).

The principal results showed that before the age of thirteen, the writers produced short texts using simple syntactic rules. Despite the brevity, the texts lacked homogeneity. The succession of statements was disorganized, without apparent semantic links or connectives. Between the ages of thirteen and fourteen, the organization of the argumentative coherence improved concomitant with increasing syntactic complexity. The texts were longer and contained more elements of subordination and coordination. Nevertheless, certain statements remained uncoordinated, causing interruptions in the flow of the text. At the age of sixteen, the argumentative texts were of good quality. Argumentation was developed from beginning to end without interruption of the argumentative flow. The texts included statements that oppose the stated point of view, and these were presented hierarchically and coordinated in such a way as to arrive at the conclusion.

Feilke (1996) interpreted these results as an indication that the capacity for written argument becomes less dependent on syntax (the texts of children of thirteen, sixteen, nineteen, and twenty-two years were not syntactically different) and more linked to the construction of textual coherence. In other words, writers progressively develop a representation of the argumentative text to construct. Little by little, they are able to take into account two opposing points of view and to use a schema to express *for* and *against* arguments. They develop their argumentation from beginning to end, without interruption.

4 LEARNING SITUATIONS

Several writing contexts should facilitate improvements in argumentative writing skill. In this chapter, two such contexts will be considered. The first focuses on cooperative writing situations. The second concerns the types of exercises that children encounter at school.

4.1 Cooperative writing of argumentative text

The advantages of cooperative writing have been detailed in many studies (Daiute, 1989; Espéret, 1991). The act of explaining one's choices to another, or of listening to the explanations of another and acting as his or her guide, encourages the acquisition of the knowledge and procedures required for writing (whether it be pair writing or computer-assisted text composition; *cf.*, Andriessen, Erkens, Overeem & Jaspers, 1996). Regarding the mastery of argumentation, some studies have shown the beneficial effect of cooperation (for these findings, *cf.* Dolz & Schneuwly, 1996).

Using a context of collective debate, Zammuner (1991) had nine- and ten-year-old students produce argumentative requests. During several group sessions, she taught some of the children a series of strategies to evaluate the argumentative orientation of statements (for or against) and to facilitate the coherent presentation of opposing points of view. The children who had participated in these debates formulated better written requests than the others. Their texts were longer and better adapted to their addressees. These children had justified their points of view and anticipated potential refutations. Their statements referred to the advantages as well as the disadvantages of a situation and were coordinated. Moreover, Zammuner (1991) concluded that the nine- and ten-year-olds that she had studied had better scores than those usually reported in the literature.

Such an improvement following an exercise of collaborative writing was observed in very young writers (aged eight) by Roussey and Gombert (1992). They asked eight-year-olds, both more and less experienced in writing, to reconstruct an argumentative text about children and television. The task was computer assisted, either performed in pairs or alone. Only the most experienced children benefited from pair work, and they constructed the texts that were the closest to expectations. In contrast, the less experienced writers suffered in the collaborative writing situation, and their performances were weaker than those of the less experienced children working alone. Analysis of the dyadic interactions of the more experienced children indicated that they had proceeded mostly by successive adjustments of adjacent statements, without having an overall view of the text.

Roussey, Farioli and Piolat (1992) evaluated the difference between peer assistance (collaborative task) and computer assistance (voice messages generated in response to errors in text completion tasks). Children the age of eight and nine, with contrasting levels of expertise in written productions, had to complete six texts (narrative, argumentative, and descriptive). In this situation, the least expert writers working alone benefited most from the computer feedback. Thus, in contrast to the usual finding, the pairs of eight- and nine-year-olds did not have the best performances and exchanged little information about their reasoning processes. Their verbal interactions contained few arguments about the formal aspects of the text. These results and those of the preceding study lead to the conclusion that at the age of eight and nine, children have not yet sufficiently acquired the argumentative schema (nor sufficient metalinguistic capacities) to guide their writing tasks and allow them to justify their choices to a peer.

More recently, a child's skill at evoking the superstructural characteristics of an argumentative text was studied by Schneuwly (1996). He analyzed the dialogues produced by adults and children from the ages of ten to fourteen as they worked in pairs to produce an argumentative text on *the usefulness of doing homework*. The statements were classed and assessed according to whether they referred to (a) the global structure of the text (*e.g., We have to have an introduction and a conclusion; We already have two arguments that go here; We need a counterargument*); (b) the thesis or the content of the arguments (*e.g., What should we write now? We have to say this*), or (c) ways to improve the text (*e.g., That's no good; Let's put that here, it's better*).

The analysis of the interactions showed that the pairs of ten-year-olds elaborated the texts step-by-step, stringing the statements one after the other based on content. This strategy of looking for semantic compatibility in adjacent statements is similar to that reported by Roussey and Gombert (1996) and Roussey, Farioli and Piolat (1992). Only from the age of fourteen on did writers plan and make frequent reference to the global organization of the text and the need to express opposing points of view. The adults, however, worked simultaneously on different levels of the text. They improved the quality of their texts by looking for 'good arguments' and the means to connect them.

These results are compatible with the judgments made by students aged eleven to sixteen (Golder & Coirier, 1994). The students had to evaluate the argumentative structure of several texts. These texts contained three or four statements and either included for and against arguments and negotiating marks (as well as other elements), or did not. The presence of arguments supporting a single point of view (justifications) seemed to be a sufficient criterion to judge a text as argumentative. The presence of counterarguments provoked difficulties in judgment of the youngest readers. Texts containing both arguments and counterarguments were often seen as nonargumentative by these children. These results underline the relationship between skill at producing counterarguments in a text (at about age thirteen, according to these authors) and skill at recognizing a text as argumentative. Indeed, one might conclude that once young writers are able to produce counterarguments in their own texts, they are also able to distinguish an argumentation from a justification in other texts.

4.2 Didactic sessions

To help young writers to compose better argumentative texts, diverse training situations in the schools have been proposed. Andrews, Costello, and Clarke (1993) directed a huge project to help children aged five to sixteen in sixteen schools. The teachers were asked to train the children in the pragmatic or formal aspects of argumentation. The choice of the type of didactic session was left to the teachers (oral debates, working from texts, role-playing of conflicts, *etc.*), and they also analyzed and evaluated the impact of training. A final report (with few details concerning the analyses) showed that training in the formal aspects had had a considerable impact on the quality of the children's productions; training in the pragmatic aspects had had much less effect. The teachers noted that even in the youngest children (aged five), argumentative writing was better constructed after training in the formal aspects of the text, even when the training and subsequent writing sessions were widely separated in time.

Brassart (1991), and Brassart and Veevaert (1992) also trained children in certain key requirements for written argumentation. The teachers ran the didactic sessions, held once a week for one hour, and lasting six months. Two types of training were proposed. The first consisted of sensitizing the students to the argumentative orientation and the search for ideas. The children worked collectively and orally to find arguments for and against many different topics. At the end of this phase, two children defended opposing points of view in a public debate. Moreover, the children analyzed individually or collectively for and against statements that were presented in cartoon form. Lastly, the children sorted *for* and *against* statements concerning several topics (alcohol, smoking, *etc.*). The second type of training consisted in developing the children's awareness of the argumentative schema. Children had to reconstruct unorganized argumentative texts. In addition, they had to find for and against connectives missing from fill-in-the-blank texts. They also had to revise an argumentative draft and rewrite a text following the argumentative structure. Lastly, they wrote alpha-omega texts as well as texts oriented toward different conclusions on the same theme.

The results showed that the eight- to thirteen-year-old children wrote better texts following training on the argumentative schema. This was most marked in the youngest children. From the age of eight years, these children were able to write argumentation that took into account opposing positions, which were well coordinated. Indeed, their performances were close to those of the twelve-year-olds.

Dolz (1996; cf., Dolz & Pasquier, 1994) defended the idea that teaching written argumentation could begin in elementary school and that it did not impose insurmountable difficulties for young students. Teaching must be well adapted to the initial argumentative skill level of the students, and it must be progressive, diversified and attractive. In this study, writers aged eleven and twelve years had didactic sessions to teach them three aspects of argumentation. They were taught (a) the contextual dimension, to encourage the writer to focus on the objective and the addressee; (b) the dimension of argumentative orientation, to help the writer determine the argumentative orientation of statements; and (c) the textualisation dimension, to encourage the coherent expression of contrasting points of view. Following these sessions, the text length and number of arguments were increased, and the texts were overall better constructed. Indeed, the writers used connectives more often to coordinate their ideas. They also took into account occasional contradictions more often. Lastly, negotiating marks and counterarguments were more numerous.

5 CONCLUSION

Does the argumentative schema become operational approaching the ages of ten to twelve, thirteen to fourteen, or sixteen to eighteen? When the research results are considered in terms of the type of writing task imposed, it becomes easier to explain the discrepancies in knowledge observed in different studies and, thus, to understand the disagreements concerning the age at which young writers master the use of the argumentative schema. Mastery of text writing, indeed, is acquired over a long period of learning that may cover anywhere from two to eight years.

To explain the discrepancies, it is no longer relevant to debate the variety of structures of the argumentative text, nor to deny the existence of such a structure (Golder, 1996). Rather, it seems much more useful to follow Coirier's suggestion (1996) and arrive at a consensus within the community of psycho-linguists as to what exactly constitutes an argumentative text. Adam (1992) sufficiently clarified the issue of the heterogeneity of texts (including narrative texts), so that this diversity does not become the 'tree that hides the forest'. To investigate when writers sufficiently possess the argumentative schema – that is, when they have the capacity to coordinate information according to the basic argumentative sequence formalized by Adam (1992) – is totally heuristic. And, as the studies in this review show, research interest in the mastery of argumentative connectives and the modes of structuring information is growing, after long having focused on the linguistic marks of negotiation and justification. The study of the different ways that information is structured in the argumentative sequence should prove highly beneficial (Gombert, 1997).

This chapter has shown how the age at which children attain mastery of the argumentative schema as a tool for the production of arguments and counterarguments is a function of the degree of constraint imposed by the writing task.

This relationship can be characterized as follows. Before the ages of twelve to thirteen, in unconstrained production, children principally write justifying texts that include arguments for their point of view. When they try to integrate counterarguments into their texts, they find them difficult to coordinate. To give coherence to their texts, these writers use different techniques and linguistic procedures (listing of counterargument statements, dialogue to express conflict, production of negotiating marks, *etc.*). Certain tasks also improve the weak performances of the youngest writers (aged ten to eleven) by facilitating the satisfactory coordination of opposing opinions in the same text. These are the following three:
1. semi-constrained tasks, in which the writers are not required to defend an imposed point of view, but are nevertheless reminded that the topic is controversial;
2. highly constrained tasks, in which the writers recompose a text either by reorganizing the sentences or by inserting connectives. In these situations, ten-year-olds were able to articulate correctly the argument and counterargument blocks. Analysis of their procedures for performing the task and the modes of correction showed that the acquisition of argumentative skill had set in;
3. training situations, notably those focused on the structural aspects of the argumentative text. In this case, even eight-year-olds were able to produce texts that took into account opposing points of view. These sessions were beneficial even for the oldest children (aged seventeen), who, before producing a text, were invited to plan it out using diverse techniques for managing opposing items of information (Dellerman, Coirier & Marchand, 1996).

It should be noted that several studies (for reviews, *cf.*, Coirier, 1996 and Golder, 1996) have shown that writers at quite a young age can be encouraged not simply to justify their point of view, but also to put it into dialogical perspective (argument + counterargument + conclusion). Approaching the age of ten, children begin to acquire the argumentative schema but cannot yet use it efficiently in situations of free productions in response to a single thematic instruction (*e.g., Should children watch television?*). In such instances, they are unable to evoke it clearly. But at this age, this cognitive tool can be used in very specific tasks that invite the writer to mobilize only certain aspects of the writing activity. The argumentative schema is thus evoked in an explicit fashion. The acquisition of this schema may be accelerated from the age of eight onwards, with didactic training. This training must be sufficiently intensive to facilitate the writing of structured argumentation in unconstrained situations approaching the ages of ten to eleven years.

How do we explain the finding of many researchers that elaborated texts are only produced much later? Why is thirteen to fourteen years of age considered to be the key age during which the writer will finally produce an argumentation, with true skill only in place approaching the ages of sixteen and seventeen?

In addition to differences in methods in the collection and analysis of texts, a more functional explanation is possible if researchers take into account the cost of the various operations performed by writers during different types of task. The efficacy of guidance by the argumentative schema could be modulated by the availability of task-dependent attentional resources (McCutchen, 1996; Swanson & Berninger, 1996). Progress in the techniques of research into text writing has improved our ability to grasp functional indices in real time (for a review on experimental designs, see Piolat & Pélissier, 1998). The most recent processing models (Hayes, 1996; Kellogg, 1996; Levy, 1997) allow researchers to take into account not only knowledge stored in long-term memory (such as text schemas), but also the functional capacities of working memory. A good illustration would be the results based on text length showing the difficulty of writers to successfully perform the beginning-end task. Children aged ten and twelve produce an elaborated argumentative text of between four and seven arguments, but are unable to coordinate a greater number in a coherent manner (Ferréol, 1997). This difficulty may be due not to insufficient mastery of the schema, but rather to a cognitive overload; that is, management of too many items of information at once (Ferréol & Piolat, 1997; Ferréol, Gombert & Piolat, 1997). It appears that younger writers cannot attempt to manage too much information if they are to benefit from the argumentative schema. When confronted with too much information, these young writers will rely on other textual indices to organize their texts.

Marchand, Coirier and Dellerman (1996) also insisted on the considerable difficulty of managing the many operations implied in argumentation. They analyzed the written productions of eleven-, thirteen, and seventeen-year-olds from many dimensions, such as the elaboration of a theme, the textual organizers, syntactic integration, errors of cohesion, and the presence of counterargu-ments. They concluded that two sources of difficulty were especially laborious: (a) the automatisation of text-writing operations that sets in between the ages of eleven and fourteen; and (b) the mastery of simultaneous performance of all required operations, which is progressively acquired up to the age of eighteen. This type of interpretation is quite interesting because it suggests that psycholinguists must not only analyze the content of written productions, but also the writing activity itself – particularly its cost.

This review of some of the questions currently facing psycholinguists has presented only the research that has taken into account the means by which writers linearise and structure their written arguments and counterarguments to defend a point of view. These studies have shown that, in certain circumstances, writers are able to create an argumentative sequence before the age of thirteen to fourteen years. It is, in fact, possible to anticipate the results of specifically chosen writing situations (*cf.*, Gombert, 1997, 1998). If one's goal is to have children abundantly justify a position, they need only be asked to defend a commonly held view. If one's goal is to have children produce argumentative texts, they should be stimulated to convince their addressees of a paradoxical point of view concerning an activity or topic that is a part of their daily lives.

For a Debate to take place the Topic must be Debatable
Developmental Evolution of the Negotiation and Debatability of Arguments

Caroline Golder & Delphine Pouit
LaCo - CNRS - University of Poitiers

ABSTRACT

In argumentation (informal reasoning), contrary to formal reasoning, all reasons are valid as long as they are accepted by the interlocutor. Argumentation can make use of formal logic, but it rests primarily upon shared beliefs. The topics of argumentative discourse are more or less debatable: there is not only one truth, but rather many arguments defending a position which can be more acceptable than others for a given addressee. To bring the addressee to accept a position, the locutor must produce acceptable arguments and negotiate his discourse. In this chapter, four determinants of argumentative discourse debatability are considered. (1) The representation of the discourse topic: to be discussed, a topic (or referent) must be represented as a debatable one; the representation of this debatability depends upon the subject's cognitive and social development. (2) The existing dominant social positions: argumentative discourses concerning debatable referents are not necessary allowed in all social instances; discourses which denote a minority position are not really debatable for everyone. (3) The locutor's involvement in his discourse. (4) The communicative purpose; whether the objective of the dialogue is to agree with or win over the interlocutor. When the communicative purpose is to debate, children present the discourse referent in a debatable way. Reaching a compromise requires the interlocutors to make concessions and to modulate their point of view.

1 INTRODUCTION

Argumentative discourse aims at modifying the addressee's representations on a specific topic. This goal involves a number of operations whose characteristics are bound by same mandatory constraint for a discourse to become argumentative: because the referents (or topics) of argumentative discourse are debatable, they have to be presented in a debatable manner. A debatable discourse is a discourse in which the speaker presents acceptable arguments (based on common values shared with his addressee), and uses linguistic devices (characterized by specific markers) to present the discourse as a negotiating one. This means that it is a 'natural' discourse, about everyday issues (an opinion discourse) as opposed to, for example, scientific discourse.

In this chapter we will present some of the theoretical elements that bestow an important role upon the notions of debatability and discursive negotiation.

These notions are supported by empirical studies on how the speaker constructs his discourse to convey the reasons behind his ideas.

To modify the addressee's representation, it is necessary for the producer and the interlocutor to accept the debate: the referent of the discourse must be put forward as debatable, it is not an objective truth, but rather subjective beliefs. To bring the interlocutor to accept the reasons behind the locutor's position (so that these reasons may be considered acceptable) the locutor must create a negotiation space. That is to say even, if he has a convincing position on the subject (according to the strength of his beliefs), he must not defend it too strongly in his discourse, otherwise his arguments might be perceived as non debatable, hence not acceptable, and the discussion would be closed.

Indeed, whether dealing with counterarguments ('We adolescents should be able to decide for ourselves, even if we sometimes make mistakes; we've got to learn our lesson'), discursive mode (for example, axiological: 'it's good', 'it's wrong',...) or with an enunciative operation ('I think that','I believe that',...), there is only one goal: to present a topic in such a manner that the addressee accepts the reasons provided to support a given position.

This negotiation dimension is evident in argumentative dialogues in which several positions are directly confronted. But negotiation is also found in written argumentative discourses. In an elaborated argumentation, the locutor is expected to envisage and to present arguments opposed to the defended position, while attributing them a lesser argumentative value. Textual and linguistic means, allowing the presentation of the referent of the discourse as debatable, are quite diversified: expressions of judgment, the modulation of judgment, counterargumentation, restriction, and the specification of the scope of arguments. These different negotiation operations appear in texts by means of linguistic indicators or marks. We will present some of the indicators which have been found to characterize negotiation operations:

1. enunciation processes: we are particularly interested in the distance the speaker establishes between himself and the discourse. This distance varies, such that the potential addressee is allowed a variable amount of space for negotiation. It can be marked by means of verbs of speaker endorsement, such as 'In my opinion', 'I find',... (Coirier, Coquin, Golder & Passerault, 1990; Golder, 1992c, 1992d; Schneuwly, 1988);
2. modulation operations such as expressions of modality: 'maybe', 'surely',... (Schneuwly, 1988);
3. concession operations or counterargumentation: 'If everybody used public transport, there should be less smog and consequently less pollution. But there are also some practical problems. Using the bus does not give the same independence as using one's own car' (Brassart, 1988, 1992; Pierault-Le Bonniec & Valette, 1987).

Yet, subtle operations of negotiation, such as irony and hinting, can be observed, especially in adult discourse (Kerbrat-Orecchioni, 1984). These argumentative 'techniques' have a 'negative' negotiation function in so far as they position the addressee in a situation where the adoption of a given point of view is so 'ridiculed' by the locutor's speech that it becomes difficult for the addressee to defend it.

In this chapter, we are concerned with the construction of the discourse aimed at rendering arguments acceptable, and we will consider some of the determinants of discourse acceptability: (1) The representation of the topic as a debatable one; (2) The existence of dominant and 'politically correct' social positions: argumentative discourses which treat nevertheless of debatable referents which denote a minority position, are not allowed in all social instances; (3) The locutor's involvement in his discourse; (4) The communicative purpose: whether the goal of the dialogue is to agree with or win over the interlocutor.

2 THE DEBATABILITY OF THE DISCOURSE TOPIC

Compared to the topics of explanation, those of argumentation are more debatable. To what extent is an argumentation different from an explanation? First, although all argumentation has an explanatory component, the aims of these two kinds of discourse are different. In explanatory discourse, the locutor explains something, which he presents as a 'settled' issue. In argumentation, on the other hand, the topic is an unsettled issue and thus, subject to discussion. While explanation can be founded solely on causality and description, argumentation needs other strategies to provide it with acceptability. In addition, the status of an argument also differs in that the reasons supporting an explanation are acceptable if they can be proven by experimentation, whereas those supporting an argumentation must be backed by the values shared by a community (Coirier, 1992; 1996).

Some referents are more debatable than others, but it is essentially the representation that the subject has of the referent[5] that determines the construction of the discourse. Topics, which are the referent of argumentative discourses, rely upon the speakers' systems of value. They are more debatable than formal topics (technical or scientific issues), which are not easily discussed as they indicate representations that accept little modifications; the topic is relatively defined prior to the production of the discourse. Thus, formal topics – having their own reality, which is external to the discourse – are not liable to have their definition remodelled by the discourse. A text which describes an itinerary with spatial and temporal relations (you turn left after the first house,...) is not really open to interpretation: in the most cases, readers construct the 'good' itinerary in their mind. Discourses in which formal topics (or referents) are presented follow strictly constructed rules. Hence, topics of formal logic require the construction of non-modifiable representations (at least for adults) since they are bound to reality. In Piaget's conservation tests, there is only one 'correct' representation that allows the subject to say that the pouring of liquid from a small glass into a larger one has not changed the quantity of poured liquid. This is not the case in natural argumentative discourse (discourse opinion), in which everything can be said provided that the listener can accept it.

It is reasonable to assume that under the effect of cognitive development and social interaction children gradually recognize the plurality of the positions attached to an argumentative topic.

The debatability of a topic varies with age level: the representation of the topic as debatable (as a natural one) constitutes a sine qua non condition in order to build an argumentative discourse. For children, problems that should be relevant to 'not debatable referent' are nevertheless treated as relevant to 'debatable referent'. It seems to be established that the negotiation textual markers translating the more or less debatable characteristics of referents, are notably differentiated according to age. This suggests that representations built upon these topics are subject to evolution (Brossard, Gelpe, Lambelin & Nancy, 1990; Espéret, Coirier, Coquin & Passerault, 1987; Golder, 1996). From a given level of cognitive development (around thirteen to fourteen years age), debatable topics give rise (in written and in verbal form) to the frequent use of restrictive marks ('Adolescents should be able to go out whenever they wish, but only during vacation periods') or modulations of certitude ('*maybe*'). Topics subject to discussion are thus presented as debatable: by not adhering to his own discourse the locutor creates a real space for debate. This possibility for debate over the topics depends on the subject's cognitive development level. To consider a topic from different points of view it is necessary to adopt a decentered position. Around three to four years of age, when thought is still *self*-centered, the sole view point that can be adopted by a child is his own: 'There is more liquid in the small glass because it is higher and because it's what I see...'. Sevenyear-old children cannot still be said to be 'egocentric', they start to negotiate their discourse in oral dialogue situations by adopting a distanciated position. Yet, they fail to consider the discourse referent under its different aspects, and especially to anticipate the counterarguments: these appear quite frequently in written situation around the age of sixteen (Coirier & Golder, 1993).

Miller's research (1986, 1987) attempts to describe the evolution of children's argumentation, focusing on whether the given arguments are acceptable or not. The analysis of interactions between children allows the author to describe the development of a collective argumentation: at three years old, no arguments are produced to justify the position adopted (stage of argumentless antagonism). However, at fourteen years old not only do the positions become justified, but the arguments employed refer to collective norms. At this stage, children are able to construct (through three cooperation principles) collective conclusions recognized as acceptable (the acceptability accorded to an argument depending on the collective values of the group). With age, children perceive the debatable dimension of argumentative topics, and present these topics in their discourse as debatable.

The perception of a topic's debatability as well as the translation of the debatability into appropriate negotiation marks, probably undergo further development beyond the age of sixteen. One may ask what is the meaning of this evolution: some adults present referents as being relevant to truth, although those referents belong to the domain of 'plausibility'.

The representation of a topic as debatable is a necessary but not a sufficient condition to produce a negotiated and elaborated discourse; other factors determine the construction of an argumentative discourse. Some of these factors are discussed below.

3 SOCIALLY DEBATABLE TOPICS

The debatability of a topic varies according to the dominant social discourses. Topics concerning natural discourse are by nature debatable (which does not necessarily mean that they are actually debated over). These topics involve the speaker's system of values (as well as those conveyed by the social environment) rather than the physical characteristics of referents. To the question: 'must immigrant children be integrated in our school system or not?' several answers are possible, based on different systems of value. We will observe that this topic's debatability is strongly constrained, in particular by dominant social discourses. Therefore the question will be more or less discussed according to whether or not the speaker perceives the production context as the basis for these discourses (*a racist discourse does not fit well within the school institution ...*).

The producer of an argumentative discourse is not engaged as an author of a scientific discourse aimed at presenting the truth, but rather as a social agent (Habermas, 1987) striving to have conclusions admitted by an interlocutor. Hence, the author of the discourse has to conform to ideological constraints imposed by the social group to which the producer belongs.

The topos, as defined by Ducrot (1983) corresponds to the socially accepted values to which the locutor refers. The topoi include 'principles' that express the practices of a social group, which orientate choices (conclusions) but do not determine them. Topoi allow the progression of the argumentative discourse, while not expressing it totally. The topos is situated between the doxa from which it is issued (the doxa is an opinion which appears as acceptable or respectable enough to the majority of people in a group) and the argument to which it leads. Arguments employing topoi (*e.g.*, 'smoking leads to cancer') are therefore acceptable (but not 'true'), that is to say, debatable with reference to other topoi (*e.g.*, 'yes but it stimulates the thought process').

There are topics for which polemic is authorized, and for which several positions are acceptable. In this case, the locutor feels free to firmly defend a position without presenting it as debatable. For example, a topic such as the right to smoke in public places, for which all positions are socially permitted (in France), should lead to a strictly defined discourse. In fact, one can complain against smoking in public places without mustering the wrath of the public. When the locutor is asked to express his opinion on such a subject, he is expected to voice his opinion firmly (whatever the position adopted), using prescriptive forms such as 'one must', and 'we have to' which constitute nonnegotiable forms of argumentative discourse. The locutor no longer places the discourse on the level of subjective – thus debatable – value judgments (' I think it is OK'), but on the level of duty, or institutional or moral obligation.

Conversely, there are topics for which there is a strong social position that the locutor cannot ignore (topics on which polemics are not authorized). The locutor will have to present his discourse in a debatable manner, thus reflecting the admittance of the dominant opinion. A topic such as the integration of immigrant children in French schools, for which there is a valued dominant social position, should lead, whatever the locutor's opinion, to a modulated discourse reflecting the main opinion of a social group. One is occasionally authorized to hold a racist discourse in some situations (for example, in the midst of certain minor political parties). In such cases, the locutor presents his opinion in a 'negotiated' manner by using enunciative processes ('I think that'), axiologicals ('it's unfair') and attenuation conditionals ('it would be nice'). It should be noted that the expression 'topics with bearing a dominant social position' does not mean that there are no other divergent positions on the subject.

What happens when pupils belonging to different age groups are asked to argue on two topics, which vary according to their level of social debatability (Golder & Coirier, 1994; Golder, 1996; in press)? We studied written protocols from one hundred children aged eleven to twelve, thirteen to fourteen, fifteen to sixteen, sixteen to seventeen, and seventeen to eighteen, whose task was to write two letters (over two weeks) in response to papers recently published in readers' letters and taken from an imaginary newspaper. The first letter argued in favor of the suppression of the right to smoke in public places (authorized debate), the second letter offered both arguments for and against the integration of immigrant children (non-authorized debate).

We noted that when the subject is risky (when the polemic is not authorized), a type of rhetorical caution is observed. When the domain is strongly ideologically constrained, there is a distancing from the discourse ('I think so', 'I believe...'), fewer value judgments are employed ('it is good', 'it is a bad thing that...'), and the impact of the judgments is attenuated through the use of conditionals ('we should... '). Also, according to the initial opinion, positions expressed regarding a socially debatable topic (authorized debate) are defended more convincingly (through the use of the prescriptive 'we must...') than they would be with a non- or little debatable topic. If the topic is socially debatable, and all positions are acceptable, it is possible to firmly assert one's position. An unexpected result concerns value judgments and attenuation conditionals. These marks, to which we first attributed a negotiation function, are less numerous when they refer to socially debatable topic. The analysis of the developmental evolution provides a first element of explanation. In young children, the frequency of use of negotiation markers (the expression of one's opinion in the form of an axiological value judgment, and the modulation of the position by means of attenuation conditionals) does not allow them to differentiate the two types of discourse. The negotiation markers are equally used in the two discourses. With age, socially debatable topics are progressively presented as such: discourse contains numerous negotiation markers. Socially nondebatable topics, on the other hand, are presented under an increasingly less negotiated form. It appears that pupils become increasingly aware of the socially dominant discourse, and do not exert caution when expressing their own opinions: their position reflects the socially dominant position. Indeed, who would dare go against a tolerant position regarding foreigners (and all the more their children)? Most of the discourses produced reflect a (seemingly) tolerant attitude among pupils toward foreign children. It is probably because they are engaged in numerous social interactions that adolescents understand the necessity to conform to dominant social discourses. Moreover, from a social developmental perspective, adolescence is often a 'conformist period': adolescents need to share ideologies with their social group.

In sum, when the referent is socially debatable, it is discussed with a great variety of arguments, and from different points of view. From a developmental perspective, the older children are better able to activate diversified argumentation fields. Thus they perceive the different points of view possible on a given topic, and articulate these points of view in a counterargumentative discourse, or at least in a negotiated discourse. The relationship that exists between the capacity to elaborate an argumentative text and sociocognitive development is evidenced here: to be able to construct a complex argumentative discourse, one has to present some knowledge and the capacity to integrate this knowledge into a coherent thought.

4 PERSONALLY DEBATABLE TOPICS

If the topic is debatable, and several arguments are thus acceptable, the speaker must present the most acceptable arguments in order to convince his interlocutor. There is no one 'good' argument for everyone, but one or many acceptable arguments for an addressee. An argument is simply 'good' for a given interlocutor.

In order to convince his interlocutor, the producer should base his arguments on common values shared with his interlocutor. For example: If I need to convince a Muslim extremist of the illegality of wearing a tchador, I should not base my argumentation on the equality of sexes. This argument is not acceptable as this religious community does not recognize it, and my argumentation will have no effect on my interlocutor. The communicative purpose of the argumentative discourse (the modification of the interlocutor's representations and beliefs) imposes constraints on the mode of discourse construction.

We will discuss here a central issue in argumentation, that of the influence of individual beliefs. Stein, Calicchia and Bernas (1995) studied the impact of individual beliefs on the manner in which an argumentation is constructed, developed, and concluded. In their research the authors asked fifteen- to eighteen-year-old teenagers to resolve conflicts verbally within a determined time of ten minutes. These conflicts dealt with moral dilemmas such as: a pupil who has changed schools mid-term receives on the same day an invitation from his former classmates and from his new classmates. For the sake of friendship should he accept or refuse the invitation of his former friends? The pupils first choose a point of view to defend, and then grade on a five-point scale their degree of commitment to the position they have taken up. They are then paired in dyads (in which children do not agree) according to their initial position. The instructions require either that they come to a compromise or that they find a solution to their disagreement. The main results reveal that the pupils provide more arguments in favor of their opinion than in favor of that of their opponent's. Inversely, they propose more arguments against their opponent's position than against their own. This result is also observed when the task requires that a compromise should be reached, and is particularly pronounced in subjects who are strongly engaged in their opinion. The authors propose the explanation that most people possess more knowledge in favor of their own beliefs than against them. In other words, they have little or no arguments that would allow them to refute their hypotheses. This lack of symmetry is also observed in the content of the discourses produced. Indeed, when the pupils are defending their own point of view, their discourse refers to ideas concerning the topic ('we may smoke because smoking is cheap, it's good I like the taste'). The argumentation against their point of view corresponds to knowledge, facts, or negative consequences ('if one smokes, one may risk lung cancer'). This asymmetry is mainly observed in the strongly involved pupils.

Yet, does this asymmetry reflect a lack of opposition information elements for a given topic, or the subjects will not to use information contrary to their point of view? Voss, Fincher-Kiefer, Wiley and Silfies (1993) shed some light on this issue. The authors presented adults with forty assertions followed by supporting elements, which vary according to their direction (for or against the assertions), to their relevance (high or low), and to the degree of agreement of the subject with the assertion. The subjects were asked to decide whether the supporting element was in favor of the assertion or against it by pressing a key on a computer keyboard. Response time was recorded and the authors found that responses were shorter for elements supporting the assertions than for those that were against them. Furthermore, subjects judged the favorable reasons more rapidly when they were in agreement with the assertions than when they were against them. Conversely, they judged the reasons against the assertions more rapidly when their own position was also against them. Finally, the highly relevant arguments were detected more rapidly than those with a low relevance. The fact that the participants succeeded in detecting arguments in both directions (for and against the assertions) suggests that both types of argument were available to them. Moreover, the difficulty in recognizing the arguments against one's own position, especially when the involvement is strong, stresses of the importance of personal beliefs in the understanding and the construction of arguments through access to information stored in memory. Finally, the role of relevance of information leads to another issue: relevance in relation to shared beliefs. An argument is not relevant as such but only in relation to the beliefs or opinions collectively accepted. This refers back to the socially dominant discourse mentioned earlier in this chapter.

We conducted a study (Golder, 1993) in order to form a better understanding of the relation between debatability and involvement (strong implication regarding one's position). The study was based on two postulates. First, that argumentation can only be elaborated when children feel concerned, involved in the debate, and when they have something to bring to the debate and feel that it is important to do so.

Many studies attest that when the topic is familiar and the children are motivated (have an incentive), even five-year-olds are capable of devising complex arguments and producing logical, coherent reasons for the position they are defending. Furthermore, when presented with a conflicting situation between two persons and asked to take sides with one of them, they are capable of coherently justifying their choice. Even though they may not be able to grasp all aspects of the opponent's reasoning, they can furnish one or two plausible reasons in support of the opposing point of view (Stein & Miller, 1993a, 1993b; Stein & Trabasso, 1982; Weiss & Sachs, 1991). In a natural interaction situation, and when they need to be convincing in order to obtain something, these argumentative abilities are displayed in even younger children. As early as four years old, the justifications provided to support their requests are combined with numerous and diversified argumentative strategies, such as arguments based on the interest of their interlocutor, and the activation of possible counter-arguments...'If you buy me a horse, I will be in charge of it every day' (Dorval & Gundy, 1990; Eisenberg, 1992; Eisenberg & Garvey, 1981; Genishi & Di Paolo, 1982; Weiss & Sachs, 1991).

The second postulate states that the perception by the locutor of the possibility for a debate over two positions is necessary for an argumentation to occur. Thus, to hold an argumentative discourse always consists in placing oneself in relation to a counter-discourse (Adam, 1992) and in providing arguments as well as counter-arguments. An argument can only take place in a debate situation in which the initial opinions of the participants are conflicting or at the very least diverging (for cases where the goal is only to reinforce the interlocutor's support to the thesis defended). The representation of the domain as presenting a strong controversy constitutes an important factor in the elaboration of argumentative discourses.

On the basis of these two postulates we reproduced an experimental situation devised by Brassart (1988), in which sixteen- to-seventeen-year-old pupils are asked to produce an argumentative discourse to conciliate two opposite positions. Two topics were proposed. One was supposed to elicit high involvement ('teenagers alone should be responsible for their spare time / It is evident that parents should be responsible for their children's spare time activities'). The other topic was labeled a low involvement topic ('Donations are the most efficient answer to hunger problems throughout the world / Technical aid brought to populations in distress is the best solution to the hunger problem') (Golder, 1993). We believe that an involving topic, which forces the participant to put himself forward in the discourse, should lead to a more elaborated text. Because the participant is concerned with the problem, he has more knowledge of the subject of the arguments and counter-arguments pertaining to the debate. It seems difficult to be concerned with a problem without having some knowledge about it (we do not consider 'degree of familiarity' and 'knowledge of the domain' to be separate variables; they are functionally tied). This better knowledge should help the participants to articulate the counter-argumentation in their discourse. On the other hand, an uninvolving topic often leads to the use of common conceptions (refer to Vigner, 1990) which are seldom correctly mastered and prove difficult to articulate in a coherent manner.

Three types of texts were observed according to the complexity of the textual organization and to the relevance with the problem: a) *failure* (no arguments for either of the positions or lack of arguments for the final position), b) *semi-success* (lack of arguments in favor of the initial position), and c) *success* (arguments and counter-arguments correctly articulated).

The highest success rate was always observed with the high subjective involvement situations. With a high involvement topic, 70 percent of the essays produced were successful. Efficient strategies are facilitated when the topic proposed allows the reference to an involving argumentative field. To account for this facilitation one simplistic explanation (though worthy of consideration) is that teenagers are often confronted with 'tight' argumentation situations when they wish to go out or watch TV late in the evening (these two topics were very frequent in the high involvement situation). The high stakes implicated in such arguments provide the incentive for the teenagers to find arguments, and especially to come up with counter-arguments, to fight those set forth by their 'opponents'. These arguments were already available for the argumentative production proposed here, leaving only the problem of incorporating them into the texts. Thus, they already possess a certain amount of arguments and counter-arguments that they only need to articulate in the proposed tasks.

The strongly involving topics lead to the highest use of negotiation marks: for example, the proportion of students who used a restriction-specification ('that's only true if, especially in the case of...') at least once, was 60 percent in the low involvement situation; it reached 90 percent in the high involvement situation.

Yet, both these topics (going out and watching TV for teenagers) are topics for which the dominant social position is quite varied: 'a little but not too much'. This intermediate point of view should be distinguished from the controversial social positions mentioned earlier concerning the right to smoke in public places. By presenting his discourse in a modulated manner, the locutor reflects this moderate position. Concerning the low involvement topic, the lack of knowledge the pupils have, or their lack of perspective regarding the social position did not allow them to integrate (in a negotiated form) the different possible arguments, and to reflect the moderated discourses that may be held concerning help to developing nations.

The debatability dimension appears again as a major aspect of written argumentative discourses. What happens, then, in oral dialogue situations when requiring that the locutor be won over to the interlocutor's opinion increases the importance of the debate?

5 COMMUNICATIVELY DEBATABLE TOPICS

If in most instances the goal of argumentative discourse is to transform the locutor's opinions (which requires the discourse to be presented under a negotiated form) it may also consist, to a lesser extent, in sharing one's ideas. In this case, the goal is more to present a point of view with adequate arguments (to share and to put forward the ideas being defended: Charolles, 1980). Therefore, the necessity for debate should bring an increase in the use of negotiation markers: reaching a compromise requires that the interlocutors make concessions, that they modulate their point of view, in summary, that they allow for a negotiation space for the other participant.

How do ten- and seventeen-year-old pupils react when they are asked to argue in a dialogue situation according to whether an interlocutory goal is present (Golder, 1992c)?

In the situation with an interlocutory stake, pupils must debate in pairs a question socially under debate in France at the time of the study: 'Should class on Saturday morning be replaced by school on Wednesday morning?'. The instructions put emphasis on the necessity to reach an agreement on whether or not an experimental zone should be set up in their school for the Wednesday morning situation.

In the situation with no interlocutory goal, the pupils are asked to elaborate together the description of an ideal town and to justify their choices. The emphasis here is the non-argumentative nature of the debate, and it is specified that there is not only one ideal town but several, and that neither is better than the others. This severely restricts the interlocutory scope of the discussion.

As both situations involve argumentative discourses that require justifications, one could have expected a similar frequency in the use of justification markers for both types of dialogues. Yet, the situation with an interlocutory goal entails a higher use of justification markers. Discourses contain several arguments, which are developed and interconnected with specification, restriction, and relations ('it's good to go school on Saturday morning because we can sleep on Wednesday morning, but only during winter periods'[1]). Thus, when the emphasis is on the necessity to expose one's point of view and to reach a consensus, the main process employed is justification. The locutor must justify his own position in order to have it accepted by his interlocutor. Conversely, when the interlocutory stake is restricted, *i.e.*, when the participants were asked to construct a common referent rather than to defend a point of view, the locutor no longer needs to defend his point of view to win the debate. In this case the locutor calls upon arguments referring to common experiences. By no longer referring to personal experience but to collective values, the locutor bases his discourse on values accepted (or supposedly accepted) by the social group to which he belongs (his school). This serves the purpose of involving the interlocutor in the dialogue referent ('School on Wednesday mornings would allow us to rest on Saturday morning'). The locutor allows the possibility for intervention in the construction of the discourse referent ('yeah, I don't care, I get up early anyway') and negotiation becomes possible.

6 CONCLUSION

In the light of the different studies presented in this chapter, it appears that the negotiation process is constrained by various situational parameters. Indeed, participants present their discourse in a negotiated manner:
1. when there are socially contrasted opinions, but also when the opinions are equally acceptable ('smoking should or should not be forbidden in public places');
2. when a modulated social position exists ('television allows to acquire knowledge but there are also other means');
3. when there is a need for cooperation, as in the elaboration of a common referent through dialogue.

The debatability of a topic appears to be a major determinant for the argumentative forms produced. Thus, a model can be proposed for the situation most likely to result in a negotiated argumentative discourse: the locutor feels involved in the debate (and knows the various arguments or counter-arguments that may be developed on the topic). Also, there are several 'socially acceptable' discourses that the participants may integrate into their discourse. Finally, the interlocutory goal to win should not be overemphasized, otherwise there will be no room left for the negotiation to take place.

It should be noted that in order to engage in argumentation the possibility for debate must exist. In writing, the locutor can manage this 'debate' dimension by 'leaving some space' for the interlocutor. On the other hand, in a dialogue situation when an interlocutory goal exists with a potential for conflict, negotiation is no longer an option. It appears that the interlocutor's presence causes the locutor to be cautious: it seems better to defend one's position than to let the interlocutor discuss it, just in case he might be right.

The interlocutor, and more generally the interlocutory situation, plays an important role in the implementation of the argumentative behavior, which is fundamentally dialogical. This situation 'mediates' the relation between the locutor and his discourse referent: not only must the discourse referent be debatable, but the situation must also allow for discussion. Further, for the situation to be favorable to discussion, the subject must be able to perceive its constraints. Indeed, if contextual parameters exist for the textual forms produced, it is because the locutor treats these, assigns a value to them, is cognitively capable of having a representation of the situational constraints (communicative purpose, interlocutor's position, *etc.*) and is capable of adapting his discourse accordingly.

From a developmental point of view, the argumentative discourse can be more, or less elaborated, depending upon the production situation. By the age of three or four, children interacting in conducive situations (*i.e.*, situations where they are motivated to convince someone of something, where their goal is to persuade), already exhibit the capacity to use relatively complex strategies: they can justify their point of view with arguments and they can take their addressee's opinions and desire into account.

Complex moral justifications were observed from the age of five (Dorval & Gundy, 1990; Eisenberg, 1992; Genishi & Di Paolo, 1982; Weiss & Sachs, 1991): subjects provided reasons which were both 'logical and sound' and close to those of adults. However, these operations do not yet pertain to very complex reasoning, and many of the results presented here lead to the following conclusion:

argumentative discourse is a relatively complex behavior which is acquired late in life.

The most important developments at the level of psycholinguistic operations take place at the ages of ten to fourteen years old (Marchand, 1993). This is not due to a gradual mastery of linguistic norms, but is caused by schooling (giving prominence in justifying points of view), and the capacity to socially extract oneself from a point of view, thereby taking into account the hearer. The studies, mostly those inspired by Piaget's work (Berkowitz, Oser & Althoff, 1987, for example), consider that before the formal operations stage (approximately age eleven), children do not possess adequate argumentative skills for engaging in 'reasoned dyadic interaction'. Children are incapable of producing 'convincing justifications'. Conflicts appear to be resolved at that age 'by power manipulation, either physical or verbal, but without recourse to collaborative justified discourse'. This 'argumentative incapacity' is assumed to be related to the degree of self-centering in children (the inability to consider another person's point of view).

According to the 'Knowledge base theory' developed by Stein and Miller (1990; 1993a; 1993b), the emergence of a complex argumentative behavior is tied to three cognitive and situation prerequisites: 1) the familiarity of the domain in question; 2) a certain amount of subject involvement, a perspective of gain; and 3) the possibility to understand and memorize the data in the problem. A most characteristic example is that of conditional reasoning. In one of the studies, the children were told a story that included a scenario of conditional promise. The results showed that from the age of eight, children could produce convincing reasons in favor of the position they are defending.

These different results appear contradictory; this contradiction could be explained if we take into account the conditions of production, the situational constraints. Some of these situational constraints have been examined in this chapter; others should be taken into account, especially those tied to the communicative purpose of the discourse.

NOTE

1   In France there is a debate concerning the most favorable day to go to school (Wednesday morning or Saturday morning). Some people think that the Wednesday is the more beneficial day because pupils can sleep at the end of the week, others think that the Saturday is more advantageous because it permits a break during the week.

Studying Argumentative Text Processing through Collaborative Writing

Anick Giroud
University of Lausanne

ABSTRACT

The aim of this chapter is to point out the significance of using collaborative writing as a methodology for the study of the processing of argumentative discourse. Our theoretical framework is based on a strong link between the social context of production (communicative purpose, relations between the writers and the addressee, etc.) and the psycholinguistic operations implemented by writers. Experimental collaborative writing provides online data as traces of the writing processes that can be compared with the final texts. We show that the study of the data collected (mainly 'metacomments' of the writers and lists of proposed formulations to be written) is a promising method for increasing our knowledge of some aspects of the argumentative procedures activated by learners (of a foreign language). In elaborating the content, we look at how the writers look for and select the arguments according to their representations constructed about the addressee. In planning the production, we examine how the text schemas influence the choices, and which kind of argumentative strategies are verbalized. In textualization, we explore how the question of the enunciative strategies is especially relevant for argumentative text processing. Due to the nature of our preliminary results, we focus our attention on the polyphonic aspect of argumentation, concluding that enunciative strategies are inextricably linked to argumentative strategies: managing voices in the text, adjusting the enunciative involvement, supporting arguments, all those operations being problematical for learners, are abundantly verbalized. Thus we propose a microgenetic study of argumentative writing activity, using collaborative work as a method of allowing the exteriorization of some internal operations.

1 INTRODUCTION TO COLLABORATIVE WRITING

The aim of this chapter is to point out the significance of using collaborative writing as a methodology for the study of the processing of argumentative text. Indeed, it seems to be a promising method for increasing our knowledge in this area, considering the specific nature of the data collected, which may inform us about the online procedures involved in argumentative text production. Thus we propose a microgenetic study of the argumentative writing activity, looking for traces of the operations processed during the production.

1.1 A learning activity

In our frame of study, collaborative writing is first of all a specific learning task: two (or three) learners have to construct and write a text together, participating equally in the production, and being equally responsible for achieving the task (*e.g.*, Damon & Phelps, 1989). The goal is to create one text, by means of interaction. The partners have to exchange ideas, plans, suggestions for formulations, and together they have to solve the problems that arise. Thus collaborative writing is used as a teaching tool: the interactions between peers are considered as a source of the potential regulation of the activity of writing. In the case of argumentative production, working with other learners offers many advantages. It seems to be helpful, for instance, when searching for arguments arising from different points of view, or for specifying the addressee. The interaction between partners writing a text together have generated some studies with different perspectives (see, for instance, Nystrand, 1986; DiPardo & Freedman, 1988; Garcia-Debanc, 1990; Zammuner, 1995), but more generally, they agree on its positive effects on the acquisition of writing.

The main advantage of collaborative writing is to offer a workspace where the learner receives immediate feedback about his[1] writing actions: he has access to how his text (or part of text) is received by someone else. Furthermore, the discussions generated by the activity make him verbalize and negotiate many things: his representations, purpose, plans, and doubts. He has to test his hypotheses, justify his propositions, and make his goals explicit. It allows him a progressively more conscious control and increases the awareness of the processes. According to the literature (for instance, Gere & Stevens, 1989; Piolat, 1990; Roussey & Gombert, 1992), the dialogues created by the activity lead to more revision processes, more critical control, and more consideration for the addressee of the text being produced.

1.2 A searching methodology

Apart from this pedagogical point of view, collaborative writing is also studied by witnessing the activity of writing in itself: the verbalizations of the writers are of great interest, in the sense that they provide a lot of information about their writing procedures. In the context of argumentation, it is highly relevant to know about the ways in which writers cope with representations of the communicative purpose, the profile of the addressee, the text genre they have to use, how they manage to deal with the polyphonic aspect of argumentation. We will show further on how researchers have access, analyzing the dialogues, to some of the argumentative strategies of writers.

David and Fayol, in their overview on the methodological aspects of studying writing production (1996), confirm that collaborative writing only recently has been exploited as a method to collect online data on the writing process. By putting two writers in an interaction situation for a collective writing task, and observing these interactions, the researcher has at his disposal two types of data: dialogues (registered and transcribed) as traces of the writing process, and texts produced as a result of the achieved task. In the dialogues, the 'text to be written' appears under various forms (Schneuwly, 1992): direct dictation (without any comments); 'variations' of a formulation (the successive states of an utterance);

'metalinguistic comments' of all kinds (*e.g.*, metagraphic, metalinguistic, metadiscursive, and metacommunicative), 'epilinguistic' evaluations, *etc*. Two categories of tools are especially relevant for our purpose: the construction of the formulations (Variations) and the metalinguistic activities (Metacomments).

The data can be analyzed according to the questions of research chosen (including native or non-native writers). In a developmental perspective, for instance, interactions between children, of different ages, or between adults, novice or expert, have been studied in a comparative way (for instance, Dolz, Pasquier & Bronckart, 1993; Dolz & Schneuwly, 1996; Garcia-Debanc, 1996), in order to discover how the capacities are progressively constructed. It can also be very useful for observing the effects of a pedagogical sequence on the writing procedure (Camps, 1995). The cooperation between participants, in an ethnomethodological perspective, has been studied through collaborative writing, with interesting results concerning the different means of solving problems which arise: asking for help, using the partner as a resource of knowledge, and so on (see for instance, Dausendschon-Gay, Gülich & Kraft, 1991; de Gaulmyn, 1992).

In the field of argumentation, the methodology has also given some promising results, concerning the influence of the text genre on the processes. Schneuwly (1992), for instance, showed that children are more concerned with choosing the right words, and modalizing their text adequately, when writing an argumentative letter, than when writing an instructive text -where the preoccupation for the addressee is more visible. It confirmed that the nature and the order of the procedures vary according to the type of text concerned. Giroud (1997), following this idea, tries to observe the traces of modalizing operations, instrumental in processing an argumentative text, in adults' collaborative writing. In an intercultural perspective, Giroud (1995) analyses the influence, on the processing, of the argumentative models of different cultures, and shows how inadequate representations of argumentative prototypes provoke 'pragmatical errors'.

When studying argumentative text production in terms of processing activities, there are many advantages in using this methodology: putting into perspective the two kinds of data (produced texts and dialogues) allows us: (a) to look for traces of the underlying operations; (b) through those traces, to make hypothesis about the processing of those operations, their quantitative importance, and their temporal distribution, their eventual combination (Bouchard, 1992, 1994; Schneuwly, 1996); (c) to study how the writing process is affected by different kinds of factors; (d) to work on and with the dynamic of the production.

In concrete terms, by using this methodology, one is able to observe what writers effectively do, even if the verbalizations only partially translate the activated processes. We have been studying adult learners of French as a Foreign Language (advanced level), engaged in a collaborative task of writing an argumentative text in the target language. In order to give the reader a concrete example of the results that can be obtained with this method, we are going to present some research about an important question for argumentative texts, namely the question of the 'polyphonic aspects' (the presence of several voices in the text). This deals with how writers create a 'network of voices' in the text, processing enunciative operations, which seems to be a particularly relevant question in setting the argumentation. From a pedagogical perspective, it might help us gaining a better understanding of how learners deal with this difficulty.

2 ARGUMENTATIVE DISCOURSE AND POLYPHONY

All authors working on argumentative discourse agree to consider the critical importance of managing the different voices for the setting of argumentation. It is well known that in any writing act, the writer has to establish a 'voice setting'. He must assign responsibility of what is being said, choosing, for instance, between 'I think this practice is unacceptable', 'A lot of people think this practice is unacceptable', 'The moralists claim that this practice is unacceptable', and thus establishing a varying distance with the content. He must also choose the kind of relationship with the intended audience, from all the existing possibilities (for instance, 'You must vote for prohibition', 'We must vote for prohibition', or 'Can you accept this terrible idea?', *etc.*)

Such enunciative procedures are part of the 'communicative structuration' (see the Geneva Psychological Model of Discourse Production, Bronckart, Bain, Schneuwly, Davaud & Pasquier, 1985; Schneuwly, 1988; Bronckart, 1996). The management of the different voices constitutes language operations, which depend on the parameters of the production context, especially the communicative purpose. Concerning the production of argumentative texts, the 'voices' strategy is essential for the discursive (rhetorical) strategy.[2] It is about convincing the audience, and activating arguments and counterarguments that must be assigned to enunciators. Therefore, the writer must elaborate enunciative strategies: choosing different plans in order to achieve his specific goal.

The decision making about the voices is critical; it is the base of the argumentative strategy, according to two perspectives: the lesser or greater distance of the writer with the utterances of his text, and the setting of other voices. Consequently, the polyphonic aspects in argumentative texts cannot be ignored: as there is always, at the origin of argumentative discourse, a controversial question on which the author takes a position, there are always (although sometimes only implicitly) two theses involved, and therefore, at least two voices.

Discussing a bioethical, social subject, the texts integrate many arguments supported by various voices (the voices of social groups or individuals). In the produced texts of the data collected, several features signal the presence of the 'Voices of the Others'[3] (lexical, graphical, syntactical marks, *etc.*), and several procedures, relevant to polyphony, are used (concession, negation, irony, *etc.*). We will come back to those manifestations which are traces of the operations of setting the enunciative strategy.

3 QUESTIONS OF RESEARCH AND METHODOLOGY

For learners, language operations present many difficulties. The question of how to signal distance and how to integrate the Voices of the Others, generates delicate technical problems: choosing the introducing verb, choosing the lexicon for the characterization of the Enunciators, adjusting the distance by procedures of modalizations, choosing the personal pronouns, and so on. Thus, the questions which arise concern mainly those difficulties: how do the learners cope with such operations? What kind of linguistic means have they at their disposal to spread the polyphony in their texts? What problems arise and how are the solutions found? How do learners react when faced with having to make decisions? What criteria are used to make those choices? How do they take into account the various constraints (contextual, communicative, linguistic, or textual)? Our present study aims to explore these questions.

We set up an experiment using a collaborative writing task. We recorded the dialogues and collected the texts of twenty pairs of learners. They were students of French as a Foreign Language at a University, who wrote, with a partner, a 'Letter to The Editor' (for a French-speaking newspaper), about a controversial debate of bioethics: 'Should in vitro fecundation be forbidden to women who have passed natural child-bearing age?' (within the dyads, partners had the same opinion on the subject). Then we put into perspective our two kinds of data, texts-produced and texts-processed.

From the enunciative configurations (*e.g.* the 'network of voices') of the final products, it is possible to characterize the enunciative strategies. Then, from the dialogues generated during the production, we can try to find the traces of the processing of those strategies. We are studying the Variations and Metacomments about the enunciative choices, such as adjusting the distance between the author and the utterance, or assigning arguments to the Voices of the others. This leads us to the possibility of forming hypotheses about the ways in which writers cope with those problems. With that purpose, observing the conflicts linked to this problematical aspect of the production seems useful.

We use the theoretical tools of Ducrot (1984), which allow us to describe how the utterances point out the existence of different voices. Ducrot (1984: 204) has conceptualized diverse enunciative levels of the text. First, he makes a distinction between the 'Speaking Subject' which is the empiric producer (the human being producing the utterance), and the different enunciative levels (which remain theoretical beings): the 'Speaker' and the 'Enunciators'. The Speaker is responsible for the enunciation (*cf.*, grammatical first person marks, such as 'I'), the Enunciators design the different sources (the voices spread all over the text) that can be marked out in the utterances.

Observing the imprint of the process of enunciation in the utterance, may provide us with clues about the enunciative operations. Such descriptors seem adequate to argumentative text analysis: the enunciative strategies can be described in terms of making decisions about the voices carrying the arguments, the choices many times verbalized by the partners (Which mark of the locutor is to be used? Are they supposed to say 'I'? Can they introduce the voice of the doctors, the brother...? *etc.*)

4   THE MANAGEMENT OF THE VOICES IN LEARNERS' ARGUMENTATIVE TEXT PRODUCTION[4]

By observing the procedures, we find interaction between different levels of operations: the voices' decision making occurs frequently, most often being determined by the choices of the argumentative/rhetorical strategies – even if sometimes we found that the voices' choice was governing the argumentative construction. The overlapping of high and low level processes is obvious. Coping with the voices is necessary at all levels of the argumentative text production processes; in 'generating content' (arguments and counterarguments); in 'planning'; in 'anchoring'[5] the text by choosing the communicative structure (selecting the discursive mode, managing the voices); and in 'textualization' (assigning contents to specific voices, lexical choices, *etc.*).

We also found, surprisingly, that a majority of the learners-writers seem to be fairly conscious of the enunciative stakes: for instance, sixteen dialogues out of twenty present a conscious and verbalized choice of the Speaker's mark. This activity sometimes generates conflicts, which reflects a high conceptualization of the enunciative management.

We will give some examples of the implementation of the processes involved in the argumentative text production by L2 learners. We limit ourselves to three aspects: at the level of generating the content, exemplifying how the activity of looking for arguments and counter-arguments, right from the beginning, has a polyphonic orientation; at the level of 'anchoring' operations, showing how the choices are linked to the argumentative strategies; at the level of the assignment of voices to arguments and counter-arguments, describing the difficulties and the way they are dealt with.

4.1 Content elaboration

The research for arguments and counter-arguments involves a polyphonic preoccupation. This implies the necessity to refer to the 'intertext' (circulating texts in the world of the learner: a press article used previously as a base of discussion, a collective debate on the subject that led to the working out of a list of arguments for and against[6], a dictionary, *etc.*) In many dialogues, generating the contents leads to a verbalization of the argumentative strategy imagined by the writers.

I shall provide an example, which illustrate how the argumentative strategy is associated with the enunciative strategy. In D1[7], two learners are looking for arguments to support their position (against the interdiction). They find A7, then A4, and then one of the partners suggests taking into account the opposite arguments:

Ex. 1:
59.F maybe it will also be necessary to see the arguments in the article, or the arguments of those who are for prohibition, to tell them that eh... for instance, I think they said that for the child, it's not good because the mother will be eh... they don't really have a mother but a grand mother, and then we could say against that, that the mother will love the child, maybe even more than a woman who is young and has not wanted a child so much[8].

So, the learner finds a counterargument in the discourse of the opponent (*I think they said that for the child it's not good*), then she justifies her suggestion introducing the concept of point of view:

Ex. 2:
61.F because here, we've got the point of view of the woman, and those who are for prohibition very often have the point of view of the child, and maybe we...

She is referring thus to her enunciative strategy, which consists of opposing points of views.

In D17, the partners verbalize a similar argumentative strategy (opposing the two points of view by presenting opposing arguments), but their comments suggest a hesitation about whether this is appropriate. They verbalize their doubts in terms of polyphonic concerns: should another point of view be introduced? Is it the appropriate argumentative strategy? We reproduce the whole discussion about this argumentative strategy, which integrates formal (E140; U153) and strategic comments (E140; E146; U155; E156), and references to the audience (E148; E150; E152).

Ex. 3:
140.E eh wait...if we begin the second paragraph with that, if we begin by admitting, of course there are some risks, but... can we begin the second paragraph with that? with of course?
141.U no
142.E no?
143.U because it is not
144.E because in fact like that
145.U logical
146.E we don't say that there are other arguments, we can just... I don't know whether we have to defend ourselves, because in fact, if we introduce the other arguments, if we say the other arguments
147.U I think we
148.E it will put in the reader's mind
149.U yes
150.E more other arguments like that
151.U yes
152.E they think of both sides, but if we just say that's how it is
153.U I think that for the purpose eh... we've only got one page and... we can't discuss everything
154.E yes we can write
155.U yes... I think it's better if we discuss only the arguments against prohibition
156.E you think we have to defend that? (...)

The suggestion of formulation of E140 is to use a concession form (*of course*) in order to present a counter-argument in an implicit way: the concession mark indicates the Speaker's attitude toward his discourse. It signals that the utterance (*of course there are some risks but*) is not assumed/supported by the authors. The proposal of introducing other points of view supported by other voices, is considered at different levels of objection. There is a formal planning consideration (E140: *can we begin the 2nd paragraph with that?*). But there are also strategic considerations about the danger of introducing opposing arguments. These refer to the predictable effect on the reader (E146: *I don't know whether we have to defend ourselves, because in fact if we introduce the other arguments, it will put in the readers' mind other arguments like that*).

The representations emerging from these comments may be regarded as quite inadequate: as if the use of counter-arguments were logically going against the current communicative purpose (to convince the audience to adopt the writer's position). The theory of argumentation suggests that it is necessary to leave a space for the opposite point of view, a space for negotiation, which will possibly lead to a movement (a change of position) of the audience. But our writers fear introducing other points of view, which have to be reported with the appropriate polyphonic means of the target language, in order to serve the author's cause.

Thus we can observe how a polyphonic choice is processed, generating a formulation which is then evaluated. This evaluation activates other levels of operations: the writers have to integrate different constraints – in that case, formal and rhetorical constraints – and calling for different kinds of representations. By studying the content elaboration, we can confirm that the argumentative processing and the polyphonic processing are almost always integrated into a generating activity. In many examples, we observed that while looking for content, the partners were simultaneously generating an argument and its opposite (correspondent counter-argument). The activity of looking for opposite pairs was helping them in their search for content.

4.2 Anchoring

We will limit ourselves to a single aspect of 'anchoring', which is a crucial one: it concerns the alternative to the Speaker's mark; writers may decide to use an explicit mark of the Speaker, or may decide to avoid any of those marks. Two kinds of negotiation are generated: discussing the option of leaving the Speaker implicit, as opposed to the option of making it explicit; or discussing the selection of a specific Speaker's mark (*e.g.*, '*I*' or '*We*').

A strategic option: what about 'taking the responsibility' for the utterance /text?
In D2, we can observe a recurring conflict about taking responsibility for the text: recurring Variations and Metacomments, and hesitations on the enunciative strategy to be used. The final text eventually presents an explicit Speaker.

The writing of the first three sentences provokes the same type of Variations: utterances supported by a neutral ('empty') enunciation (no Speaker), and utterances explicitly supported by marks of a First Speaker. The conflict remains for a long time – throughout the Variations of formulations to be written – between J, who systematically introduces the mark [nous] (*we, the authors*), and R who systematically refuses or avoids this marking out, choosing to neutralize the enunciation. This strong conflict, materialized by the collaborative nature of the activity, is to continue through numerous negotiations: from J36, the beginning of the redaction of sentence 1, to R423, thus 400 turn takings. We will now provide more details about analyzing the different sequences where enunciative strategies are verbalized.

Let us consider the conflicts opposing the enunciative options.

Sentence 1
In the first part of the sentence, we find the opposition: J36/R37: *we refer / in reference to the article* R45/47 is rejecting the marked utterance invoking stylistic reasons. J finally agrees (with no comment) writing down the unmarked formulation. For the second part of the sentence, J69 makes the same enunciative proposal: *we want to express our.* R74 finally agrees again, opting for the same mark: *we had*.

Sentence 2
The same opposition arises several times:
A/ First attempt: R100: *it is true that it's an act against nature*; J101: *we want to give*. The J101's proposition generates a first negotiation (Metacomment):

Ex. 4:
103.J do we want to say we?
104.R no

B/ Second attempt: J105: *we do know that it is a very ambiguous subject*; R108: *indeed, this is a subject.* J 109 again initiates a Metacomment in order to make the conflict explicit:

Ex. 5:
109.J but do you want to remain neutral or do you want...
110.R no no
111.J do you want to take... because it's necessary to... eh...

Thus she is verbalizing the alternative of their enunciative strategy, staying neutral (avoiding marks of the Speaker) or taking position (by introducing those marks). Once again, she is taking the initiative of the negotiation, but R remains unconvinced.

C/ Third attempt: in front of R's mutism, J113 reiterates a marked proposition, *we, we would like*, trying to justify it (because you always want to give your opinion):

Ex. 6:
113.J we us, we would like... because you always want to give your advice
114.R yes absolutely
115.J as we, we are giving... because
116.R but we are going to make a little introduction, saying that it is true that... eh... people eh...
117.J indeed
118.R it is true that... indeed... indeed
119.J the the...
120.R this subject... creates much controversy, many controversial opinions, no? is it possible to say that in French?
121.J eh... no, indeed...
122.R this subject eh... creates... some critics... creates
123.J creates <writing> many (...)

R118 marks her opposition to this new attempt, by proposing the formulation *it is true that*, associated with a timid justification (*we are going to make a little introduction*), which seems to convince J to renounce once again to the marked option.

Sentence 3
A/ The same conflict reappears, at the beginning of writing the third sentence. Considering the Variations:

> J145: after a long reflection, we / after a lot of reflection on that
> R148: it is true that / it is true that an old woman who is not anymore able to give birth
> J149: it is true that the power of nature
> R150: it is true that an old woman can't give birth to a child in a natural way.

The J145 proposition is rejected by R148 counter-proposition, generating Variations that do not affect the enunciative configuration. R is in a strong position here, she doesn't feel the need to justify herself: R146, as a reply to the marked proposition of J145, asks her partner to read again the text already written. When the reading is finished, she imposes a new formulation, suppressing again the explicit mark of the Speaker we, replaced by a modalizing marker (epistemic mode: *it is true that*).

> Ex. 7:
> 145.J <writing> mh...ok>...we would like to give our opinion on the subject of in vitro fecundation...indeed, this subject creates a lot of criticism for the prohibition...and against...after thinking a lot, we... ok it gives an introduction eh... after thinking a lot about that, we...
> 146.R eh read me the text... referring
> 147.J wait... <reading> referring to your eh... no... referring to the article printed in the paper Liberation on twenty eighth of December ninety three, we would like to give our opinion on the subject of in vitro fecundation... indeed this subject creates many criticism for the prohibition and against>
> 148.R and against... full stop... eh... then next line, we write it is true that... eh... it is true that... an old woman who is not anymore able to give birth
> 149.J it is true that the nature power (...)

Once again, J149 is giving up. However, those proposed utterances have not yet been written down. The two partners keep digressing from the writing to the referent. Then, they change their organization and decide to write a draft, take notes, digressing again for a long time.

B/ When they finally come back to finish the writing of the third sentence, J404 makes a new proposition. The Variation integrates a mark of the Speaker (*we realize that it is clearly against nature*), that now supports the whole R100 proposition concerning CA5, as they were writing the second sentence (*it is true that it is an act that goes against nature*): using R's proposal with only a modification of the enunciative configuration in order to explicit the involvement of the Speaker explicit. R does not reject clearly this proposition, but initiates a new digression, which again delays the writing.

The recurrence of the conflict throughout the interaction is quite spectacular: both strategies (involve the Speaker/erase the Speaker) are in conflict throughout the dialogue. It causes the writers to verbalize references to enunciative strategies (*staying neutral* or *taking position*, introducing enunciative marks of the Speaker, *telling their opinions*, *etc.*), references which would probably have remained implicit (unconscious?) without the necessity of justifying the proposed formulations. Thus the partners prove their capacity to conceptualize (in order to justify), afterwards, the operations processed.

A strategic choice: What mark must be chosen?
Choosing the appropriate mark is often verbalized, in various ways, within a brief comment or a long discussion. When justifying their propositions, a majority of the writers refer to:

1. The text genre concerned, as in D15:

Ex. 8:
12.T how do we want to begin? because we are both of us eh... we are going to use feminine first person
13.I yes
14.T I am
15.I yes, like that, like a letter
16.T yes, ok, so (...)

2. The argumentative strategy to be adopted, as in D20:
Initiating the redaction of the first sentence, G43 verbalizes the option of taking a specific point of view. The partners have already been through a phase of elaborating the arguments, where the construction of a specific, common representation of a character emerged: the aged woman concerned by this IVF problem. G41 begins by proposing an interrogative modality:

Ex. 9:
40.E how do we begin?
41.G maybe with a question
42.E which one?
43.G eh... are the women eh... maybe let's put ourselves in the women's position... of that age... don't we, we women more than fifty, have the right to eh... to want to be mother or to want to have a child?
44.E can we begin like that? don't we...

The first Variation (*are the women / don't we, women*) presents an important enunciative modification, with the addition of a first person mark, explicitly involving the Speaker. What is more, the redundancy *we* and *women more than fifty* enhances the movement, and gives more specific information about the 'profile' of the Speaker. G43's Metacomment (making the enunciative strategy explicit) appears right on the boundary of the two Variations: it describes the enunciative change: *let's put ourselves in women's position*; there is a choice of positioning, of anchoring, to be made, and this choice is highly conscious. In fact, the whole formulation proposed is filled with marks of the Speaker's involvement: *e.g.*, interro-negative modality (highly rhetorical), deontic modality (*we don't have the right*). This enunciative configuration results in calling out to the audience, and denying the opposite thesis. The following Meta-comments confirm the level of the activity. We are in an 'anchoring' problematic and the partners are referring to the question of the addressee (the audience of the text), linked to the question of the official Speaker (the signature):

Ex. 10:
45.G mh... but who are we addressing? the population? or the politicians? or...

46.E the public opinion
47.G yes, yes
48.E we can first write the letter, then put
49.G wait... eh two signatures... we could put eh... we are two fifty three and fifty four year old women... and we want to ask the public opinion haven't we got the right to be mother?

In order to evaluate her own proposition, G45 (*but who are we addressing?*) calls for their representation of the situational context, by questioning the addressee's status. After E48's answer, defining the addressee as *public opinion*, the partners will keep on proposing Variations, which reinforce the degree of involvement of the Speaker:

G53: we are two fifty three and fifty four year old women and we want to ask the public don't we have the right to be mothers
E54: we / we women of / sixty year old
E56: we / we confirm / that it is possible to bring up a child
G57: that it is
E61: who can stop me / who can
G62: who can say
E63: forbid me
E65: who is going to decide
G66: who can
E67: if I / if I able or unable to grown the child
G68: who can decide on my freedom
E69: who can decide on my destiny and my children's destiny

The change from the plural mark (*we*) to the singular mark (*I*) is very clear in E61 and it will not be modified afterwards. E54/56 rejects the interro-negative proposition suggesting a new Variation (whose Speaker's marks still remain strong). E58 justifies her opposition by a Metacomment:

Ex. 11:
58.E because it's a bit ridiculous, isn't it? haven't we got the right to be?
59.G yes, because those are completely different questions... how did you say?
60.E maybe we can write who can... who can
61.G who can tell
62.E forbid me
63.G yes, that will be good... that would be good as...
64.E who who is going who is going to decide (...)

The transformation from *we* to *I* corresponds to a metalinguistic pause in the following Variations: as if the partners were taking a distance from the activity at this point of the construction. Many metaelements are clear (*e.g.*, G59: *those are completely different questions /how did you say?*; E60: *maybe we can write*, and even G63, commenting afterwards: *yes it will be good / it would be good*, evaluating the formulations).

The interrogative modality (explicitly suggested by G41) is conserved, associated with a first person singular. Consequntly, the first enunciative option chosen by the writers, which was the use of a 'enunciation modality'[9], seems independent from the utterance content; the interrogative form remains a permanent frame for the writing (the textualization). Within this frame, they create Variations about marking the Enunciator, and choosing a voice for the utterance. A second level of enunciative 'problem solving' appears.

However, the strategic choice of the mark *I* has not yet been justified. The explanation comes *a posteriori*, through a verbalization of the argumentative strategy. G74 initiates a metasequence about choosing a point of view, which leads her to make her argumentative strategy explicit, previously mentioned in G43 (*maybe let's put us in the women position*), by means of the following Metacomments[10]:

Ex. 12:
74.G (...) so... maybe we could eh... tell about as if she had a similar experience (...) and so for instance tell that this woman... this woman had she has lived a similar situation... she had a child or she made an in vitro insemination and then she had a child she could well bring up her child, and then... she she has a normal life with her family and her child and all that... and so, like that, this woman is trying to convince the other women or those who are against, that they can have a normal life
75.E yes but I don't think it's good to do that to convince the other women to do the same
76.G yes but we're not going to do it... it's not convincing the others but saying that it's not fair to forbid... something that was a good thing for her... that maybe it gave her a lot of satisfaction, that she is happy because of that, that she lived a normal life like all the other women, that her family is a normal family like all the other families and that her son or daughter eh... are like all the other kids... (...) or maybe... that this woman is a woman who wants to do it, and so she tries to convince.

The strategy consists in introducing a narrative sequence, where the Speaker (*this woman*) tells her experience. Concerning the referential content of the narration, two options are generated: the woman has experienced IVF already, or she wants to. By telling her story, *she is trying to convince*. The narrative tool is therefore considered as an appropriate means for argumentative efficiency, since they agree on it. After this long verbalization about the argumentative strategy, the actual writing can begin again.

To sum up: first, within a single intervention (G43), we went from a neutral enunciation (*are the women*) to a marked enunciation (*are we, women*), through an anticipated Metacomment on the enunciative strategy being developed (changing of point of view/Speaker's voice). In this case, the conceptualization of the enunciative change occurred before the formulation of this change.

Secondly, we went from the mark *we* to the mark *I*, with no direct justification. The change occurs in E61 and remains stable. Subsequently, G74, when initiating the generating of the second sentence, will be based on that enunciative option, already used in the first sentence (*who can decide about my freedom of choosing my destiny?*) to verbalize her argumentative strategy. In that case, it seems that the conceptualization of the change occurs *a posteriori*. Disclosing her strategy, suggesting the narrative content, G refers to *this woman, she,* and not any more to *the two women* mentioned at the beginning. It is as if the enunciative choice (*I*) had generated the argumentative strategy, not the other way round.

This is a good example of the inextricability of the operations processed during the text production. Once again, it appears to be difficult to separate the levels of the operations and their relationships.

Finally, what have we learnt from studying verbalizations of the choice of the Speaker's mark? Processing this operation, the partners are calling for three types of representations: they are using references to the text genre concerned and its conventions; they are verbalizing enunciative strategies which seem to them to correspond to the proposed formulations; and they are verbalizing their argumentative strategies. Several times we were surprised, when studying the Metacomments, by the high level of conceptualization of the activity. The necessity to explain and justify, during the conflicts, implies an effort to make the operations conscious: de facto, the Comments themselves seem to play an important role in constructing the writing.

In addition, we noticed once more the interaction between the operations: the 'anchoring' choice is a complex global processing whose functioning is hard to describe. The Speaker's mark choice is also strongly linked with the choice of mentioning or not the addressee, with the problem of referring more, or less to the situational context (all operations being part of the anchoring process). So aspects other than those presented here should be integrated in the discussion.

However, our partial study of the anchoring processing leads us to some reflections. First of all, let us keep in mind that anchoring operations are very often verbalized: either in choosing the enunciative modality (a Speaker?), an allocutary mark (a reference to the addressee?), or when presenting more, or less explicitly the referent (the level of implicit content?). The problems are very often discussed in two ways: a conflicting way (two conflicting propositions are in competition), and a collaborative way (adjusting the representations linked to the parameters of the situation, in order to agree about a common image of the addressee, the social context, the communicative purpose).

In fact, only three or four dialogues do not present any verbalizations of anchoring choices. The partners, in these cases, begin the writing without wondering about the subject: the proposed formulations are not questioned on the enunciative level, as if it were obvious. T18, for instance, is surprising: we were expecting that the choice of a very specific enunciative option (a direct call for the reader, by using recurring injunctive modalities) would result from a negotiation. The absence of any Metacomment on the subject suggests the hypothesis that the enunciative configuration used was so obvious to the partners that it did not need to be discussed.

Secondly, we want to keep in mind that the choices, as we can observe them in studying the verbalizations, are more often achieved by agreeing on common features of the parameters of the situation: the Metacomments help partners to precise and adjust representations which are to determine choices. In addition to this problem of agreeing on appropriate representations, the problem of agreeing on appropriate tools (enunciation tools) has to be solved.

So it seems that in dealing with argumentation, the learners are regularly faced with anchoring choices.

4.3 Managing the 'Voices of the Others'

Another aspect of the enunciative operations is keeping the writers busy: they are faced (in an argumentative text more than in others) with the problem of assigning specific voices to arguments or counterarguments. They can choose between two general options: introducing the 'doxa' voice (the common opinions of society, *people*, *we*, designating nobody in particular), or a specific Secondary Enunciator (a specific social group: the doctors, the woman, the opponents, the media, or an individual character).

Let us point out first that this type of operation is more often visible through the Variations than through the Metacomments. This is understandable, perhaps, considering the more 'technical' nature of the difficulties to work out: *e.g.*, name the Enunciator 2, find the adequate verb for introducing the reported discourse,[11] choose the appropriate modality, *etc*. The partners approach the problem by testing with the Variations the (limited) possibilities of supporting arguments. The extent and the frequency of the lists of Variations give us indications of the degrees of difficulty experienced by the writers.

A longitudinal study of some dialogues provides interesting results. We found comments confirming that the assignment of utterances to Secondary Enunciators is not a random activity; on the contrary, it is an activity controlled by the argumentative strategy. We will go through two eventualities: the assignment of an argument (in favor of the writer's thesis) and of a counterargu-ment (against the writer's thesis).

The polyphonic management of the arguments
In D14, the will to use the doctor's voice is verbalized right from the beginning of the content elaboration (E51: *we must also listen to the doctor's advice*). This comment concerns both the writers (for the research of arguments) and the readers (who will listen/be informed of the opinions of the doctors). This voice, then, will be reported in the text,[12] functioning as an authority argument: Sentences 11 and 12 result from this choice.

The study of the writing of these two sentences informs us about the chronological aspect of the operations. Designating the Enunciator (the voice of the doctors) is the first choice, next is the choice of the Introducing Verb, then the choice for the content of the argument supported (thus matching the syntax order).

In Sentence 11, the polyphonic implementation does not seem to generate major problems, other than the negation of the verb.

Ex. 13:
295. E eh... from the medical point of view, we can see
296. D yes now I go already to second...
297. E yes <writing> medical>
298. D the doctors
299. E it is not
300. D we can already put the doctors the doctors
301. E is it not sure?
302. D yes... the doctors advise advise... advise?
303. E mhmh... don't advise, rather
304. D yes don't advise...
305. E <writing>... have... children...
306. D a pregnancy or have children
307. E mhmh... at this age...>
308. D for the dangers they pose for the mother as much as for the mother as for the child...
309. E <writing>... mhmh... the mother... as for the child...>

This passage illustrates the beginning of the writing of Sentence 11. The comments of the partners performing this activity proviede us with interesting clues about the way the language operations are processed. For instance, we can observe that the Enunciator is proposed in a previous formulation, when the writers do not yet know what is going to be enunciated: (D298/D300: *the doctors / we can already put the doctors*).

It is also worth noting that the option chosen concerning this enunciative modality is not questioned afterwards. The Introducing Verb proposed determines the choice of Related Reported Discourse. The Variations produced here concern only the assertive/negative modality (D302: *advise* / E303: *don't advise*). The process of writing appears as a meticulous construction with visible chronology: choosing the Enunciator, then choosing the kind of reported discourse, after which begins the textualization of the argument itself. The choice of the Enunciator results in a strategic decision, which is higher in the hierarchy of operations.

The same movement is visible in Sentence 12, although in that case, the writing generates more difficulties, resulting in many lexical Variations of the Enunciator and the Introducing Verb. It begins with a proposition of E309, whose Metacomment seems to confirm what has just been said: *and also we can take as an argument the fact that the other doctors refused*. This comment looks very explicit: it is verbalizing a strategy, which consists in introducing a Voice of the Others. The specific (and difficult, for learners) processing of this operation creates numerous lexical Variations concerning the Enunciator:

D310: one has testified / there has been a testimony
E311: there is in England / the English doctors
D312: Professor Craft, an eminent expert at London Fertility
D314: the professor's staff
E315: the whole staff
D316: the doctor / the first / the English doctor that she
D318: he
D320: the first doctor who saw her
D324: the doctors who had
E325: the English doctor
D326: who had seen her before

This long list is proof of the difficulty writers meet in trying to establish the right voice. We are interpreting the first three Variations as metalinguistic marks of the argumentative strategy: the aim is to make an authority voice speak with a strong social image, whose opinions have to be trusted. The plan is to present a testimony whose content is less important than the fact that there is a testimony. Through these Variations, the partners try to individualize the Enunciator, specifying more and more: from a defined group (E311: profession and nationality) to an individual subject (D312 gives his name, his title, adding an esteemed socio-professional qualification which enhances the efficiency of the authority argument: *an eminent expert*). D314 then comes back to a collective determination (*the professor's staff*). It seems that the partners are testing the effect of the different options on each other. The writing is going on through the negotiation.

A second type of Variation emerge, which concerns the choice of the Introducing Verb: *testify/forbid/refuse* are both metalinguistic verbs, both potentially performative, both indicators for the Related Reported Discourse. Therefore, the

Variation does not concern the kind of Reported Discourse to be used, which was decided long before (in E51) with regard to the argumentative strategy: using an authority argument. The partners did not suggest neutral verbs –such as 'to explain', for instance – which would have focused on the content of the Reported Discourse. They are only concerned with the 'Saying' [Le Dire], the act of enunciating produced by prestigious characters.

Example D14 illustrates a kind of mechanism which is originated by the choice of a strategy that we can try to reformulate: we will resort to an authority argument, we will call on the doctor's help. From this choice, a whole series of operations are intitiated where new choices are necessary (determining the Enunciator, selecting the Introducing Verbs, choosing the verb modality (negation/assertion/interrogation), choosing the temporal mode, *etc.*). The negotiations generated by the activity give us partial access to the functioning of this mechanism: we note that all of the decisions to be made at the level of the textualization are determined by the underlying choice of the strategy (argumentative *and* polyphonic).

The polyphonic management of the counterarguments
Studying the introduction of counterarguments in the texts leads to the same reflections. In different dialogues, we found the traces, upstream, of making decisions about an argumentative strategy. Take for instance D11: *introduce an argument from those who are in favor of IVF*, which indeed implies a polyphonic enunciative strategy, being formulated in such a way. The partners are faced with the problem of how to do, to which they react by suggesting enunciative solutions: begin with a question / quote a sentence / mention the addressee you are opposing. Nevertheless, the polyphonic option has been decided already.

This leads us to an important aspect of the dynamic of the processing: high level strategic choices create new constraints for writers, at each level of the operations (content elaboration, planning, communicative structuration, textualization, and revision).

We will develop a single example of the enunciative managing of counterarguments, with D1, where the operation is causing many difficulties. As in many other dialogues, the partners for T1 have stated in the content elaboration phase their wish to introduce counter-arguments (F59). The idea is recalled in initiating the writing of Sentence 3, by C387's proposition: *everybody speaks about the child <long pause> but isn't it probable that such a woman loves....*This formulation will function as a frame, an argumentative and enunciative frame, for the writing of Sentences 3 and 4 (Sentence 3 presenting the counter-argument, Sentence 4 refuting it).

In Sentence 3, the problem becomes how to assign a voice to the counterargument (CA2). A long list of Variations show that the two partners have great difficulty in making the choices. In order to pass from *everybody speaks about the child*, the first formulation proposed, to *those who claim for the prohibition are worrying about the fact the children might suffer from a mother who is too old*, the last formulation written, the authors must process a series of operations that illustrate very well what textualization is. The primitive utterance *everybody speaks about the child* contains the three areas of difficulty the writers have to face, materialized by four lots of Variations:
1. To formulate the Enunciator 2: *everybody / those who are for the prohibition / those who represent this interdiction / those who claim for this interdic-

tion / those who claim for the interdiction / those who speak / those who plan.
2. To formulate the verb for introducing reported discourse: they temporarily keep the verb *to speak*, then they add a second verb, *to worry*, ending with the suppression of the first one.
3. To formulate the reported content: (1) with the verb *to speak: about the child / always about the child who will be disadvantaged with a mother who is too old / about children disadvantaged by / about children suffering from a life with a mother who is too old / only about children*; (2) with the verb *to worry: that their children / her child / of their children / only of their children / that their children suffer from a mother who is too old / only / on / to / to their children / that the children suffer from a mother who is too old / to the children and their happiness / that the little kids.*
4. To adopt the adequate syntax, according to the different considered formulations. On one hand, the construction of the verb *to worry* generates some hesitations about the appropriate syntactical connection (*worry about / to / of / on / towards*). On the other hand, the two verbs in French (for Introducing Reported Discourse: *to speak* and *to worry*) are competitive: they generate repetitions of the word children.

We will not go further on in the description, which implies more details based on the French language. We simple want to stress that the attempt for textualizing the sentence can be considered to have failed: the last formulation, syntactically inappropriate, does not satisfy the writers, who seem aware of not having been successful in solving the problem:

Ex. 14:
440.F a bit cold... that the children suffer from a woman who is too old... maybe it is... find another word
441.C well we can eh maybe we can go on and look for it, the exact structures, afterwards

The C441 comment (*look for the exact structures afterwards*) is a way of getting out of the dead end. In fact, no more allusion will be made in the dialogue to modify the writing of Sentence 3. But in the produced text, the Variation *only speak about the children* has been crossed out. These different movements clearly reveal a number of difficulties the writers have to face: they have to pay attention to all kinds of constraints (syntactical, textual, pragmatical, enunciative) and they cannot do it simultaneously. That is why the construction of a sentence may take a long time, untill the revision phase.

In the end, we realize that, in order to go from *everybody speak about the children* to the utterance finally written, the two partners processed multiple operations of textualization, more, or less interdependent from each other. We observe a big difference in expressing subjectivity between the two ends of the chain: in the final sentence, the characterization of Enunciator 2 is more specific, and it presupposes the existence of the opposite camp. The voice of 'doxa': *everybody*, previously selected, is transformed into the voice of a limited group, *those who claim for the interdiction*. By restricting and weakening the Enunciator, the writers make it clearer that the Speaker is not supporting the counterargument.

The same movement (increasing subjectivity) is clear for the Introducing Verb: from the most neutral verb (*to speak*) to a verb expressing feelings (*to worry*).

This latter verb, being used as an Introducing Verb, causes problems of syntactical construction, even for native writers. Finally, the modification realized on the formulation of the counterargument seems to be linked to the writers' worry of being more specific (verbalized by F436: *because like that, (...) it is clear why they are suffering*). They can refute CA2 with A2 only if they stress it.

As in the previous examples, the argumentative and enunciative structure is set upstream (*everybody speaks about the children; but isn't it probable that...?*) and determines the other operations. It is a polyphonic strategy: the counter-argument is to be supported by a 'Voice of the Others', in order to be refuted by the voice (highly modalized) of the Enunciator 1 (*e.g.*, the Speaker) and it was already present in F59.

We could go on mentioning examples illustrating the processing of assigning voices to the utterances. They are numerous and more often than not show the choices processed under the control of an argumentative strategy, sometimes verbalized during the task, which is determined by the representations of the writers. We saw how these representations first concerned some parameters of the situation of production (references to the addressee, to the newspaper, and to the text genre and its conventions, are verbalized). Secondly, they concerned the referential content (the position of the partners, for or against, radical or moderate, consensual or divergent, the degree of personal implication, being more or less concerned by the question of IVF, the knowledge of the writer, and so on).

5 CONCLUSION

In conclusion, we think that this study increases our knowledge about the processing of argumentative texts by learners. Collaborative writing methodology offers much information about the operations in process. However, its great interest lies in materializing the dynamic of the processing. It shows that the different levels of operations, as defined by models of production (Hayes & Flower, 1980; Bronckart *et al.*, 1985; Bronckart, 1996) remain theoretical. In fact, they often function simultaneously, and their articulation is very complex. Considering again the questions we were proposing, we are able to provide partial answers. As two partners are working out the writing task, the activity leads to two possibilities: either to conflict, or to collaborative interaction, both being observable in the dialogues.

The polyphonic work is controlled by the argumentative strategy, often verbalized previous to the writing. The problem solving can be seen as going through several steps: (a) becoming aware of the problem (conceptualizing the choices); (b) taking in account the different constraints of the production situation; (c) using criteria directly determined by their representations of the production situation; (d) mastering the polyphonic instruments, considering that the learners have a limited range of tools, hesitate, and keep on testing them in the Variations they produce.

The dynamic aspect of the data highlights an important feature of the processing. The three areas we developed (generating the content, anchoring, and assigning the voices) are fully integrated. The polyphonic work we set out to describe is made of interacting procedures at different levels, which we detailed: choosing the speaker's mark, choosing the enunciative modalities, and choosing the Voices of the Others, being narrowly linked to the textualization choices (syntax, connections, lexicalization), and the argumentative strategy choices.

We discovered specific procedures for the elaboration of the content, based either on searching for opposite pairs of arguments and counter-arguments, or on searching for counterarguments first in order to be able to refute them. During the writing, numerous enunciative choices are verbalized, evaluated, and negotiated, with the argumentative purpose in mind: it seems that, for a majority of the learners studied, the activity of argumentation is basically a polyphonic activity, whatever the culture of origin.

The advantages of collaborative writing methodology are numerous for our purpose. However, we are conscious of its limitations. We have underlined how the verbal interaction of the writers modified the dynamic of the processing, and we know that our observations depend on the verbalizations of the partners. What is verbalized is a very small part of what is going on. Nevertheless, this partial piece of information allows us gain a better understanding of the processing of the argumentative text, providing clues about how two writers cope with it. The research should be extended to more aspects of the writing procedures, from a qualitative and quantitative perspective.

ANNEX 1

Texts produced quoted in the chapter, with their approximate translation (keeping as faithfully as possible the original style, including errors).

T1

Non à l'interdiction
(1) Heureusement nous vivons dans une société où la liberté individuelle a une grande valeur. (2) Depuis des dixaines d'années les femmes ont lutté pour le droit d'avortement mais actuellement on est de nouveau en train d'augmenter les restrictions de leur liberté en interdisant la technique de fécondation in vitro pour les femmes ménopausées. (3) Ceux qui proclament cette interdiction s'inquiètent que les enfants souffrent d'une mère trop agée. (4) Mais est-ce que ce n'est pas probable qu'une femme qui prend les risques d'un accouchement à l'âge de 50 ans soit la meilleure mère par rapport aux mères qui ont leurs enfants à cause d'un 'accident'. (5) D'ailleurs nous trouvons beaucoup de petits éduqués par leur grands-parents ce qui ne choque pas les défenseurs de l'interdiction.
(6) Devrons-nous pas interdire aux hommes de devenir père à l'âge de 50 ans?

No to prohibition
Happily we live in a society where individual liberty is highly valued. For several decades, women have struggled for the right of abortion but at present we are once again in the process of increasing the restrictions of their freedom by prohibiting the technique of in vitro fecundation for menopausal women. Those who call for this prohibition are worried that the children will suffer from having a mother who is too old. But isn't it probable that a woman who takes the risk of giving birth at the age of 50 would be a better mother compared to those mothers who have their children as a result of an 'accident'. We find a lot of kids brought up by their grand parents which does not shock those in favor of prohibition. Shouldn't we prohibit men over 50 from becoming fathers?

T2

Non à l'interdiction!
(1) En référence à l'article paru dans le journal 'Libération' le 28 décembre 1993, nous aimerions donner notre avis sur le sujet de la fécondation 'in vitro'. (2) En effet, ce sujet suscite beaucoup de critiques pour l'interdiction et contre.
(3) Nous sommes de l'avis que cette découverte est très importante parce qu'elle peut permettre aux hommes et plus particulièrement aux femmes de mieux organiser leur vie. (4) Prenons une femme qui, à trente ans, n'a pas eu la chance de trouver un partenaire juste et qui se trouve dans un état où elle est presque obligée de fonder une famille et d'avoir des enfants. (5) Pourquoi est-elle obligée? (6) C'est bien la nature qui la soumet à un délai restreint pour pouvoir accoucher. (7) Alors, pourquoi devons-nous être contre la fécondation 'in vitro'? (8) Regardons les avantages que cette méthode peut nous apporter! (9) D'abord, cela donne à un couple un délai plus large pour fonder une famille. (10) Puis les deux partenaires peuvent profiter de leurs loisirs et de leur temps libre. (11) Et enfin, c'est ce qui leur permet de mieux s'engager dans leurs domaines professionnels. (12) Plus tard, cela peut aussi attribuer à une bonne éducation de l'enfant.
(13) Tout de même, il ne faut pas abuser de cette possibilité. Des lois restrictives devraient être crées.

No to prohibition!
Referring to the article which appeared in the paper 'Libération' on 28th decembre 1993, we would like to give our opinion on the subject of 'in vitro' fecundation. Indeed this subject creates a lot of criticism for the prohibition and against it.

We are of the opinion that this discovery is very important because it can allow men and more particularly women to organize their lives better. Let's take a woman who at thirty years old, did not have the good luck to find the right partner and who finds herself in a situation where she is almost obliged to start a family and have children. Why is she obliged? It really is nature which submits her to a fertility time limit. So why must we be against in vitro fecundation? Let's look at the advantages which this method can bring us! First of all, it gives a couple more time to start a family. Then both partners can profit from their leisure and their free time. And finally, it is what allows them to be more involved in their professional fields. Later, this can also attribute to a good education of the child.

All the same, one must not abuse this possibility. Restrictive laws should be created.

T14

(1) Suite à la publication dans le journal 'Libération' d'un reportage consacré au cas exeptionnel d'une femme britannique de 59 ans qui a accouché de jumeaux, l'opinion publique commence à se poser des questions.
(2) Nous personnellement, nous sommes restés choqués par ce cas. (3) Premièrement, nous n'approuvons pas l'action de la mère. (4) On a l'impression qu'elle avait voulu les enfants uniquement pour elle-même. (5) Après avoir décidé de consacrer sa vie à sa carrière, à la fin elle a compris qu'il lui manquait qchose. (6) Ces réaction égoïstes doivent être mises en cause.

(7) A quel point une femme de 60 ans, peut-elle se charger de l'enfant? (8) A-t-elle assez d'énergie pour l'élever? (9) Par rapport à l'enfant, on ne sait pas comment il sera vu par son entourage? (10) Ca ne va pas être facile, car il y a la différence de l'âge très grande avec sa mère et comment supporter les réactions de ses camarades. (11) Du point de vue médical, les médecins ne conseillent pas d'avoir les enfants à cet âge à cause du danger que cela présente autant pour la mère que pour l'enfants. (12) En plus, le médecin anglais qui l'avait vu avant, le lui avait refusé. (13) Bien sûr, le cas peut être considéré comme une réussite de la médecine. (14) Mais si on permettait ça, on devrait aussi accepter les demandes des femmes plus âgées.
(15) Le cas cité va contre les règles morales qui font partie de nos habitudes. (16) Il faudrait pas laisser trop aller les décisions brusques car cela pourait amener l'anarchie.
(17) Quand on est dans la situation de choisir si on va avoir un enfant, on doit pas prendre des décisions à la légère. (18) Il faut pas seulement prendre en compte les satisfactions personnelles, mais penser aussi à l'avenir de l'enfant. (19) La société devrait porter la responsabilité d'imposer les limites à ces actions.

Following the publication in the paper 'Libération' of a report about an exceptional case of a 59 year old british woman who gave birth to twins, public opinion is beginning to ask questions.

We personally were shocked by this case. First of all, we don't approve the action of the mother. One has the impression that she wanted these children only for herself. After having decided to dedicate her life to her career, finally she understood that she was missing something. This egotistical reaction must be questionned.

To what extent can a 60-year-old woman look after a child? Does she have enough energy to bring them up? As for the child, one doesn't know how he/she will be seen by his/her peers? That is not going to be easy, seeing the age difference between the mothers; will the child be able to bear the reactions of his friends?

From the medical point of view, doctors do not advise childbirth at this age because of the danger which this presents as much for the mother as for the child. In addition, the English doctor consulted in the first place had refused her the procedure.

Of course, the case can be considered as a success for medicine. But if one allows it in the first place, one should also accept the demands of older women.

The case cited goes against moral rules which are part of our customs. One shouldn't embark upon sudden decisions because this could bring anarchy.

The decision to have a child should not be taken lightly. One must not only take into account personal satisfactions, but also think of the future of the child. Society should take the responsibility of imposing limits on these actions.

T15

Non à l'interdiction!
Je suis contre la loi qui interdit la technique de fécondation in vitro pour les femmes âgées.

Premièrement on a déjà assez de lois et je pense que chaque loi empêche l'homme en général de prendre ses propres responsabilités. Comme ça on se réfère toujours à la loi.

Pour moi se pose jamais la question d'une fécondation in vitros, parce que je voudrai jamais prendre les risques qui existent sans doute pour moi-même; je pense aussi aux enfants pour qui une mère agée est peut-être un problème. Mais je veux que les femmes peuvent garder la liberté de décider pour elles-mêmes.

Deuxièmement on n'a pas des preuves que les femmes 'agees' sont moins saines. En plus elle vivent plus les probabilités de vie sont plus élevées que autrefois, les conditions de la vie sont devenues mieux.

Troisièmement qui peut prouver que les mères jeunes aiment plus leurs enfants.

No to prohibition!
I am against the law which forbids the in vitro fecundation technique for older women.

First of all, we already have enough laws and I think that each law stops one in genereral taking his own responsibilities. Thus, we'll always refer to the law.

For me, the question of in vitro fecundation will never have to be asked, because I would never take the risks which exist. I must also think about the children for whom an old mother is maybe a problem. Though I would want women to be able to have the freedom to decide for themselves.

Secondly we don't have any proof that these older women are less able. In addition, women live longer, life expectation is higher, the standard of living is also improved.

Thirdly, who can prove that young mothers would love their children more.

T 17

Non à l'interdiction
(1) Il ne faut pas interdire la technique de fécondation in vitro pour les femmes ménopausées. (2) La base d'argument c'est que cela doit être seulement le choix de la femme. (3) Nous ne pouvons pas commencer à mettre les réstrictions sur les systèmes réproductifs des femmes. (4) Même si nous sommes contre l'idée, nous devons réspecter le droit de la femme de choisir.
(5) Il y a tellement des arguments pour l'interdiction, comme les femmes ménopausées sont trop agées, trop faibles, et il y a plus de risques. (6) Mais, honnêtement, il y a toujours des risques pour les femmes à n'importe quel âge et les risques devraient être discuter entre la femme et son médecin et après c'est toujours la femme qui doit décider. (7) De toute façon, si une femme a un coeur très faible ou si elle a d'autres maladies, nous ne pouvons pas l'empecher d'avoir des enfants, c'est toujours son choix si elle va prendre des risques ou pas. (8) Quelques-uns disent que la femme va mourir avant que l'enfant puisse s'occuper de lui-même, mais la possibilité de mourir se pose à chaque jour pour tout le monde. (9) Où pouvons-nous mettre la ligne d'âge?
(10) Il est nécessaire que nous laissions les femmes le pouvoir de gouverner leurs propres corps. (11) Ce n'est à nous ni de décider ni d'imposer les destins des femmes. (12) Elles doivent conserver à n'importe quel âge le droit de choisir pour elle-même.

No to prohibition
One must not prohibit the in vitro fecundation technique for menopausal women. The basis of argument is that this must be only the choice of the woman. We cannot begin to put restrictions on the women reproductive rights. Even if we are against the idea, we must respect the right of the woman to choose.

There are so many arguments for prohibition: menopausal women are too old, too weak, and there are more risks. But, honestly, there are always risks for women at whatever age and the risks should be discussed between the woman and her doctor and then it should be the woman who decides. Even if a woman has a very weak heart or if she has other illnesses, we cannot stop her from having children, it is always her choice. Some say that the woman will die before the child can look after himself, but the possibility of dying is present everyday for everybody. Where can we draw the line of mortality?

It is necessary to leave to women the power to govern their own bodies. It is not for us to decide or to impose the fate of women. They must keep at whatever age the right to choose.

T20

Qui peut décider sur la liberté de choisir mon destin?
Je suis profféseure au colège depuis 30 ans.

J'ai consacré tout ce temps à élever les enfants d'autres, et je n'ai pas eu l'oportunité d'avoir une famille et mes propres enfants.

Aujourd'hui à 54 ans j'ai rencontré l'homme de ma vie et il m'a demandé de l'épouser, bien qu'il est beaucoup plus jeune que moi.

On a décidé de former une veritable famille et on voudrait avoir un enfant.

J'ai consulté plusieurs medecins car j'ai reçu la menopause il y a déjà quelques années et la seule posibilité d'avoir un enfant ça serait par le moyen de l'insemination in vitro.

Mon mari et moi, on croyait que cette décition c'était toute à fait normale, et on a été surpris par la reaction des autres, qui pensaient que je n'avais pas l'âge pour le faire.

Qu'une mère soit bonne ou pas ça ne dépend pas de son âge si non de sa capacité.

Je crois que les jeunes mères ont très peu de temps pour se consacrer à ses enfant. Elles sont beaucoup d'activités. et elles veulent encore faire beaucoup des choses pour elles-mêmes; tandis que les mères de notre âge, apart d'avoir une éxperience de vie plus grande, on a l'envie de rester déjà chez nous et dediquer tout notre temps à notres enfants. D'autre part je ne vois pas quel peut être la difference entre ma famille et les autres et quels conséquences peuvent produire sur mon enfent.

J'ai évidement beaucoup réflechis avant de faire ce pas, j'ai mis sur la balance toutes les conséquences et j'arrivé à la concluson que je pouvait être une mère comme toutes les autres.

Alors, pourquoi on veut décider sur ma vie?
Fin

Who can decide on my freedom to choose my destiny?
I have dedicated all this time to educating the children of others, and I did not have the opportunity to start a family.

Today at the age of 54 I met the man of my life and he asked me to marry him, though he is much younger than me.

We decided to form a real family and we would like to have a child.

I have consulted several doctors because I have entered the menopause some years ago and the only possibility to have a child would be by means of in vitro insemination.

My husband and I thought that this decision was completely normal, and we were surprised by the reactions of others, who think I don't have the right age to do that.

A mother being good or not doesn't depend on her age, but on her capacity.

I think that young mothers have little time to dedicate to their children. They have a lot of activities, and they still want to do a lot of things for themselves; whereas mothers of our age, apart from having a greater life experience, already have the desire to stay at home and dedicate all our time to our children. On the other hand I don't see what can be the difference between my family and the others and what the possible consequences could be for my child.

Obviously I thought a lot before making this step, I weighed up the pros and cons and I reached to the conclusion that I could be a mother like all the others.

So, why do they want to decide about my life?

The End

ANNEX 2

Extracts of the dialogues quoted in the chapter

Conventions for the transcription of the dialogs
- overlaps: underlined utterances
- pauses: - (1 to 2 seconds), - (2 to 5 seconds), - (more than 5 seconds)
- partial words:....dation
- interrogative intonation:?
- comments from the transcriber: <relit>.....>; <A écrit>..........>; <rire>
- not understandable utterance: ***

Ex. 1
59.F peut-être il faudra aussi eh - voir les arguments dans l'article ou bien - les arguments - de ceux qui sont pour l'interdiction - pour un peu - eh - comment dire - pour un peu leur dire qu'ils ont <inaudible> qu'ils eh - eh - par exemple - je crois que - qu'ils ont dit pour l'enfant c'est pas bien parce que la mère elle sera - eh ils n'ont pas vraiment une mère mais une grand-mère et puis - on pourrait dire eh contre ça que même la mère elle va aimer son enfant - plus peut-être qu'une femme qui a - qui est jeune - et qui a pas - tellement voulu un enfant -
60.C oui c'est - oui -

Ex. 2
- 61.F parce que là - on a le - le point de vue de de la femme si tu veux et ceux si si - ceux qui sont pour l'interdiction ont très souvent le point de vue de l'enfant - et peut-être on
- 62.C oui c'est vrai
- 63.F on devrait aussi -
- 64.C faut comparer -
- 65.F mhmh - alors (...)

Ex. 3
- 140.E (...) eh - attends peut-être - si on commence le deuxième paragraphe avec ça - si on on commence - par admettre bien bien sûr il y a des risques - mais - est-ce qu'on peut commencer le deuxième paragraphe avec ça? - avec bien sûr - parce que comme ça on
- 141.U non
- 142.E non?
- 143.U parce que il n'y a pas de -
- 144.E parce qu'en fait comme ça -
- 145.U logique
- 146.E on ne dit pas qu'il y a des autres arguments - si on peut juste - je sais pas si il faut si il faut nous défendre et - si - parce qu'en fait - si on introduit - les autres arguments si on dit les autres arguments -
- 147.U je crois qu'on
- 148.E ça mettra dans la tête des des lecteurs -
- 149.U ouais
- 150.E les autres arguments comme ça -
- 151.U ouais
- 152.E ils pensent -
- 153.U je crois parce que
- 154.E ils pensent à les deux mais si on juste dit - les choses comme voilà ça c'est ça c'est comme -
- 155.U je crois que pour le but - eh nous avons - nous n'avons - qu'une page - et bon - on ne peut discute - tout
- 156.E ouais ouais on écrit eh - chaque quatres lignes -
- 157.U <rire>
- 158.E on peut écrire
- 159.U ouais -
- 160.E eh -
- 161.U je crois que c'est mieux - si on discute - si on ne discute que - disons - les arguments - contre l'interdiction
- 162.E tu crois qu'il faut défendre ça - il faut il faut - non non je - je te demande c'est tout hein moi je - je sais pas - eh -

Ex. 4
- 103.J est-ce qu'on veut dire nous?
- 104.R non

Ex. 5
- 109.J mais tu veux rester neutre ou tu veux
- 110.R non - non

111.J tu veux prendre – parce qu'il faut – eh

Ex. 6
113.J nous nous aimerions
114.R tu vois il il
115.J parce que tu veux toujours dire ton avis
116.R oui tout à fait
117.J puisque que nous nous donnons – parce que
118.R mais on va – on va faire une petite introduction – qui va dire que il est vrai que – eh les gens – eh
119.J en effet
120.R il est vrai que ce – en effet – en effet eh
121.J les les –
122.R ce sujet – suscite beaucoup de controverse de de d'avis controverse non? c'est possible de dire ça en français?
123.J eh – non en effet –
124.R ce sujet – eh – suscite – de – la critique – suscite
125.J suscite <écrit> beaucoup de

Ex. 7
145.J <écrit> mh – ok – mh nous aimerions donner notre avis sur le sujet la fécondation in vitro – en effet ce sujet suscite beaucoup de critiques pour l'interdiction – et contre – après avoir bien réfléchi – nous – voilà ça donne une *** une introduction – eh – après avoir beaucoup réfléchi là-dessus – nous –
146.R eh – lis-moi un peu le texte – en référence
147.J attends – en référence à votre ar...eh – ah non – en référence – à l'article paru dans le journal Libération – le vingt-huit décembre mill neuf cent nonante trois – nous aimerions donner notre avis sur le sujet de la fécondation in vitro – en effet ce sujet suscite beaucoup de critiques pour – l'interdiction et contre –
148.R et contre – point – eh – puis – alors eh à la ligne – on écrit il est vrai que – eh – eh – il est vrai que – eh une femme âgée – qui n'est plus en pouvoir – de – de – de mettre au monde
149.J il est vrai que que la nature pouvoir

Ex. 8
12.T comment – on veut commencer – parce que nous sommes tous les deux eh – on va parler à la première personne du féminin
13.I oui mh
14.T je – suis
15.I oui – comme ça – comme une lettre quoi
16.T oui – d'accord – alors

Ex. 9
40.E comment nous commençons –
41.G peut-être avec une question –
42.E quelle – laquelle? –
43.G eh – est-ce que les femmes eh: – peut-être mettons-nous: peut-être dans la position des femmes – de cet âge – est-ce que nous les femmes de:

plus de cinquante ans on a pas le droit de: eh -- de vouloir être mère ou de vouloir - avoir un enfant
44.E *** commencer comme ça - est-ce que nous?

Ex. 10
45.G mh mhmh - eh mais on se dirige à qui? -
46.E mh?
47.G on se dirige à qui? - à la population - ou: les politiciens - ou: -
48.E à l'opinion publique -
49.G ouais - ouais c'est ça -
50.E on peut écrire la lettre et puis -
51.G ouais
52.E après mettre -
53.G attends - eh: deux signatures - on pourrait mettre eh: nous sommes deux femmes de: - eh cinquante trois et: cinquante quatre ans - et on: veut demander à l'opinion publique est-ce que nous n'avons pas le droit d'être mère? -

Ex. 11
58.E parce que si: - c'est un peu ridicule - non est-ce que nous n'avons pas le droit d'être non? -
59.G oui c'est que ça - sont des questions complètement différentes - un de de bon <bas> c'est plutôt la même chose> - mh: - comment tu avais dit?
60.E peut-être on peut écrire - qui - peut m'em... qui - peut -
61.G qui - peut dire
62.E interdire à moi -
63.G qui oui: ça sera bien - ça serait bien comme:
64.E qui qui va dé... qui va décider -

Ex. 12
74.G sur - la liberté - alors sur la liberté - de - choisir - mon destin > - destin - alors - peut-être on pourrait - eh: - non ça va pas - non moi je disais de raconter comme si: elle avait eu une expérience eh similaire -
75.E mhmh - ***
76.G et alors - par exemple raconter que cette femme - mh: - cette femme elle a eu elle a vécu: une: une situation similaire - elle a: eu - un enfant - ou ou elle a fait une une insémination in in vitro - et: puis elle a eu un enfant elle a pu bien élever son enfant - et: et puis: - elle elle mène une vie normale avec sa famille et son enfant -
77.E mhmh
78.G et tout ça - et alors que - de - cette façon cette femme elle essaie de convaincre les autres femmes - ou ou: ceux qui sont contre - de voir que: - ils peuvent avoir une vie - normale
79.E oui tu tu sais je pense que: que c'est possible mais moi je ne pense pas que c'est c'est c'est bien - faire ça pour convaincre les les autres femmes pour eh - faire la même chose
80.G oui mais c'est que on va - on va pas le faire - c'est pas convaincre les autres sinon - dire que - c'est pas juste - d'interdire - une chose que peut-être que pour elle - c'était une bonne chose - que c'était une

chose que peut-être l'a: l'a donné beaucoup de satisfactions: qu'elle est heureuse à cause de ça qu'elle a mené une vie normale comme tous les autres femmes – que sa famille c'est une famille normale comme tous les autres familles et que son fils ou fille eh: sont comme tous les autres enfants – ou l'aborder d'autres points de vue *** –
81.E que peut décider qui peut décider – la liberté de choisir mon destin
82.G ou peut-être – que cette femme c'est une femme qui veut le faire –
83.E mhmh
84.G et alors elle essaie de convaincre
85.E oui je pense que c'est mieux parce que nous nous avons moi je je eh: je ne suis pas très sûre que c'est bien – <rires>
86.G <rires> bon – alors <relit> qui peut décider sur la liberté de choisir – mon destin >– mh: – on doit – décrire un peu – cette phrase
87.E la situation
88.G ouais – eh: j'ai: cinquante six ans –

Ex. 13
295.E mhmh – eh du point de vue médical on peut voir –
296.D ouais maintenant je passe déjà à deuxième
297.E oui <écrit> – > médical –
298.D les médecins –
299.E ce n'est pas
300.D on peut déjà mettre les médecins les médecins
301.E ce n'est pas sûr? –
302.D ouais – les médecins a conseillent – conseillent – conseillent?
303.E mhmh – ne conseillent pas – plutôt –
304.D ouais ne conseillent pas – <E écrit>
305.E avoir – d'enfants
306.D une grossesse> ou avoir des enfants –
307.E mhmh – <écrit> à cet âge – >
308.D pour les dangers qu'il présente pour – la mère – tant pour la mère como pour l'enfant –
309.E mhmh – <écrit> mhmh – la mère – que pour l'enfant – > (...)

Ex. 14
440.F un peu froid – que les enfants souffrent d'une mère trop âgée – (x s.) c'est peut-être – trouver un autre mot
441.C bon – on peut – eh peut-être qu'on – nous pouvons – continuer –
442.F mh
443.C et – le – chercher – les strcutures exactes après –
444.F ouais

NOTES

1 In order to facilitate reading, we will use only the masculine marks to refer to the learners of both sexes.
2 A strategy being defined as a set of means carried out to achieve a goal, those means being materialized in linguistic forms/features in the texts: writers have to choose (construct a strategy), between different plans, those which are the most adequate in order to achieve their argumentative goal.

3   [la Voix des Autres]
4   See Annex 1, for the texts produced, quoted in the chapter (English and French versions).
5   See the Geneva Model of Discourse Production (Bronckart *et al*, 1985): the anchoring is the way in which the writer links his discourse to the enunciative situation in which it is produced (presence or absence of marks of the material situation of production, selection of temporal aspects, references to the addressee, etc.).
6   Listed from A1 to A10, and from CA1 to CA10; A is used in the text for 'argument', CA for 'counterargument'.
7   Dialogue from Group 1 (D1) corresponding to the Text 1 (T1).
8   All the extracts of the dialogues are translated from the French interlanguage of the learners. In order to facilitate the reading, specific marks of oral characteristics have been suppressed. For original dialogues, see Annex 2.
9   [modalité d'énonciation]: an utterance always has an 'enunciation modality': assertion, interrogation, injunction, etc.
10 For French text, see Annex 2.
11 Verbs Introducing Reported Discourse: those metalinguistic verbs which are used to report the discourse of someone else, which we will designate as Introducing Verb'.
12 By means of 'Related Reported Discourse' [Discours Rapporté Narrativisé]: the doctors advise to / refuse to....

Argumentation and Constructive Interaction

Michael Baker
GRIC - COAST, CNRS & Université Lumière Lyon II

ABSTRACT

Research on collaborative learning currently emphasizes the need to understand the processes at work in communicative interactions between learners, as a means of discovering interactive learning mechanisms. Within this general research program, we concentrate on the specific case of argumentative interactions, with the aim of describing how they can be constructive. A constructive interaction is defined as one in which new meanings or knowledge are coelaborated, and/or one that fulfills some specific (constructive) function with respect to cooperative activity. Our main proposal is that in order to address this research problem we need to combine analyses of argumentative interactions along five theoretically separable dimensions: dialectical, rhetorical, epistemological, conceptual, and interactive. Respectively, these consider argumentative interactions in terms of rational criticism, cognitive effects on participants, the nature of knowledge involved, the form of cognitive representations, and coelaboration of meaning and knowledge. We present a detailed analysis of an extended interaction sequence, taken from a corpus that was collected in a physics classroom. The analysis reveals how the interactive pressure imposed by the necessity to resolve interpersonal conflicts forces meanings and knowledge to evolve, as well as the basic function of argumentation in this context: the filtering of flawed proposals.

Conflict is dissipated in much the same way as is the tension of a spring when you melt the mechanism (or dissolve it in nitric acid). This dissolution eliminates all tensions. (Wittgenstein, 1980, pp. 9/9e)	Der Konflikt löst sich etwa, wie die Spannung einer Feder in einem Mecha-nismus, den man schmilzt (oder in Salpetersäure auflöst). In dieser Lösung gibt es keine Spannungen mehr.

1 INTRODUCTION

Researchers working on collaborative learning have recently turned their attention to the interdisciplinary study of the dynamics of communicative interactions (*e.g.*, Resnick, Levine & Teasley, 1991; Pontecorvo, 1993). In one sense, this shift of emphasis is linked to the recognition that, without powerful theories and specific models of cooperative learning, the search for interactive learning mechanisms will be essentially blind (see *e.g.*, Mandl & Renkl, 1992; Dillenbourg, Baker, Blaye & O'Malley, 1995). In a wider sense, it is motivated by the emergence of new paradigms in cognitive science – such as 'situated learning' (Lave, 1988) or 'cognitive interactionism' (Suchman, 1987) – that emphasize the role of interactions in learning (*i.e.*, both communicative interactions within groups of persons, and interactions between persons and the socially constituted material world).

Within this general research program we focus on the specific case of argumentative interactions produced in collaborative problem solving situations. Our aim is to understand the cognitive-interactional processes that operate within these interactions, and to describe some ways in which they can be considered to be *constructive* interactions.[1]

The term 'constructive interaction' was coined by Miyake (1986), to describe the way in which the conceptual points of view of people who are trying to understand a complex physical device (a sewing machine) go through successive iterations, between understanding and nonunderstanding. In our sense, an interaction can be 'constructive' in at least two ways.

First, an interaction is constructive if it literally leads to the co-construction or building of something - meaning, understanding, solutions to problems, and sometimes knowledge. Constructive interaction in this sense relates to the problem of *emergence* from communicative interaction: how can it be that new knowledge or understanding arises from interaction with others, that is not easily reducible to a simple function of the participants' knowledge and contributions? Note that in this case we are not directly concerned with 'Constructive' interaction, with a capital *C*, *i.e.*, the construction of representations that are accepted as correct from a normative point of view. Rather, our aim is to describe the potentially productive transformations that are manifest throughout the students' interaction, some of which may turn out to be Constructive.

Secondly, an interaction can be constructive to the extent that it generally contributes in some way to cooperative goal-oriented activity. In the case of collaborative problem solving, an example is when one student points out something that enables the students to realize that they do not in fact understand their current joint solution, which leads to its *deconstruction* to leave the part of it that is useful. To ask to what extent an argumentative interaction is constructive in this second sense is to inquire as to its *function* with respect to collaborative problem solving. Does it lead to the addition of new knowledge to the common ground (Clark & Schaefer, 1989), or is it rather a means of eliminating solutions? Does it lead to better mutual understanding or simply to confusion?

Our main proposal is that understanding how argumentative interactions can be constructive in these two senses requires combining analyses along five theoretically separable dimensions: *dialectical, rhetorical, epistemological, conceptual,* and *interactive*. We illustrate these analytical dimensions with respect to an interaction sequence drawn from a corpus of collaborative problem solving dialogues collected in a physics classroom.

2 COMMUNICATIVE, ARGUMENTATIVE, AND CONSTRUCTIVE INTERACTIONS: SOME WORKING DEFINITIONS

Our aim here is to propose an approach to analyzing *interactions* that are both *communicative* and *argumentative*, in order to understand how they may be *constructive*. We therefore need to provide working definitions of these key terms.[2]

2.1 Inter-action and communicative interaction

We use the term *interaction* (or 'inter-action', literally 'action between') to distinguish situations in which *actions* of *agents* are mutually *dependent* (c.f., Kerbrat-Orecchioni, 1990, p. 17). Classically, action is distinguished from behavior in that the former presupposes the operation of the will – of intentionality – whether the agent is conscious of this or not at the time of acting, whereas the latter does not necessarily do so. An agent is an entity that is, at least, capable of acting intentionally on the basis of cognition. Actions are mutually dependent when they are each set off or caused by others, and when they are related in a certain way. Usually this means that the interdependent actions are directed towards the achievement of a common goal, possibly in relation to a common plan. An example of interaction involving interdependent physical actions is the case where two people attempt to transport a piano up a staircase: one person pushes to the right so that another can lift the piano up a step, the raising of the piano causes the first to push again, and thus they can both advance in achieving the common goal of moving the piano upwards.

This definition of interaction, as essentially *interpersonal*, would therefore exclude the case where agents act on their physical environment, the *reaction* of which then leads to a modification in the agents' actions. For example, people using hammers to strike in nails, successively modify their hammering actions as a function of the reaction of the nails and wood. Thus, theorists of situated learning, such as Lave and Wenger (1991), speak of people 'interacting', 'negotiating' or even 'conversing' with their environment. In our terms, such phenomena would be described as 'action/reaction' rather than 'interaction' since one of the parties (the physical environment) is not an agent, capable of intentional action. As we define them, what interaction and action/reaction have in common, is interdependency,[3] and the fact that at least one human agent is involved in the situation described.

Communicative interaction is therefore interaction that involves communication, *i.e.*, sequences of mutually dependent communicative actions. In our terms, an action is communicative if – minimally – it is performed by a speaker with the intention of producing a more or less specific cognitive effect in a hearer, by means of the hearer's recognition of the speaker's intention to produce that effect (Grice, 1957).[4] Although communicative actions can be nonverbal,[5] we are concerned here primarily with *verbal* actions, *i.e.*, with the utterance of interconnected sequences of speech acts, whose aim is to enable interlocutors to share their mental states. The actions will be interdependent to the extent that speakers' actions and thoughts mutually influence each other. The piano-moving example described above involves nonverbal and noncommunicative interaction. In reality, such cases usually involve (verbal and nonverbal) communicative interaction to some extent – for example, when the piano is stuck, and a discussion arises concerning how to unblock it. In what follows, when we refer to communicative interactions, we mean verbal communicative interactions.

2.2 Argumentative interaction

We view *argumentative interaction* as a specific type of communicative interaction. Although nonverbal communicative acts (such as banging one's fist on the table) can be used in argumentative interactions, we do not deal with them here. Within the literature, many different views exist on what argumentation is (see *e.g.*, Plantin, 1990; van Eemeren, Grootendorst & Henkemans, 1996). Not all of these view it as a form of communicative interaction, as defined above (*e.g.*, argumentation as a text, argumentation as a type of speech act, and argumentation as a form of logical proof). For our purposes here, an argumentative interaction is a communicative interaction that satisfies only two minimal conditions (to be described shortly). These conditions correspond to a minimal definition of a dialectical approach to argumentative interactions. To that extent, *an argumentative interaction is simply a verbal communicative interaction in which the dialectical dimension is present.*

The two characteristics that a communicative interaction must minimally possess in order to be viewed as an argumentative interaction are as follows.

2.3 Minimal conditions for argumentative interactions

1. Opening phase: A verbal conflict must be mutually recognized by the participants, with respect to one or more views[6] attributed to one or more of the participants; a verbal conflict is an expressed difference of positions[7] (for/against, pro/contra) or attitudes (*e.g.*, belief/non-belief) with respect to the view(s).
2. Argumentation phase: Following the opening phase, participants must each make at least one communicative act that is globally in accordance with the positions expressed in the opening phase. These communicative acts reveal some degree of stability in the positions with respect to the view(s) expressed in the opening phase. Communicative acts produced in an argumentative interaction that are in accordance with a for/pro position are termed defenses, and those that correspond to the against/contra position are termed attacks.

Normative theories of argumentation may adopt far stricter criteria (*e.g.*, van Eemeren & Grootendorst, 1984). We are not claiming that these two conditions are necessary and sufficient for all that has been termed argumentation, but simply that they constitute a useful working definition that can be used for analyzing argumentative interactions produced in collaborative problem solving situations.

In an idealized case, the opening phase would be as follows:
[Move 1] X: 'The battery is a transformer of energy.' (expression of a view)
[Move 2] Y: 'No it isn't, it doesn't receive energy!' (attack on X's view)
[Move 3] X: 'Yes it is, it makes electricity from chemicals.' (defense of own view)
At the end of the opening phase, both X and Y have expressed their different positions (pro and contra) with respect to X's view by attacking or defending that view at least once. There are several ways in which this idealized schema can be modified, whilst nevertheless preserving its essential structure. For example:
- X's view in move 1 need not necessarily be expressed – it could already be part of the common ground (Clark & Schaefer, 1989) concerning what X believes; however, in this case, once attacked, X could try to avoid verbal conflict by saying 'I didn't say that'.
- Y's attack, corresponding to a contra position in move 2, could be expressed in several different ways:
  - by a simple denial ('No it isn't!');
  - by saying something that is mutually understood to be an attack on X's proposal or belief (*e.g.*, 'But it doesn't take in energy!');

- or by proposing a different view concerning the matter at hand (*e.g.*, the common problem to be solved) where the two views are mutually believed to be contradictory (i.e., proposing a counterthesis).
- In move 3, X could attempt to defend his view by making a counterattack, such as one that attempts to invert the 'burden of proof' (*e.g.*, 'could you tell me why not?').

At the end of the opening phase, although opposed positions have been expressed, the participants could then let the matter drop, in which case argumentative interaction would have been initiated, but not pursued. According to the second condition, therefore, the participants must make at least one further communicative act that confirms the relative stability of these positions, *i.e.*, the willingness to engage in argumentative interaction. Once positions are initially established, they can of course shift. The point is that at any give stage, positions must be established and mutually recognized.

In most cases, a third phase will occur, in which the participants discuss how the verbal conflict should be *closed*. Who is right or wrong? Who has won or lost? What should be done/believed? However, we have found that in many cases, students simply move on to something else, and leave the closure (*e.g.*, resolution) implicit. For this reason, the closing phase is not strictly essential to an analysis of real argumentative interactions. What is basically required is that participants take opposed positions with respect to a view, and act communicatively in order to give reasons for and against the view in a way that is coherent with their positions and a minimal commitment to them. This minimal argumentative interaction schema is summarized in Table 1. Parts that are enclosed in square brackets '[]' are optional,[8] '...' indicates that further moves of this type may be made. From Table 1 it can be seen that just four moves (2 to 5) are required for argumentative interactions.

Table 1   Minimal idealized schema for analysis of argumentative interactions.

Phase	Moves
(1) *Opening phase* (initial expression of views and mutual recognition of opposed positions with respect to them)	[Move 1 - X: expression of view(s) *v*] Move 2 - Y: attack on *v* (contra position) Move 3 - X: defence of *v* (pro position)
(2) *Argumentation phase* (communicative acts in accordance with positions)	Move 4 - Y: attack on *v* (confirmation of relative stability of contra position) Move 5 - X: defence of *v* (confirmation of relative stability of pro position) [...]
[(3) *Closing phase* (discussion of outcome)]	[Move 6 - Y: clarification of position with respect to *v* and outcome of argumentation phase Move 7 - X: clarification of position with respect to *v* and outcome of argumentation phase]

Most theoretical approaches to the study of argumentation specify the goals of arguers (*e.g.*, Walton, 1989). Thus, as we shall discuss below, rhetorical approaches (Perelman & Olbrechts-Tyteca, 1958/88) see argumentation as an attempt to persuade, whereas dialectical approaches (Barth & Krabbe, 1982) see it as an attempt to play and win a verbal game. Given our aim of analyzing collaborative problem solving interactions, we do not consider to be specific goals are necessary to a minimal and operational definition of argumentative interactions, for two reasons. First, students may have various different goals in engaging in argumentative interactions – *e.g.*, attempting to persuade, to convince, to appear reasonable, to cooperatively search for a common solution, to avoid losing face. We do not want to restrict our definition to a single goal, since this would exclude much of what is manifestly argumentative interaction in the situations that we study. Secondly, in practice it is very difficult to infer students' goals in argumentative interactions.

Constructive interaction
Whilst any communicative interaction can be constructive, our concern here is with the specific case of argumentative interactions. As mentioned in the introduction, the first sense in which a communicative interaction can be constructive is when it leads to the (co-)construction of something – a problem solution, meaning, knowledge, *etc*. The epistemological, conceptual, and interactive dimensions of argumentative interactions described below address this aspect. The epistemological dimension is intended to encapsulate the way in which students who argue in terms of different types of reference knowledge can come to a common point of view with respect to the problem to be solved, as a result of confronting their knowledge in argumentative interaction. The conceptual dimension concerns the way that students divide up their understanding of what is being discussed. It enables us to understand how some forms of conceptual change could result from engaging in argumentative interactions. Finally, the interactive dimension describes the interdependencies between students' communicative actions, how the way in which they build on each other's contributions can lead to the co-construction of knowledge.

The second sense in which a communicative interaction – and an argumentative interaction in particular – can be constructive is when it fulfills some specific function with respect to the cooperative problem solving task. Our aim in this case is to ask what that function might be. For example, the clarification of a concept that relates to something that is being discussed, contributing a new element to the problem solution, enabling the students to recognize that their previous solution is unacceptable, and so on. An argumentative interaction which is not constructive in this second sense, would be one that had no incidence at all on the students' subsequent cooperative problem solving (*e.g.*, 'arguing for the sake of it').

In summary, therefore, a constructive argumentative interaction is one that serves some specific purpose or function with respect to the activity in which the participants are engaged (*e.g.*, cooperative problem solving), and/or which leads to (co-)construction of knowledge or understanding. Knowledge co-construction during argumentative interaction can be viewed as a specific function with respect to the participants' broader activity. In general terms, our inquiry is therefore directed towards understanding the function of argumentative interaction in task-based communicative interactions, or to answering the question 'why argue, what difference does it make?'.

3 DIMENSIONS OF ARGUMENTATIVE INTERACTIONS

Relatively little research has hitherto been carried out specifically on the role of argumentative interactions in cooperative learning. Most has concentrated on studying the production and understanding of argumentative discourse[9] (*e.g.*, Voss, Blais & Means, 1986; Golder, 1996) rather than interaction, or else on studying argumentative interactions in situations that were not designed to promote learning (*e.g.*, Resnick, Salmon, Zeitz, Wathen & Holowchak, 1993). However, in both cases, researchers have often applied models of argumentation that were designed for analyzing texts rather than interactions. For example, Resnick and colleagues (*op. cit.*) applied Toulmin's (1958) argument graphs to the analysis of discussions between university students of contentious issues (such as 'nuclear power'). The argument graphs were extended to include the different types of reasoning underlying supports, backings, *etc.*, as well as thematic links, reformulations of utterances, implicit claims, conclusions, and premises.

We argue that, first, in order to understand how argumentative interactions can be constructive, we need to use models of argumentation that are inherently dialogical and pragmatic. Secondly, the analysis of argumentational dimensions (dialectical and rhetorical) needs to be supplemented by the analysis of other dimensions (epistemological, conceptual, and interactive) if we are to understand the nature of constructive argumentative interactions (and, ultimately, how they relate to collaborative learning). Thirdly, the different dimensions need to be analytically separate, precisely so that we can study how they function with respect to each other.

From our theoretical point of view, the only dimension that is *strictly* argumentational – that defines argumentative interactions as such – is the *dialectical dimension*. The approach to analyzing argumentative interactions that we have described above is thus derived from a more general dialectical model (see below). What we term the rhetorical dimension is concerned with the cognitive effects on speakers and hearers that result from engaging in an argumentative interaction. Clearly, cognitive effects can be produced by engaging in any type of communicative interaction since their production is a defining characteristic of communication itself (see above). The term 'rhetorical' is therefore used here simply to refer to the specific case of cognitive effects produced in argumentative interactions, and also to indicate the relations between this dimension, as we define it, and other areas of argumentation theory (see Van Eemeren, Grootendorst & Henkemans, 1996). The other three dimensions – epistemological, conceptual, interactive – can also be present, to a greater or lesser extent, in any communicative interaction that is produced within the context of a knowledge-based activity (*i.e.*, involving the communication, acquisition, co-construction, discovery, *etc.*, of knowledge). Our aim here is thus to study how these dimensions operate in the specific case of argumentative interactions.

We discuss each dimension below and indicate in each case how their study is relevant to our objectives as stated in the introduction.

3.1 The dialectical dimension

Along the dialectical dimension, argumentation is viewed as a sort of interactive game, a 'verbal jousting tournament', the objective of which is, of course, for someone to emerge as the winner (and someone else as the loser). There may be different reasons (goals) why participants play the game; for example, desiring personally to win, or else attempting to put different views to a critical examination (Walton, 1989). Our analysis approach is based on the formal dialectics of Barth & Krabbe (1982). We shall only give a brief outline of this approach here, sufficient for understanding the analyses that follow.[10]

Dialectics begins from a conflict situation: <A, B, Con, T>. A and B are the participants in the dialogue, *Con* a set of concessions (statements that are agreed by the participants prior to debating), and T the thesis to be debated. The minimal starting point is that one participant, for example A, has made a statement U, and the other has raised doubts with respect to U. A makes one defensive move with respect to U, which now becomes the thesis, T. The participants have now adopted specific dialectical roles: A becomes the proponent, and B the opponent. These roles condition participants' commitments to theses, concessions, and to making certain types of moves in specific contexts.

The moves in the game are specific speech acts: assertions (U), requests for defensive moves (U? - 'how do you defend U?'), hypothetical statements ((?)U - 'I am prepared to defend U for the purposes of this debate'), and a special speech act U! that indicates that the interlocutor has made a 'foul move'. Such foul moves are defined with respect to a set of general rules that govern the debate and that, ideally, are agreed by the participants prior to debating. For example: a participant cannot both assert a statement then attack it, since this would correspond to adopting both a pro and a contra position with respect to that statement within the same argumentation sequence. Other rules operate to generally make the debate converge on a determined outcome (*e.g.*, no repeating of moves indefinitely, all attacked statements to be immediately defended) and to decide what that outcome is (*e.g.*, if B has no more legal moves at his disposition with which to reply to an attack, then he has lost). There are of course also specific rules that determine what counts as an attack or a defense of a particular statement (*e.g.*, A? and B? are attacks on $A \wedge B$') that will correspond to a domain model in task-oriented dialogues. There are two basic types of conflicts: 'simple', in which a single thesis is debated, and called into doubt by the opponent, and 'mixed', in which each participant proposes a thesis (thesis and counterthesis).

We are not, of course, claiming that such idealized models can, as such, account for all aspects of real argumentative interactions, particularly those produced by students. For example, van Eemeren and Grootendorst (1984) have pointed out that concessions are not fixed prior to debating, but are continually negotiated throughout argumentative interactions. Rather, we view such abstract dialectical models as providing a basic structure, and functional components, with respect to which we can search for correlates in real interactions: what are the general rules that govern argumentative interactions between students? what is the range of speech acts that they use? how are outcomes determined? With respect to the latter question, Trognon (1990) has shown that the basic predictions of such dialectical models - who has won or lost? - conform to human intuitions in certain cases. This result is promising for cognitive studies of argumentation since it enables us to address the question of how argumentation outcomes influence the subsequent course of collaborative problem solving (*e.g.*, does the loser's belief drop in his thesis?).

3.2 The rhetorical dimension

Traditionally, rhetoric is the art of persuading an auditorium, a group of listeners. The means used do not of course have to be rational, their simple aim is efficacy in persuasion. Significantly, the sophist or rhetorician is able to argue both in favor of and against any given opinion (see *e.g.*, Ducrot & Schaeffer, 1995: 140-151).

We generalize the use of the term 'rhetoric', first, to any type of *epistemic effect* that is produced, as a result of argumentative interaction. Epistemic effects are concerned with the status of representations from the point of view of individuals, their attitudes with respect to them – being in a state of knowing, believing, suspecting that something is the case, viewing it as plausible, certain, or as a defensible opinion, etc. In interactions, these attitudes can shift, or be revised.[11] Changes of epistemic status can often be more subtle than revisions of beliefs to nonbeliefs. For example, as the result of an argumentative interaction, students may view a proposal that they had hitherto viewed as certain, as uncertain, yet defensible (Nonnon, 1996). Such a change may in fact turn out to be constructive, since, once the students have realized that they do not fully understand something, they may be motivated to seek out the required knowledge.

Secondly, such effects can be produced with respect to *all participants* in the interaction: the uttering of a particular sequence of speech acts in an argumentative discussion can have effects on the speaker as well as on the hearer. This possibility can be compared with the 'self-explanation' effect (Chi, Bassok, Lewis, Reimann & Glaser, 1989; Chi & vanLehn, 1991; Webb, 1991): subjects who produce explanations can learn from so doing, as well as those who receive them.

Within a computational approach to speech-act theory (*e.g.*, Cohen, Morgan & Pollack, 1990), certain types of cognitive effects that result from engaging in argumentative interactions can be modeled as relatively stable perlocutionary effects of speech acts (van Eemeren & Grootendorst, 1984).

3.3 The epistemological dimension

The epistemological dimension deals with the nature of the knowledge that is involved in argumentative interactions – the knowledge that is appealed to, and which underlies the interaction. We distinguish three aspects: (1) the intrinsic properties of knowledge, (2) the knowledge domain, and (3) the source of the knowledge. Properties that are intrinsic to a different types of knowledge include its degree of inherent ambiguity, its complexity, and the existence of alternative solutions or conceptual points of view. By a domain we mean a body of knowledge as possessed by a recognized social group of experts (such as researchers in psychology or mathematics, or international scientific bodies). There are of course sub-domains: for example, organic and inorganic chemistry. The source of knowledge can be either considered from the point of view of the individual's capabilities, or in terms of the social-institutional positions of individuals or groups. Thus individuals may acquire knowledge through perception (including information acquired from other people), action, or reasoning. The social-institutional status of the person(s) from whom knowledge is acquired is important: knowledge acquired from a teacher, a parent, or a friend does not have the same status.

Analyzing the nature of the knowledge involved in argumentation is important given that some types of knowledge used as arguments or counter-arguments may be perceived as having more strength or weight. For example, an argument that appeals to an undeniable fact of everyday experience (fire burns) may have more weight than one that depends on individual reasoning. Secondly, in cognitive terms, some types of knowledge may be more firmly anchored (DiSessa, 1988), or 'epistemically entrenched' (Gardenförs, 1992), than others.

3.4 The conceptual dimension

The conceptual dimension of argumentative interactions is concerned with the *form* of knowledge, the way in which it is *represented*, in the universe of reference (the 'external' task whose achievement is the reason why the communicative interaction takes place). It is thus not the same as the epistemological dimension that deals with the *nature* of knowledge. An example will perhaps make this clear. Suppose that the topic of an educational interaction is 'living beings', such as plants and animals. In such an interaction, along the epistemological dimension, students may appeal to different types of knowledge – of physiology, paleontology, botany, *etc.* – coming from different sources (what they learned in school, in everyday life during a visit to the zoo, *etc.*). Now suppose that the teacher asks 'what is the main difference between plants and animals?' Establishing such a difference is a conceptual matter, it requires performing a type of *linguistic-cognitive operation*, termed *differentiation*. Such operations are 'the means by which discourse performs ... cognitive work on representations' (Vignaux, 1990: p. 307; see also Vignaux, 1988). For example, a student might reply 'animals have legs and can move, whereas plants are fixed to the ground by their roots'. Such differentiations (the separating of representations or concepts from each other) are the bases for *determinations*, *i.e.*, characterizations of the object of discourse, *e.g.*, qualifications or properties which are being attributed ('animals have legs'). It is not possible to predicate or to evaluate propositions (predications) unless one can, to some extent, differentiate concepts.

The conceptual dimension relates directly to two important aspects of argumentative interactions that have already been described by argumentation theorists. The first aspect concerns the fact that in order to argue effectively, participants are often obliged to *clarify* their interpretations of utterances (Naess, 1966). The second relates to the fact that debates often shift towards 'deeper', more fundamental, or general issues (Walton, 1992).[12] We shall describe how the *interactive pressure*[13] that requires conflicts to be resolved verbally in argumentation triggers such operations. This pressure may in turn lead concepts to evolve (*e.g.*, to the correct differentiation: 'The difference between plants and animals lies in the way that they obtain their *energy* – via photosynthesis or by digestion.').

3.5 The interactive dimension

In the specific case of argumentative interactions, the interactive dimension encapsulates the processes by which knowledge [epistemological dimension] or concepts/representations [conceptual dimension] are transformed, reformulated, refined, elaborated, or *negotiated* in communicative interaction.

We adopt Roulet and colleagues' (Roulet, Auchlin, Moeschler, Rubattel & Schelling, 1985; Roulet, 1991) distinction between *interactive* and *interactional* completeness in a model for interactions based on the concept of negotiation. Interactive completeness is a condition for interactional completeness. If someone wants to sell you a carpet, then you can agree to buy it or not. Similarly, if someone provides you with some information, you can agree with it or not. This is *interactional* negotiation, operating on the level of agreement/nonagreement, or acceptance/nonacceptance. However, in order to know whether you agree or not (with buying the carpet, or with the information content), in the first case you have to know the price, the type of carpet, *etc.*, and in the second you have to understand the information. So a subdialogue can be entered into in order to determine the price, the color, *etc.*, and what the information means (explanatory dialogue), which corresponds to *interactive* negotiation.

In the case of collaborative problem solving dialogues, students are usually required to reach some degree of *agreement* with respect to the solution to the problem (interactional negotiation). However, in order to attain such agreement, they often need to transform initial proposals into some new proposal that is acceptable to each and which satisfies the constraints of the problem (interactive negotiation, driven by the need to reach agreement on the interactional level).

In Baker (1994, 1995) we described a general model of collaborative problem solving, based on the idea that it is fundamentally a negotiation (interactive) that operates on the 'knowledge level'.[14] Initial proposals may be *transformed* in interaction in four basic ways. They may be *extended* (*e.g.*, new propositions or predicates conjoined, inferences draw) or *restricted* (*e.g.*, their range of validity, propositions, or predicates 'removed' – 'I agree with x, but not that it is F'); their *foundations* may be examined (justification, explanation), or they may be *reformulated*. Usually, repetition (zero reformulation at the knowledge level) serves a specific purpose at another communicative level: checking mutual understanding, summarizing the current common solution so that agreement can be decided. In this way, collaborative problem solving can be described succinctly (Baker, 1995), to give a picture of the extent to which the students are genuinely collaborating, rather than solving the problem in a parallel way.

The reason why the interactive dimension is important here is perhaps obvious: students may be led to transform initial proposals into more refined concepts and knowledge, which may then be internalized.

In argumentative interactions, there is pressure on individuals to avoid *intrapersonal* conflict, or cognitive dissonance (Festinger, 1957), and special *interactive pressure* (Bunt, 1995) to resolve interpersonal conflicts. Argumentative interactions are often emotionally charged. This is not necessarily negative, since there may be an interplay between knowledge-based and socially-based argumentation (debate vs. dispute). We adopt the working hypothesis that *these pressures operating in argumentative interactions may lead meanings and knowledge to evolve*.

3.6 Some relations between the dimensions

Dialectical and *rhetorical* dimensions of argumentation are intrinsically related given that the former is intimately associated with attitude formation – the taking of stances, positions, for or against proposals. Once participants engage in an argumentative interaction, they must step back from their proposals, examine their foundations, defend or attack them, and, in general, *reflect* upon their knowledge.

Such reflection may itself be a cause of change in attitudes (see our earlier remarks concerning the self-explanation effect in an interactive context). As mentioned above, argumentation outcomes may also be the causes of attitude shifts.

However, argumentative interactions are not always resolved in a strictly dialectical way, *i.e.*, with refutation or successful defense (and concession), leading to the designation of a winner and a loser. This is where *dialectical*, *interactive*, and *conceptual* dimensions relate to each other. Thus, some argumentative interactions may be resolved (or rather 'dissolved') by negotiating a compromise (*interactive*) that combines and refines alternative proposals. Others may be 'defused' by differentiating the *conceptual* framework into two parts, that enables each participant to be 'right', but within a separate framework (*e.g.*, 'You are right in the case of elastic impacts and I am right in the case of inelastic impacts' – see Baker, 1991). Clearly, the *conceptual* dimension is related to the *epistemological* one, given that the nature of the knowledge involved determines how it can be conceptualized.

Finally, as mentioned above, *dialectical*, *rhetorical*, and *epistemological* dimensions interrelate given that the nature of the knowledge involved determines the extent to which participants will be willing to change their minds with respect to it (rhetorical), and that some types of knowledge (epistemological) provide more forceful arguments (dialectical).

4   THE TASK AND THE CORPUS

The corpus from which the sequence analyzed here was taken, was collected in a physics class of a secondary school (*lycée*) in the Lyon area (France). The class was experimental to the extent that a new teaching sequence, on the theory and model of energy in physics, was being tried out on the students (aged sixteen to seventeen). The students were not specializing in sciences for their examinations (*baccalauréat*) – this was 'physics for literary students'.

The students' task was designed for learning about modeling in physics, and the theory/model of energy in particular (Tiberghien, 1994, 1996; Devi, Tiberghien, Baker & Brna, 1996). In the part of the energy modeling teaching sequence discussed here, students are asked to produce qualitative models (diagrams) called 'energy chains' in order to represent energy storage, transfer, and transformation in a series of three simple experimental situations. Figure 1 shows example energy chains (correct, and students' solution) for an experimental situation where a battery is linked to a bulb by two wires.

The didactic rationale of this task is that by attempting to instantiate the simple qualitative model for energy in concrete cases, the students will be led to co-construct an understanding of the concepts of 'energy' and 'model'. This will involve coelaborating the semantics of the model, given its syntax and lexicon, together with a domain of reference (Tiberghien, 1996).

Students worked in pairs, with the person whom they normally sat next to. Within the same class, twenty students, ten pairs, drew the energy chains on paper. The students were given a sheet that expressed simple definitions of elements of the energy chain (*e.g.*, 'a reservoir stores energy'), the law of conservation of energy, and a set of syntactic rules to which the diagrams had to conform (*e.g.*, 'A complete energy chain must start and end with a reservoir'). They were also given experimental apparatus (battery, wires, bulb, a small motor, a dynamo, a weight, and string). Spoken dialogue was tape-recorded, then transcribed, and paper copies were collected.

Figure 1 Energy chains (correct solution and example students' solution) for an experiment where a bulb is connected to a battery by two wires.

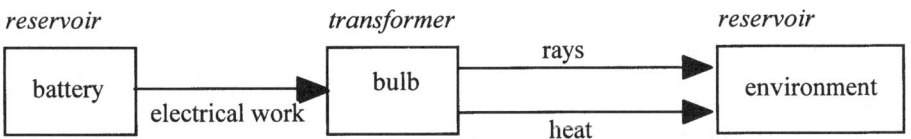

Example students' solution :

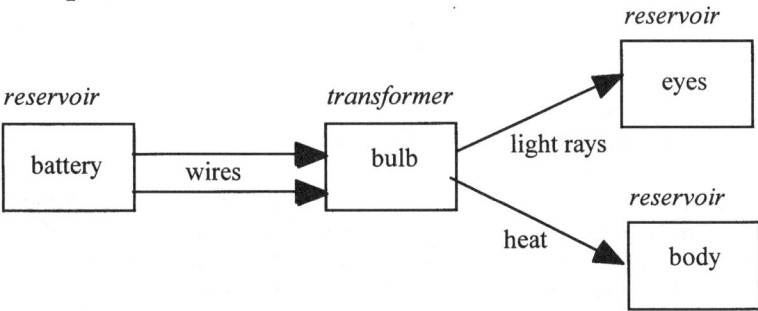

This task was chosen for the study of argumentative and constructive interactions given that it is exploratory and constructivist, and requires the use of a range of different types of knowledge (see analyses below). Together, these factors lead to a task situation which provides a wide 'negotiation space' (Dillenbourg & Baker, 1996), or which is potentially highly 'debatable' (Golder, 1996; Golder & Pouit, this volume).

5 AN EXAMPLE OF ARGUMENTATION SEQUENCES AND ITS ANALYSIS

We present and analyze an extract from the corpus described above. The example illustrates many, but of course not all, of the possible interrelations between the analytical dimensions described earlier. Other possible and real phenomena (those occurring elsewhere in the corpus) will be discussed in the next section.

In the analyses we indicate the incidence of different dimensions as follows:
D – dialectical dimension,
R – rhetorical dimension,
E – epistemological dimension,
C – conceptual dimension,
I – interactive dimension.

The extract is divided into subsequences for purposes of exposition, that follow on directly from each other (for reasons of space, short sections that are inessential to the argumentative interaction itself are omitted; this is indicated by '<...>').

This extract is taken from a communicative interaction between a boy and a girl (whom we shall call John and Mary – J and M).[15] They attempted to produce an energy chain for a simple experimental situation in which a battery is linked to a bulb by two wires (the bulb shines when connected to the battery by the wires). Our analysis illustrates the following specific cases of relations between all five dimensions:

1. implicit negotiation (I) of knowledge as a means of argumentative attack (D);
2. explicit negotiation (I) as a means of argumentative defense and resolution (D);
3. the role of different types of knowledge (E) to which each student appeals within dialectical processes (D);
4. a specific relation between dialectical outcomes (D) and changes in positions or attitudes[16] (R); and
5. conceptual differentiation (C) as a means of attempting to find a negotiated (I) resolution to the argumentative interaction (D).

Subsequence 1: John's thesis is proposed and refuted

Prior to the sequence analyzed here, the students had already agreed that the battery was a reservoir of energy, and the bulb a transformer of it. Their problem at this stage was to determine the nature of the transfer(s) of energy between the two. John's proposal – which becomes his thesis – is shown in Figure 2 (see line 180 in Table 2).

Figure 2 John's thesis.

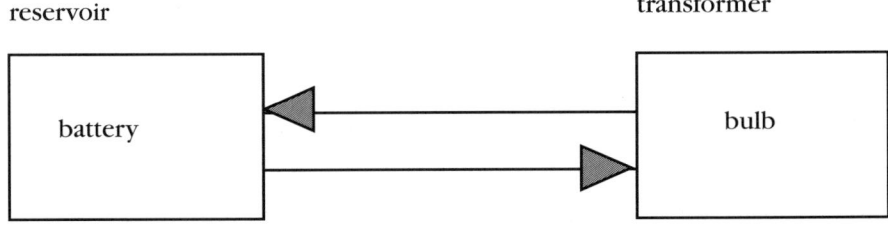

Table 2 First subsequence.

Line	Loc	Dialogue
178	J:	Right, there, there's the ...
179	M:	... transformer. Do the transfer arrow
180	J:	There are several of them to be done. One there [battery to bulb]. Should we put another one there? [bulb to battery]
181	M:	Pprrrttt!
182	J:	You see, it leaves from a reservoir and it comes back to a reservoir.
183	M:	Is that right!?
184	J:	A reservoir to begin with and a reservoir to end with.
185	M:	Have we got two batteries John?
186	J:	No!
187	M:	Have we got two batteries!?
188	J:	No
189	M:	Then why do you say such a load of rubbish!
190	J:	What have we forgotten then?

The dialectical structure of this sequence provides the basic framework within which relations with other analytical dimensions can be shown (Table 3).[17]

Table 3 Dialectical structure of first subsequence†

Transcr. line	Dialectical moves	Mary	John	Pragmatic character of dialectical move
180	(a)		(A ∧ B)	John's thesis
181	(b)	(A ∧ B)?		Expression of doubt; (indirect) request for defense of (a)
182	(c)		C	Direct defense of (a)
183	(d)	C?		Request for defense of (c)
184	(e)		C'	Direct defense of (a)
185	(f)	D		Attack on (a)
186	(g)		◆D	Concession of D
187	(h)	D		Attack on (a)
188	(i)		◆D	Concession of D
189	(j)	⊗ (A ∧ B)		Explicitation of argumentation outcome: John's thesis is *refuted*
190	(k)		◆(j)	Concession of the argumentation outcome: refutation (j)

† Propositions: A = 'There is a transfer from battery to bulb'; B = 'there is a transfer from bulb to battery; C = 'there must be an a reservoir at the beginning and the end of an energy chain'; D = there are not two batteries in the experiment'. ' X' ' indicates a reformulation of X. Argumentation speech acts: U = statement; U? = request for defense: 'how do you defend U?' Dialectical moves: ◆U = statement U conceded; ◆(n) = dialectical move n conceded; ⊗U = explicitation of argumentation outcome: 'U is refuted in this debate'.

The analysis shown in Table 3 can be seen as a more detailed instantiation of the general schema for argumentative interactions discussed previously (see Table 1), using elements of Barth and Krabbe's (1982) dialectical model,[18] but without claiming to perform dialogic logic proofs (we are describing real argumentation). Thus, in Table 3, dialectical moves (a)-(c) correspond to the opening phase, moves (d)-(h) to the argumentation phase, and moves (i)-(k) to the closing phase. The analysis is of course highly idealized, and deliberately only takes into account a single dimension (D), precisely so that other dimensions can be analyzed with respect to it. For example, the idealized dialectical function of Mary's utterance (Table 2, line 181) ' Pprrrttt!' is to raise doubts, and indirectly request defense; John's question (Table 2, line 190) 'what have we forgotten then?' is interpreted as a concession of the refutation of his thesis.

With respect to other dimensions, the first important point to be noted here is that John auto-reformulates (I) his defense 'C' of his thesis (moves (c) and (e) in Table 3). Initially (line 182) he says that his thesis is justified because 'it [energy?, electricity?] leaves from a reservoir and comes back to a reservoir'. He then reformulates this proposal in order to move towards a more direct statement of the energy chain rule, provided by the teacher 'A complete energy chain must start and end with a reservoir.' This makes clear how a more legitimized form of knowledge (E) supports his thesis. In essence, his ingenious proposal is that since the transfer leaves from a reservoir (battery) and comes back to one (the same battery, the arrows go round in a circle), his thesis satisfies the energy chain rule. From the combination of dialectical and interactive analyses, we can thus see that this reformulation is elicited by the *interactive pressure* of Mary's request for a defense (move (d) in Table 3).

The second important point concerns the nature of Mary's attack ('Have we got two batteries?'), glossed as the proposition: 'D = there are not two batteries in the experiment') and the underlying reasoning that links it to John's thesis, thus proposing that it is refuted. This is perhaps not obvious, although it appears to be fully understood by the students. Our interpretation is that Mary's refutation depends on an implicit elaboration (I) of the energy chain rule cited above, *i.e.*: 'R1': An energy chain must start and end with a reservoir, *and the first and last reservoirs cannot correspond to the same physical object.*' Her reasoning is basically as follows. Since R1', and given the concession that 'the battery is a reservoir', then this would imply that there must be *two different batteries*. This is manifestly false (there is only one battery on the table before them). So John's proposal is refuted (or at least, the energy chain rule is no defense for it).

The third point concerns the different types of knowledge (E) to which each student appeals in their dialectical moves (D). Mary appeals, in the final analysis, to basic facts of perceptual experience: there is only one battery! As such, these facts cannot be refuted, although the reasoning based on them could be. John appeals to knowledge whose source is the teacher (the energy chain rules). *However*, this is manifestly not the type of knowledge that underlies the solution that he proposes: the energy chain transfers go round in a circle like an electrical circuit, knowledge of electricity in fact underlies his solution. Thus argumentation is not simply a matter of rendering knowledge and reasoning explicit, but rather may involve *a posteriori* reconstruction, and the use of the most convincing arguments to hand (Baker, 1996a, 1996b; Baker, to appear). As we shall see, these basic epistemological stances remain relatively constant throughout the whole sequence.

Finally, we note that factors of interaction management (making sure that the other has received and understood the message) interfere with strict dialectical rules – *e.g.*, the repetition of attacks and defenses in Table 3, (f)-(i). One basic dialectical rule is, however, always adhered to: an attack must be followed by a defense.

Subsequence 2: Mary's counter-thesis

In the subsequent subsequence, Mary begins by explaining her way of thinking about the problem (a linear causal model – line 191 of Table 4), and proposes a counterthesis (Figure 3), now that John's thesis has been refuted.

Figure 3   Mary's counter-thesis.

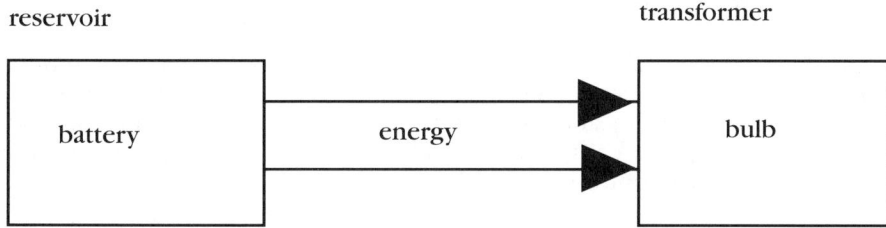

Table 4   Second subsequence.

Line	Loc	Dialogue
191	M:	But no. I.....You know there, it's obvious that it's like that [two arrows both from battery to bulb]. I thought that. Look, there's the wire. Wait ... Me, I thought it was like that! That the two wires...You see, the energy goes from there [the battery]. It goes ttssouiii across the two wires and arrives there [the bulb]. You understand. So they're like that the two arrows. You understand what I'm trying to say? I mean that it goes from there, there's a wire like that from the reservoir, there's a wire that goes from the reservoir and carries it to the battery, you agree? And it's like that, there's the other wire. Me, I would have done it like that.
192	J:	Yes, but that's no good! Look what they say 'An energy chain ... '
193	M:	I don't give a damn
194	J:	What?
195	M:	I'm telling you I don't give a damn. For me it's like that.
196	J:	Yes but a complete energy chain begins and ends with a reservoir.
197	M:	Yes, but I've got it. But me, I'm telling you, it's not because they wrote that that we have to do that [John's solution]
198	J:	Uhh, but precisely, we do have to!

This subsequence illustrates two main phenomena. Firstly, epistemological stances (E) remain constant (see above): Mary appeals to perceptually-based facts, and John to the rules of the model. It is significant that Mary's thesis is based on linear causal reasoning, which is nevertheless anchored in the perceptual world, since she says that the transfers correspond to the wires[19]. Secondly, the subsequence gives a good illustration of one type of relation between D and R dimensions: *dialectical refutation of a thesis does not necessarily lead to dropping a pro position with respect to it.* John accepted that his thesis was refuted (D) at the end of subsequence 1; however, this has *not* produced the effect that he drops his thesis (R). In fact, he uses the same argument (energy rule) that was a defense of his own thesis as an attack on Mary's. Mary's defense in fact appeals to her conception of the logical relations between the two theses debated: it is not because her thesis is not entirely satisfactory that his thesis is right.

Subsequence 3: Mary finds a compromise, yet hesitates ...

The students are now at something of an impasse: John's thesis has been refuted, although he has not, apparently, changed his mind about it; Mary's thesis has been shown to be inadequate, since it does not satisfy the energy chain rule. Mary therefore tries to find a compromise (Table 5) to resolve the conflict (D), that combines elements of both solutions (I).

Table 5   Third subsequence.

Line	Loc	Dialogue
199	M:	In my opinion, in my opinion, it leaves from both sides, so ... But you know, there could be two arrows in each direction ... I'm going to tell you ...
200	J:	Yeah, it doesn't begin and end with a reservoir, so it's not a complete energy chain
201	M:	John, John, I'm going to tell you s'mthing
202	J:	Yes
203	M:	They put 'if there are several modes of transfer, you must have an arrow for each mode of transfer'. You understand? So there are two directions of ar rows. There's that one [battery to bulb] and that one [bulb to battery]. It could be that there are two arrows in this direction [battery to bulb] and one in the reverse direction [bulb to battery], you agree? Well, be logical. Eh!
204	J:	That's all we have to put apart from that?
205	M:	Uh, well me, I would have put the arrows in the other direction
206	J:	You put other arrows here?
207	M:	It leaves from a reservoir and it goes to the transformer, I don't give a damn if it comes back to the ...
208	J:	... and you take that off? <silence> You take that off?
209	M:	Uh, no! Dunno about that! I was just thinking about that. Because you see, me, I say to myself ... Look: y've got the battery and y've the two wires, the energy, it goes across the two wires, so, it goes from the reservoir and it does that. You understand. It's not that it goes through the wire, in my opinion, eh?, it's not that it leaves in the wire, passes through the transformer and then it comes back to the reservoir in the other wire. You see what I mean? It's that

		it goes from there [battery] and across the two wires, it arrives there [bulb], so it's the same direction, the arrows.
		<...>
224	J:	We can't put an arrow in that direction like that and in that direction. That doesn't mean anything
225	M:	[she reads the sheet] 'One indicates on each arrow the mode of transfer. If there are several modes of transfer, you must have an arrow for each mode of transfer'. Me, that's how I understood it. But we don't give a damn, everyone does it how he wants, we thought about it like that, the others haven't done it

Mary's proposal begins (lines 199, 203, 225 of Table 5) with the cognitive operation of *determination* (C) of the concepts /transfer/mode/: each of the transfers is now to be conceptualized as a different *mode* of transfer (either 'energy' or 'electricity'). Under our interpretation, this enables Mary to allow both partners to be 'right' and thus to resolve the conflict (D) by negotiating a compromise (I) that superficially combines the conflicting proposals. When in line 207 she states 'I don't give a damn if it comes back ...' then (as shown by the later dialogue) she proposes that the common solution could have only arrows from battery to bulb, if their mode is 'energy' (her solution), but that this is not incompatible with there being a third transfer, which comes back to the battery, since this could be a different mode of transfer ('electricity'). What she appears to be proposing as a compromise is shown in Figure 4. It can be seen that her proposal combines and reconceptualizes elements of the two opposed theses (Figures 2 and 3).

Figure 4   Mary's compromise solution.

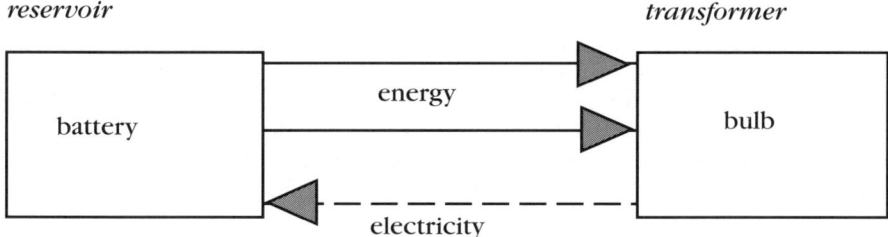

However, Mary hesitates (end of line 209), retracts, and returns to her own thesis, given that John does not accept her proposal (line 224), and perhaps because she has understood the incoherence or superficiality of her compromise.

The final refutation ...

The complete sequence is resolved by refutation in the subsequence shown in Table 6.

Table 6   Fourth subsequence.

Line	Loc	Dialogue
226	J:	Ah but, there's no return, that's it, we slipped up. There's no return, they're right [the dyad on the next table]
227	M:	But that's what I've been trying to tell you. That arrow there [bulb to battery] means that the energy, it passes from the transformer to the reservoir. That's never been seen. Otherwise, that [the bulb] never goes out. You see what I mean?
228	J:	Pass me your eraser?

Significantly, it is John who refutes his own thesis, but by appealing to information outside this dyad's interaction (the solution of the students on the next table). Mary reformulates (I) this refutation (line 227), saying that that is what she had been trying to say all along. The refutation (D) is conclusive since it appeals to everyday knowledge (E): bulbs never shine forever. John concedes, Mary has won. This does not, however, necessarily mean that Mary's solution will be mutually accepted (R).

5   DISCUSSION: CONSTRUCTIVE MECHANISMS IN ARGUMENTATIVE INTERACTIONS

For the case of collaborative problem solving interactions, we have seen how the dialectical framework of argumentative interactions imposes a special *interactive pressure* (to resolve verbal conflicts) on the participants. This pressure stimulates students to draw on different types of knowledge, to determine and differentiate concepts, to negotiate the meaning of key terms in the domain of reference, and to combine elements of solutions as compromises. To paraphrase Wittgenstein's striking expression (Wittgenstein, 1980, pp. 9/9e), verbal conflicts are usually *dissipated* or *dissolved* rather than *resolved*, in a strictly dialectical sense. The interactive and interactional phenomena described above, thus constitute an answer to our first question in this specific case: how are argumentative interactions constructive, in the sense of leading to coelaboration or emergence of meaning and knowledge?

Our second question concerned constructive interaction in the sense of the overall function of argumentative interaction with respect to collaborative problem solving: how might it be seen as contributing to this activity? It appears that one intuitively plausible possibility can be eliminated in this case: argumentation does not always function as a means of augmenting shared knowledge. It is not primarily a means by which a proposal, when successfully defended, then becomes accepted by all parties involved. Usually, and in the cases described above, its function is to *eliminate* 'flawed' proposals (Baker, 1996a, 1996b), *i.e.*, those with respect to which it is mutually recognized that there is at least one counterargument. Thus, in the above example, John's solution was eliminated by refutation; Mary's solution remained as a plausible candidate, yet John still maintained that it was not acceptable since it did not satisfy the energy chain rule. This process may be ultimately constructive in our second sense to the extent that unfruitful problem solving paths are not taken by the students.

Such elimination can also be constructive in the first sense to the extent that it leads to a joint attempt to understand *why a proposal is not acceptable* (rather than leading to discussion of why a proposal is acceptable). In simple terms: if no one has found anything wrong with a proposal, then why inquire into its foundations? It is only when something appears to be wrong that the need to explain and understand is felt and acted upon. Therein may lie the real key to understanding the constructive interaction (in both senses) engendered by argumentation. It is true that when one of two competing proposals is eliminated from consideration, the remaining one may be considered as the 'common' solution. But this does not necessarily mean that it is mutually believed. Rather, it may be mutually *accepted* (Cohen, 1992), 'for the sake of argument', given the basic contract of the interaction that at least some 'common' solution must be proposed at the end of the session (something, although not completely agreed, is better than nothing).

6 CONCLUSIONS AND FURTHER WORK

The analyses presented here go some way towards furthering our understanding of how argumentative interactions produced in collaborative problem solving situations can be constructive, in the sense of leading to coelaboration of meaning and knowledge, and in the sense of fulfilling a specific role in the collaborative activity. Our main proposal is that the analysis of strictly argumentational aspects (*i.e.*, dialectics and rhetoric) cannot alone give us the key to these problems, which lies rather in understanding the interrelations between five analytically distinct dimensions. We have seen how argumentative interactions can lead to reconstruction rather than expression of knowledge, how the pressures they exert on participants can lead to coelaboration of meaning, and how they act as filters of flawed proposals.

For the present, our analysis approach has been applied to corpora of communicative interactions in the domain of learning physics (the present chapter; Baker, 1991, 1996a, 1996b). However, as Golder (1996) points out, one does not argue about anything, with anyone and in any social-institutional situation. Therefore, the extent to which this approach can lead to insight into the constructive processes involved in a wider range of tasks and situations remains to be determined. Our results are presently limited to domains of school physics that are relatively 'closed' (a determinate set of correct solutions exists). And yet, these domains provide a sufficiently wide space of debate given that they require the students – especially in qualitative modeling tasks – to draw on a wide variety of types of knowledge. In more 'open' domains, such as social science and humanities subjects, an even wider space of debate exists, since argumentation in terms of different theoretical and methodological approaches is an integral part of these domains from the very outset (Goodyear & Stone, 1992). It is therefore reasonable to conjecture that the approach described here will find application beyond the specific tasks to which it has been applied up to the present, provided that the tasks are 'knowledge-rich', and especially when they are also open-ended. In fact, it is difficult to conceive of an argumentative interaction occurring with respect to a task that was neither 'knowledge rich' nor open-ended: in that case there could be little to argue about. Elaborating a theoretical analysis of the nature of problem solving situations-tasks that allow the emergence of both argumentative interactions and collaborative learning remains a fascinating goal for future research.

A second specificity of the task analyzed here resides in the fact that the students were asked to reach agreement on a single solution to the problem: would similar constructive processes be likely to occur if this constraint was relaxed? We speculate that – in the cases where students simply 'worked together' (spontaneously or by request), and could propose divergent individual solutions – this would in fact alleviate many unproductive aspects of argumentative interactions along the interactive dimension, such as the generation of false or 'too easy' compromises. Once people are engaged in communicative interaction, they cannot always avoid addressing conflicting views, adopting positions, and justifying themselves, without losing 'face' on a social level. In such cases, they become committed to following the driving forces, the interactive dynamics, of argumentative interactions through to the end. This would usually require making the terms of debate more precise, along the conceptual dimension, and eventually seeking a cooperative or constructive resolution to the social and cognitive conflict of views.

ACKNOWLEDGEMENTS

The corpus analyzed here was collected in collaboration with other colleagues, of whom I would like to particularly thank Andrée Tiberghien, as well as the teachers and pupils who participated in the study. I am also grateful to Andrée Tiberghien and to Matthieu Quignard for their comments on this work, and to reviewers of this book for their help in clarifying the expression of my ideas. This research was financed by the Centre National de la Recherche Scientifique (CNRS).

NOTES

1. The terms *interaction*, *communicative interaction*, *argumentative interaction* and *constructive interaction* will be discussed in more detail below. For the present, we assume an intuitive understanding on the part of the reader.
2. Our brief discussion necessarily touches upon fundamental and contentious issues in cognitive science concerning the nature of cognition and action, that we can of course not resolve: our aim is simply to clarify our own position with respect to these matters.
3. *C.f.*, Lave (1991), p. 67: '[situated social practice] emphasizes the relational interdependency of agent and world, activity, meaning, cognition, learning and knowing.'
4. For example, if a speaker S, in a certain context, makes the utterance 'The door!', directed towards a hearer H, this counts as a communicative action to the extent that S intends to produce the cognitive effect in H 'H understands that S wants H to shut the door', by means of H's recognition of S's intention 'S intends me, H, to understand that S wants me to shut the door'. If S had no such intention (e.g., S had no intention that H should recognise his intention; S knew that H intended to shut the door in any case), then this does not count as a communicative action. In this case S would have made a locutionary act

(the uttering of words having a linguistic meaning), but not an illocutionary, or communicative, act (Austin, 1962; Searle, 1969).
5   For example, X could push Y towards a door with the communicative intention that Y understand that X wants Y to leave.
6   In this quite general definition we use the term 'view' in order to avoid theoretical commitments with respect to the public or private nature of argumentation. A view could be interpreted as a proposition, a propositional attitude, a (public) statement, or even a speech act. In terms of a dialectical model of argumentative interactions, the view with respect to which participants adopt opposed positions is termed a thesis.
7   In Barth & Krabbe's (1982) dialectical theory, such positions are termed 'dialectical roles', and can be either 'proponent' or 'opponent'.
8   The three phases can be compared with the stages for rational discussions described by van Eemeren & Grootendorst (1984).
9   By 'discourse' we mean a spoken or written linguistic product (*e.g.*, a speech, a text) that is not produced in a communicative interaction.
10 See van Eemeren, Grootendorst & Henkemans (1996), chapter 9, pp. 246-273, for a general introduction.
11 See research on belief revision in artificial intelligence, for example Gardenförs (1992).
12 Walton (1992) gives the example of a debate on the desirability of the institution of tipping in the USA, that becomes a debate on the more fundamental issue of what should be the role of the state in regulating work practices.
13 Strictly speaking, we should distinguish *interactive* pressure – the obligation to respond in interaction, to think of one's reply in real time – from *interactional* pressure, which concerns social aspects of interaction (see Muntigl & Turnbull, 1998) such as loss or preservation of 'face' (the person who is refuted may lose face, resolution of the verbal conflict must be negotiated so that face is preserved).
14 Note that interaction management, rights and obligations, self and other-images, *etc.* may also be negotiated (see *e.g.*, Moeschler, 1985).
15 All students' names have been changed, and all dialogues have been translated from the original French by the author. The complete corpus (in French) is publicly available at: http://sir.univ-lyon2.fr/GRIC-COAST/DRED/
16 The extract shows a micro-level rhetorical shift (of position, or attitude, with respect to a view) within the argumentative interaction sequence itself. Analysis of more global rhetorical changes would require analysing the students' communicative interaction after the argumentative interaction sequence. For example, if a student continues to propose a thesis that was refuted, then this implies no direct rhetorical change as a function of the dialectical dimension (see Baker 1996a, 1996b for a detailed discussion of this issue).
17 We provide such an analysis of this short section simply in order to illustrate the method. For more details see Baker (1996a, 1996b).
18 We add one additional symbol '♦' to indicate moves that have the function of conceding – either a statement, or else a claim concerning the outcome of the argumentation itself – and a second, '⊗', to indicate explicitation of the argumentation outcome.
19 Note that this is in fact false. Mary has not understood that in modelling, there is no necessary one to one correspondence between entities to be modelled and elements of the model – it is not because there are two wires that there

must be two *transfers* of energy; there should be only one transfer, of electrical work, from the battery to the bulb.

Software for Problem Solving through Collaborative Argumentation

Arja L. Veerman
Department of Educational Sciences, Utrecht University
Tamsin Treasure-Jones
Computer Based Learning Unit, University of Leeds

ABSTRACT

In this chapter we focus on how to provoke and support collaborative argumentation in order to optimize open-ended problem solving in network-based learning environments. Taking task characteristics into consideration, support could be designed for the important cognitive processes of collaborative argumentation. Based upon studies of five network-based environments, we propose a framework that considers both characteristics of the task and structured interaction. Our main finding is that structuring interaction at the interface does not necessarily provoke argumentation. The initiation of argument seems to be related to task characteristics, such as use of a competitive instructional task design. However, our review shows that both task characteristics and structured interaction play an interconnected role in supporting argumentation during collaborative problem solving.

1 INTRODUCTION

One of the main principles of constructivist learning theory is the negotiated construction of knowledge through dialogue. Understanding is achieved through interaction within an environment (Salomon, 1997), in which students, tutors, the task information, and (electronic) tools are available. It is believed that learning is achieved when we are presented with conflicts, and manage through negotiation (alone or in a group) to produce a solution: 'cognitive conflict or puzzlement is the stimulus for learning and determines the organization and nature of what is learned' (Savery & Duffy, 1996). In Piaget's terms this describes the need for accommodation when current experience can not be assimilated in existing schema: the sociocognitive conflict (Piaget, 1977). Such learning through negotiation can consist of testing understanding and ideas against each other as a mechanism for enriching, interweaving, and expanding understanding of particular phenomena. Active engagement in collaborative argumentation during problem solving fits this principle by giving prominence to conflict and query as mechanisms for enriching, combining, and expanding understanding of problems that have to be solved (Savery & Duffy, 1996). After all, as VonGlaserfeld (1989) has noted, other people are the greatest source of alternative views to challenge our current views, and hence to serve as the source of cognitive conflict that stimulates learning.

We consider an argument to be a structured connection of claims, evidence, rebuttals *etc.*. A minimal argument is a claim for which at least doubt or disbelief is expressed (van Eemeren, Grootendorst & Snoeck Henkemans, 1995). Such doubt or disbelief can be expressed by an individual (if working alone) or by a partner in an argumentative dialogue. In response to such doubts, a complex structure may be produced, potentially including features such as chaining of arguments, qualifications, contraindications, counter-arguments, and rebuttals. Hence the argument is the product, the structure linking claims, evidence, and rebuttals. The process by which the argument is produced, we refer to as argumentation.

Our interest lies in argumentation structures that are built by groups of students involved in collaborative problem solving. During problem solving, we expect students to make various claims about the domain and the potential solutions. It is possible that during the problem solving no doubt is expressed regarding the claims and solutions, and hence no argument emerges in the dialogue. However, such a situation seems unlikely, and we believe would not produce the best solution for the problem. Certainly, if the students have not produced reasons to support the claims and solutions during the problem solving process itself, then we have no reason to believe that they will be able to produce such reasons at a later date. Therefore, we believe that students should be encouraged to use argumentation processes to build argument structures during problem solving. The argumentation processes discussed in this chapter are: (a) argument elaboration: produces support for claims and chains arguments together; (b) critical checking: evaluates the strength and relevancy of information, in order to integrate it into the argument structure and/or in order to assess the validity of its current position in the argument structure; (c) multiple viewpoints: consideration of alternative claims and counterarguments in order to choose the preferred claim/solution and to produce rebuttals where necessary.

This chapter addresses how such argumentation processes can be supported in electronic environments. We will consider academic students actively engaged in collaborative argumentation in order to solve open-ended problems such as writing papers, constructing hypotheses, or designing computer-based learning programs. These types of problems are characterized by the existence of justifiable beliefs and multiple acceptable viewpoints, as described by Baker (1992). In working on problems together, students first have to establish a (partially) shared focus, which can be changed, maintained, or refined during the problem solving process (Roschelle, 1992). The focus determines the concentration on thematic parts (subproblems) of the problem to be solved. Subsequently, information relevant to the sub-problem must be generated and gathered from mental or material resources. The next phase is to critically check its strength (Is the information true?) and relevance (Is the information appropriate?), before integrating it into the problem solving process (for instance, by assimilating new information in a writing assignment). Finally, after discussing alternative solutions, the strongest and most relevant one must be chosen (Erkens, 1997).

1.1 Argumentation in problem solving assignments

In constructivism, learning is philosophically viewed as enriching understanding in interaction with the environment (Savery & Duffy, 1996). Knowledge is actively constructed, connected to the individual's cognitive repertoire and to a broader, often team-based, and interdisciplinary context in which learning activities take place (Salomon, 1997). Constructivism seems to be influenced not only by a Piagetian perspective on individual cognitive development through sociocognitive conflict, but also by the sociocultural approach emphasizing the process of interactive knowledge construction in which the appropriation of meaning through negotiation plays a central role (Greeno, 1997). From a constructivistic perspective, collaborative argumentation during problem solving can be regarded as an activity encouraging learning through mechanisms such as externalizing knowledge and opinions, self-explanation, reflecting on each other's information, and reconstructing knowledge through critical discussion.

Several studies show the positive effects of collaborative argumentation during open-ended problem solving (Burnett, 1993; Erkens, 1997). Burnett analyzed the dialogues between students engaged in a collaborative writing task, and found that students who became involved in 'substantial conflict' during the writing assignment ended up considering more alternative solutions, and finally produced better papers. 'Substantial conflict' not only involved the considering of multiple perspectives, but also a critical evaluation of these alternatives. Students who did not engage in this type of conflict tended to compromise too soon and produced poorer solutions. Another example is the study of Erkens (1997), in which pairs of students solved partly predefined problems. He found that during and after phases of information checking, argumentation significantly contributed to the success of the final problem solution.

In almost every part of the problem solving process, difficulties may arise. Students can fail to understand each other or to maintain focus on the same thematic content. They can be biased towards agreement, and consequently fail to query or counter doubtful information. Elaboration may not be focused on key concepts and misconceptions may not be recognized. Argumentation might help to minimize some of these problems. In collaborative argumentation it is essential to evaluate new information, to stimulate the amount and variety of elaboration, and to consider multiple perspectives. This can be achieved by a critique of information (either through expressing doubt, or by generating counter-arguments), producing justifications, and considering pro and contra arguments in relation to each other. Unfortunately, collaborative argumentation does not always arise spontaneously and does not always embody the most important features that contribute to the problem solving process. Several studies (Baker, 1996; Pilkington & Mallen, 1996; Veerman, 1996) have shown that engaging in discussion depends on task characteristics, including the domain, the learning goals, the instructions, and the expected product. Therefore, argumentation may have to be provoked: for instance, through task design. In network-based environments, structured interaction may encourage students to engage in critical argumentation. Moreover, essential cognitive processes in collaborative argumentation could be *supported*, such as: critical evaluation of information, multiple perspective taking, (varied) elaboration.

1.2 Computer mediated communication

In this chapter we will concentrate on students taking part in text-based argumentation via computer mediated communication (CMC) systems such as chatboxes or newsgroups available on the Internet. As with Face-to-Face communication (F2F), in CMC participants have to span a transactional distance. This 'psychological and communication space to be crossed', is a space of potential misunderstanding between the creation and interpretation of participants' utterances (M.G. Moore, 1993; Pea, 1993). The meaning of an utterance in F2F communication can be conveyed by use of visual and inflective cues, such as face expression and intonation (Mason, 1992). Most CMC systems do not enable these multi-modal forms of communication, and hence there is an increased risk of misinterpretation (M.G. Moore, 1993). Without understanding each other, only feigned arguments occur, not leading to knowledge development.

In addition, printed text appears to encourage a sense of closure. A printed text is often assumed to have reached a state of completion. Subjects are seduced into believing and accepting ideas and statements which they see in print as true, simply because they are in written form (Mason, 1992). It is not clear whether students treat text in a CMC environment in the same manner as printed text, or whether it is regarded as an ongoing dialogue. Although students share the same communicational context, they might be not as critical of new information or possible problem solutions as they would be in F2F settings.

To *provoke* and *support* argumentation in CMC systems, text-based interaction can be structured at the interface. Appropriated to task characteristics, students can be provided with dialogue markers, sentence openers, and turn-taking control. These options might improve shared understanding, focus maintenance, or critical assessment of new information. Additional options for free text interaction could stimulate elaboration, whereas careful use of turn-taking control and dialogue rules could guide the interaction without constraining it. In addition, graphic representation of arguments might support the exploration of multiple perspectives and the identification of misconceptions and gaps.

To examine how to *provoke* and *support* collaborative argumentation in CMC systems, this chapter first considers the role of collaborative argumentation in problem solving. Important cognitive processes in collaborative argumentation during open-ended problem solving will be discussed. Secondly, the characteristics of open-ended problem solving tasks, including specific learning goals and instructional design, will be linked to collaborative argumentation. In order to discuss how task characteristics could be related to electronic support for collaborative argumentation in CMC systems, we will review five examples of network-based environments, comparing features of structured interaction intended to *provoke* or *support* collaborative argumentation. To conclude this review, we suggest that structuring interaction is marginally effective in *provoking* argumentation, but more clearly contributes to its *support*. However, since each experiment has different task and interface characteristics we have to consider these findings as suggestions for future research questions rather than conclusions in themselves.

2 COLLABORATIVE ARGUMENTATION IN OPEN-ENDED PROBLEM SOLVING

Collaborative problem solving is frequently used to promote learning. Discussion can be particularly productive when problems are characterized by globally defined task goals and incomplete available knowledge (Erkens, 1997). These open problem solving tasks, such as answering an essay question, are characterized by

participants having incomplete knowledge of the subject, and having to use (justified) beliefs and values to work on multiple acceptable strategies, viewpoints, and problem solutions (Baker, 1992). Collaborative argumentation allows students to discuss their incomplete or conflicting knowledge, and to use each other as a source of information and evaluation. However, engaging in discussion does not necessarily result in good collaboration, argumentation, or problem solving. For instance, failure to note a misconception that has been made explicit in the dialogue will not advance the problem solving process. Also, a compromise solution, proposed and accepted in order to avoid conflict, may be worse than either of the conflicting solutions (Baker, 1996). The questions considered in this chapter, therefore, are:
(1) In which phases of solving open-ended problems is collaborative argumentation most productive? (2) What characteristics can be identified (of the task, the instruction and of structured interaction) that (a) provoke argumentation, (b) support the following cognitive processes in collaborative argumentation: *critical checking of new information, exploration of multiple perspectives, and (varied) elaboration.*

2.1 Focus

In collaborative problem solving, students have to initiate and maintain a shared focus of the problem (Erkens, 1997). They have to agree on the overall goal, descriptions of the current problem state, and available problem solving actions (Roschelle & Teasley, 1995). Focusing on the thematic content is essential for the global and local level of communication. Through the global level, students keep track of the main goals or concepts. Through the local, or direct level, students can discuss relations between different features of (sub-)goals or concepts. Both 'problem spaces' (Bereiter & Scardamalia, 1987: 13) need to be coherent (Erkens, 1997: 3.3.1; van Wijk, 1995). Because focus plays an important role in the interpretation and understanding of communicative utterances, failure to maintain a shared focus will result in a decrease of mutual understanding and problem solving quality (Erkens, 1997).

A range of problems related to focus has been identified in collaborative problem solving (Erkens 1997). Erkens transcribed thirty protocols of ten- to twelve-year-olds students working in pairs on a problem solving task called *The Camp Puzzle*, and analyzed seven dialogues in depth. In this task, students had to derive the personal characteristics of six children by combining given statements. However, the information required to solve the task had been distributed between the two students. Therefore, the students had to exchange information and negotiate their inferences and task strategy. Erkens found that low-performing dyads exhibited greater difficulties in focusing than high-performing dyads. Problems arose because students became confused about the shared focus, or students changed their shared focus before reaching a solution to the previous subproblem. Specifically, focus confusion occurred when students: did not elaborate on each others' utterances; became fixed upon their own focus and therefore only interpreted incoming information from their own perspective; did not develop their own viewpoint, did not negotiate about focus and simply followed the focus taken by their partner.

Changing focus before solving a sub-problem caused difficulties either because the sub-problem was forgotten and never solved, or because students returned to the problem later and repeated their earlier mistakes.

Baker & Bielaczyc (1995) studied students working in C-CHENE, a computerized tool for collaborative problem solving in the domain of physics. They claim that failure to maintain a shared focus is one of the main problems leading to missed opportunities. These are situations in which students could have used each other as a resource for learning, but did not.

Collaborative argumentation might be of help in initiating the problem solving process. Through argumentation, the focus on the task goal and the themes can be determined. Collaborative argumentation can support the discussion of what focus to share and maintain. Although this does not have to lead to knowledge development, it is an essential precondition for fruitful problem solving. In the next section, we will discuss the role of argument checking processes in open-ended problem solving.

2.2 Argument checking

Having started the collaborative problem solving process with a (partly) shared focus, students can progress by generating or gathering information relevant to the current problem. This could be information retrieved from memory, or new information from resources such as books or the Internet. Students should be involved in informing, elaboration, and questioning at this stage in order to ensure that relevant information is known and understood by all participants. Students should check new information against their existing knowledge. The following are examples of the sort of questions students should use to evaluate the new information: 'Is the new information relevant to the current problem?', 'Is the new information consistent with existing knowledge or is there a conflict?' and 'How reliable is the new information?'. When new information is considered doubtful or disbelieved, then students can check the information by means of clarification questions (Bunt, 1989) or (counter)arguments.

Checking new information does not only involve logical cognitive processes. It also depends on the problem context, prior knowledge, interest, beliefs, and values of the individual problem solvers (Toulmin, Rieke & Janik, 1984; Baker, 1994; Stein & Miller, 1991). Therefore, checking information is to some extent subjective. To scrutinize information critically, Petty and Cacioppo (1986) described an approach for argument checking. Their model describes how to check new information along the *central route*, which involves treating it as being 'problematic'. In scrutinizing information along the central route, relevant knowledge is used in order to evaluate the information argumentatively on its *strength* and *relevance*. Thus, information can be related to existing knowledge, leading to acceptance, doubt, or disagreement. Especially in the case of doubt or disagreement, questions or counter-arguments can be generated to evaluate the information. Although the central route is the most 'objective' approach, the cognitive effort involved is tremendous. The more complex the problem under discussion, the harder it will be to scrutinize every chunk of new information in this manner. Instead of taking the central route, checking can also proceed along a second, less reliable but easier and faster *peripheral route*. Here, in contrast to the central route, evaluation is the result of associations with affective cues, or the result of making inferences about the probable correctness of information, and the desirability of a certain problem solving strategy or solution. Affective cues such as the source's expertise, the dominance of a peer student, or simply the sum of given arguments can be used as 'evidence' in checking new information. Scrutinizing information along this route requires less cognitive effort, but the problem solving is less 'objective' than when the central route is followed.

Previous research (Chan, 1995; Baker & Bielaczyc, 1995; Erkens, 1997) has identified problems associated with checking information during collaborative problem solving. Chan studied 108 students (54 in grade nine and 54 in grade twelve) learning biological evolution theories, which contradicted their beliefs. Comparisons were made between situations in which conflict was maximized and minimized. The specific goal was to evaluate whether students using *problem-centered* discourse moves gained more, as shown by the post-test scores. The production of problem-centered moves is comparable to processes of checking information along the central route (Petty & Cacioppo, 1986). Students using problem-centered moves identified problems in their partner's statements and reformulated problems into questions of inquiry. They connected new information to existing information, tested it by countering, and looked for inconsistencies. Chan found a significant difference between the average number of problem-centered moves in high-achieving pairs (fourteen) and low-achieving pairs (two). Situations in which conflict was maximized were more advantageous for students than situations with minimized conflict.

Baker and Bielaczyc (1995) also found that missed opportunities occur when students are biased towards early agreement, and therefore process each other's information before checking it critically. Taking this learning approach, identified as *problem-minimization* (Bereiter & Scardamalia, 1993), means that checking processes are not following the central route, but they are aimed at minimizing problems or necessary belief revision.

In Erkens' study (1997), the checking processes of low-achieving problem solving pairs were compared to those used by high-achieving problem solving pairs. Several problems were identified in the processes used by the low-achieving pairs. Difficulties occurred when transmitted information was doubtful or unclear, but was not queried or countered in the dialogue. Even when check-questions were asked, elaborations and justifications were not asked for or given. Incorrect inferences were made without checking the resources, and no questions were asked to elaborate on other possible problem solutions. Better problem solving pairs used more checking procedures and a variety of arguments; they questioned new information and elaborated on justifications.

In processing discussed information, possible problem solutions have to be produced. These solutions have to be evaluated and, for some assignments, a final solution has to be chosen (*e.g.*, decision making tasks). When evaluating problem solving solutions, Erkens (1997) found that low-achieving pairs encountered the same difficulties with checking as when they evaluated gathered information. When a proposed solution was doubtful or unclear, again, few check-questions were asked and no counter-arguments were produced. Better problem solving pairs checked their proposed solutions and discussed argumentatively which solution to choose, using a variety of argument types and elaborating on the arguments.

Although argumentation in collaborative problem solving dialogues can occur in every stage of the problem solving process, argumentation is crucial during two particular phases (Erkens, 1997). Argumentation can contribute significantly to the problem solving process when new information is considered. This information should be critically discussed before being integrated into the existing knowledge structures. This is also the case when solutions are evaluated argumentatively before a definitive solution is selected. Argumentation to share or maintain focus, results in satisfying preconditions for productive collaborative problem solving, it does not necessarily advance the construction of knowledge.

2.3 Exploration of multiple perspectives

Another aspect also influences the contribution argumentation can make in collaborative open problem solving tasks. In argumentation, students have to take into account contrasting points of view. Holding different points of view can result in different evaluations of the information's strength and relevance, and the problem solution's acceptability. In open-ended problem solving, students have to elaborate on multiple perspectives in order to relate, compare, and differentiate the effects of various problem solving activities or possible problem solutions. However, biased behavior in argumentative discussions can inhibit students in their collaborative problem solving process. In biased discussions, students do not share information efficiently, but focus only on a small amount of information available.

Using as a basis the 'Biased Simpling Model of Discussion', Hightower and Sayeed (1995) studied students discussing which candidate to choose for a specific job. The Biased Simpling Model of Discussion predicts that students will (1) favor their own positions and attack opposing positions, thus producing imbalance in the argument, (2) accept group preferences, (3) elaborate on shared information rather than distributed information, and (4) concentrate on perspectives with a high proportion of information available. In Hightower's experiment, 93 students working in groups of three were provided with partly shared and partly distributed information about several imaginary candidates for a job. Their task was to discuss and finally select the candidate they thought would be most suitable for the job, based upon the information given. Fifteen groups worked using the Electronic Discussion System (EDS), a synchronous tool supporting Computer Mediated Communication (CMC). The other groups worked in a Face-to-Face condition. Results of the study confirmed the predictions based upon the Biased model. Biased behavior occurred when defending their own positions and attacking opposing points of view. This phenomenon is strongly supported by several other studies on argumentative discussions (Veerman & Andriessen, 1997; Kuhn, 1991; Voss & Means, 1991; Stein, Cacclichia & Bernas, 1996). Independent, of the mode of communication (F2F or CMC), Hightower also found that the discussion was more biased when there was a large amount of shared information. Students aimed for consensus by focusing on the most popular information in the group. In addition, it was found that a high information load provoked biased discussions. Most interestingly, Hightower found more biased behavior in the CMC environment than the F2F setting. She concluded that students have to put more effort into transmitting information in CMC discussions versus F2F discussions. In crossing the 'transactional distance' reaching mutual understanding is more difficult, and, therefore, biased discussions occur more easily.

To summarize, using the following processes during the evaluation of new information and acceptable problem solutions, can optimize the following problem solving process:
1. critical assessment of new information,
2. exploration of multiple perspectives,
3. varied elaboration.

The characteristics of the task, instruction, or structured interaction might support these cognitive processes in collaborative argumentation. In CMC systems, particular attention must be paid to reaching mutual understanding, critically assessing new information, and preventing biased behavior.

However, whilst it is important to consider the problems students encounter during argument, the first step is to encourage students to engage in argumentative discussions. Several studies (Baker, 1996; Pilkington & Mallen, 1996; Veerman, 1996) have shown that whether students start critical discussions depends on task characteristics, including the domain, the learning goals, the instructions, and the expected product. Providing students with predefined and conflicting information or competitive forms of instruction combined with a joint solution, can provoke argumentative discussions. This issue will be pursued in the next section.

3 COLLABORATIVE ARGUMENTATION AND TASK CHARACTERISTICS

In open-ended problem solving tasks, collaborative argumentation has to be initiated, especially in the phases prior to integrating new knowledge into existing knowledge structures and deciding on the most acceptable problem solution. One critical task feature for argumentation is that the subject matter is debatable. Normative loaded subjects, such as abortion or discrimination, are likely to inhibit argumentative discussion for social reasons (Golder, 1998). Discussions do not always start spontaneously and may have to be provoked. Spontaneous discussions are likely to arise when doubt is expressed about specific statements, arguments, or conclusions. Grouping students with conflicting opinions (Stein, Calicchia & Bernard, 1996) or involving students in preparatory individual work prior to collaboration (Bull & Broady, 1997) increases the likelihood of conflict, and hence, spontaneous argument. Instructing students about role-playing activities, such as defending or attacking predefined and conflicting stances (Veerman & Andriessen, 1997), can also provoke discussions. In addition, students can be given different goals concerning the 'closure' of arguments. For example, they could be instructed to reach consensus, to win discussions, or to stop a discussion when an impasse is reached. Also, students may be asked to create an individual or joint *final product* based upon their argumentative discussion (*e.g.*, an oral presentation or an argumentative text).

Defining learning goals and the expected final product can encourage students to *engage* in argumentative discussions, but this alone can not overcome the difficulties students have in critical argumentation *during* discussions. However, knowing that the final product will be assessed can act as a motivation, increasing the effort put into the argument evaluation by the students. Besides, although creating a joint product stimulates positive interdependency (Erkens, 1997), students tend to accept each other's information without critical assessment of new information in relation to existing information (Suthers & Weiner, 1995: formative evaluations; Veerman & Andriessen, 1997). Moreover, students tend towards a partial and biased search through the problem space (Hightower & Sayeed, 1995). Therefore, instructions should aim to encourage a critical, multiple-sided, and elaborated argumentative discussion. Two options for effective instructional design will be discussed in the next two paragraphs.

One approach to providing support through instruction would be to advise students to be competitive, critique each other's information, and not to accept new information without being convinced of its strength and relevance. In this situation students must be thorough and persuasive, finding as many reasonable arguments as possible in order to convince the other person to accept their point of view. However, if a final joint product is required, students must reach a consensus at the end of their discussion. This can be solved by instructing students to produce justifications for their position and to present it to the other students during an argumentative discussion in which they attempt to refute the other position and rebut attacks on their position. Finally, they are instructed to drop all advocacies and seek a synthesis that takes both perspectives and positions into account in order to construct a joint product (Johnson & Johnson, 1993; Veerman & Andriessen, 1997).

A second example is to provide students with predefined stances. By providing predefined stances, the global focus of the discussion is made explicit. Students are aware of each other's stance and thus have fewer problems interpreting each other's utterances and constructing mutual understanding. Since the problem space has been clearly defined, information checking procedures can focus on relevance to the predefined stances within the boundaries of the problem space. However, providing students with predefined stances might not support information checking based on critical argumentation. One possible problem is that students will not feel motivated to critique their partner's information. Enforcing predefined stances without making concessions to personal beliefs and values may mean that the student does not feel any responsibility to critically defend a statement. To support critical argumentation, in this setting, students could be asked to produce the stances themselves. Thus, students will have personally constructed the stance, and therefore feel responsible for it (Veerman & Andriessen, 1997). Because of the predefined stances the problem space is bounded, aiding the process of checking information.

Another issue that is related to the task and its influence on argumentation is the problem solving domain. Although the domain does not directly affect the quality of collaborative argumentation, it influences the methods used to check new information. In rich problem solving areas including scientific information, students could be instructed to check information critically using scientific theories and empirical or logical evidence, rather than personal information. In less rich problem solving domains, personal-oriented arguments could be valued based upon the beliefs and values shared by social communities or authorized individuals (Freeman, 1992). When scientific arguments are used, checking on strength can be based upon theories, empirical evidence, or logical reasoning chains extracted from verifiable resources. However, 'correct' scientific information resources will not decisively settle all arguments. The interpretation of information can differ and the relevance of information can be a matter of discussion. In academic learning, students aim to check arguments on verifiable resources whenever it is possible. Raising this issue through instruction could be useful.

To summarize, instructional support can be usefully given at the start of the discussion and during the negotiation process of the discussion. Taking into consideration the domain, goal, and content of the task, instruction can be tailored towards optimizing checking procedures in collaborative argumentation, and towards optimizing the scope and variety of elaboration in argumentation. In network-based environments support could be provided for these important but problematic processes by structuring the interaction at the interface.

4 NETWORK-BASED ENVIRONMENTS FOR SOLVING PROBLEMS THROUGH ARGUMENTATION

Five systems have been chosen for this review. The selection of the systems is constrained by focusing on features affecting collaborative argumentation as described in the earlier sections.

First, the chosen CMC systems are all designed for educational tasks in which the emphasis is on collaborative argumentation as a method to optimize problem solving, or as a final learning goal. There are published results available on the use of all five systems and, in particular, data related to argument usage. Secondly, the chosen network-based environments are all designed for symmetrical interaction. This means that participants do not have formal differences in power and status (as tutors and students do), and although prior knowledge will vary, students are expected to have comparable cognitive backgrounds. Furthermore, four of the systems are designed for synchronous communication, whereas one system is designed for asynchronous communication. In synchronous forms of communication, both interlocutors have to be present at the same time; for example, when using computerized chat boxes or a telephone. In asynchronous communication, the interaction can be delayed by hours, days, or weeks, as is the case with e-mail, because the multiple participants do not have to be present and use the system at the same time.[1] The selected CMC systems, including the asynchronous environment, were only used for short task assignments, rather than assignments completed over a period of weeks or months. In addition, we only considered CMC tasks in which a product or closing of the discussion was required. When considering the electronic features of the CMC systems, we searched for a range of environments that demonstrated different approaches to structuring the interaction in order to support communication, and more specifically, argumentation. In Table 1, the selected systems are listed with short remarks on the structured interaction.

For each system, we will briefly describe the mode of communication, the main learning goal(s), and the support for argumentation (aimed at the process or product) provided through structuring the interaction. In discussing the systems, success at provoking and supporting argumentation, characteristics of the task, instruction, and structured interaction will be considered.

4.1 The Dialab system

The Dialab system (D. Moore, 1993) is a synchronous communication tool, designed to teach argument and critical thinking skills using a rigid, logic-based dialogue game (MacKenzie, 1985). Students use the Dialab system in pairs. The Dialab system mediates argumentative dialogues between students, applying rules from MacKenzie's dialogue game (DG). DG defines a set of dialogue moves (allowable move types), a set of commitment rules (used to monitor the statements each player has committed to during the dialogue), and a set of dialogue rules (which determine which move types can follow each other).

Table 1 Selected CMC systems and characteristics of structured interaction.

CMC system	Structured interaction
Dialab	Rigid turn-taking control Rigid communication rules
Conference MOO	No turn-taking control Mixture of structured communication rules and free input of text
CTP	Semienforced turn-taking control in task window No communication rules
CLARE	Asynchronous turn taking Double-layered rigid communication rules
Belvédère	No turn-taking control Graphically represented communication rules in task window

When using the system, one of the students starts by choosing a move from the set of sentence openers (for example *I assert that*, *Is it the case that*...) as shown in Figure 1. Each of these sentence openers is represented within the system as a type of dialogue move (for example *Statement* or *Question*). Once the student has chosen a sentence opener, the system displays the selected move type at the bottom of the Input window (see 'Player 3 Input' window in Figure 1). Although the interaction is partly restricted to a menu-based interface, after a move has been chosen, free text can be entered into the system. Thus, Player 1 is allowed to choose the statement move 'I assert that...' and put in free text after this utterance '.....in education computers are a waste of money'. Turn taking is rigidly enforced and a participant can only make one dialogue move per turn. Their opponent will not see this move until they choose to send it, by pressing the DONE button. There is no mechanism for interrupting a turn, or for chatting in an unrestricted manner. Following a turn, the computer system updates the sender's commitment store (using the commitment rules) and the move and statement records. Control now passes to Student 2, who must choose a move. Based on the preceding move type, the dialogue rules determine which move types Student 2 can choose in response. For example, a question cannot be followed by another question. Within the freetext entry, the student can explicitly refer to a statement in the statement record. Hence, by choosing the sentence opener *Why*... and pointing at Statement 1, the responding student's move will become 'Why are computers in education a waste of money?' (in the system's internal representation: challenge statement 1).

The commitment rules keep track of each participant's commitment store; these are updated following each turn, and are visible to both participants. Besides adding all of the statements made by a student to their commitment store, the system will also add those statements, made by their opponent, that they have neither challenged nor explicitly expressed no commitment to. Figure 1 shows the interface, as

Figure 1   Screendump of the Dialab MOO.

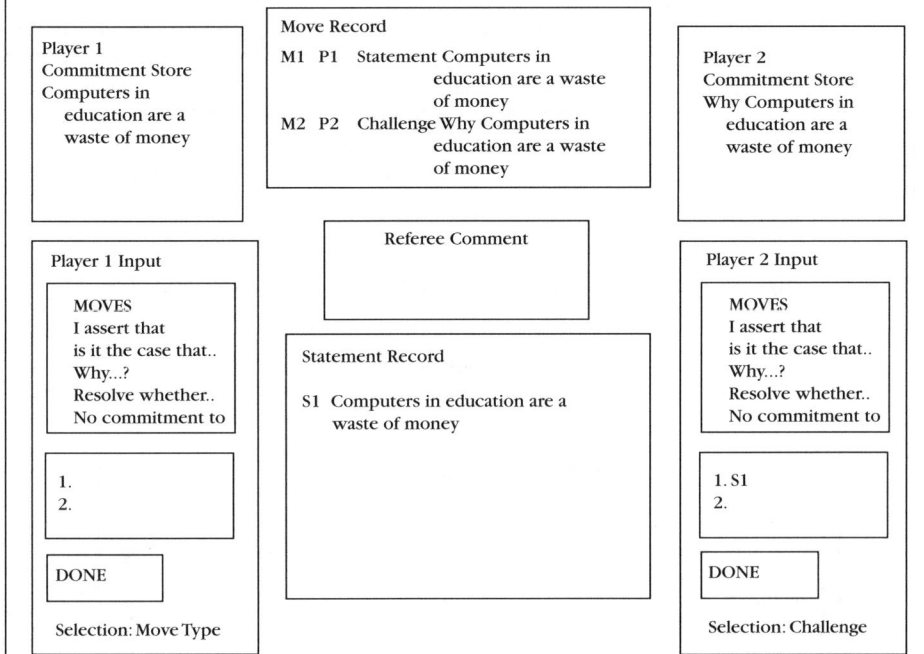

it would appear once the updating is complete following Student 2's move. Finally, win-lose rules are applied to the collaborative dialogue identifying situations in which a participant has won or lost the game (for example, by showing inconsistency in their commitment store). The dialogue ends once one participant has 'won' the game.

4.2 Conference MOO

A Multiple Object-Oriented system (MOO) is a synchronous, text-based virtual environment. Multiple users can connect to a MOO at the same time and interact with each other in these two-dimensional virtual spaces, which are divided into text-based buildings, (class) rooms, and hallways. They can make appointments, arranging where to meet and whom to invite. The flow of communication in a MOO is comparable to that in any synchronous chat. A Multiple-line message can be created and not seen by other participants until the writer 'sends' it. Once 'sent', messages then appear in the shared chat history. One difference between an average chat box and a MOO, is that participants can perform actions (such as wave to each other, wink, smile, and hence express feelings through recognized nonverbal gestures). In a MOO, participants can conduct multiple private conversations as well as public group conversations. The flow of different lines of interaction is not structured. The display of private and public messages from different conversations and on different topics is ordered according to the time they were sent.

In this section we discuss a MOO designed specifically for a scheduling task. Pairs of students have to schedule a conference, taking several constraints into account, such as the number of talks, different themes, and the technical equipment available in each conference room (Jermann & Schneider, 1997). The conference MOO consists of two distinct tools: the first is dedicated to the communication (see: Figure 2) and the second is dedicated to the problem representation (see: Figure 3).

Figure 2   Interface of the communication tool of the conference MOO.

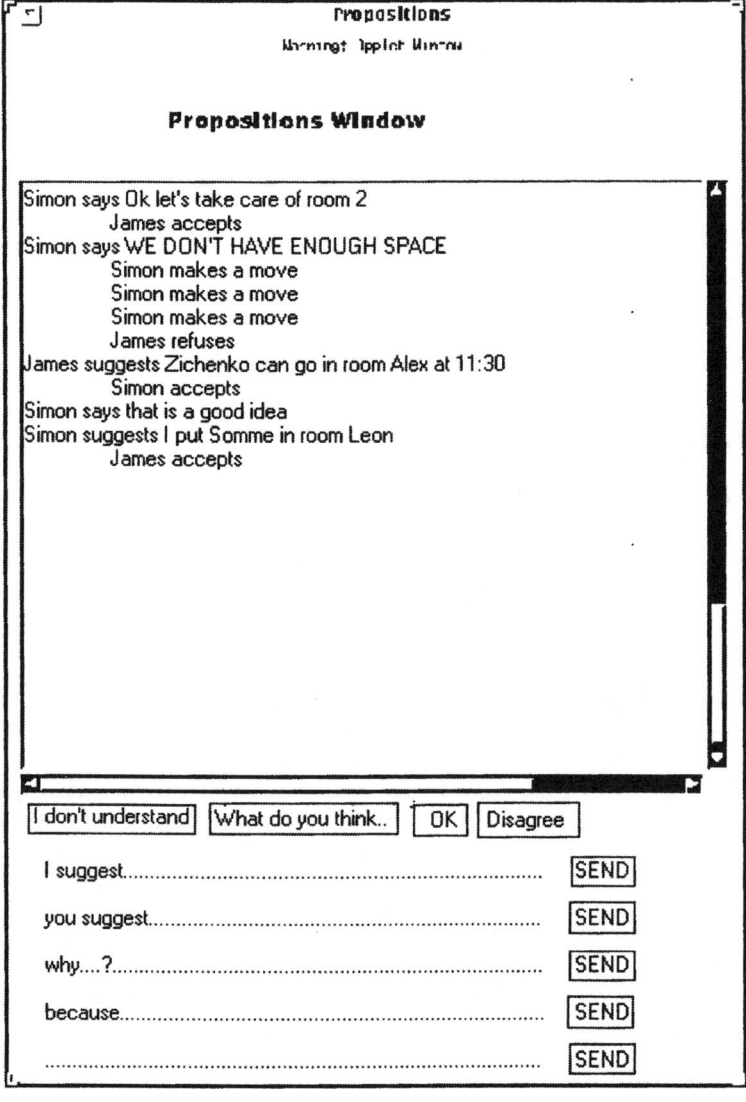

SOFTWARE FOR COLLABORATIVE ARGUMENTATION   217

The communication tool, which provides two modes for communication, is particularly interesting. It comprises a free mode to fill in text fields and a structured mode for delivering utterances by using buttons. The communication tool is intended for synchronous, text-based communication. Students can communicate by pressing buttons, using sentence openers, or by entering free text. A dialogue history displays the utterances and allows students to reply to a particular utterance by selecting it. The reply will be indented underneath the utterance to which it refers. When no item is selected in the dialogue history, the new utterance is added to the end of the history list. This structuring method is common in asynchronous, web-based discussion systems that use 'threading'. Students can choose to communicate using the 'semi-structured' interface or the 'free-text' mode. They are allowed to combine both modes in their communication.

In the semi-structured version of the Conference MOO, four buttons are available, labeled *I don't understand*, *What do you think*, *I agree*, and *I disagree*. In addition there are four text fields containing the sentence openers *I propose*, *You propose!*, *Why*, and *Because*. Free text can be entered after these sentence openers.

Figure 3   Interface of the task window of the conference MOO.

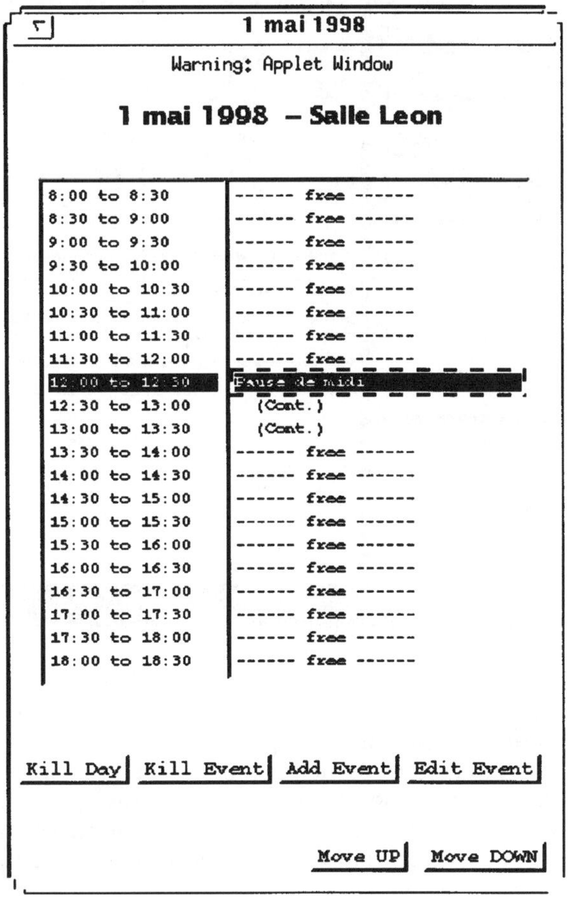

The task window (Figure 3) represents the problem students have to solve collaboratively. In the task window, conference rooms are listed with twenty-one available time slots. Students use this window to create a schedule. Once an event is allotted, it can be moved up and down and it can be edited. The task is finished once the students have allocated a room and a time for all of the talks.

4.3 The CTP system

The CTP system (Collaborative Text Processing) is a synchronous network tool (Andriessen, Erkens, Overeem & Jaspers, 1996). The tool consists of a shared word processor, a chatting tool, and private information resources, and is intended to support collaborative distance writing of argumentative texts. In this version of the program the collaboration and the sharing of windows is restricted to pairs of students. The working screen of the program displays several private and shared windows (see: Figure 4).

Figure 4   Screendump of the CTP system.

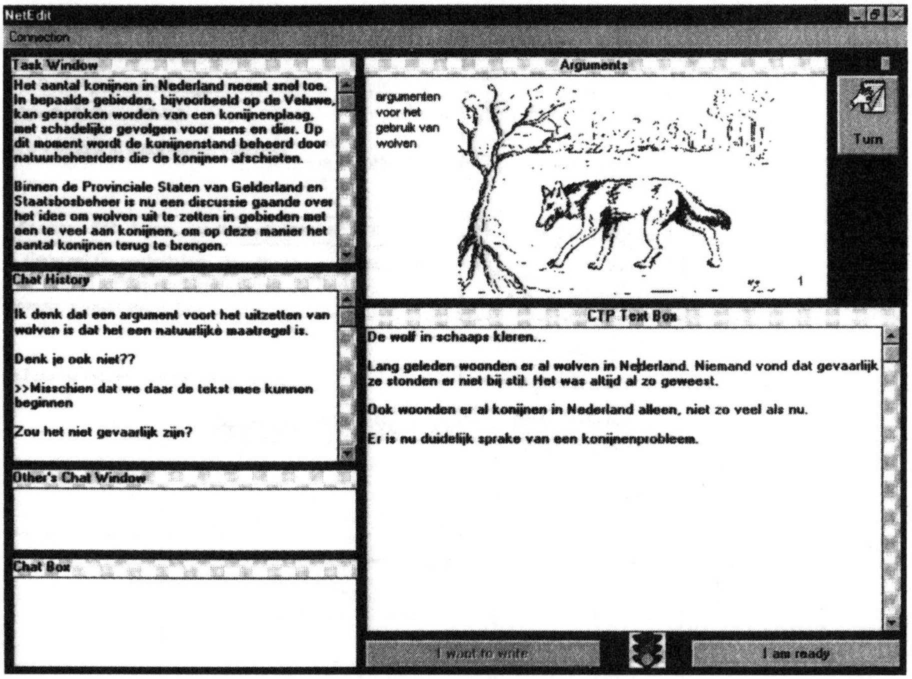

Figure 4 shows a Task and Argument Window at the top of the screen. The Task Window displays the assignment. The Argument Window displays the supporting information given to individual participants. These task-related arguments (in this example, considering the case of encouraging hunting versus increasing the number of wolves to stop the expansion of rabbits ruining Dutch forests) can be presented in text or pictures. Online communication between the writing partners is achieved using a text-based chat box. In the shared text window (CTP Text Box) the participants may enter, edit, and revise the text they are currently writing. Here, putting text into the window is neither constrained nor prompted by menu-based interfaces or preselected utterances. Participants are free to write what they want and express it in any manner. However, turn-taking control of the window is provided using a traffic light mechanism.

4.4 The CLARE system

The CLARE system (Wan & Johnson, 1994) is an asynchronous network tool, developed in order to facilitate meaningful learning through collaborative knowledge construction. Two main phases of (a) Exploration, and (b) Consolidation are involved in the use of the CLARE system. During the Exploration phase, students work individually on summarizing and evaluating text-based study material. These summaries and evaluations are collected in the system's database. During the Consolidation phase, students compare, deliberate, and integrate each other's summaries and evaluations. Similarities and differences between each other's work are the input for asynchronous group discussions. The group size in this phase is not constrained, but the greater the number of students the more complex the task of comparing and discussing will become. Finally, based upon the previous activities, students have to integrate their own knowledge with that of others in order to create a shared knowledge base.

CLARE supports the phases of exploration and consolidation in different ways. The teacher chooses a text, and divides this into sections. The text is then included as a hypertext document within the CLARE system (see lower left-hand window in Figure 5). Students can move around this document using standard navigational links (*e.g.*, Next, Up, and Previous).

Figure 5 Screendump of the CLARE system.

CLARE: RPC-Base						CLARE: RPC-Base										
Session	Edit	Compare	Argument	Integrate	Utilities	ID	User	PR	CL	CO	ME	EV	TH	SU	IN	OT	T^h
Problem 1: Software engineers						236	Peter	1	10	2	0	1	2	3	0	0	19
Author implies that software engineers						240	Curt	1	7	1	0	1	2	1	0	1	14
must be controlled by a figure in authority.						232	Rosa	1	2	3	0	1	0	1	3	1	12
Problem 2: Software Crisis																	
A correct programme must be devised.																	

Session Edit Compare Argument Integrate Utilities	Session Edit Compare Argument Integrate Utilities
hands, throw out the methodoligy, close the door and hack, I become a lapsed software engineer. a member of Hackers, Anymomous, perhaps you do too,	**Name:** Software discipline
	Description: Author implies that software engineers must be controlled...
When I say 'we did not have time to do it right, ...	**Summarisations:** {--> summarises} **Evaluations:** **Integrations:**

Whilst working through the text, students have to summarize and evaluate sections of the text. They are able to highlight parts of the document and use nodes to label the type of section they are summarizing or evaluating. Possible nodes include *Problem*, *Evidence* and *Claim*. The student's choice of node determines the type of template (Figure 5; bottom right-hand corner) generated, into which they enter their short summaries. A link is automatically added between the highlighted text in the left window, the chosen node, and the completed template. Students can now add evaluative remarks to the summary by using nodes such as *Critiquing* or *Question*, which also have associated templates. When the students finish their individual exploration of the text, the group-oriented phase of consolidation starts. The interface changes with this phase. A comparative view of some selected summaries (chosen by matching the node type and text selection) is shown at the top left of the window. Students can add comments and critiques to each other's summaries and evaluations by using the 'Deliberation' node. Students can add as many comments as they like, and build on each other's remarks. In this way, the students engage in a structured asynchronous discussion. Students have access to all of the information in the CLARE database, including the summaries, evaluations, comments, disagreements, or conclusions.

4.5 Belvédère system

Belvédère is a synchronous network-tool developed by the Learning Research and Development Center at the University of Pittsburgh (Learning Research and Development Center, 1996). Among many other applications, Belvédère can be used for constructing argumentative diagrams online, with individuals or groups of students of any size (see: Figure 6). Constructing argumentative diagrams by organizing arguments according to specific problem statements is believed to be a useful learning activity during the planning phase of an ill-structured problem solving task.

Figure 6   Screendump of the Belvédère system.

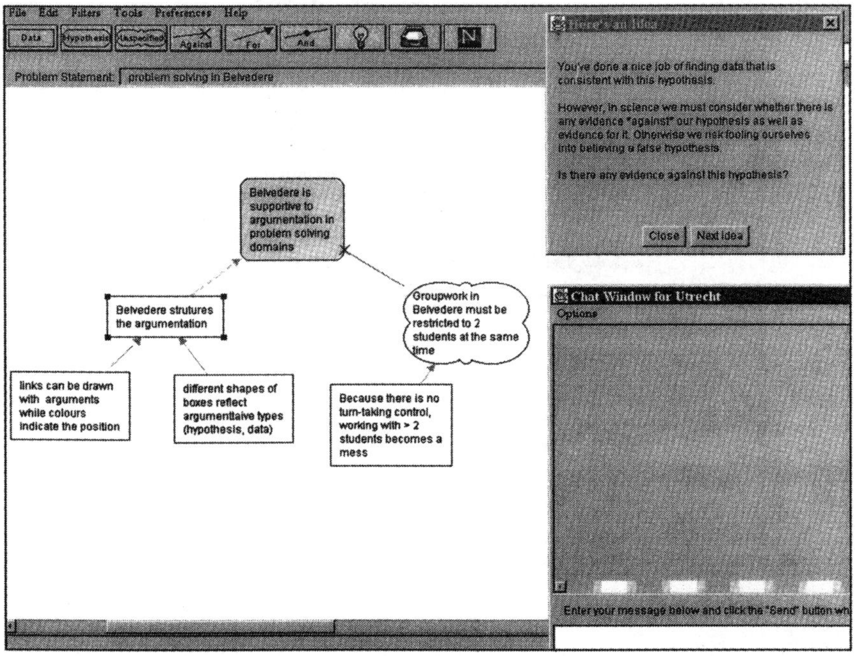

The working screen of the program displays private and shared windows. To communicate with a partner the student has a text-based chat box, as in the CTP system, or a typical MOO, in which multiline messages can be created and sent. Messages will then be displayed, coupled with the writer's name, in the shared chat history. Adding data into the diagram is constrained; students must use the predefined set of boxes (*hypothesis, data, unspecified*) and links (*for, against, and*). These are shown in the menu bar in Figure 6. Links can be given a thickness reflecting a participant's confidence in the information. The thicker the line, the more certain the student is about the input. Participants' names can be displayed alongside their contributions. Thus, students can keep track of who is responsible for each component in the argument diagram. An electronic coach (the 'bulb') is available to give help on demand. The coach gives advice on how to improve the argumentative structure of a diagram.

5 DISCUSSION OF THE SYSTEMS

In every system, an effort has been made to structure the interaction through the interface. In some systems the interaction is structured within the communication windows (Dialab), in other systems the interaction is structured within the task screens (CTP, Belvédère) and some systems structure interactions at both task and communication level (Conference MOO, CLARE). This structure has been provided for several reasons.

Text-based communication can lead to misunderstanding (M.G. Moore, 1993) because nonverbal and paralinguistic cues are not available to support the interpretation of messages. The meaning of utterances must be inferred mainly from the text-based language. To support students in maintaining a shared focus and reaching a shared understanding, interaction can be structured electronically. Turn-taking facilities can help students to keep track of their interactive process. Predefined sentence openers in communication windows such as 'I propose...' or 'Why do you think...', and discourse acts such as *Question* or *Critique* can represent the generation mechanism of an utterance, therefore making explicit the (underlying) goal of an utterance. Buttons, shaped boxes, and links, such as those used in the Belvédère system, can also represent discourse acts graphically and ease the interpretation process.

Another reason to structure interaction in network-based environments is to encourage students to focus on specific parts of the communication or problem solving process. Generally, structuring interaction can lead to an increase of task-oriented behavior, and a decrease of off-task behavior (Baker & Lund, 1997). Specifically, by using a defined (sub)set of discourse acts and sentence openers, students can be encouraged to take part in certain discourse and problem solving activities such as argumentation in order to evaluate an alternative solution.

Moreover, students could be supported in problematic activities such as checking arguments before integrating them into the problem solving process. For instance, in Belvédère, students can present their confidence in claims and evidence by annotating the boxes with comments such as *strongly believe*.

Structuring the interaction in task- or communication windows of network-based environments can help students to understand each other, to share the same focus or to improve their collaborative argumentation. The main question in this section, therefore, is how interaction can be structured to *provoke* and *sup-*

port collaborative argumentation in order to optimize open-ended problem solving. In the next sections, this issue will be explored, and related to the task characteristics and instruction provided in the empirical studies conducted with each of the selected systems.

5.1 Structuring interaction to provoke discussion

Except for the Conferencing MOO system, all the systems have been used for educational purposes, and a considerable amount of argumentation was generated during their use (D. Moore, 1993; Jermann & Schneider, 1997; Andriessen *et al.*, 1996; Wan & Johnson, 1994; Veerman & Andriessen, 1997). Table 2 shows the proportion of argumentative utterances observed during the studies conducted with each of the five systems. In calculating the proportion of argumentative utterances, the sum of the following utterance types: (a) questions triggering arguments, (b) problem statements, (c) argument-oriented pro and contra statements, (d) elaborations of arguments, is divided by the total number of utterances produced in the dialogue or in the final product. Studies with the Dialab system and the Conference MOO calculated the argumentative utterances in the dialogues, whereas the study with the CTP system reported only those argumentative utterances present in the final product (the written text). For the CLARE system, the proportion of argumentative utterances refers to those present in the asynchronous database, whereas the Belvédère study gives approximate figures for the argumentative utterances produced both in the dialogue and the final product (the argumentative diagram). In the Belvédère study the total number of utterances was not measured exactly. This was because non-task-related utterances were mostly counted as one unit, instead of being divided into separate units of utterances. Therefore, we had to estimate the proportion of argumentative utterances based on the rough data available from both the dialogues and diagrams.

Table 2   System design, task characteristics and the proportion of observed argument.

System	Structured	Argumentative task interaction	Observed argument (dialogue)	Observed argument (product)
Dialab	Yes	Yes	1.00	—
CTP	No	Yes	unknown	.91
Belvédère	Yes	Yes	ca. .90	ca. .95
CLARE	Yes	Task problems	.35	dialogue = product

In the pilot study using the Dialab system, seven academic students, previously trained in using the dialogue game, used a partially implemented system. The aim of the system was to support students in a 'fair and reasonable' discussion. An experimenter played the role of the system (as it would perform when fully implemented). The students communicated using standard chat boxes, but had to identify their move type. The experimenter intervened when they broke the dialogue or commitment rules. The interface provided them with specific argumentative dialogue moves, and their task was to engage in the discussion and try to win an argumentative about Capital Punishment. Because of the restricted interface, students were forced to use argumentative utterances, although they could choose to make only assertions or confirmations.

In the CTP system, 74 students in academic social sciences worked on a collaborative writing task. Each pair was instructed to write two texts, (1) considering the problem of the overpopulation of rabbits, and (2) considering labor policy. Pairs were randomly assigned to different conditions in order to encourage a fruitful discussion as part of the writing process. Students were provided with predefined arguments in (a) a textual format, or (b) graphical representations. Except for turn-taking facilities in the task window, interaction was not structured. Despite this, in each experimental condition the proportion of argumentative utterances in the text ranged from a minimum of .87 to a maximum 1.00. The average proportion, as shown in Table 1, was .91.

Similar studies have been undertaken with the Belvédère (Veerman & Andriessen, 1997) and the CTP system (Andriessen et al, 1996). In the Belvédère study, fourteen students working in pairs produced conflicting stances about three different aspects of a conceptual design task. Each aspect had to be discussed in separate sessions using Belvédère. Three argumentative diagrams had to be submitted as the final product. The average proportion of argumentative utterances was circa .90 in the dialogues and circa .96 in the diagrams. When comparing the proportion of arguments produced in the Belvédère system and the CTP system no significant difference was found despite the provision of argumentative moves such as *Hypotheses, Data, For*, and *Against* in the task window of the Belvédère system.

In the study using the CLARE system (Wan & Johnson, 1994) it seemed that the amount of argumentation dropped to a proportion of .35 mainly because of problems at the task level. In this study tewnty-four upper-level undergraduates in Software Engineering worked in groups of four. Prior to engaging in a collaborative discussion, they had to identify, individually, the main problem and four major claims in a given text. None of the subjects correctly identified the main problem while summarizing the text, and only half of the subjects found major claims and connected evidence. As a result, it appeared that students used the wrong kind of dialogue markers to summarize and discuss parts of the text. Because the use of dialogue discourse markers was interconnected (*e.g.*, selecting *evaluation* brought up primitives as *critique, question*, and *suggestion*) the misappropriation of dialogue markers escalated. These problems, occurring both at the task level and in structuring the interaction at the interface, decreased the possibility of good argumentation occurring in the discussions.

In contrast to the studies described above, little argumentation occurred during the use of the Conference MOO. Ten pairs of academic students had to solve a scheduling task and had flexible access to dialogue acts. An analysis of Jermann and Schneider's raw data shows that less than 10 percent of the total amount of utterances could be coded as argumentative. Argumentative utterances were made mostly by the use of the dialogue acts: why, *I disagree*, and *because*. The main difference between the Conference MOO and other studies described is that of task type. In the MOO, the problem solving task was semiclosed. Although the solution could be reached by multiple strategies, all the information needed to solve the problem was provided to all of the students. No competitive instruction was given and students worked together *without needing* to produce argumentative discussions. In this case, little argument occurred, despite the provision of argumentative markers.

To conclude, based upon the studies described above, it seems obvious that structuring the interaction at the level of the interface does not on its own provoke discussion. Task characteristics such as predefined and conflicting information may stimulate the need for discussions when the information is divided between the students. Also, competitive forms of instruction combined with the production of a joint solution can stimulate students to engage in argumentative discussions. However, the experiments with the five systems in this review did not compare students given the same task in structured versus unstructured interfaces. Therefore, we need to be tentative about these findings.

5.2 Structuring interaction to support collaborative argumentation

As discussed in the previous section, structuring the interaction by using dialogue moves, controlling turn taking or allowing students to indicate their confidence in claims (such as in the Belvédère system) does not necessarily *provoke* discussion. However, interaction structuring might support collaborative argumentation in order to optimize problem solving. Compared to F2F situations, in CMC systems interaction can be structured electronically; for example by providing students with dialogue markers or turn-taking control. In F2F situations instruction can be given – for example, concerning the use of questions or arguments – but this would not directly support the discussions *online*. Providing instruction might not be enough to improve focus maintenance, to limit misunderstanding, or to support dialogue management (all of which are preconditions for fruitful argumentation). Furthermore, instruction may not be sufficient to support the argumentation processes of critical checking, argument elaboration and the consideration of multiple viewpoints (Veerman & Andriessen, 1997). In CMC systems, electronic support through structuring interaction could be focused on important preconditions and on cognitive processes essential to collaborative argumentation. In Table 3 we summarize the main mechanisms used in the five systems reviewed, and the activities they are supposed to *support* in collaborative argumentation during problem solving.

In this section, we will discuss the five systems, consider which argumentative dialogue moves were supported, what methods were used to structure interaction, and whether these approaches appear to *support* collaborative argumentation. Our findings are offered as suggestions for the improvement of collaborative argumentation through structuring interaction in CMC systems. Systems designed using these suggestions can then be used to test their validity.

Dialab system / CLARE

In the Dialab system, students are forced to use specific types of argumentative dialogue moves. Also, students are forced to enter one speech act (move) in each turn. The argumentative move types are connected to specific sentence openers. These include sentence openers for information checking, including question asking or countering arguments. For example, the dialogue move *Challenge* is connected to the sentence opener *Why*.... The dialogue history is explicitly used to select new moves. Since communication is restricted, it is likely that there will be few problems concerning the focus of the argument and shared understanding.

Table 3   Mechanisms of structured interaction to support activities in collaborative argumentation.

Mechanism	Activity support
Turn-taking	- Dialogue management - Social aspects: handle interruptions and dominance
Dialogue moves / sentence openers	- Shared understanding due to explicit goal of the message - Encourages use of argument moves - Encourages specific problem solving activities
Graphical argument structure	- Shared understanding - Encourages use of argument moves - Visual identification of gaps and conflicts in the argument - Consideration of multiple perspectives and balance
Explicit use of dialogue history in new moves	- Dialogue management - Focus and shared understanding
Confidence ratings	- Encourage checking of weak claims

Moreover, dialogue management is rigidly structured and can hardly be misunderstood. The results of the study showed that students could be trained to use the dialogue game properly. They were able to identify their move types accurately, and followed the dialogue rules. The argument produced was fair and reasonable. However, the 'win-loss' design of Dialab may mean that students are tempted to shift focus when they realize that their argument is losing with the current focus. This would lead to unresolved (sub)arguments, undermining critical checking along the central route in argumentative discussions. This would not necessarily cause problems for the task the system was designed for, but if it were to be used for collaborative problem solving, then this issue would need to be addressed. In open-ended problem solving, a strict rule set combined with rigid turn-taking control is inappropriate when students are trying to solve a problem for which they do not yet have the full and unquestionable information. Specifically, allowing students to enter only one move in a turn cannot encourage elaboration. The study with the CLARE system (Wan & Johnson, 1994) supports this claim. In this study it is found that such restricted input mechanisms can actually inhibit elaboration.

Conference MOO
In the Conference MOO, the use of structure at the interface and the freetext input are combined. In Jermann & Schneider's study, results indicated that the use of the free versus the structured interface is dependent on the content type of the utterance. From the total number of utterances (n=1039), 58 percent concerned task *category*, 22 percent task *strategy* and 20 percent task *management*. Contributions concerning the task *category* and the task *strategy* are expressed more often through the structured section than through the free section. Management

contributions are expressed mostly by using free text entry. This interface shows how interactivity can be structured at the interface, providing both restricted and unrestricted input modes. Admittedly, little argumentation occurred during the use of this system, but this has been previously explained in terms of the chosen *task* rather than the interface design. Students worked together *without* a specific need for producing argumentative discussions. In collaborative argumentation students can have the same kind of preferences as in the MOO Conference system, using restricted or free input modes for different types of contributions. Allowing free input could, for instance, stimulate task management whereas collaborative argumentation could be enhanced by providing specific sentence openers representing check-questions and counter arguments at the interface. Additionally, the interface could also include dialogue moves and sentence openers designed to prompt the exploration of multiple viewpoints, and elaboration.

Belvédère system
In the Belvédère system, graphical dialogue moves are implemented in the task-window and unrestricted communication takes place in the text-based chat box. By using predefined graphical boxes representing argumentative dialogue moves, students can identify information serving as claims and evidence. Arguments can be connected as preferred by using graphical links defined as *For*, *Against*, and *And*. Electronic advice on argument structure is provided on request. This is largely based on the argument structure defined by Toulmin (1958). The study with Belvédère (Veerman & Andriessen, 1997) involved seven pairs of students who produced conflicting stances and then argued about the conceptual task of designing specific learning goals. Comparing the twenty-one dialogues with the twenty-one diagrams produced (seven pairs x three tasks) shows that producing argumentative diagrams increases multiple perspective taking and elaboration.

CTP system
The study of the CTP system (Andriessen *et al.*, 1996) showed that, in the written product, students explored multiple viewpoints and elaborated on their arguments, despite the fact that no dialogue moves or turn-taking control was available in the communication window. Improved elaboration could be related to some of the task characteristics, in particular the fact that students were provided with pictorial information. The pictorial information gave rise to a greater number and variety of elaborations in the written products than did the textual information. The only turn-taking control within CTP was in the task window; this regulated the coordination between students, creating a final product rather than affecting the argumentation processes.

In conclusion, providing a combination of structured and unrestricted interaction modes within both the task and communication windows might support argumentation during collaborative problem solving. In the communication window, combining free-text entry with well designed argument dialogue moves or sentence openers, can stimulate critical checking procedures in collaborative argumentation without restricting the argumentation or problem solving. In the task window, graphic argumentative dialogue acts improve consideration of multiple viewpoints and elaboration. However, task characteristics such as providing students with predefined stances also play an important role in improving the exploration of different viewpoints. Further research is needed to explore how these graphic dialogue acts produce improved viewpoint exploration and elaboration. In addition, turn-taking control in the communication window must be designed carefully, so that it does not inhibit elaboration. Controlling turn taking in the task window regulates the coordination in producing a final product. Therefore, although it provides no direct support for the processes of collaborative argumentation, this may support the problem solving process.

6 CONCLUSIONS

In this chapter, we have considered how to provide computer-based support for argumentation during collaborative problem solving. We found that, in specific phases of the collaborative problem solving, information checking (along the central route), exploration of multiple viewpoints, and elaboration are important processes. Taking into account the problem solving domain, learning goals, and the final product, instruction can be tailored towards optimizing checking procedures, consideration of multiple viewpoints, and the variety of elaboration in collaborative argumentation. The choice of domain, the characteristics of the final product (individual or joint), and the mode of interaction (competitive or cooperative) all form part of the 'instruction'. Electronic support, provided by structuring the interaction, can also be designed to encourage and support the main cognitive processes involved in collaborative argumentation. In order to discuss how task characteristics in open-ended problem solving tasks might be related to electronic support for collaborative argumentation, we reviewed five examples of network-based environments, and compared their approaches to structuring the interaction and supporting argumentation.

The central question addressed was how to structure interaction, *provoke* discussion, and *support* collaborative argumentation in order to optimize open-ended problem solving. First of all, we found that mutual understanding and focus maintenance are essential for engagement in fruitful discussions. These preconditions can be facilitated not only by task characteristics (*e.g.*, instructing students to construct conflicting stances as an input for discussion), but also by structuring interaction (*e.g.*, the use of explicit sentence openers, dialogue moves, graphical argument, or dialogue history). Secondly, we found that structuring the interaction does not necessarily *provoke* argumentation. This seems to have more to do with task characteristics such as the competitive instructional design of the task. Notably, the provision of argument moves in the Belvédère system did not produce more argument than the unstructured CTP interaction interface. However, the task chosen for the Conference MOO system appeared to have a negative effect on the production of argument, despite the provision of argument moves at the interface. Tasks that do provoke argument appear to have at least some of the following characteristics:
1. multiple acceptable solutions exist,
2. competitive instructions (students are instructed that they must spend some time arguing),
3. role playing or pre-defined conflicting stances are used,
4. required information is split between the group members,
5. students with conflicting original beliefs are grouped together,
6. an initial individual work stage in which students construct their own stance or solution,
7. a joint product is required.

Such task characteristics appear to provoke collaborative argumentation. Support can also be provide through structured interaction at the interface (Dialab and

Belvédère both used this approach), although our review suggests that this may have a negative effect if the structure is not well designed or is not suitable for the current task. Considering the interaction, structuring dialogue acts in a hierarchical manner (as was done in CLARE), and thus making them interdependent was clearly disadvantageous. A mistake in choosing the first dialogue move can result in a whole sequence of inappropriate dialogue acts or sentence openers being used, and hence cause problems in the discussion. In addition, control of turn taking can discourage elaboration when it prevents multiple moves being made in one turn. Therefore, it is preferable to place no restrictions on turn-taking control in the communication window, or on the use of dialogue moves, so that any dialogue act can be used in combination with and following any other dialogue act (this includes dialogue moves, sentence openers, and free-text). Hence, a richer set of interactional moves is available that may be suitable for different interactive contexts. Enabling communication using built-in argumentative dialogue acts, sentence openers *and* free-text input can stimulate critical checking procedures without inhibiting students' argumentation and problem solving. In addition, graphic argumentative dialogue acts in the task window can add value to the exploration of multiple perspectives and elaboration. Finally, turn-taking control can be used in the task window, regulating the coordination process needed to create the final product.

It is obvious that when designing environments to provoke discussions and to support argument in collaborative problem solving, both task characteristics and structured interaction at the interface must be taken into account, and the interaction between the two must be considered thoroughly. However, our framework is tentative because further research is needed in this area. It is our aim to suggest the directions in which research might usefully proceed. Encouraging the important argument processes of information checking along the central route, exploration of multiple viewpoints, and elaboration of the arguments is affected by the choice of the problem solving domain, the task characteristics, and the choice between asynchronous or synchronous modes of communication in network-based environments. Further research could be done comparing students working on the same task in structured versus unstructured interfaces, taking into account graphic or text-based dialogue moves, sentence openers, the availability of free-text entry, and turn-taking control in both task and communication windows. Also, we need to have a stronger idea of how certain task goals can be supported by structuring the interaction. In the evaluation of our systems, mismatches were observed between the task goals and characteristics of structured interaction. This seems to suggest that software may have to be written specifically for a range of problem types, rather than attempting to build one generic system for all.

The importance of continuing this line of research is obvious considering the increase of network-based learning environments in the last decade. Since educators and educational designers have discovered the Internet, the need for research results detailing how to provide effective support for electronic discussions during collaborative problem solving has increased, yet the answers are not easily forthcoming. Hopefully, during the next decade further studies will be conducted in this area and the results will be made available to the many education practitioners who want to make use of this new technology.

NOTE

1 Although the division between asynchronous and synchronous modes of commu-nication appears to be clear, it must be kept in mind that asynchronous systems can be used for sending messages almost simultaneously, and synchronous systems can be used as asynchronous systems (Dillenbourg & Traum, 1997).

References

Adam, J.M. (1990). *Eléments de linguistique textuelle: Théorie et pratique de l'analyse textuelle*. [Textual linguistic: Theory and textual analysis]. Liège: Mardaga.
Adam, J.M. (1992). *Les textes: types et prototypes. Récit, description, argumentation, explication et dialogue*. [Texts: Types and prototypes: narration, description, argumentation, explanation and dialog]. Paris: Nathan.
Akiguet, S. (1992). *Le traitement de l'argumentation écrite par l'enfant de 9 à 11 ans. Rôle des connecteurs et du schéma prototypique* [Processing of written argumentation by 9-11 years old children. Role of the connectors and of the prototypical schema]. Thèse de Doctorat. Aix-en-Provence.
Akiguet, S. (1997). Amorce de la compétence argumentative écrite chez des enfants de neuf, dix et onze ans. [Beginning of the argumentative competence in 9-11 year old children]. *Archives de Psychologie, 65,* 29-48.
Akiguet, S., & Piolat, A. (1996). Insertion of connectives by 9- to 11-year-old children in an argumentative text. *Argumentation, 10,* 253-270.
Alamargot, D., & Chanquoy, L. (Eds.) (in press). Through the Models of Writing Processes. In G. Rijlaarsdam & E. Espéret (Series eds.) & D. Alarmargot & L. Chanquoy (Vol. Eds.). Studies in Writing: Vol. 7. Through the Models of Writing Processs. With commentaries by John R. Hayes and R. Kellogg. Amsterdam: Amsterdam University Press.
Albro, E. R., & Stein, N.L. (1999). Children's memories for conflicts with liked and disliked peers. Unpublished manuscript. Whittier College.
Andrews, R., Costello, P., & Clarke, S. (1993). *Improving the quality of argument, 5-16.* Hull: University Press.
Andriessen, J. (1991). Children's reflection on coherence during text construction. *European Journal of Psychology of Education, 6 (2),* 257-266.
Andriessen, J., Coirier, P., Roos, L., Passerault, J.M., & Bert-Erboul, A. (1996). Thematic and structural planning in constrained argumentative text production. In G. Rijlaarsdam, H. van den Berg & M. Couzijn (Eds.), *Current Trends in Writing Research: What is writing? Theories, Models and Methodology* (pp. 237-251). Amsterdam: Amsterdam University Press.
Andriessen, J., Erkens. G., Overeem, E., & Jaspers, J. (1996, September). *Using complex information in argumentation for collaborative text production*. Paper presented at the UCIS '96 conference, Poitiers, France.
Angell, R. B. (1964). *Reasoning and logic*. New York, NY: Appleton-Century-Crofts.
Anscombre, J.-C. & Ducrot, O. (1983). *L'argumentation dans la langue*. [The argumentation in the language]. Bruxelles: Mardaga.
Anscombre, J.-C. & Ducrot, O. (1986). Argumentativité et informativité. [Argumentativeness and informativeness]. In M. Meyer (Ed.), *De la métaphysique à la rhétorique*. [From metaphysics to rhetoric]. (pp. 79-94). Brussel: Editions de l'Université de Bruxelles.
Antaki, C., & Leudar, I. (1990). Claim-backing and other explanatory genres in talk. *Journal of Language and Social Psychology, 9,* 279-292.
Apothéloz, D. (1990). The development of cohesion in writing: preliminary research on anaphoric procedures and thematic planning in texts by children. In M. Spoelders (Ed.), *A contribution of C&C to the International Litteracy Year* (pp. 57-70). Lier: Van In and C&C.
Apothéloz, D., & Brandt, P.Y. (1992). Les organisations raisonnées: justifier, argumenter, étayer. [Reasoned organizations: justifying, arguing and supporting]. *Travaux du Centre de Recherches Sémiologiques, 60,* 55-88.
Apothéloz, D., & Mieville, P. (1989). Cohérence et discours argumenté [Coherence and the argumentative discourse]. In M. Charolles (Ed.), *The resolution of discourse* (pp.68-87). Hamburg: Buske Verlag.

Applebee, A., Langer, J.A., Jenkins, L.B., Mullis, I.V.S., & Foertsch, M.A. (1990). *Learning to write in our nation's schools: Instruction an achievement in 1988 at grades 4, 8, and 12*. Princeton, NJ: Educational Testing Service.

Aristotle. (1960). *Rhetoric*. Translated by L. Cooper. New York, NY: Appleton-Century-Crofts.

Austin. J.L. (1962). *How to Do Things with Words*. London etc.: Oxford University Press.

Baker, M. (1992). Modeling Negotiation in Intelligent Teaching Dialogue. In R. Moyse & M.T. Elsom-Cook (Eds.), *Knowledge Negotiation* (pp. 199-240). London: Academic Press Limited.

Baker, M. (1996). *Argumentation and Cognitive Change in Collaborative Problem-Solving Dialogues*. COAST Research Report Number CR-13/96, France.

Baker, M., & Bielaczyc, K. (1995). Missed opportunities for learning in collaborative problem-solving interactions. In J. Greer (Ed.), *Proceedings of AI-ED 95 - 7th World Conference on Artificial Intelligence in Education* (pp. 210-218). Charlottesville: Association for the Advancement of Computing in Education (AACE).

Baker, M.J. (1991). The Influence of Dialogue Processes on the Generation of Students' Collaborative Explanations for Simple Physical Phenomena. *Proceedings of the International Conference on the Learning Sciences*, (pp. 9-19). Evanston Illinois, USA, August 1991.

Baker, M.J. (1994). A Model for Negotiation in Teaching-Learning Dialogues. *Journal of Artificial Intelligence in Education*, 5(2), 199-254.

Baker, M.J. (1995). Negotiation in Collaborative Problem-Solving Dialogues. In R.-J. Beun, M.J. Baker & M. Reiner (Eds.), *Dialogue and Instruction: Modeling Interaction in Intelligent Tutoring Systems* (pp. 39-55). Berlin: Springer-Verlag.

Baker, M.J. (1996a). *Argumentation and Cognitive Change in Collaborative Problem-Solving Dialogues*. (Research Report N° CR-13/96). The COAST Research Team, Lyon [http://sir.univ-lyon2.fr/GRIC-COAST/coast.rapports.eng.html].

Baker, M.J. (1996b). Argumentation et co-construction des connaissances [Argumentation and co-construction of knowledge]. *Interaction et Cognitions*, 1, 2/3, 157-191.

Baker, M.J. (*in press*). Argumentative Interactions and Cooperative Learning. *Escritos* [in Spanish translation].

Baker, M.J., & Lund, K. (1997). Promoting reflective interactions in a computer-supported collaborative learning environment. *Journal of Computer Assisted Learning*, 13, 175-193.

Bakhtine, M. (1981). La structure de l'énoncé [The structure of the utterance]. In T. Todorov, *Bakhtine. Le principe dialogique*. Paris: Editions du Seuil.

Baron, J. B. (1991). Beliefs about thinking. In J. F. Voss, D. N. Perkins & J. W. Segal (Eds.), *Informal reasoning and education* (pp. 169-186). Hillsdale, NJ: Lawrence Erlbaum Associates.

Baron, J. B. (1995). Myside bias in thinking about abortion. *Thinking and Reasoning*, 1, 221-265.

Barth, E.M., & Krabbe, E.C.W. (1982). *From Axiom to Dialogue: A Philosophical Study of Logics and Argumentation*. Berlin etc.: Walter de Gruyter.

Bassano, (1991). Opérateurs et connecteurs argumentatifs: une approche psycholinguistique. [Argumentative operators and connectors]. *Intellectica*, 11, 149-191.

Bassano, D. & Champaud, C. (1987a). Argumentative and informative functions of French intensity modifiers *presque* (almost), *à peine* (just, barely) and *à peu près* (about): an experimental study of children and adults. *Cahiers de Psychologie Cognitive*, 7 (6), 605-631.

Bassano, D. & Champaud, C. (1987b). La fonction argumentative des marques de la langue [Thee argumentative function of linguistic markers]. *Argumentation*, 1 (2), 175-199.

Bassano, D. & Champaud, C. (1987c). Fonctions argumentatives et informatives du langage: le traitement des modificateurs d'intensité au moins, au plus et bien chez l'enfant et chez l'adulte [Argumentative and informative functions of language: the processing of the modifications of intensity au moins, au plus et bien by children and adults]. *Archives de Psychologie*, 55 (212), 3-30.

Beale, W.H. (1986). *Real Writing. Argumentation, Reflection, Information.* (2nd ed.). Glenview, Ill.: Scott, Foresman & Co.
Beaudichon, J. (1982). *La communication sociale chez l'enfant* [The social communication in children]. Paris: Presses Universitaires de France.
Benoit, W.L., Hample, D. & Benoit, P.J. (Eds.). (1992). *Readings in Argumentation*. Berlin etc.: Foris (PDA 11).
Bereiter, C., & Scardamalia, M. (1987). *The Psychology of Written Composition.* Hillsdale, NJ: Erlbaum.
Bereiter, C., & Scardamalia, M. (1993). *Understanding expertise.* La Salle, IL: Open Court.
Bereiter, C., Burtis, P.J., & Scardamalia, M. (1988). Cognitive operations in constructing main points in written composition. *Journal of Memory and Language, 27*, 261-278.
Berk, U. (1979). *Konstruktive Argumentationstheorie* [Constructive argumentation theory]. Stuttgart: Frommann-Hotzboog (Problemata 72).
Berkowitz, M.W., Oser, F., & Althoff, W. (1987). The development of sociomoral discourse. In W. Kurtines & J. Gewirtz (Eds), *Moral development through social interaction.* New York: John Wiley & Sons.
Bernardi, B. de (1996). *Interestingness and argumentative text production.* Paper presented at the First International Workshop on Argumentative Texts. University of Barcelona, Spain, October 23-25, 1996.
Bernardi, B. de, & Antolini, E. (1996). Structural differences in the production of written arguments. *Argumentation, 10* (2), 175-196.
Bernas, R. S., & Stein, N. L. (1995). Case-based reasoning: Decision making and conceptual change. Paper presented at the Psychonomic Society Meetings, November, Los Angeles.
Bernas, R.S., & Stein, N.L. (1996). Argumentative reasoning and decision making in abortion cases: Paper presented at the Psychonomic Society Meetings, November, Chicago.
Bernas, R.S., & Stein, N.L. (1997). Predicting changes in positions on abortion on the basis of content and structural complexity of arguments. Paper presented at the Psychonomic Society Meetings, November, Philadelphia.
Bernas, R.S., & Stein, N. L. (1998a). Decision Making and Changes of Opinion During the Process of Arguing. Paper presented at the ISSBD Meetings, July, Bern, Switzerland.
Bernas, R.S., & Stein, N.L. (1998b). The relationship between outcomes in an argument and memory for the argument. Unpublished manuscript, University of Chicago.
Berninger, V.W., & Swanson, H.L. (1994). Modification of the Hayes and Flower model to explain beginning and developing writing. In E. Butterfield (Ed.), *Advances in cognition and Educational Practice. Vol. 2: Children's writing: Toward a process theory of development of skilled writing* (pp. 57-82). Greenwich: CT: JAI Press.
Billig, M. (1987). *Arguing and thinking: A rhetorical approach to social psychology.* Cambridge, England: Cambridge University Press.
Billig, M., Condor, S., Edwards, D., Gane, M., Middleton, D., & Radley, A. (1989). *Ideological dilemmas.* London: Sage.
Biro, J. & Siegel, H. (1992). Normativity, argumentation and an epistemic theory of fallacies. In F.H. van Eemeren, R. Grootendorst, J.A. Blair & C.A. Willard (Eds.), *Argumentation Illuminated* (pp. 85-103). Amsterdam: SICSAT/ISSA (SICSAT 1).
Black, J.B., & Bower, G.H. (1980). Story understanding as problem solving. *Poetics, 9,* 223-250.
Blair, J.A., & Johnson R.H. (Eds.). (1980). *Informal Logic. The First International Symposium.* Point Reyes, CA: Edgepress.
Blair, J.A., & Johnson, R.H. (1987a). Argumentation as dialectical. *Argumentation, 1* (1), 41-56.
Blair, J.A., & Johnson, R.H. (1987b). The current state of informal logic. *Informal Logic 9* (2/3), 147-151.
Bock, J.K. (1982). Toward a cognitive psychology of syntax. *Psychological Review, 89,* 1-47.
Boggs, S.T. (1978). The development of verbal disputing in part-Hawaiian children. *Language in Society, 7,* 325-244.

Borel, M.-J. (1989). Comment dit-on d'une *logique* qu'elle est *informelle?* [How do you say about logic that it is informal?]. In: M.-J. Reichler (Ed.). L'interpretation des textes.. (pp. 115-156), Paris: Editions de Minuit.

Borel, M.-J., Grize, J.-B., & Miéville, D. (1983). Essai de logique naturelle. [An essay about natural logic]. Bern: Peter Lang.

Boscolo, P. (1995). The cognitive approach to writing and writing instruction: A contribution to a critical appraisal. *Current Psychology of Cognition, 14(4)*, 343-366.

Bouchard, R. (1992). Erreurs pragmatiques, profils interactionnels et situation de production du discours [Pragmatical errors, interactional profiles and situation of discourse production]. In R. Bouchard (Ed.), *Acquisition et enseignement / apprentissage des langues,* (pp. 446-452). Grenoble: Lidilem.

Bouchard, R. (1994). De l'oral à l'écrit en français langue étrangère: les procédés d'intégration discursive [From oral to written in French as a Foreign Language: discursive integration procedures]. *Bulletin Suisse de Linguistique Appliquée, 59*, 103-126.

Bourdin, B., & Fayol, M. (1994). Is written language production more difficult than oral language production? A working memory approach. *International Journal of Psychology, 29(5)*, 591-620.

Braet, A. (1984). *De klassieke statusleer in modern perspectief. Een historisch-systematische bijdrage tot de argumentatieleer* [Classical theory of status in modern perspective. A historical-systematic contribution to the theory of argumentation]. Groningen: Wolters-Noordhoff.

Braine, M. D. S., & Rumain, B. (1983). Logical reasoning. In P. H. Mussen (Serie Ed.) & J. H. Flavell, & E. M. Markman (Vol. Eds.), *Handbook of child psychology: Vol. 3, Cognitive development.* (pp. 263-240). New York, NY: Wiley.

Brandt, P.-Y. (1989). *La justification par la négative dans l'argumentation enfantine* [Justification by the negative in children's argumentation]. Bern: Peter Lang.

Brassart, D.G. (1987). *Le développement des capacités discursives chez l'enfant de 8 à 12 ans: le discours argumentatif (étude didactique)* [Development of discursive abilities in 8-12 year old children: argumentative discourse]. PhD thesis. Université de Strasbourg: Strasbourg.

Brassart, D.G. (1988). La gestion des contre-arguments dans le texte argumentatif écrit chez les élèves de 8 à 12 ans et les adultes compétents [The management of counter arguments in written argumentative texts by students from 8 to 12-year-olds and competent adults]. *Journal Européen de Psychologie de l'Education, 1*, 51-69.

Brassart, D.G. (1989). La gestion des contre-arguments dans le texte argumentatif écrit chez les élèves de 8 à12 ans, et les adultes compétents [Monitoring of written counter-arguments by in 8-12 year old children]. *European Journal of Education, 4, 1*, 51-69.

Brassart, D.G. (1990). Retour(s) sur Mir Rose, ou comment analyser et représenter le traitement argumentatif (écrit)? [Coming back to 'Mir Rose': How to analyze and to represent written argumentation]. *Argumentation, 4,* 299-332.

Brassart, D.G. (1991). Les débuts de la rédaction argumentative. Approche psycho-linguistique didactique [Development of written argumentation: Psycholinguistic didactic approach]. In M. Fayol, J.E. Gombert, H. Abdi & D. Zagar (Eds.), *La production d'écrits de l'école maternelle au collège* (pp. 95-124). Dijon: CRDP.

Brassart, D.G. (1992). Negation, concession and refutation in counterargumentative composition by pupils from 8 to 12 years old and adults. *Argumentation, 6,* 77-98.

Brassart, D.G. (1996). Does a prototypical argumentative schema exist? Text recall in 8 to 13 year old. *Argumentation, 10 (2),* 163-174.

Brassart, D.G., & Veevaert, A. (1992). *Enseigner, apprendre le texte argumentatif.* [Teaching, learning the argumentative text]. Lille: CRDP.

Brewer, W.F. (1980). Literary theory, rhetoric, and stylistics: implications for psychology. In R.J. Spiro, B.C. Bruce & W.F. Brewer (Eds.), *Theoretical issues in reading comprehension* (pp. 231-239). Hillsdale, N.J.: Lawrence Erlbaum.

Brewer, W.F., & Lichtenstein, E.H. (1982). Stories are to entertain: a structural-affect theory of stories. *Journal of Pragmatics, 6,* 473-486.

Britt, M.A., Rouet, J.F., Perfetti, C.A., & Georgi, M.C (1994). Learning from history texts: from causal analysis to argument models. In G. Leinhardt, S. Beck & K. Stainton (Eds.), *Teaching and learning in history* (pp. 47-84). Hillsdale, NJ: Lawrence Erlbaum.

Bromberg, M., & Dorna, A. (1985). Modèles argumentatifs et classe de prédicat [Argumentative models and predicate class]. *Psychologie Française, 30,* 51-58.

Bronckart, J.-P. (1996). *Activité langagière, textes et discours.* [Linguistic activity, texts and discourse]. Lausanne: Delachaux et Niestlé.

Bronckart, J.-P., Bain, D., Schneuwly, B., Davaud, C., & Pasquier, A. (1985). *Le fonctionnement des discours. Un modèle psychologique et une méthode d'analyse* [The functioning of discourse. A psychological model and a method of analysis]. Paris: Delachaux & Niestlé.

Brossard, M., Gelpe, D., Lambelin, G., & Nancy, B. (1990). Comparaison à l'école élémentaire entre deux types de discours: discours d'opinion et discours physique [Comparison in elementary school between two types of discourse: opinion discourse and physical discourse]. Colloque L'explication, Paris V.

Bruxelles, S., Ducrot, O., & Raccah, P.-Y. (1995). Argumentation and the lexical topical fields. *Journal of Pragmatics, 24,* 99-114.

Bull, S., & Broady, E. (1997). Spontaneous peer tutoring from sharing student models. In B. du Boulay & R. Mizoguchi (Eds.), *Proceedings of Artificial Intelligence in Education* (pp. 143-150). Kobe: IOS Press.

Bunt, H.C. (1989). Information dialogues as communicative action in relation to partner modelling and information processing. In M.M. Taylor, F. Neel, & G. Bouwhuis (Eds.), *The structure of multimodal Dialogue* (pp. 47-75). Amsterdam: Elsevier Sciences Publishers.

Bunt, H.C. (1995). Dialogue Control Functions and Interaction Design. In R.J. Beun, M.J. Baker & M. Reiner (Eds.), *Dialogue and Instruction, Modeling Interaction in Intelligent Tutoring Systems,* (pp. 197-214). Berlin, Springer-Verlag.

Burleson, B.R. (1979). On the analysis and criticism of arguments: some theoretical and methodological considerations. *Journal of the American Forensic Association, 15,* 137-147.

Burnett, R. E. (1993). Decision-making during the collaborative planning of co-authors. In A. Penrose, & B. Sitko (Eds.), *Hearing ourselves think: Cognitive research in the college writing classroom* (pp. 125-146). NY: Oxford University Press.

Camps, A. (1995). Production de textes en situation de groupe. [Production of texts in group situation]. *Bulletin Suisse de Linguistique Appliquée, 61,* 119-136.

Chaikan, S. (1980). Heuristic versus systematic information processing and the use of source versus message cues in persuasion. *Journal of Social and Personality Psychology, 39,* 752-766.

Champaud, C. (1994). L'argumentation [Argumentation]. *Psychologie Française, 39 (2),* 193-203.

Chan, C.K.K. (1995). Collaborative processing of incompatible information. *Proceedings of the Seventeenth Annual Conference of the Cognitive Science Society* (pp. 346-351). Hillsdale, N.J.: Lawrence Erlbaum Publishers.

Chanquoy, L. (1996). *Connectives and argumentative texts. A developmental study.* Paper presented at the First International Workshop on Argumentative Texts. University of Barcelona, Spain, October 23-25, 1996.

Chanquoy, L. (1998). *La rédaction de textes: Mémoire de travail et niveaux de traitement* [Text editing: working memory and levels of processing]. Note de synthèse pour l'Habilitation à Diriger des Recherches. Université de Provence.

Chanquoy, L. (in press). Thinking skills and the acquisition of connectives by children. In J.H.M. Hamers, J.E.H. van Luit & B. Csapo (Eds.), Thinking skills and teaching thinking. Amsterdam: Swets & Zeitlinger.

Chanquoy, L., & Costeplane, J. (1995). *The use of connectives in three types of text written by children.* Paper presented for the 6th European Conference for Research on Learning and Instruction. Biennial Meeting. University of Nijmegen, The Netherlands, August 26-31, 1995.

Chanquoy, L., & Fayol, M. (1991). Etude de l'utilisation des signes de ponctuation et des connecteurs chez des enfants (8-10 ans) et des adultes [Study of the use of punctuation markers and connectors by children (8-10 years old) and adults]. *Pratiques (numéro spécial 'la ponctuation')*, 70, 107-124.

Chanquoy, L., & Fayol, M. (1995). Analyse de l'évolution de l'utilisation de la ponctuation et des connecteurs, dans deux types de texte [Analysis of the evolution of the use of punctuation markers and connectors in two types of texts]. Etude longitudinale du C.P. au C.E.2. *Enfance*, 2, 227-241.

Charolles, M. (1980). Les formes directes et indirectes de l'argumentation [Direct and indirect forms of argumentation]. *Pratiques*, 28, 7-44.

Charolles, M. (1986). La gestion des orientations argumentatives dans les textes [The management of argumentative orientations in texts]. *Pratiques*, 49, 87-101.

Chi, M.T.H., & VanLehn, K.A. (1991). The Content of Physics Self-Explanations. *Journal of the Learning Sciences*, 1(1), 69-105.

Chi, M.T.H., Bassok, M., Lewis, M.W., Reimann, P., & Glaser, R. (1989). Self-Explanations: How Students Study and Use Examples in Learning to Solve Problems. *Cognitive Science*, 13 (2), 145-182.

Chittenden, G. E. (1942). An experimental study in measuring and modifying assertive behavior in young children. *Monographs of the Society for Research in Child Development*, 7 (1, Serial No. 6).

Clark, H.H., & Haviland, S.E. (1977). Comprehension and the given-new contract. In R.O. Freeddle (Ed.), *Discourse production and comprehension* (pp.1-40). Hillsdale: Lawrence Erlbaum Associates.

Clark, H.H., & Schaefer, E.F. (1989). Contributing to Discourse. *Cognitive Science*, 13, 259-294.

Clark, R.A., & Delia, J.G. (1976). The development of functional persuasive skills in childhood and early adolescence. *Child Development*, 78, 1008-1014.

Cohen, J., Morgan, J., & Pollack, M. (1990). *Intentions in Communication*. Cambridge Mass.: MIT Press.

Cohen, L.J. (1992). *An Essay on Belief and Acceptance*. Oxford: Clarendon Press.

Coirier, P. (1992). The textual setting of natural reasoning. Paper presented at the Vth Conference of the European Society for Cognitive Psychology. Paris (France), September 12-16.

Coirier, P. (1996). Composing argumentative texts: cognitive and/or textual complexity. In G. Rijlaarsdam, H. van den Bergh, & M. Couzijn (Eds.), *Theories, models and methodology in writing research* (pp.317-337). Amsterdam: Amsterdam University Press.

Coirier, P. (1999). Les types de textes: Une approche de psychologie cognitive [Text types: a cognitive psychological approach]. In G. Skytte and F. Sabatini (Eds.), *Linguistica testuale comparativa* (pp. 11-36). Copenhagen: Museum Tusculanum.

Coirier, P., & Andriessen, J. (in preparation). Conceptual and textual Constraints in composing argumentative Texts.

Coirier, P., Andriessen, J., Chanquoy, L., & De Bernardi, B. (1997). *Argumentative text writing: From planning to translating*. Paper presented at the Vth European Congress of Psychology: Invited Symposium on 'Psychology and the study of written text production', Dublin (Ireland), July, 6th-11th.

Coirier P., Broggio E., & De Bernardi, B. (1996). Systemic relations between compositional skills in 12- to 18- years-olds: some empirical data. *E.A.R.L.I. SIG Writing Conference*, Barcelona, Spain, 23-25 October.

Coirier, P., Coquin-Viennot, D., Golder, C., & Passerault, J.M. (1990). Le traitement du discours argumentatif: recherches en production et en compréhension [Processing of argumentative discourse: research on production and comprehension]. *Archives de Psychologie*, 58, 315-348.

Coirier, P., Gaonac'h, D., & Passerault, J.M. (1996). *Psycholinguistique textuelle. Approche cognitive de la compréhension et de la production des textes* [Textual psycholinguistic: Cognitive approach of text comprehension and production]. Paris: Armand Colin.

Coirier, P., & Golder, C. (1993). Production of supporting structure: developmental study. *European Journal of Psychology of Education, 2*, 1-13.
Coirier, P., & Golder, C. (1993). Writing argumentative text: a developmental study of the acquisition of supporting structures. *European Journal of Psychology of Education, 2,* 169-181.
Coirier, P., & Marchand, E. (1994). Writing argumentative texts: a typological and structural approach. In G. Eigler & T. Jechle (Eds.), *Writing: Current Trends in European Research* (pp. 163-182). Freiburg: Hochschul Verlag.
Cole, P. & J.L. Morgan (Eds.). *Syntax and Semantics 3: Speech Acts*. New York: Academic Press.
Corgan, V.C. (1987). Perelman's universal audience as critical tool. *Journal of the American Forensic Association, 23* (3), 147-157.
Couzijn, M. & Rijlaarsdam, G. (1996). Learning to read and write argumentative text by observation. In G. Rijlaarsdam, H. van den Bergh, H. & M. Couzijn (Eds.), *Effective teaching and learning of writing. Current trends in research* (pp 253-273). Amsterdam: Amsterdam University Press.
Couzijn, M. (1999). Learning to write by observation of writing and reading processes: effects on learning and transfer. In D. Galbraith & G. Rijlaarsdam (Eds.), Effective Strategies for the Teaching and Learning of Writing [Special issue]. *Learning and Instruction, 9* (2), 109-143.
Couzijn, M.J. (1995). *Observation of Writing and Reading Activities: Effects on Learning and Transfer*. Dordrecht: Dorfix.
Crammond, J.G. (1998). The uses and Complexity of Argument Structures in Expert and Student Persuasive Writing, *Written Communication, 15 (2)*, 230-268.
Crawshay-Williams, R. (1957). *Methods and Criteria of Reasoning. An Inquiry into the Structure of Controversy*. London: Routledge & Kegan Paul.
Daiute, C. (1989). Play as Thought: Thinking Strategies of Young Writers. *Harvard Educational Review, 59,* 1-23.
Damer, T.F. (1987). *Attacking Faulty Reasoning*. 2nd ed. Belmont, CA: Wadsworth (1st ed. 1980).
Damon, W., & Phelps, E. (1989). Critical distinctions among three approaches to peer education. *International Journal of Educational Research, 13* (1), 9-19.
Dausendschon-Gay, U., Gulich, E., & Kraft, U. (1991). Ecrire ensemble: les corrections [Writing together: revisions]. In R. Bouchard, J. Biliez, J.-M. Coletta, V. de Nuchèze & A. Millet (Eds.), *Acquisition et enseignement/apprentissage des langues* [Acquisition and languages teaching/learning] (pp. 425-437). Grenoble: Lidilem.
David, J., & Fayol, M. (Eds.). (1996). Comment étudier l'écriture et son acquisition? [How to study writing and its acquisition?]. *Etudes de Linguistique Appliquée, 101,* 5-7.
Dearin, R.D. (Ed.). (1985). A special issue to honor the memory of Chaim Perelman. *Journal of the American Forensic Association, 22* (2), 63-95.
Dellerman, P., Coirier, P., & Marchand, E. (1996). Planning and expertise in argumentative composition. In G. Rijlaarsdam, H. van den Bergh, & M. Couzijn (Eds.), *Theories, models and methodology in writing research* (pp. 182-195). Amsterdam: Amsterdam University Press.
Denhière, G., & Baudet, S. (1992). *Lecture, compréhension de texte et Science Cognitive* [Reading, text comprehension and cognitive science]. Paris: P.U.F.
Devi, R., Tiberghien, A., Baker, M.J., & Brna, P. (1996). Modelling Students' construction of energy models in physics. *Instructional Science, 24,* 259-293.
Dillenbourg, P., & Baker, M.J. (1996). Negotiation Spaces in Human-Computer Collaboration. Proceedings of COOP'96, *International Conference on Design of Cooperative Systems*, Juan-les-Pins, France, June 1996.
Dillenbourg, P., & Traum, D. (1997, August). *The relationship between interaction and problem solving in virtual collaborative environments*. Presented at the 7th European Conference for Research on Learning and Instruction. Athens, Greece.

Dillenbourg, P., Baker, M.J., Blaye, A., & O'Malley, C. (1995). The evolution of research on collaborative learning. In H. Spada, & P. Reimann (Eds.), *Learning in Humans and Machines* (pp. 189-205). London: Pergamon.

DiPardo, A., & Freedman, S.W. (1988). Peer response groups in the writing classroom: Theoretic foundations and new directions. *Review of Educational Research*, 119-149.

DiSessa, A. (1988). Knowledge in Pieces. In G. Forman & P. Pufall (Eds.), *Constructivism in the Computer Age*. Hillsdale NJ: Lawrence Erlbaum Associates.

Dolz, J. (1996). Learning argumentative capacities. A study of the effects of a systematic and intensive teaching of argumentative discourse in 11-12 year old children. *Argumentation*, *10* (2), 227-251.

Dolz, J., & Pasquier, A. (1994). Enseignement de l'argumentation et retour sur le texte [Learning argumentation with text reviewing]. *Repères*, *10*, 163-178.

Dolz, J., & Schneuwly, B. (1996). Apprendre à écrire ou comment étudier la construction des capacités langagières [Learning to write or how to study the construction of the linguistic abilities]. *Études de Linguistique Appliquée*, *101*, 73-86.

Dolz, J., Pasquier, A., & Bronckart, J.P. (1993). L'acquisition des discours: Emergence d'une compétence ou apprentissage de capacités langagières? [Discourse acquisition: emerging competence or learning linguistic skills?]. *Etudes de Linguistique Appliquée*, *92*, 23-37.

Dorval, B., & Gundy, F. (1990). The development of arguing in discussions among peers. *Merrill-Palmer Quarterly*, *36*, 389-409.

Doxtader, E.W. (1991). The entwinement of argument and rhetoric: a dialectical reading of Habermas' theory of communicative action. *Argumentation and Advocacy*, *28* (2), 51-63.

Ducrot, O. (1980). *Les échelles argumentatives* [Argumentative scales]. Paris: Les éditions de Minuit.

Ducrot, O. (1983). Opérateurs argumentatifs et visée argumentative [Argumentative operators and argumentative goal]. *Cahiers de Linguistique Française*, *5*, 7-36.

Ducrot, O. (1984). *Le dire et le dit* [Saying and what is said]. Paris: Les éditions de Minuit.

Ducrot, O. (1995). Les modificateurs déréalisants [Modificators for non-accomplishing]. *Journal of Pragmatics*, *24*, 145-165.

Ducrot, O. (1996) Slovenian Lectures/[Conférences slovènes]. Argumentative Semantics/ [Sémantique argumentative]. Edited by I.Z. Zagar; English translation Sebastian McEvoy. Ljubljana: ISH [Institut za humanisticne studije Ljubljana].

Ducrot, O., & Schaeffer, J.-M. (1995). (Eds.). *Nouveau Dictionnaire Encyclopédique des Sciences du Langage* [New Encyclopedic dictionnary of sciences of language]. Paris: Editions du Seuil.

Dunn, J. (1988). *The beginnings of social understanding*. Cambridge: Harvard University Press.

Dijk, T.A. van, & Kintsch, W. (1983). *Strategies of discourse comprehension*. New York: Academic Press.

Eckerman, C., & Stein, M. (1982). The toddler's emerging interactive skills. In K. Rubin & W. Ross (Eds.). *Peer relations and social skills*. New York: Springer-Verlag.

Eemeren, F. H. van (1994). The study of argumentation as normative pragmatics. In F. H. van Eemeren, & R. Grootendorst (Eds.), *Studies in pragma-dialectics* (pp. 3-8). Amsterdam: Sic Sat.

Eemeren, F.H. van (1986). Dialectical analysis as a normative reconstruction of argumentative discourse. *Text*, *6*, 1-16.

Eemeren, F. H. van, & Grootendorst, R. (1994). Rationale for a pragma-dialectical perspective. In F. H. van Eemeren, & R. Grootendorst (Eds.), *Studies in pragma-dialectics* (pp. 11-28). Amsterdam, Sic Sat.

Eemeren, F.H. van, & Grootendorst, R. (1984). *Speech Acts in Argumentative Discussions. A Theoretical Model for the Analysis of Discussions Directed towards Solving Conflicts of Opinion*. Berlin: Walter de Gruyter.

Eemeren, F.H. van, & R. Grootendorst (1988). Rationale for a pragma-dialectical perspective. *Argumentation*, *2*, (2), 271-291.

Eemeren, F.H. van, & Grootendorst, R. (1992) (Eds.). *Special issue of the review Argumentation on "Relevance"*. Dordrecht: Reidel.
Eemeren, F.H. van, & Grootendorst, R. (1992). *Argumentation, Communication, and Fallacies. A Pragma-Dialectical Perspective*. Hillsdale, NJ: Lawrence Erlbaum Associates.
Eemeren, F.H. van, Grootendorst, R., & Snoeck Henkemans, A.F. (1995). *Argumentatie* [Argumentation]. Groningen, The Netherlands: Woltersgroep.
Eemeren, F.H. van, Grootendorst, R., & Snoeck Henkemans, F. (1996). *Fundamentals of Argumentation Theory: A Handbook of Historical Backgrounds and Contemporary Developments*. Mahwah New Jersey: Lawrence Erlbaum Associates.
Eemeren, F.H. van, Grootendorst, R., Blair, J.A. & Willard, C.A. (Eds.). (1987a). *Argumentation: Across the Lines of Discipline. Proceedings of the First International Conference on Argumentation 1986*. Dordrecht etc.: Foris (PDA 3)
Eemeren, F.H. van, R. Grootendorst, J.A. Blair and C.A. Willard (Eds.) (1987b). *Argumentation: Perspectives and Approaches. Proceedings of the Conference on Argumentation 1986*. Dordrecht etc.: Foris (PDA 3A).
Eemeren, F.H. van, Grootendorst, R., Blair, J.A. & Willard, C.A. (Eds.). (1991). *Proceedings of the Second International Conference on Argumentation*. Amsterdam: SICSAT/ISSA (SICSAT 1A en 1B).
Eemeren, F.H. van, Grootendorst, R., Blair, J.A. & Willard, C.A. (Eds.). (1992). *Argumentation Illuminated*. Amsterdam: SICSAT/ISSA (SICSAT 1).
Eemeren, F. H. van, Grootendorst, R., Jackson, S., & Jacobs, S. (1993). *Reconstructing argumentative discourse*. Tuscaloosa, AL: The University of Alabama Press.
Eemeren, F.H. van, Grootendorst, R., Snoeck Henkemans, A.F., Blair., J.A., Johnson, R.H., Krabbe, E.C.W., Plantin, C., Walton, D.N., Willard, C.A., Woods, J., & Zarefsky, D.(1996). *Fundamentals of Argumentation Theory. A Handbook of Historical Backgrounds and Contemporary Developments*. Mahwah, N.J.: Lawrence Erlbaum.
Eisenberg, A. R., & Garvey, C. (1981). Children's use of verbal strategies in resolving conflicts. *Discourse Processes*, 4, 149-170.
Eisenberg, A.R. (1992). Conflicts between mothers and their young children. *Merrill-Palmer Quarterly*, 38, 21-44.
Elbow, P. (1981). *Writing with Power. Techniques for Mastering the Writing Process*. Oxford: Oxford University Press.
Erkens, G. (1997). *Cooperatief probleemoplossen met computers in het onderwijs: Het modelleren van cooperatieve dialogen voor de ontwikkeling van intelligente onderwijssystemen* [Cooperative problem solving with computers in education: Modelling of cooperative dialogues for the design of intelligent educational systems]. Ph.D. thesis, Utrecht University, the Netherlands.
Erkens, G., & Andriessen, J.E.B. (1994). Cooperation in Problem Solving and Educational Computer Programs. *Computers in Human Behavior*, 10, 107-125.
Espéret, E. (1991). The development and the role of narrative schema storytelling. In G. Piérault-Le Bonniec & M. Dolistsky (Eds.), *Language basis... Discourses bases*. Amsterdam: John Benjamins Publishing.
Espéret, E., Coirier, P., Coquin, D., & Passerault, J.M. (1987). L'implication du locuteur dans son discours: discours argumentatifs formel et naturel [Locutor's involvement in his own discourse: formal and natural argumentative discourse]. *Argumentation*, 1, 149-168.
Farrell, T.B. (1977). Validity and rationality: the rhetorical constituents of argumentative form. *Journal of the American Forensic Association*, 13, 142-149.
Farrell, T.B. (1979). Habermas on argumentation theory. Some emerging topics. *Journal of the American Forensic Association*, 16, 77-82.
Favart, M., & Passerault, J.M. (1996). Functionality of cohesion devices in the management of local and global coherence: two studies in children's written production of narratives. In G. Rijlaarsdam, H. van den Berg & M. Couzijn (Eds.), *Current Trends in Writing Research: What is writing? Theories, Models and Methodology* (pp. 349-365). Amsterdam: Amsterdam University Press.

Fayol, M. (1986). Les connecteurs dans les récits écrits. Etude chez l'enfant de 6 à 10 ans [The connectors in written narratives. A study with 6-10 years old children]. *Pratiques, 49*, 101-113.

Fayol, M. (1989). Une approche psycholinguistique de la ponctuation: étude en production et compréhension [A psycholinguistic approach of punctuation: a study of production and comprehension]. *Langue Française, 81*, 21-39.

Fayol, M. (1991). Text typologies: A cognitive approach. In G. Denhière & J.P. Rossi (Eds.), *Texts and Text Processing* (pp. 61-76). Amsterdam: North Holland Press.

Fayol, M. (1992). L'écrit: perspectives cognitives [Writing: cognitive perspectives]. In A. Bentolila (Ed.), Les entretiens nathan, lecture et écriture, actes II, Paris: Nathan.

Fayol, M. (1997). *Des idées au texte. Psychologie cognitive de la production verbale, orale et écrite* [From ideas to text: Cognitive psychology of spoken and written production]. Paris: P.U.F.

Fayol, M., & Abdi, H. (1988). Influence of script structure on punctuation. *European Bulletin of Cognitive Psychology, 8*, 265-279.

Fayol, M., & Monteil, J.M. (1988). The notion of script: From general to developmental and social psychology. *Cahiers de Psychologie Cognitive, 8*, 335-361.

Fayol, M., & Schneuwly, B. (1987). La mise en texte et ses problèmes [Textual formulation and its problems]. In J.L. Chiss, J.P. Laurent, J.C. Meyer, H. Romian & B. Schneuwly (Eds.), *Apprendre/enseigner à produire des textes écrits* (223-240). Bruxelles: De Boeck.

Feilke, H. (1996). From syntactical to textual strategies of argumentation. Syntactical development in written argumentation texts by students aged 10 to 22. *Argumentation, 10* (2), 197-212.

Ferréol, M. (1997). How do children reconstruct an argumentative text? The role of the number of arguments and the availability of the topic. Graphic presentation at the 7th *Early; 97*, Athens, *August 26-30*.

Ferréol, M., & Piolat, A. (1997, Mars). *Gestion de textes argumentatifs de longueur différente en fonction de l'âge et de la capacité mémorielle des participants* [Monitoring of argumentative text: Effect of age, working memory span and length of texts]. Session de posters à l'Atelier de Conjoncture de la Société Française de Psychologie 'Mémoire de Travail et Développement'. Chambéry, France.

Ferréol, M., Gombert, A., & Piolat, A. (1997, August). Effects of the length of texts on the writing of an argumentative text. In J. Andriessen (chair), *Writing an argumentation.* Symposium conducted at the 7th European Conference for Research on Learning and Instruction. Athens, Greece.

Festinger, L. (1957). *A theory of cognitive dissonance.* Stanford: Stanford University Press.

Fisher, R., & Brown, S. (1988). *Getting together: Building a relationship that gets to yes.* Boston: Houghton Mifflin.

Fisher, R., & Ury, W. (1981). *Getting to yes: Negotiating agreement without giving in.* USA: Penguin.

Fisher, W. R. (1987). *Human communication as narration.* Columbia, SC: University of South Carolina Press.

Flower, L.S. (1981). *Problem Solving Strategies for Writing.* New York: Harcourt Brace Jovanovich.

Flower, L.S., & Hayes, J.R. (1977). Problem solving strategies and the writing process. *College English, 39*, 449-461.

Flower, L.S., & Hayes, J.R. (1981). A cognitive process theory of writing. *College Composition and Communication, 32*, 365-387.

Foss, S.K., Foss, K.A. & Trapp, R. (1985). *Contemporary Perspectives on Rhetoric.* Prospect Heights, Illinois: Waveland Press. (2nd ed. 1991).

Frederiksen, C.A. (1975). Representing logical and semantic structure of knowledge acquired from discourse, *Cognitive Psychology, 7*, 358-371.

Frederiksen, C.A. (1987). Cognitive models and discourse analysis. In C.R. Cooper and S. Greenbaum (Eds.), *Written Communication Annual: An International Survey of Research and Theory, Vol. 1: Studying Writing: Linguistic approaches* (pp. 227-267). Beverly Hills, CA: Sage.

Freeman, J. B. (1992). Relevance, warrants, backing, inductive support. *Argumentation, 6,* 219-235.
Freeman, J.B. (1988). *Thinking Logically. Basic Concepts for Reasoning.* Englewood Cliffs, N.J.: Prentice-Hall.
Fulkerson, R. (1996). The Toulmin model of argument and the teaching of composition. In B. Emmel, P. Rosch, & D. Tanney (Eds.), *Argument revisited; argument redefined: Negotiating meaning in the composition classroom* (pp. 45-72). London: Sage.
Galbraith, D. (1996). Self-monitoring, discovery through writing and individual differences in drafting strategies. In G. Rijlaarsdam, H. van den Berg & M. Couzijn (Eds.), *Current Trends in Writing Research: What is writing? Theories, Models and Methodology* (pp.121-141). Amsterdam: Amsterdam University Press.
Galbraith, D. (1999). Writing as a Knowledge Constituting Process. In G. Rijlaarsdam & E. Espéret (Series Eds.) & M. Torrance & D. Galbraith (Vol. Eds.) *Studies in writing: Vol. 4. Knowing what to write: Conceptual Processes in Text Production* (pp. 139-160). Amsterdam: Amsterdam University Press.
Garcia-Debanc, C. (1990). *L'élève et la production d'écrits.* [The learner and the production of written work]. Metz: Centre d'analyse syntaxique de l'université de Metz.
Garcia-Debanc, C. (1996). Tâches d'écriture et processus rédactionnels: de l'observation aux implications didactiques? [Writing tasks and writing processes: from observation to pedagogical implications?]. *Etudes de Linguistique Appliquée, 101,* 46-59.
Gardenförs, P. (Ed.). (1992). *Belief Revision.* (Cambridge Tracts in Theoretical Computer Science 29), Cambridge: Cambridge University Press.
Garnham, A., & Oakhill, J. (1994). *Thinking and reasoning.* Oxford, UK: Blackwell.
Gaulmyn, M.-M. de (1992). Rédaction: reformulation et traduction. Les ratures, ça nous intéresse [Writing: reformulation and translation; deletions, we find that interesting]. In R. Bouchard, J. Biliez, J. -M. Coletta, V. de Nuchèze, & A. Millet (Ed.), *Acquisition et enseignement/apprentissage des langues* [Acquisition and languages teaching/learning] (pp. 461-469). Grenoble: Lidilem.
Genishi, C., & Di Paolo, M. (1982). Learning through argument in a preschool. In L.C. Wilkinson (Ed.), *Communicating in the classroom* (pp. 49-66). New York: Academic Press.
Gere, A., & Stevens, R.S. (1989). The language of writing groups: How oral response shapes revision. In S.W. Freedman (Ed.), *The acquisition of written language: Response and revision* (pp. 85-105). Norwood, N.J.: Ablex.
Gilbert, M. (1997). Coalescent argumentation. Mahwah, NJ: Lawrence Erlbaum Associates.
Giroud, A. (1995). L'articulation entre les diverses compétences mobilisées dans l'activité d'écriture en FLE [Articulation beween the different competences involved in the activity of writing in French as a foreign language]. *Revue de Phonétique Appliquée, 115/116/117,* 213-226.
Giroud, A. (1997). Comment des apprentis-scripteurs négocient l'écriture d'un texte: la gestion des modalisations [How learner writers negotiate the writing of a text: managing the modalizations]. *Cahiers du Français Contemporain, 4,* 305-326.
Glynn, S.M., Britton, B.K., Muth, K.D., & Dogan, N. (1982). Writing and revising persuasive documents. *Journal of Educational Psychology, 74* (4), 557-567.
Golden, J.L., & J.J. Pilotta (Eds.). (1986). *Practical Reasoning in Human Affairs. Studies in Honor of Chaim Perelman.* Dordrecht etc.: Reidel. (Synthese Library 183).
Golder, C. (1992a). Justification et négociation en situation monogérée et polygérée dans les discours argumentatifs [Justification and negotiation in individually and multyply managed argumentative discourse. *Enfance, 46,* 99-112.
Golder, C. (1992b). Le discours argumentatif: impact de la finalité communicative sur les formes textuelles produites [Argumentative discourse: the impact of communicative finality on produced textual forms]. *Pratiques, 73,* 119-125
Golder, C. (1992c). Production of elaborated argumentative discourse: the role of cooperativeness. *European Journal of Psychology of Education, 7,* 49-57.
Golder, C. (1992d). Mise en place de la conduite de dialogue argumentatif: la recevabilité des arguments [Acquisition of argumentative dialogue behaviour: the argument's admissibility]. *Revue de Phonétique Appliquée, 102,* 31-43.

Golder, C. (1993). Framed writing of argumentative monologues by sixteen-and seventeen-year-old students. *Argumentation, 7*, 343-358.
Golder, C. (1996). *Le développement des discours argumentatifs* [Development of argumentative discourses]. Lausanne: Delachaux & Niestlé.
Golder, C. (in press). Debatable topic or not: do we have the right to argue? *European Journal of Psychology of Education.*
Golder, C., & Coirier, P. (1994). Argumentative text writing: Developmental trends. *Discourse Processes, 18*, 187-210.
Golder, C., & Coirier, P. (1996). The production and recognition of typological argumentative text markers. *Argumentation, 10*, 2, 271-282.
Golder, C., & Pouit, D. (1999). For the debate to take place the theme must be discussible. Developmental evolution of the negotiation and admissibility of the arguments. In G. Rijlaarsdam & E. Espéret (Series Eds.) & J. Andriessen & P. Coirier (Vol. Eds.), *Studies in Writing: Vol. 5. Foundations of argumentative text processing*. Amsterdam: Amsterdam University Press.
Gombert, A. (1997). *Comment les rédacteurs de 10 à 13 ans se justifient-ils et argumentent-ils? Rôle du thème rédactionnel, de l'opinion consensuelle et de la thèse défendue* [How do 10-13 year old writers justifying and argument?]. PhD Thesis, Université de Provence.
Gombert, A. (1998). L'étayage de deux points de vue contraires. ...Etude chez de jeunes rédacteurs de 10 à 13 ans [Sustaining of contradictory perspective among 10-13 year old writers]. In R. Vion (Ed.), *Les sujets et leurs discours. Enonciation et interaction* (pp. 23-45). Aix en Provence: Presses de l'Université de Provence.
Gombert, A., & Roussey, J.Y. (1993). Computer-assisted training effects on argumentative text writing skills in children. In G. Eigler, & T. Jechle (Eds.), *Writing. Current trends in European Research* (pp. 183-196). Freiburg: Hochschul Verlag.
Goodwin, M. H. (1990). *He-Said-She-Said: Talk as social organization among Black children*. Bloomington, IN: Indiana University Press.
Goodyear, P., & Stone, C. (1992). Domain Knowledge, Epistemology and Intelligent Tutoring in Social Science. In R. Moyse, & M. Elsom-Cook (Eds.), *Knowledge Negotiation* (pp. 69-96). London: Academic Press.
Göttert, K.-H. (1978). *Argumentation. Grundzüge ihrer Theorie im Bereich theoretischen Wissens und praktischen Handelns* [Argumentation. Foundations of theory pertaining to theoretical knowledge and practical action]. Tübingen: Niemeyer.
Gottman, J. (1994). *Why marriages succeed or fail*. New York: Simon & Schuster.
Govier, T. (1985). *A Practical Study of Argument*. Belmont: Wadsworth.
Govier, T. (1987). *Problems in argument analysis and evaluation*. Dordrecht: Holland/Providence RI - U.S.A: Foris.
Govier, T. (1989). Critical thinking as argument analysis? *Argumentation, 3*, 115-126.
Greeno, J.G. (1997). Response: On claims that answer the wrong question. *Educational Researcher, 20* (1), 5-17.
Grice, H.P. (1957). Meaning. *The Philosophical Review, LXVI* (3), 377-388.
Grice, H.P. (1975). Logic and conversation. In P. Cole, & J.L. Morgan (Eds.), *Syntax and Semantics 3: Speech Acts* (pp. 45-58). New York: Academic Press..
Grize, J.B. (1982). *De la logique à l'argumentation* [From logic to argumentation]. Genève: Librairie Droz. (Travaux de droit, d'économie, de sciences politiques, de sociologie et d'anthropologie 34).
Grize, J.B. (1990). *Logique et langage* [Logic and language]. Paris: Ophrys.
Grize, J.B. (1996). Logique naturelle et communication [Natural logic and communication]. Paris: Presses Universitaires de France.
Gross, A. G. (1990). *The rhetoric of science*. Cambridge, MA: Harvard University Press.
Guercin, F., Roussey, J.-Y., & Piolat, A. (1990). Time series: a tool for analyzing complex cognitive activities. Application to the study of text revising strategies. *CPC/European Bulletin of Cognitive Psychology, 1*(10), 79-110.
Habermas, J. (1981). Theorie des kommunikativen Handelns [The theory of communicative action]. Frankfurt: Suhrkamp.

Habermas, J. (1987). *Théorie de l'agir communicationne* [Theory of communicative action]. Paris: Fayard.
Halpern, D. F. (1996). *Thought and knowledge.* Mahwah, N.J.: Erlbaum.
Hample, D. (1977). The Toulmin model and the syllogism. *Journal of the American Forensic Association, 14,* 1-8.
Hayes, J.R. (1996). A new framework for understanding cognition and affect in writing. In M.C. Levy & S.E. Ransdell (Eds.), *The science of writing. Theories, Methods, Individual differences and Applications* (pp. 1-27). Mahwah, N.J.: Laurence Erlbaum Associates.
Hayes, J.R., & Flower, L.S. (1980). Identifying the organization of writing processes. In L.W. Gregg, & E. R. Steinberg (Ed.), *Cognitive processes in writing* (pp. 3-30). Hillsdale, N.J.: Lawrence Erlbaum Associates.
Hayes, J.R., & Nash, J.G. (1996). On the nature of planning in writing. In C.M. Levy & S. Ransdell (Eds.), *The Science of Writing* (pp. 29-55). Mahwah, New Jersey: Erlbaum.
Hays, J.N., Brandt, K.M., & Chantry, K.H. (1988). The impact of friendly and hostile audiences on the argumentative writing of high school and college students, *Research in the Teaching of English, 22,* 39-416.
Healy, P. (1987). Critical reasoning and dialectical argument. *Informal Logic, 9* (1), 1-12.
Henle, M. (1962). On the relation between logic and thinking. *Psychological Review, 69,* 366-378.
Hidi, S., & Baird, W. (1988). Strategies for increasing text-based interest and students' recall of expository text. *Reading Research quarterly, 23* (4), 465-483.
Hightower, R., & Sayeed, L. (1995). The impact of computer-mediated communication systems on biased group discussion. *Computers in Human Behaviour, 11,* 33-44.
Hillocks, G., Jr. (1986). *Research on Written Composition. New Directions for Teaching.* Urbana, Il.: ERIC Clearinghouse on Reading and Communication Skills.
Isnard, N, & Piolat, A., (1994). The effects of different types of planning on the writing of argumentative text. In G. Eigler & T. Jechle (Eds.), *Writing: Current trends in European Research* (pp.121-132). Freiburg: Hochschul Verlag.
Jackson, S. & Jacobs, S. (1980). Structure of conversational argument. Pragmatic bases for the enthymeme. *Quarterly Journal of Speech, 66,* 251-265.
Jackson, S. & Jacobs, S. (1989). About coherence. In J.A. Anderson (Ed.), *Communication Yearbook, 12* (pp. 146-156). Newbury Park, CA: Sage.
Jacobson, N., & Gottman, J. (1998). *When men batter women.* New York: Simon and Schuster.
Jeffery, G.C., & Underwood, G. (1996). The role of working memory in the development of a writing skill: learning to co-ordinate ideas within written text. In G. Rijlaarsdam, H. van den Bergh, & M. Couzijn (Eds.), *Theories, models, and methodology in writing research* (pp. 268-282). Amsterdam: Amsterdam University Press.
Jermann, P., & Schneider, D. (1997). Semi-structured interface in collaborative problem-solving. *http://tecfa.unige.ch/tecfa/publicat/jermann-papers/lsnne97/lsne-97-1.html.* TECFA, University of Geneva, Switzerland.
Johnson, D. W., & Johnson, R. T. (1993). Creative and Critical Thinking Through Academic Controversy. *American Behavioral Scientist, 3*(1), 40-53.
Johnson, R. (1991). The place of argumentation in the theory of reasoning. *Communication and Cognition, 24* (1), 5-14.
Johnson, R.H., & Blair, J.A. (1977). *Logical Self-defense.* Toronto: McGraw-Hill Ryerson. (2nd ed. 1983, 3rd ed. 1993).
Johnson, R.H., & Blair, J.A. (1980). The recent development of informal logic. In: J.A. Blair, & R.H. Johnson (Eds.), *Informal Logic. The First International Symposium* (pp. 3-28). Point Reyes, CA: Edgepress.
Johnson, R. H., & Blair, J.A. (1991). Context of informal reasoning: Commentary. In J. F. Voss, D. N. Perkins, & J. W. Segal (Eds.), *Informal reasoning and education* (pp. 131-152). Hillsdale, N.J.: Lawrence Erlbaum Associates.
Johnson-Laird, P. N. (1983). *Mental models.* Cambridge, MA: Harvard University Press.
Jose, P.E. (1988). Liking of plan-based stories: The role of goal importance and goal-attainment difficulty. *Discourse Processes, 11,* 261-273.

Jose, P.E., & Brewer, W.F. (1984). The development of story liking: Character identification, suspense, and outcome resolution. *Developmental Psychology, 20,* 911-924.
Kellogg, R.T. (1993). Observations on the psychology of thinking and writing. *Composition Studies, 21,* 3-41.
Kellogg, R.T. (1996). A model of working memory in writing. In M.C. Levy & S.E. Ransdell (Eds.), *The science of writing. Theories, Methods, Individual differences and Applications* (pp. 57-71). Mahwah, NJ: Laurence Erlbaum Associates.
Kerbrat-Orecchioni, C. (1984). Discours politique et manipulation: du bon usage des contenus implicites [Political discourse and manipulation: on the proper use of implicit contents]. In C. Kerbrat-Orecchioni, & M. Mouillaud (Eds.), *Le discours politique.* Lyon: Presses Universitaires de Lyon.
Kerbrat-Orecchioni, C. (1990). *Les Interactions Verbales (Tome 1)* [Verbal Interactions (Vol 1)]. Paris: Armand Colin.
Kienpointer, M. (1983). *Argumentationsanalyse.* [Analysis of argumentation]. Innsbruck: Verlag des Instituts für Sprachwissenschaft der Universitäts.
Kienpointner, M. (1991a). Argumentation in Germany and Austria: an overview of the recent literature. *Informal Logic, 13* (3), 129-136.
Kienpointner, M. (1991b). Rhetoric and argumentation-relativism and beyond. *Philosophy and Rhetoric, 24* (1), 43-53.
Kintsch, W., & van Dijk, T.A. (1978). Toward a model of text comprehension and production. *Psychological Review, 85,* 363-394.
Klein, W. (1985). Argumentationsanalyse: ein Begriffsrahmen und ein Beispiel [Analysis of argumentation: a framework and an example]. In J. Kopperschmidt & H. Schange (Eds.), *Argumente [Argumentation].* München: Finck.
Kneupper, C.W. (1978). Teaching argument: An introduction to the Toulmin model. *College Composition and Communication, 29,* 237-241.
Knudson, R E. (1994). An Analysis of Persuasive Discourse: Learning How to Take a Stand. *Discourse Processes, 18 (2),* 211-230.
Kopperschmidt, J. (1977). *Überzeugen - Problemskizze zu den Gesprächschancen zwischen Rhetorik und Argumentationstheorie* [Persuasion...]. In M. Schecker (Ed.), *Theorie der Argumentation* [Theory of Argumentation] (pp. 203-240). Tübingen: TBL Verlag Gunter Narr.
Kopperschmidt, J. (1978). *Das Prinzip der vernünftigen Rede* [The principle of rational reason]. Stuttgart: Kohlhammer.
Kopperschmidt, J. (1980). *Argumentation. Sprache und Vernunft II* [Argumentation: Speech and Cognition]. Stuttgart: Kohlhammer.
Kopperschmidt, J. (1985). An analysis of argumentation. In T.A. van Dijk (Ed.), *Handbook of Discourse Analysis,* vol. 2 (Dimensions of discourse), 159-168.
Kopperschmidt, J. (1987). The function of argumentation: a pragmatic approach. In: F.H. van Eemeren, R. Grootendorst, J.A. Blair, & C.A. Willard (Eds.), *Argumentation: Across the Lines of Discipline. Proceedings of the First International Conference on Argumentation 1986* (pp. 179-188). Dordrecht : Foris (PDA 3).
Kopperschmidt, J. (1989). *Methodik der Argumentationsanalyse.* [The method of analysis of argumentation]. Stuttgart: Fromann-Holzbog.
Kopperschmidt, J. (Ed.). (1990). *Rhetorik. Bd. 1: Rhetorik als Texttheorie.* Darmstadt: Wissenschaftliche Buchgesellschaft.
Kuhn, D. (1991). *The skill of argument.* Cambridge, U.K.: Cambridge University Press.
Kuhn, D. (1995). Microgenetic study of change: What has it told us? *Psychological Sciences, 6*(3), 133-139.
Kuhn, D. (1996). The effects of evidence on attitudes: Is polarization the norm? *Psychological Science, 7* (2), 115-120.
Lapintie, K. (1998). Analysing and evaluating argumentation in planning. *Environment and Planning B: Planning and Design, Vol. 25,* 187-204.
Lave, J. (1988). *Cognition in Practice.* Cambridge: Cambridge University Press.

Lave, J. (1991). Situated Learning. In L.B. Resnick, J.M. Levine, & S.D. Teasley (Eds.), *Perspectives on Socially Shared Cognition* (pp. 63-82). Washington D.C.: American Psychological Association.
Lave, J., & Wenger, E. (1991). *Situated Learning: Legitimate peripheral participation*. Cambridge: Cambridge University Press.
Learning Research and Development Center (1996). Advanced Cognitive Tools for Learning. *http://advlearn.lrdc.pitt.edu/belvedere/index.html*. University of Pittsburgh, Pittsburgh.
Leech, G.N. (1983). *Principles of Pragmatics*. London and New York: Longman.
Leinhardt, G., Stainton, C., Virji, S., M., & Odoroff, E. (1994). Learning to reason in history: Mindlessness to mindfulness. In M. Carretero & J. F. Voss (Eds.), *Cognitive and Instructional Processes in History and the Social Sciences* (pp. 131-158). Hillsdale, NJ: Erlbaum.
Levelt, W.J.M. (1981). *The speaker's linearization problem*. Phil. Trans. Roy. Society. London B295, 305-315.
Levelt, W.J.M. (1989). *Speaking: from intention to articulation*. Cambridge, Mass.: MIT Press
Levinson, S.C. (1983). *Pragmatics*. Cambridge: Cambridge University Press.
Levy, C.M. (1997). The " R " that psychology forgot: Research on writing processes. *Behavior Research Methods, Instruments and Computers, 29,* 137-145.
Lorenzen, P. & Lorenz, K. (1978). Dialogische Logik [Dialogic logic]. Darmstadt: Wissenschaftliche Buchgesellschaft.
Lundquist, L. (1987). Toward a procedural analysis of argumentative operators in texts. In: F.H. van Eemeren, R. Grootendorst, J.A. Blair, & C.A. Willard (Eds.), *Argumentation: Perspectives and Approaches. Proceedings of the Conference on Argumentation 1986* (pp. 60-69). Dordrecht: Foris (PDA 3A).
Luscher, J. (1989). Connecteurs et marques de pertinence: l'exemple de *d'ailleurs*. [Connectives and markers of relevance: The case of *anyway*]. *Cahiers de Linguistique Française, 10,* 101-145.
MacKenzie, J.D. (1985). No logic before Friday. *Synthese, 63,* 329-341.
Maier, R. (1989). Natural logic and norms in argumentation. In: R. Maier (Ed.) *Norms in Argumentation. Proceedings of the Conference on Norms 1988* (pp. 49-65). Dordrecht: Foris (PDA 8).
Mandl, H., & Renkl, A. (1992). A plea for 'more local' theories of cooperative learning. *Learning and Instruction, 2,* 281-285.
Marchand, E. (1993). Le développement des compétences textuelles et argumentatives de 11 à 17 ans [The development of textual and argumentative skills: from 11 to 17 years]. Mémoire de recherche de DEA. Université de Poitiers, Juin.
Marchand, E., Coirier, P., & Dellerman, P. (1996). Textualization and polyphony in argumentative composition. In G. Rijlaarsdam, H. van den Berg, & M. Couzijn (Eds.), *What is writing? Theories, Models and Methodology* (pp. 366-380). Amsterdam: Amsterdam University Press.
Mason, R. (1992). The textuality of computer networking. In R. Mason (Ed.), *Computer Conferencing: The Last Word* (pp. 22-35). Victoria, British Columbia: Beach Holme Publishers Limited. .
Maynard, D.W. (1985). On the functions of social conflict among children. *American Sociology Review, 50,* 207-223.
McCleary, W.J. (1979). Teaching deductive logic: A test of the Toulmin and Aristotelian models for critical thinking and college composition. Unpublished dissertation, University of Texas.
McCutchen, D. (1984). Writing as a linguistic problem. *Educational Psychologist, 19,* 226-238.
McCutchen, D. (1987). Children's discourse skill: form and modality requirements of schooled writing. *Discourse Processes, 10,* 267-286.
McCutchen, D. (1988). 'Functional automaticity' in children's writing: A problem of metacognitive control. *Written Communication, 5,* 306-324.

McCutchen, D. (1996). A capacity theory of writing: Working memory in composition. *Educational Psychology Review, 8* (3), 299-325.
McCutchen, D., Covill, A., Hoyne, S. H., & Mildes, K. (1994). Individual differences in writing: Implications of translating fluency. *Journal of Educational Psychology, 86 (2)*, 256-266.
McKerrow, R. E. (1977). Rhetorical validity: an analysis of three perspectives on the justification of rhetorical argument. *Journal of the American Forensic Association, 13*, 133-141. (Repr. in Benoit, Hample & Benoit (Eds.). (1992), 297-311).
Means, M. L., & Voss, J. F. (1996). Who reasons well? Two studies of informal reasoning among children of different grade, ability and knowledge levels. *Cognition and Instruction, 14*, 139-178
Meyer, B. J. F. (1975). *The organization of prose and its effect on memory*. Amsterdam: North-Holland.
Meyer, M. (1982a). Argumentation in the light of a theory of questioning. *Philosophy and Rhetoric, 15*, 81-103.
Meyer, M. (1982b). *Logique, langage et argumentation* [Logic, language and argumentation]. Hachette. [English translation in Meyer, M. (1986a)].
Meyer, M. (1986b). *De la problématologie. Philosophie, science et langage* [About problematology. Philosophy, science and language]. Bruxelles: Mardaga.
Meyer, M. (Ed.). (1986c). De la métaphysique à la rhétorique [From metaphysics to rhetoric]. Brussel: Editions de l'Université de Bruxelles.
Miller, M. (1986). Argumentation and cognition. In M. Hickmann (Ed.), *Social and functional approaches to language and thought (pp. 225-249)*. New York: Academic Press.
Miller, M. (1987). Argumentation and cognition. In M. Hickmann (Ed.), *Social and functional approaches to language and thought* (pp. 225-249). San Diego, CA: Academic Press.
Miller, M. (1987). Culture and collective argumentation. *Argumentation, 1*, 127-154.
Miller-Jones, D. (1991). Informal reasoning in inner-city children. In J. F. Voss, D. N. Perkins, & J. W. Segal (Eds.), *Informal reasoning and education* (pp. 107-130). Hillsdale, NJ: Lawrence Erlbaum Associates.
Miyake, N. (1986). Constructive Interaction and the Iterative Process of Understanding. *Cognitive Science, 10* (2), 151-177.
Moeschler, J. (1980). La réfutation parmi les fonctions interactives marquant l'accord et le désaccord [Refutation between interactive functions indicating agreement and disagreement]. *Cahiers de Linguistique Française, 1*, 54-78.
Moeschler, J. (1982). *Dire et contredire* [Asserting and countering]. Bern: Peter Lang.
Moeschler, J. (1985). *Argumentation et Conversation: Eléments pour une analyse pragmatique du discours* [Argumentation and Conversation: Elements for a pragmatic discouse analysis]. Paris: Hatier-Crédif.
Moeschler, J. (1989a). Pragmatic connectives, argumentative coherence and relevance. *Argumen-tation, 3*, 321–339.
Moeschler, J. (1989b). *Modélisation du dialogue. Représentation de l'inférence argumentative* [Modelling dialogue. The representation of argumentative inference]. Paris: Hermès.
Moore, D. (1993). *Dialogue Game Theory for Intelligent Tutoring Systems*. Unpublished PhD thesis, Leeds Metropolitan University.
Moore, M. G. (1993). Theory of transactional distance. In D. Keegan (Ed.), *Theoretical principles of distance education* (pp. 22-38). London: Routledge.
Muntig, P., & Turnbull, W. (1998). Conversational structure and facework in arguing. *Journal of Pragmatics, 29*, 225-256.
Murray, D. M. (1987). *Write to Learn* (2nd ed.). New York: Holt, Rinehart & Winston.
Naess, A. (1966). *Communication and argument. Elements of applied semantics*. London: Allen & Unwin.
Naess, A. (1975). *Communication und Argumentation. Eine Einführung in die angewandte Semantik* [Communication and argumentation. An introduction into applied semantics]. Kronberg: Scriptor Verlag.

Newell, A., & Simon, H. A. (1972). *Human problem solving*. Englewood Cliffs, N.J.: Prentice-Hall.
Nickerson, R. (1986). *Reflections on reasoning*. Hillsdale, N.J.: Erlbaum.
Nølke, H. (1992). Semantic constraints on argumentation: from polyphonic micro-structure to argumentative macro-structure. In: F.H. van Eemeren, R. Grootendorst, J.A. Blair, & C.A.Willard (Eds.). *Argumentation Illuminated* (pp. 189-200). Amsterdam: SICSAT/ISSA (SICSAT 1).
Nonnon, E. (1996). Activités argumentatives et élaboration de connaissances nouvelles: le dialogue comme espace d'exploration [Argumentative activities and elaboration of new knowledge: The dialogue as exploration area]. *Langue Française, 112* (December 1996), 67-87.
Nystrand, M. (1986). Learning to write by talking about writing: A summary of research on intensive peer review. In M. Nystrand (Ed.), *The structure of written communication: Studies in reciprocity between writers and readers* (pp. 179-211). Orlando: Academic Press.
Öhlschläger, G. (1979). Beiträge zur Theorie und Praxis der Argumentation [Contributions to theory and practice of argumentation]. *Zeitschrift für Germanistische Linguistik, 7*, 83-103.
O'Keefe, D. J. (1977). Two concepts of argument. *Journal of the American Forensic Association, 13*, 121-128.
O'Keefe, B. J., & Benoit, P. J. (1982). Children's arguments. In J. R. Cox & C. A. Willard (Eds.), *Advances in argumentation theory and research* (pp 154-183). Carbondale: Southern Illinois University Press.
Pea, R.D. (1993). Learning scientific concepts through material and social activities: Conversational analysis meets conceptual change. *Educational psychologist, 28* (3), 265-277.
Pennington, N., & Hastie, R. (1993). The story model for juror decision making. In R. Hastie (Ed.), *Inside the Juror: The Psychology of Juror Decision* (pp. 192-221). Cambridge: Cambridge University Press.
Perelman, C. & L. Olbrechts-Tyteca (1958/1969). *La nouvelle rhétorique: traité de l'argumentation* [The New Rhetoric. A Treatise on Argumentation]. Bruxelles: l'Université de Bruxelles.
Perelman, C., & Olbrechts-Tyteca, L. (1958/1969). *The new rhetoric. A Treatise on argumentation*. Trans. by J. Wilkinson & P. Weaver. Notre Dame: University of Notre Dame Press.
Perelman, C., & Olbrechts-Tyteca, L. (1958/1988). *Traité de l'argumentation. La nouvelle rhétorique* [The new rhetoric: A treatise on argumentation]. Bruxelles: Editions de l'Université de Bruxelles.
Perfetti, C.A., Britt, M.A., Rouet, J.F., Georgi, M.C., & Mason, R.A. (1994). How Students Use Texts to Learn and Reason about Historical Uncertainty. In J.F.Voss & M. Carretero (Eds.), *Cognitive and Instructional Processes in History and Social Sciences* (pp. 257-284). Hillsdale, N.J.: Lawrence Erlbaum Associates.
Perkins, D. N. (1989). Reasoning as it is and could be: An empirical perspective. In D. M. Topping D. C., Crowell, & V. N. Kobayashi (Eds.), *Thinking across cultures: The third international conference on thinking* (pp. 175-194). Hillsdale, N.J.: Lawrence Erlbaum Associates.
Perkins, D. N., Allen, R., & Hafner, J. (1983). Difficulties in everyday reasoning. In W. Maxwell (Ed.), *Thinking: The expanding frontier* (pp. 177-189). Philadelphia: Franklin Institute Press.
Perkins, D. N., Farady, M. & Bushey, B. (1991). Everyday reasoning and the roots of intelligence. In J. F. Voss, D. N. Perkins & J. W. Segal (Eds.), *Informal reasoning and education* (pp. 83-105). Hillsdale, NJ: Lawrence Erlbaum Associates.
Petty, R. E., & Cacioppo, J.T. (1986). *Communication and Persuasion: Central and peripheral routes to attitude change*. New York, N.Y.: Springer-Verlag.

Petty, R.E., & Cacioppo, J.T. (1986). The elaboration likelihood model of persuasion. In L. Berkowitz (Ed.), *Advances in experimental social psychology* (Vol. 19, pp. 123-205). San Diego, CA: Academic Press.

Piaget, J. (1977). *The development of thought: Equilibration of cognitive structures*. New York: Viking Penguin.

Pièraut-Le Bonniec, G., & Vallette, M. (1987). Développement du raisonnement argumentatif chez l'adolescent [Development of argumentative reasoning in adolescents]. In G. Piéraut-Le Bonniec (Ed.), *Connaitre et le dire* (pp. 263-275). Bruxelles: Mardaga.

Pilkington, R.M., & Mallen, C. (1996). Dialogue games to support reasoning and reflection in diagnostic tasks. In P. Brna, A. Paiva, & J. Self (Eds.), *Proceedings of EuroAIED* (pp. 213-220). Lisbon: Fundacao Calouste Gulbenkian.

Pinto, R.C. (1995). The relation of argument to inference. In F.H. van Eemeren, R. Grootendorst, J.A. Blair, & C.A. Willard (Eds.), *Perspectives and Approaches* (pp. 271-286). Proceedings of the Third ISSA Conference on Argumentation. Amsterdam: Sic Sat.

Piolat, A. (1990). *Vers l'amélioration de la rédaction de texte* [Towards the improvement of text writing]. Dossier d'habilitation à diriger des recherches, Université de Provence, Aix-en-Provence.

Piolat, A., & Pélissier, A. (1998). Etude de la rédaction de textes: contraintes théoriques et méthodes de recherches [Study of text writing: Theoretical constraints and research methods]. In A. Piolat & A. Pélissier (Eds.), *La rédaction de textes. Approche cognitive* (pp. 225-269). Lausanne: Delachaux & Niestlé.

Piolat, A., & Roussey, J.-Y. (1996). Intérêts et limites de l'étude assistée par ordinateur des processus rédactionnels [Interest and limit of computer assisted studies for written processes]. *Etudes de Linguistique Appliquée, 101*, 33-45.

Plantin, C. (1990). *Essais sur l'argumentation: introduction linguistique à l'étude de la parole argumentative* [Essay on argumentation: linguistic introduction to argumentative speech research]. Paris: Kimé.

Pontecorvo, C. (Ed.). (1993). Discourse and Shared Reasoning. [Special issue]. *Cognition and Instruction, 11* (3 & 4).

Pontecorvo, C., & Girardet, H. (1993). Arguing and reasoning in understanding historical topics. *Cognition and Instruction, 11*, 365-395.

Popper, K.R. (1972). *Objective Knowledge: An Evolutionary Approach*. Oxford: Clarendon Press.

Popper, K.R. (1974). *Conjectures and Refutations. The Growth of Scientific Knowledge*. 5th ed. London: Routledge & Kegan Paul.

Pouit, D., & Golder, C. (1996). Peut-on faciliter l'argumentation écrite? Effets d'un schéma de texte, d'une liste d'idées et d'un thème familier [Can we facilitate written argumentation? Effects of a textual schema, a list of ideas and a familiar theme]. *Archives de Psychologie, 64*, 179-199.

Quasthoff, U. (1978). The uses of stereotype in everyday argument. *Journal of Pragmatics, 2*, 1-48.

Ramage, J.D., & Bean, J.C. (1992). *Writing arguments (2nd edition)*. New York: MacMillan.

Ray, J.W. (1978). Perelman's universal audience. *Quarterly Journal of Speech, 64*, 361-384.

Reboul, A. (1988). Les problèmes de l'attente interprétative: Topoi et hypothèses projectives [Problems of interpretative expectation: topoi and hypotheses]. *Cahiers de Linguistique Française, 9*, 87-114.

Reboul, O. (1988). Can there be non-rhetorical argumentation? *Philosophy and Rhetoric, 21* (3), 220-223.

Reboul, O. (1990). Rhétorique et dialectique chez Aristote. *Argumentation, 4* (1), 35-52.

Reichler, M.-J. (Ed.). (1989). *Perspectives méthodologiques dans les sciences du langage* [Methodological perspectives in the language sciences]. Bern: Peter Lang.

Reinard, J.C. (1984). The role of Toulmin's categories of message development in persuasive communication. Two experimental studies on attitude change. *Journal of the American Forensic Association, 20* (4), 206-223.

Rescher, N. (1988). The range of rationality. In N. Rescher Ed.), *Rationality: A philosophical inquiry into the nature and the rationale of reason* (pp. 1-18). Oxford, England: Clarendon Press.

Resnick, L.B., Levine, J.M., & Teasley, S.D. (Eds.). (1991). *Perspectives on Socially Shared Cognition.* Washington D.C.: American Psychological Association.

Resnick, L.B., Salmon, M.H., Zeitz, C.M., Wathen, S.H., & Holowchak, M. (1993). Reasoning in conversation. *Cognition and Instruction, 11* (3 & 4), 347-364.

Rest, J. (1983). Morality. In P.H. Mussen, J. H. Flavell, & E. M. Markman (Eds.), *Cognitive development: Handbook of child development.* New York: Wiley.

Rijlaarsdam, G., & van den Bergh, H. (1996). The dynamics of composing - An agenda for Research into an interactive compensatory model of writing: Many questions, some answers. In C.M. Levy & S. Ransdell (Eds.), *The Science of Writing* (pp. 107-125). Mahwah, N.J.: Erlbaum.

Rijlaarsdam, G., van den Bergh, H., & Couzijn, M. (1996a). *Effective Teaching and Learning of Writing. Current Trends in Research.* Amsterdam: Amsterdam University Press.

Rijlaarsdam, G., van den Bergh, H., & Couzijn, M. (1996b). *Theories, Models and Methodology in Writing Research.* Amsterdam: Amsterdam University Press.

Rips, L. (1994). *The psychology of proof.* Cambridge, MA: The MIT Press.

Rogoff, B. (1990). *Apprenticeship in thinking: Cognitive development in social contexts.* New York: Oxford University Press.

Roschelle, J. (1992). Learning by collaborating: Convergent conceptual change. *The journal of the learning sciences, 2* (3), 235-276.

Roschelle, J., & Teasley, S.D. (1995). Construction of shared knowledge in collaborative problem solving. In C. O'Malley (Ed.), *Computer-supported collaborative learning.* New York: Springer-Verlag.

Ross, M., & Holmberg, D. (1990). Recounting the past: Gender differences in the recall of events in the history of a close relationship. In M. Olson & M. P. Zanna (Eds.), *Self-inference processes: The Ontario Symposium* (Vol. 6, pp. 135-152). Hillsdale, N.J.: Lawrence Erlbaum Associates.

Rottenberg, A.T. (1985). *Elements of argument.* New York: St. Martin's.

Rottenberg, A.T. (1994). *Elements of argument: A textured reader (4th edition).* Boston: St. Martin's.

Rouet, J.F., Favart, M., Gaonac'h, D., & Lacroix, N. (1996). Writing from Multiple Sources: The Representation of Arguments and Evidence in Novice and Expert History Students. In G. Rijlaarsdam, H. van den Bergh & M. Couzijn (Eds.). *Current Trends in Writing Research: What is writing? Theories, Models and Methodology* (pp. 44-60) Amsterdam: Amsterdam University Press.

Roulet, E. (1992). On the structure of conversation as negotiation. In H. Parrett & J. Verschueren (Eds.) *(On) Searle on Conversation* (pp. 91-99). Amsterdam: John Benjamins.

Roulet, E., Auchlin, A., Moeschler, J., Rubattel, C., & Schelling, M. (1985). *L'articulation du discours en français contemporain* [Discourse stucture in contemporary French language]. Bern: Peter Lang.

Roussey, J.Y., & Gombert, A. (1992). Ecriture en dyade d'un texte argumentatif par des enfants de 8 ans [Cooperative writing of argumentative text in 8 year old children]. *Archives de Psychologie, 60,* 297-315.

Roussey, J.Y., Akiguet, S., Gombert, A., & Piolat, A. (1995). Etude de l'utilisation du schéma argumentatif par des rédacteurs âgés de 8 à 11 ans [Study of the use of argumentative schema by 8-11 year old children]. *Enfance, 2,* 205-214.

Roussey, J-Y., & Gombert, A. (1996). Improving argumentative writing skills: Effect of two types of aids. *Argumentation, 10,* 283-300.

Roussey, J-Y., Farioli, F., & Piolat, A. (1992). Effects of social regulation and computer assistance on the monitoring of writing. *European Journal of Psychology of Education, 7* (4), 295-309.

Rowan, K.E. (1988). A contemporary theory of explanatory writing. *Written Communication, 5* (1), 23-56.
Rumelhart, D.E., & Norman, D.A. (1978). Accretion, tuning and restructurating: Three modes of learning. In J.W. Cottin, & R. Klatzky (Eds.), *Semantic factors in cognition* (pp. 246-267). Hillsdale, N.J.: Lawrence Erlbaum.
Salomon, G. (1997, August). *Novel constructivist learning environments and novel technologies: Some issues to be concerned.* Invited key-note address presented at the 7th European Conference for Research on Learning and Instruction (EARLI), August 26-30, 1997, Athens, Greece.
Sandhya, S., & Stein, N.L. (1998). A narrative and self assessment study of marital satisfaction in Indian Couples. Unpublished manuscript. University of Chicago.
Santos, C. M. (1996). *Good reasoning: to whom? when? how?: An investigation of belief effects on syllogistic and argumentative reasoning.* PhD thesis, University of Sussex, UK.
Santos, C. M. (1997). *The effects of beliefs and values on the argumentation process in a dialogic situation.* Manuscript submitted for publication.
Santos, C. M. (1998, July). Myside bias: argumentation flaw or pragmatic strategy? In C. M. Santos & N. L. Stein (Convenors), *The study of argumentative thinking in everyday contexts*. Symposium conducted at the XVth Biennial Meetings of the International Society for the Study of Behavioural Development (ISSBD). Bern, Switzerland.
Santos, S. L. (1993). *The construction of arguments: A comparison of the strategies employed in experimental and naturalistic settings.* PhD thesis, University of Cambridge, UK.
Santos, S. L. (1995). Argumentation in a naturalistic setting. In F. H. van Eemeren, R. Grootendorst, J.A. Blair, & C.A. Willard (Eds.), *Proceedings of the Third ISSA Conference on Argumentation, Vol. III. Reconstruction and Application* (pp. 30-41). Amsterdam.
Santos, S. L. (1997). *Uma exploração de variantes e invariantes da argumentação em linguagem natural* [Exploring variant and invariant aspects of argumentation in natural language]. (Tech. Rep. No. 520723/95-3). Brasília: CNPq (Brazilian National Research Council).
Santos, S. L., & Vasconcelos, S. B. (1998). *The impact of text structure on children's argumentative writing.* Manuscript submitted to publication.
Savery, J.R., & Duffy, T.M. (1996). Problem based learning: An instructional model and its constructivistic framework. In B. Wilson (Ed.). *Constructivist learning environments: Case studies in instructional design* (pp. 135-148). Englewood Cliffs, N.J.: Educational Technology Publications.
Schank, R.C., & Abelson, R.P. (1977). *Scripts, Plans and Understanding.* New York, N.J.: Lawrence Erlbaum.
Schecker, M. (Ed.). (1977). *Theorie der Argumentation.* Tübingen: TBL Verlag Gunter Narr.
Schneuwly, B. (1986). Activité langagière ou action langagière complexe - Discussions et recherches allemandes [Linguistic activity or complex speech acts - German discussions and researches]. *Bulletin de Psychologie, 38,* 595-606.
Schneuwly, B. (1986). Quelle typologie des textes pour l'enseignement? Une typologie des textes [Which text typology for teaching?]. *Actes du IIIème Colloque International de Didactique du Français 'Apprendre/Enseigner àProduire des Textes Ecrits'* (pp. 53-63). Bruxelles: De Boeck.
Schneuwly, B. (1988). *Le langage écrit chez l'enfant. La production des textes informatifs et argumentatifs* [The written language of children. Production of informative and argumentative texts]. Neuchâtel et Paris: Delachaux & Niestlé.
Schneuwly, B. (1990). Production de textes écrits, types de textes et types d'activité [Written texts production and types of texts]. In M. Fayol, J. E. Gombert, H. Abdi & D. Zagar (Eds.) *La production d'écrits* (pp. 71-81). Dijon: CRDP.
Schneuwly, B. (1991). Différences entre les processus de production de trois genres: Du dialogue entre énonciateurs au texte écrit [Differences between production processes of three text genres: From dialogue between enunciators to written text]. *Repères, 3,* 45-65.

Schneuwly, B. (1996). Content and formulation writing argumentative texts in pairs. *Argumentation, 10,* 213-226.

Schneuwly, B., Rosat, M.C., & Dolz, J. (1989). Les organisateurs textuels dans quatre types de textes écrits. Etude chez des élèves de 10, 12 et 14 ans [Textual organizers in four types of written text. A study with 10, 12, and 14 years old pupils]. *Langue Française, 81,* 52-69.

Scinto, L.F.M. (1984). Architectonics of texts produced by children and the development of higher cognitive function. *Discourse Processes, 7,* 371-418.

Searle, J.R. (1969). *Speech Acts. An Essay in the Philosophy of Language.* Cambridge: Cambridge University Press.

Searle, J.R. (1979). *Expression and Meaning. Studies in the Theory of Speech Acts.* Cambridge: Cambridge University Press.

Shantz, C., & Shantz, D. (1985). Conflict between children: Social-cognitive and sociometric correlates. In W. Damon & M. Berkowitz (Eds.), *New directions in child development (Vol. 29): Peer conflict and psychological growth* (pp. 3-21). San Francisco: Jossey-Bass.

Siegel, H. (1987). *Relativism Refuted. A Critique of Contemporary Epistemological Relativism.* Dordrecht etc.: Reidel. (Synthese Library 189).

Stein, L. S., Calicchia, D. J., & Bernas, R. S. (1996). Conflict talk. Understanding and resolving arguments. In T. Givon (Ed.), *Typological studies in language: conversational analysis* (pp. 233-267). Amsterdam: John Benjamins.

Stein, N. L., & Albro, E. R. (1997). The structure and content of parent-child conflict negotiations. Paper presented at SRCD, April, Washington, D.C.

Stein, N. L., & Broaders, S. (In press). Predicting Psychological Well-Being from Beliefs and Goal Appraisal Processes During the Experience of Emotional Events. In S. Goldman, P.L. Van den Broek & A. Graesser (Eds.), *Essays in Honor of Tom Trabasso.* Mahwah, NJ: Lawrence Erlbaum Associates.

Stein, N. L., & Glenn C. G. (1979). An analysis of story comprehension in elementary school children. In R. O. Freedle (Ed.), *New directions in discourse processing* (pp. 53-120). Norwood, N.J.: Ablex.

Stein, N.L., & Liwag, M.D. (1997). A goal-appraisal process approach to understanding and remembering emotional events. In P. van den Broek, P. Bauer, & T. Bourg (Eds.), *Developmental spans in event comprehension and representation* (pp 199-235). Hillsdale, NJ: Lawrence Erlbaum Associates.

Stein, N. L., & Miller, C.A. (1990). I win - you lose: The development of argumentative thinking. In J. Voss, D. Perkins, & J. Segal (Eds.), *Informal reasoning and instruction* (pp. 265-290). Hillsdale, N.J.: Lawrence Erlbaum Associates.

Stein, N. L., & Miller, C.A. (1993a). A theory of argumentative understanding: Relationships among position preference, judgments of goodness, memory, and reasoning. *Argumentation, 7,* 183-204.

Stein, N. L., & Miller, C. A. (1993b). The development of memory and reasoning skill in argumentative contexts: Evaluating, explaining, and generating evidence. In R. Glaser (Ed.), *Advances in instructional psychology (Vol. 4)* (pp. 285-335). Hillsdale, NJ: Lawrence Erlbaum Associates.

Stein, N.L., & Ross, M. (1996). Discussing conflicts: Similarities and differences in husband's and wife's description of the same conflicts. Paper presented at the Psychonomic Society, Chicago, IL.

Stein, N. L., & Trabasso, T. (1982). Children's understanding of stories: A basis for moral judgment and dilemma resolution. In C. Brainerd & M. Pressley (Eds.), *Verbal processes in children: Progress in cognitive development research* (pp. 161-188). New York: Springer Verlag.

Stein, N. L., & Trabasso, T. (1989). Children are understanding of changing emotion states. In C. Saarni & P. Harris (Eds.), *The Development of Emotional Understanding* (pp. 50-77). New York, N.Y.: Cambridge University Press.

Stein, N. L., Bernas, R. S., & Calicchia, D. J. (1997). Conflict talk: Understanding and resolving arguments. In T. Givon (Ed.), *Conversation: Cognitive, communicative and social perspectives*. Amsterdam: John Benjamins.

Stein, N. L., Bernas, R. S., Calicchia, D. J., & Wright, A. (1995). Understanding and resolving arguments: The dynamics of negotiation. In B. Britton & A. G. Graesser (Eds.), *Models of understanding* (pp. 257-287). Hillsdale, N.J.: Lawrence Erlbaum Associates.

Stein, N. L., Bernas, R. S., Calicchia, D. J., & Wright, A. (1996). A model of argument understanding: the dynamics of negotiation. In B. Britton, & A. Graesser (Eds.), *Models of Understanding Text* (pp. 257-287). Hillsdale, NJ: Lawrence Erlbaum Associates.

Stein, N.L., Calicchia, D., & Bernas, R. (1995). Understanding and resolving arguments: do compromise instructions help? Paper at the EARLI symposium: cognitive processes in the learning and teaching of argumentation skills, Nijmegen, Holland, 27 August.

Stewart, K.L., Kowler, M.E., & Bullock, C. (1987). *Essay Writing for Canadian Students* (2nd ed.). Scarborough, Ont.: Prentice-Hall.

Stratman, J.F. (1994). Investigating Persuasive Processes in Legal Discourse in Real Time: Cognitive Biases and Rhetorical Strategies in Appeal Court Briefs. *Discourse Processes, 17*, 1-57.

Suchman, L. (1987). *Plans and situated actions: The problem of human-machine communication*. Cambridge: Cambridge University Press.

Suthers, D., & Weiner, A. (1995). GroupWare for developing critical discussion skills. http://www.pitt.edu/~suthers/belvedere University of Pittsburgh, Pittsburgh.

Swanson, H.L., & Berninger V.W. (1996). Individual differences in children's working memory and writing skill. *Journal of Experimental Child Psychology, 63,* 358-385.

Tesla, C., & Dunn, J. (1992). Getting along or getting your own way: The development of young children's use of argument in conflicts with mother and sibling. *Social Development, 1,* 107-121.

Tiberghien, A. (1994). Modeling as a basis for analyzing teaching-learning situations. *Learning and Instruction, 4,* 71-87.

Tiberghien, A. (1996). Construction of prototypical situations in teaching the concept of energy. In G. Welford, J. Osborne, & P. Scott (Eds.), *Research in Science Education in Europe* (pp. 100-114). London: Falmer Press.

Toulmin, S. (1976). *Knowing and acting*. New York: Macmillan.

Toulmin, S., Rieke, R., & Janik, A. (1984). *An introduction to reasoning*. New York: Macmillan Publishing.

Toulmin, S.E. (1958). *The uses of argument*. Cambridge, England: Cambridge University Press.

Trabasso, T., & Stein, N. L (1997). Narrating, representing, and remembering event sequences. In P. van den Broek, P. Bauer, & T. Bourk (Eds.), *Developmental spans in event comprehension and representation* (pp. 237-270). Hillsdale, N.J.: Lawrence Erlbaum Associates.

Trabasso, T., & Stein, N. L. (1994). Using goal-plan knowledge to merge the past with the present and the future in narrating events on-line. In M. Haith, J. Benson, R. Roberts, & B. Pennington (Eds.), *The development of future-oriented processes* (pp. 323-349). Chicago: University of Chicago Press.

Trabasso, T., & van den Broek, P. (1985). Causal thinking and the representation of narrative events. *Journal of Memory and Language, 24,* 612-630.

Travaux du Centre de Recherches Sémiologiques (1992). *Les organisations raisonnées* [Motivated organizations], *n° 60,* Neuchâtel: Université de *Neuchâtel*.

Travaux du Centre de Recherches Sémiologiques (1995). *Raisonnement et calcul* [Reasoning and calculation], *n° 63,* Neuchâtel: Université de Neuchâtel.

Trognon, A. (1990). Relations Intersubjectives dans les Débats. [Intersubjective relations in debats]. In A. Berrendonner & H. Parret (Eds.), *L'Interaction Communicative* [Communicative Interaction] (pp. 195-213). Berne: Peter Lang.

Ury, W. L. (1991). *Getting past no: Negotiating with difficult people*. New York: Bantam.

Veerman, A.L. (1996, October). *Argumentation during solving ill-structured problems.* Paper presented at the First International Workshop on Argumentative Text Processing, Barcelona.

Veerman, A.L., & Andriessen, J.E.B. (1997, September). *Academic learning and writing through the use of educational technology.* Presented at the conference on Learning and Teaching Argumentation, Middlesex University, London.

Verbiest, A. (1991). A new supply of argumentative indicators? In: F.H. van Eemeren, R. Grootendorst, J.A. Blair, & C.A. Willard (Eds.), *Proceedings of the Second International Conference on Argumentation* (pp. 448-454). Amsterdam: SICSAT/ISSA (SICSAT 1A en 1B).

Vignaux, G. (1988). *Le Discours Acteur du Monde: Enonciation, argumentation et cognition* [World actor's discourse: utterance, argumentation and cognition]. Paris: Ophrys.

Vignaux, G. (1990). A Cognitive Model of Argumentation. In F.H. van Eemeren, R. Grootendorst, J.A. Blair, & C.A. Willard (Eds.), *Proceedings of the Second International Conference on Argumentation*, (Vol.1), pp. 303-310.

Vignaux, G. (1992). From negation to "notion": cognitive processes and argumentative strategies. *Argumentation, 6* (1), 29-39.

Vigner, G. (1990). Argumenter et disserter: parcours d'une écriture [To argue and to write: the development of one's writing]. *Pratiques, 68,* 17-55.

Völzing, P.-L. (1979). *Begründen, Erklären, Argumentieren. Modelle und Materialien zu einer Theorie der Metakommunikation* [Backing, explaining, arguing. Models and means for a theory of metacommunication]. Heidelberg: Quelle & Meyer.

VonGlaserfeld, E. (1989). Cognition, construction of knowledge, and teaching. *Synthese, 80,* 121-140.

Voss, J. F., & Means, M. L. (1991). Learning to reason via instruction in argumentation. *Learning and Instruction, 1,* 337-350.

Voss, J. F., Fincher-Kiefer, R., Wiley, J., & Silfies, L. N. (1993). On the processing of arguments. *Argumentation, 7,* 165-181.

Voss, J. F., Greene, T. R., Post, T. A., & Penner, B. C. (1983). Problem solving skill in the social sciences. In G. H. Bower (Ed.), *The psychology of learning and motivation: Advances in research and theory, 17* (pp. 165-213). New York: Academic Press.

Voss, J.F., Wiley, J., & Sandak, R. (in press). *Text processing.* (Tentative). Mahwah, NJ: Erlbaum.

Voss, J.F., Blais, J., & Means, M.L. (1986). Informal reasoning and subject matter knowledge in the solving of economics problems by naive and novice individuals. *Cognition and Instruction, 3* (4), 269-302.

Voss, J.F., Perkins, D. N., & Segal, J. W. (Eds.). (1991). *Informal reasoning and education.* Hillsdale, NJ: Lawrence Erlbaum Associates.

Voss, J.F., Vesonder, G.T., & Spilich, G.J. (1979). Text generation and recall by high knowledge and low knowledge individuals. *Journal of Verbal Learning and Verbal Behavior, 6,* 651-667.

Vye, N. J., Goldman, S. R., Voss, J. F., Hmelo, C., Williams, S., & Cognition and Technology Group at Vanderbilt. (1997). Complex mathematical problem solving by individuals and dyads. *Cognition and Instruction, 15,* 434-484.

Walton, D. (1982). *Topical Relevance in Argumentation.* Amsterdam: John Benjamins.

Walton, D. N. (1992). *Plausible Argument in Everyday Conversation.* Albany, NY: State University of New York Press.

Walton, D.N. (1989). *Informal Logic.* Cambridge: Cambridge University Press.

Wan, D., & Johnson, P.M. (1994). Experiences with CLARE: a Computer-Supported Collaborative Learning Environment. *Proceedings of the 1994 ACM Conference on Computer Supported Work*, Chapel Hill, North Carolina.

Webb, N.M. (1991). Task-related verbal interaction and mathematics learning in small groups. *Journal for Research in Mathematics Education, 22* (5), 366-389.

Weck, G. de (1991). *La cohésion dans les textes d'enfants. Etude du développement des processus anaphoriques* [Cohesion in children's texts. Study of the development of anaphoric processes]. Neuchâtel: Delachaux et Niestlé.

Weck, G. de, & Schneuwly, B. (1993). Anaphoric Procedures in Four Text Types Written by Children. *Discourse Processes, 17 (3),* 465-477.

Weiss, D.M., & Sachs, J. (1991). Persuasive strategies used by preschool children. *Discourse Processes, 14*, 55-72.

Wenzel, J.W. (1979). Jürgen Habermas and the dialectical perspective on argumentation. *Journal of the American Forensic Association, 16* (2), 83-94.

Wenzel, J.W. (1980). Perspectives on argument. In: J. Rhodes & S. Newell (Eds.), *Proceedings of the 1979 Summer Conference on Argument* (pp. 112-133). Falls Church: SCA.

Wijk, van C. (1995). *Levels of competence in writing*. Presented at the 5th European workshop on natural language generation, Leiden.

Wilkins, M. C. (1928). The effect of changed material on the ability to do formal syllogistic reasoning. *Archives of Psychology, 16*.

Willard, C.A. (1979a). The epistemic function of argument: reasoning and decision-making from a constructivist/interactionist point of view. *Journal of the American Forensic Association, 15*, 169-191.

Willard, Ch.A. (1979b). The epistemic function of argument: reasoning and decision-making from a constructivist/interactionist point of view (Part II). *Journal of the American Forensic Association, 15*, 211-220.

Willard, Ch.A. (1983). *Argumentation and the Social Grounds of Knowledge*. Alabama: The University of Alabama Press.

Willard, Ch.A. (1989). *A Theory of Argumentation*. Tuscaloosa etc.: The University of Alabama Press.

Witte, S.P., & Cherry, R.D. (1986). Writing processes and written products in composition research. In C.A. Cooper, & S. Greenbaum (Eds.), *Studying Writing: Linguistic Approaches* (pp. 112-153). Beverly Hills etc.: Sage. Written Communication Annual. An International Survey of Research and Theory 1.

Wittgenstein, L. (1980). *Culture and Value*. G.H. von Wright (Ed.). Oxford: Basil Blackwell.

Woods, J., & Walton, D. N. (1982). *Argument: The Logic of the Fallacies*. Toronto: McGraw-Hill Ryerson.

Woods, J., & Walton, D. N. (1989). *Fallacies: Selected Papers, 1972-1982*. Dordrecht/Providence: Foris Publications, PDA 9.

Woodworth, R. S., & Sells, S. B. (1935). An atmosphere effect in formal syllogistic reasoning. *Journal of Experimental Psychology, 18*, 451-460.

Zammuner, L. (1991). Children's Writing of Argumentative Texts: Effects of Indirect Instruction. *European Journal of Education, 6* (2), 243-256.

Zammuner, V. L. (1987). For or against: The expression of attitudes in discourse. *Text, 7*, 411-434.

Zammuner, V.L. (1995). Individual and cooperative computer-writing and revising: Who gets the best results? *Learning and Instruction*, 101-124.

Zarefsky, D. (1995). Argumentation in the tradition of speech communication studies. In F. H. van Eemeren, R., Grootendorst, J. A. Blair, & C. A. Willard (Eds.), *Perspectives and Approaches* (pp. 32-52). Proceedings of the Third International Conference on Argumentation. Vol. 1. Amsterdam: Sic Sat, 5A.

SUBJECT INDEX

academic discussions 55
acceptability 10, 27, 48, 61-63, 65, 67, 68, 90, 94
  of a statement 90
  of reasons 4
  of the reason 32
acceptable reasons 12
acceptable to the addressee 86
accuracy of argument understanding 98
active open-mindedness 89
addition 68
  compensation 72
  confirmation 72
  transformation 65
addressee 7, 9, 10, 137, 167
addressee's acceptability 90
  familiarity 6
  interests 6
  opinions 4
  representation 138
adequate presentation 62
adversative connectives 122
affective cues 208
aim of argumentation 3
allocutary mark 162
alpha-omega paradigm 22, 23
alpha-omega task 126, 128
alpha-orientation 24
alpha-thematization 24
American academic debate 53
American Forensic Association 56
analysis of argumentation structures 56
  of fallacies 48
analytic overview 61, 62, 64, 66, 68, 69, 73
  of argumentation 59, 60
analytic transformation 60, 62, 65, 66, 68
  of deletion 63
  route 62
analyzing argumentative texts 100
anaphora 19, 20
anaphoric references 119
  reprises 129
anchoring 153, 156, 159
  choice 162

operations 154
antagonist 50, 70
anticipation of counterarguments 81
appropriateness 10
  of a reason 92
appropriativity 5
arguers' attitudes and beliefs 91
arguing 26
argument acceptability 12
  checking processes 208
  elaboration 204
  generation 100
  knowledge 103
  model 16
  representation 113
  structure 94, 119
argumentation 15, 29
  based on the dissociation of elements 47
  based on the structure of reality 46
  establishing the structure of reality 46
  perspective 15
  phase 181, 194
  processes 204
  schemes 46, 48
  stage 51
  structure 70, 204
  theory 43
argumentative attack 192
  competence 77
  connectives 121, 122
  connectors 51
  constraints 8, 21, 23
  defense 192
  dialogue 5, 138, 204
  direction 51
  discourse 50, 149
  incapacity 148
  interaction 179, 181, 192, 194, 198-200, 201
  letter 151
  operator 51, 52
  orientation 9, 23, 25
  power 51
  principles 51
  process 14, 19

processing 156
prototypes 151
requirements 25
schema 15, 117, 121, 123-126, 129, 131, 133, 134
sequence 133, 135
situation 4, 8, 81, 94
skills 82
square 120
strategy 54, 144, 152, 154, 155, 159, 161, 162, 163, 165, 167
structure 9, 127, 132, 167
text 6, 131, 133
utterances 222
writing 88, 129
argumentativity 52
assertion 102, 186
assisted insertion task 122
substitution task 122
Association for Informal Logic and Critical Thinking 56
assumptions 116
asynchronous discussion systems 217
modes of communication 228, 229
network-tool 219
attentional resources 121
attenuation conditionals 141, 142
attitudes 89
attributes arguers 93
audience acceptability 90, 91, 94
authorized debate 141
automatic recovery of ideas 9
retrieval 9
automatization 19, 135
axiological value judgment 142

background knowledge 99
backing 14, 45, 46
beginning-end task 128
beliefs 77, 83, 85, 116, 208
Belvédère 213, 220, 221, 223, 224, 226, 227, 228
benefits 97
bias 78, 82, 86, 116
biased behavior 210
Biased Simpling Model of Discussion 210

causal conjunctions 130
relationships 122
thinking 13
central route 208, 228
chaining of arguments 204
chatting tool 218
checking processes 209
claim 3, 8, 14, 15, 45, 100, 220
CLARE 213, 219, 221, 222, 223, 224, 225, 228
clarification questions 208
clarify 35
clarity 72
clarity rule 67
classical rhetoric 52
classification of argumentation schemes 56
closing phase 183, 194
CMC 211, 213, 224
co-construction 180
of knowledge 184
cognitive activities 3
development 15, 139
dissonance 189
effect 179, 181, 185
load 15
overload 25, 28, 135
processes 227
representation 17, 179
structures 118
coherence 4, 40, 119, 121, 122, 125, 130, 134
coherent argumentation 13, 22
presentation of opposing points 130
cohesion devices 20
markers 119
collaboration 7
collaborative argumentation 203, 205, 211, 224, 226, 227
argumentative text production 7
discussion 223
distance writing 218
knowledge construction 219
learning 179, 185
learning situations 7
problem solving situations 199
problem solving 180, 181, 186, 198, 204, 228

task 131
text processing 218
writing 15, 124, 131, 149, 150, 167
collective argumentation 90
  norms 140
  valid statements 90
commitment rules 213, 214
  set 48
common frame of reference 7, 16
  principles 85
  values 143
communication tool 217
communicational context 206
communicative constraints 153
  goal 4, 17
  interaction 179, 181, 192, 199, 200, 201
  purpose 137, 139, 143, 149, 150, 152, 155
  rationality 54
  rules 66, 67
  situation 10
  structuration 152
communicatively debatable topics 146
competent argumentative reasoning 87
competitive instructions 227
completeness 78, 82, 86
complex moral justifications 6
  reasoning 6
  syntax 19, 20
complexity of argument understanding 98
comprehensibility 61, 62, 63, 65, 67, 68
  of arguments 98
compromise 4, 109, 110, 111, 143, 190, 197, 207
compromisers 115
compromises 200
computer assistance 131
Computer Mediated Communication 205, 210
computer-assisted text composition 130
conceptual devices 4
  differentiation 192
  dimension 184, 185, 188, 190, 200
  planning 21
conceptualization 20
  process 25
concession 15, 129, 152, 186, 190, 194
  form 155
  mark 155
  operations 138
concision 69
concluding 70
  stage 51
conclusion 88, 120
Confcrcncc MOO 213, 215, 217, 221-223, 227, 335
confidence ratings 224
confirmation of deletion 64
  of non-deletion 64
conflict 8
  intervention 6
  resolution 104, 116
  situations 186
  talk 76, 102
conflicting beliefs 227
  opinions 211
confrontation 70
  stage 51
congruency effects 6
connectives 19, 20, 26, 117, 119, 121, 122, 129, 130
  of concession 129
consensus to win 211
contraindications 204
constrained writing tasks 126
construction of argumentative texts 61
constructive interaction 179, 180, 184, 200
constructivism 54, 204
constructivist learning theory 203
content dimensions 75, 94
  elaboration 154
  generation 22
  memory 115
  space 13
context 94
  of production 127
contextual constraints 153
  dimension 75, 77, 91, 94, 133
  factors 127
contrast 35

control of social relationships 98
  of turn taking 228
controversial issue 33
conversational argument 51
convince 4
cooperative goal-oriented activity 180
  problem solving task 184
  problem solving 6, 16
  writing 6, 121, 130
cooperativity 6
coordinating arguments and counterarguments 126
coordination 19, 130
co-orientation of arguments 23
counterargument 17, 32, 78-81, 83, 84, 86, 89, 91, 92, 94, 100, 119, 121, 154, 155, 204, 208
counterargumentation 8, 15, 86, 87, 138, 145
counterargumentative discourse 142
counter-discourse 144
credibility 100
criteria for good argument 75, 90
critical argumentation 212
  assessment of new information 211
  checking of new information 207
  checking procedures 226
  checking 204
  control 150
  discussion 50, 60, 61
  epistemology 11, 86, 87
  evaluation of information 205
  reasoning 76, 87
  thinking skills 213
critique of information 205
critiquing 220
CTP system 213, 218, 221, 222, 223, 226

data 45, 221
datum 45
debatability 4, 7, 26, 137, 144, 147
debatable 8, 26, 137, 138, 191
  referent 139
  topics 26
debate situation 144
decision making 40, 101
deconstruction 180

deductive reasoning 30
  rules 3
defence 102
definition of argumentative texts 76
  of argumentation 43
degree of familiarity 145
deletion 60
  confirmation 72
  introduction 64, 67, 70
  transformation 65
deletion-compensation 67
deletion-confirmation 66
deontic modality 159
descriptive approaches 85, 94
  dimension 43, 44
  text 131
descriptivists 56
desires 83
determinants of argumentative discourse 137
  of discourse acceptability 138
Devil's advocate experiment 81
diagrammatic organization 14
Dialab system 213, 221, 222, 224, 227
dialectic 50, 53
dialectical approach 181
  dimension 185, 189, 190, 201
  framework 198
  model 186, 194
  moves 194
  outcomes 192
  processes 192
  refutation 196
  roles 201
  rule 195
  stages 70
  theory 201
dialectics 199
dialogical dimension of argumentation 120, 129
  perspective 134
dialogue 203
  game 213
  history 224, 227
  logic 47, 54, 55
  management 224, 225
  markers 206
  move 213, 214, 224, 226-228

rules   206, 214, 225
difference of opinion   70
differentiation   188
dimension of argumentative orientation   133
disagreement   7, 15, 102, 108, 111
disarrangement   62
discourse   201
    production   17
discursive logical operations   53
    negotiation   13, 27, 137
    orientation   119
discussible   211
discussion of the conflict   105, 114
dispositio   17
dispositions   89
    arguers   93
dissociation   46
distance   152
distanciated positions   140
distancing from the discourse   142
dominant social positions   138
doxa   141, 166
    voice   163
dual structures   127
dyadic interactions   131

early emergence hypothesis   97
EAT   8, 11, 12, 17, 20, 21, 27
effective argumentation techniques   46
effective argumentative communication   5
efficiency rule   68
efficient argumentation   12
egocentric   90, 140
elaborate   35
elaborated argumentation   1, 7, 15, 17, 26, 87, 119, 138
elaborated argumentative text   1, 6, 8, 20, 21, 25, 28, 88, 117, 135
    writing   27, 87
elaborated discourse   140
    text   21, 27, 129, 145
elaboration   226, 227
    of a theme   135
    of the arguments   228
Electronic Discussion System   210
electronic environments   204

text production   8
embedded texts   127
embedding   15
emotion   101
end statement of goals   110, 111
enunciation   153, 156
    constraints   166
    markers   20
    modality   161
    processes   138
    sources   16
    strategies   7
enunciative change   159, 161
    choices   153
    configuration   153, 159, 162
    level   153, 162
    management   154, 165
    modality   162, 167
    modification   159
    operation   138, 151, 153, 156, 162
    option   161
    procedures   152
    processes   141
    strategies   149, 153, 154, 156, 157, 158, 162, 165
    structure   167
enunciator   163, 165
epilinguistic evaluations   151
epistemic effect   187
    mode   158
    status   197
epistemological continuum   86
    dimension   184, 185, 187, 188, 190
    stances   196
    understanding   89
errors of cohesion   135
ethnomethodological   151
ethos   34
evaluate the argumentative orientation
    of statements   130
evaluation   21, 27
    of argumentative text   29, 40
    of arguments   11, 39
    of ideas   2
    of social relationships   98
    process   17
everyday argument   88, 116
    discourse   53

disputes 98
　emotional contexts 101
　reasoning 76, 82
　settings 100
　tasks 41
evidence 14, 100, 220
expected final product 211
experimental setting 79, 81
expert knowledge 13
　performance 37
experts 15, 39
explanatory dialogue 189
　discourse 139
explicit conclusion 120
　negotiation 192
exploration of multiple perspectives 207
exploration phase 219
extended text 8
extra-logical dimensions 76

face-to-face communication 205, 224
　condition 106
　interaction 103-105, 107
factual appraisals 112
failed texts 126
failure text 145
fallacies 43, 48, 49, 51, 55
　of ambiguity 49
fallacy 88
familiar topic 5, 6, 7, 144
field-dependent elements 45
field-invariant elements 45
fixed conclusion 121
　opposing position 121
flawed proposals 198, 199
focus maintenance 227
formal argumentative analysis 100
　aspects of argumentation 132
　dialectics 49, 186
　logic 44, 55, 99, 104
　logic-based context 29
　operations stage 148
　reasoning 11, 87, 137
　repertoire 88
　task situation 30
　validity 87
formality 69

foul move 186
free text 226, 228
free-association of ideas 14
free-text mode 217
French as a Foreign Language 151, 153
functional approach 1, 3, 4
　capacities of working memory 135
　constraints 10

generating argumentative text 35, 49
　content 153, 154
Geneva model 54
Geneva Psychological Model of Discourse Production 152
genuine evidence 87, 89
global organization of the text 131
goal driven 102
goal of the text 3
goal-oriented 38
goals in argumentation 94
　of argumentation 86
good argument 75, 86, 91-93
　reasoning 11, 86
　support 11
grammatical constraints 19
graphic argumentative dialogue acts 228
　dialogue moves 228
graphical argument structure 224
　argument 227
　dialogue 226
　marks 152
Grice's Cooperative Principle 66

hierarchical organization 18, 21, 119
　structure 13
high involvement topic 145
highly constrained tasks 121, 134
　productions 121
hinting 138
hypothesis 221, 223
hypothetical statements 186

idea evaluation 10
idea generation 1, 9, 21
　generation process 10, 17, 27
　organization in a text 13
　retrieval 9

ideal evaluation process   27
    selection process   27
identical deletion-compensation   64, 67
ideological constraints   141
illocutionary verbs   53
ill-structured problem solving task   220
ill-structured problems   35
implicit negotiation   192
implicitness   62
individual beliefs   143
    recomposition   124
inference processes   89
inferential chain   86
informal context   29
    logic   47, 48
    reasoning process   3
    reasoning   11, 41, 76, 78, 87, 137
    task situation   30
information checking   205, 212, 227
    processing model   30
inherent bias   97
initial reasons   115
    statement of goals   110
initiator of the argument   108
initiators of the discussion   109
injunctive modalities   162
insertion of connectives   121
instructive text   151
integration of goals   100
interaction   181, 200
    management   195
interactional moves   228
    negotiation   189
    pressure   201
interactive completeness   188, 189
    contexts   104
    dimension   184, 185, 189, 200
    knowledge construction   205
    pressure   188, 189, 194, 198, 201
interdisciplinary collaboration   55
interest   208
internalized dialogues   6
International Society for the Study of Argumentation   56
interpersonal relationships   98
interrogative modality   160
interro-negative modality   159
    proposition   160

interruption of the argumentative flow   130
intersentential organization   21
intrapersonal conflict   189
intrasentential organization   20
intrinsic properties of knowledge   187
introducing verb   164, 165, 167
involvement   144
    discourse   137
    of the speaker   160
involving topics   145
irony   138

joint product   227
justification   15, 45, 86, 119, 146, 205
    markers   146
    of viewpoints   76, 85
    process   14
justify one's point of view   122
justifying a favored position   102

knowledge base theory   148
    co-construction   184
    domain   187
    of the domain   4, 145
    to-be-retrieved   9
    transformation   13

lack of clarity   62
learning goals   205, 211
    situations   130
length of text   130
lexical choices   19, 21, 26, 153
    marks   152
lexicalization   19
linear marking   129
    organization   21
    sequence of information   17
linearization   2, 17, 21, 22
    of the information   119
    process   17, 19, 25, 27
linearizing-translating   28
linguistic coding   2, 17, 20, 21
    coding process   19
    constraints   153
    coordination   23
    devices   3, 4, 19, 20, 27, 137
    expertise   20, 26

indicators 138
means 55
procedures 134
relationships 15
skills 20
tools 128
linguistic-cognitive operation 188
local coherence 23
locus of argumentation 79
locutor's involvement in discourse 139
logic 53
logical cognitive processes 208
   coherence 100
   criteria 93
   errors 100
   reasoning 11, 104
   rules 12
   thinking 41
logic-based arguments 31
   deductive reasoning task 41
   tasks 31
logic-discursive schematization 3
logos 34
long-term memory 9

makes-sense epistemology 11, 86
marked enunciation 161
marks of negotiation 129
mediation talks 55
memory retrieval 112
mental schemas 13
   structures 97
metacognitive framework 89
   knowledge 91
   prompts 77, 78, 83, 91
metacomment 149, 151, 156, 157, 159, 161, 164
metacommunicative 151
metadiscursive 151
metagraphic 151
metalinguistic 151
   capacities 131
   comments 151
   marks 164
   pause 160
metasequence 161
microstructure of text 13
minimal argumentation 8

level 87
minimal argumentative operations 6
   structure 11
modal adverbs 53
modalization 26, 129
modalizing marker 158
   operations 151
model of a critical discussion 51
model of argument understanding 97, 98
model of good argument 88, 94
moderated discourses 145
modulated social position 147
modulation 14, 26
   of certitude 140
   of the position 142
   operations 138
modus ponens 31
   tollens 31
monological situations 120
MOO Conference System 226
moral codes 102
   dilemmas 12, 143
   gain 5
   obligation 141
   values 9
motivation 211
multidimensional conceptual structure 21
   structure 19, 27
multidisciplinary collaboration 55
Multiple Object-Oriented system 215
multiple perspective taking 205, 226
multiple perspectives 210, 211
multiple viewpoints 204, 226-228
mutual understanding 227
my-side arguments 78
   bias hypothesis 79
narration 20
narrative condition 111
   schema 117
   sequence 161
   text 118, 123, 131
   understanding 98
narratives 39
natural argumentation 11
   argumentative discourse 139
   logic 53, 57

naturalistic setting 79, 81
nature of knowledge 179, 188
negation 152
negative appraisals 112, 113
   negotiation function 138
   personal consequence 107
   reasons 97
negotiated discourse 142
   resolution 192
negotiation 55, 87, 99, 101, 102, 119, 157, 203, 205
   dimension 138
   function 142
   markers 142
   marks 88, 145
   operations 138
   process 212
   space 138, 191
neutral enunciation 161
   verbs 165
non-argumentative connectives 122
   texts 128
non-authorized debate 142
Non-deletion-confirmation 67
non-formal reasoning 54
non-identical deletion compensation 64, 67
non-polemic topic 10
nonverbal cues 221
normative approach 94, 85
   approach to argumentation 47, 54
   dimension 43, 44
   reconstruction 61, 62
   rules 12
   theorists 44
normativists 56
norms of argumentation 12
not debatable referent 139
novice reasoning 39
novices 39
number of nominalizations 130

omega thematization 24
omega-orientation 24
Ontario Society for the Study of Argumentation 56
open problem solving tasks 206, 211
open task 127

open-ended problem solving 203, 205
opening 70
   phase 181, 194
   stage 51
operational difficulty 121
operators 30, 37
opponent 81, 102, 186, 201
opponent's position 83, 97
opposing a position 114
   claims 8
   elements 92
   points of view 134
   position 84, 116
   reasons 107
   views 83
opposing-opinion task 128
opposite claim 8, 12
   standpoint 6
oral argument skill 98
   argumentation 104
   argumentative skill 99
   debates 132
   dialogue situations 140, 145
ordering statements 121
organization 1, 21, 22
   devices 19
   of argument knowledge 116
   of ideas 2
   of texts 15
   of the knowledge 104
   process 27
organizational structures 98
organizing process 13, 15
   strategies 14
orientation of arguments 10
original beliefs 227
other-side arguments 78
outcome of the conflict 105
outlined organization 14
outlines 14
own position 83

pair work 124, 131
   writing 130
paralinguistic cues 221
parameters of textual coherence 130
   of the situation 3
pathos 34

peer assistance 131
peripheral route 208
perlocutionary effects 187
permutation 61, 68
  confirmation 72
  transformation 65
personal beliefs 144
  individual dispositions 86
  knowledge 82
  pronouns 152
personally debatable topics 142
perspective of gain 6, 148
persuasion 33, 24
phenomenology 54
planning 2, 153
plausibility 140
  of the reason 32
plausible narratives 93
pluralistic approach 48
polemic 141
  topic 10
polemicity 7
policy making 55
politeness rule 106
polyphonic 7, 88, 165
  aspects 150, 151, 152
  choice 156
  discourse 88
  implementation 163
  management 163
  option 165
  orientation 154
  pre-occupation 154
  processing 156
  strategy 167
  work 167
polyphony 51, 149, 152
positive appraisals 112, 113
  benefits 102
  reasons 97
  value 116
practical reasoning 76
pragma-dialectic approach to argumentation 61, 90
  model 60
  rules 51
  theory 12
pragma-dialectics 48, 49, 56

pragma-linguistics 47
pragmatic aspects of argumentation 132
  component 28
  connectives 53
  constraints 3, 5, 7, 13, 166
pragmatical errors 151
pre-argumentation level 87
preconditions 8
predefined stances 212
preference 107
premise 88, 120
presence of counterarguments 135
present specific case 35
presentation addition 65
  deletion 65
  permutation 65
  substitution 65
presentation transformation 63, 66, 72
  of addition 68
  of permutation 68
  of substitution 68
  route 62
primary text 62, 64
principle of ownership 107
prior-knowledge 77, 82, 83, 114, 116, 208, 213
prior-thought 82
private contexts 104
probabilistic situation 33
problem context 208
  representation 216
problem solving 203
  operators 35
  perspective 15
  structure 35
problem space 207, 212
  state 207
  statement 35
problematology 54
problem-centered discourse 209
  moves 209
problem-minimization 209
procedural knowledge 16
procedures of modalizations 152
proficiency in language 10
profile of the addressee 150
proponent 186, 201

protagonist 50, 70
prototypical argumentative sequence 124
  schema of argumentation 14
  schemas 118
  sequences 120
  superstructure 120
provoke argumentation 206, 207, 227
  collaborative argumentation 206, 221
  discussion 224, 227, 228
pseudo evidence 87, 89
psycholinguistic operations 149
punctuation 19, 21, 129
purposes of participants 91

qualification 100, 204
qualifier 14, 45, 46
quality of arguments 93
  of the argumentation 16
quantity of knowledge 10
quasi-logical argumentation 46
question 220
radical argumentativism 51, 57
rational criticism 179
rationality 44, 99
real world contexts 98
reasonable argumentation 44
reasonableness 53, 90
reasoning 17, 26, 29, 33, 101
  operators 35, 40, 41
  process 19, 83
  structure 35
reasons for opposing a favored position 83
  an opponent's position 83
  each point of view 105
reasons for refuting a position 106
reasons for supporting a favored position 83
  a position 106
  an opponent's position 83
  each point of view 105
rebuttal 14, 45, 78, 83, 115, 204
recognition of opposing arguments 76, 85
  of the conflict 105, 106, 114
recognized disagreement 5

recomposition of argumentative text 123
  of text 117, 121
reconstruct an argumentative text 131
reconstructing knowledge 205
recursion 2
redundancy 62
references to the audience 155
referential content 167
  domain 3
  field 16
  planning 2
reflection-minded attitude 60
refutations 119, 131, 190, 194
  of counter arguments 4
  of position 107, 119, 190, 194
regulation 150
relevance 10, 32, 43, 48, 55, 208
  of information 212
relevant arguments 143
  information 61, 62
reliability of information 4
reorganization of a text 121
repercussions of the argument 105
  of a topic 140
  of argumentative discourse 137
  of the argumentative text 130
  of the audience 11
  of the topic 137 138, 139
requests 186
research program of informal logic 56
resolution 109, 183
  of the argument 112
  strategies in argumentation 75, 76
resolving a difference 50
  the conflict 105, 114
resource of knowledge 151
restriction-specification 145
restrictive marks 140
retraction 48
retrieval of arguments 10
retrieving process 10
revised text 62, 70
revising 2
revision processes 150
revisions 125
rewriting procedure 62
  the analytic overview 63

rhetoric 52, 53, 55, 199
rhetorical approach to argumentation 57
  argument structures 99
  changes 201
  dimension 185, 187, 189, 190
  space 13
  strategies 4, 13
  structures 98
role of negations 54
role-playing 227
  activities 211
  of conflicts 132
role-play instruction 79

scaffolding procedure 78
  technique 77, 78, 84
search processes 89
secondary enunciator 163
selection of ideas 2
  process 17
self-explanation effect 187, 190
semantic choices 21
  compatibility 131
  links 130
semi-constrained productions 121
  tasks 134
semi-structured interface 217
semi-success text 145
semi-successful texts 126
sentence formulation 21, 22
  openers 19, 206, 226-228
shared beliefs 137
  focus 207, 208
  understanding 224
simultaneous performance 135
situation model 16
  modelling 86
situational constraints 147
  context 33, 85, 162
  parameters 147
social acceptability 9
  codes 102
  context 85, 149
  dissension 53
  environment 140
  interaction 139
  positions 137

social-epistemological approach to argumentation 54
socially accepted values 141
  debatable topic 140, 142
sociocognitive conflict 203, 205
software 203
sound argumentation 44
soundness 87
  of reasons 13
source memory 115
  of the knowledge 197
sources of organization 13
space for negotiation 138, 155
speaker's mark 162
specific audience 11
  processing 5
specificity 69
specified interlocutor 12
speech act theory 54, 187
  acts 186
Speech Communication Association 56
spontaneous use of connectives 123
Standard Treatment 55
standards of sound argumentation 91
  of validity 88
stand-off 109-111, 113
standpoint 45
state argument 35
  assertion 35
  claim for defense 36
  claim for prosecution 37
  conclusion 35
  constraint 35
  disagreement 37
  evidence 37
  fact 35, 37, 38
  interpretation 36, 38
  need for search 36
  observation 36
  of the art 43
  outcome 35
  qualifier 35
  reason support defense claim 36
  reason supporting claim 37
  reason 35
  recapitulation 36
  solution 35
  strategy 36

subproblem   35
stock issues   53
strategic choice   161
   comments   155
   considerations   155
   control   10
   recovery of ideas   9
   selection of information   9
structure of argumentative texts   121
   of the argumentation   60
structured interaction   205
   interfaces   228
structuring dialogue acts   228
   interaction   224, 227
   of information   120
stylistic dimensions   69
subject involvement   148
subjective appraisals   112
   involvement   6
   value judgments   141
subordination   15, 19, 130
substantial conflict   205
substitution   61, 68
   confirmation   72
   transformation   65
successful defense   190
   texts   126, 145
succession of statements   130
sufficiency   10, 48
summarize   35
superstructures   118
support   35
   argument   228
   argumentation   206
   collaborative argumentation   206, 221, 224, 227
   of a position   102, 114, 115
supporting element   92, 143
   own position   103
   reason   32, 107
supports to arguments   78
syllogism   30, 33, 99
symbolic interaction   54
symmetrical condition   80
   interaction   213
synchronous communication   213
   modes of communication   228, 229
   network-tool   220

syntactic integration   135
   parameters   130
syntactical constraints   166
   marks   152
system of values   140
systematic rewriting   62

taking position   157
task assignments   15
   category   225
   environment   5
   features   77
   management   225, 226
   strategy   225
   type   223
task-dependent attentional resources   134
task-oriented behaviour   221
teaching tool   150
temporal connective   129
   marking   129
   mode   165
text genre   150, 151, 159, 162, 167
   linguistics   54
   organization   9
   schemas   118, 125, 149
text-based communication   221
   dialogue moves   228
textual coherence   130
   connectives   119
   constraints   21, 153, 166
   devices   19, 20, 27
   elaboration   129
   markers   126, 128
   models   4
   organization   4, 19, 135
   organizers   26
   requirements   23, 24
   thematization   25
textualization   149, 153, 161, 165, 167
   dimension   133
   indices   129
textualizing operations   19
thematic constraints   21
   continuity   20, 21, 24, 27
   elaboration   19
   organization   21
   quality of argumentative texts   127

structure   19
thematization   20, 23, 25
theory of argument knowledge   101
    of emotional understanding   101
    of logic   50
    of relevance   53
think aloud protocols   35
top-down strategies   15
topic   79, 82, 105, 114, 137
    continuity   21
    elaboration   9
    expertise   9
    familiarity   9
    of the argument   105
    structure   13, 16
topical fields   52
topic's debatability   140
topoi   8, 11, 12, 14, 27, 51-53, 141
topos   51, 52, 57, 141
training situations   134
    strategies   98
transformation   60
    of deletion   64
    of the analytic overview   66
translating   2, 17
    process   1, 13, 21
trial and error   124
turn-taking   224
    control   206, 227, 228
type of audience   91
    of interaction   77, 81
    of setting   77, 79
typology of texts   120

unassisted insertion task   122, 123
    substitution task   122, 123
unbiased argument   92
unconstrained writing   127
    productions   121
    writing task   117, 128, 129
unexpressed premises   12, 56, 71
unfamiliar topic   9
unidimensional structure   19
uninvolving topic   145
unstructured interfaces   228
use of conditionals   142
usefulness   10

validity   100
    of arguments   12
    of conclusions   41
value judgments   104, 142
values   77, 83, 85, 208
variations   151
varied elaboration   205, 207
Venn diagrams   100
veracity of facts   4
    of information   4
verb modality   165
verbal conflict   181, 198
voices of the others   152, 167

warrant   14, 45, 100
web-based discussion system   217
well-known topic   9
who initiated the argument   108
    the event   105
win-lose rules   214
win-loss   109, 110, 111, 113
    design   225
winners   115
writing argumentative texts   60
    process   59

NAME INDEX

Abelson 118
Adam 118-121, 124, 125, 127, 133, 144
Akiguet 88, 117, 119, 123, 125
Albro 98, 99, 102, 113
Allen 83, 88
Althoff 148
American Forensic Association 56
Andrews 132
Andriessen 118, 139, 210-212, 218, 222-224, 226
Anscombre 51-53, 57
Antolini 88, 127, 128
Apothéloz 119
Aristotle 35, 40, 99
Association for Informal Logic and Critical Thinking 56
Auchlin 53, 188
Austin 57, 201

Bain 152
Baker 179, 189-191, 194, 199, 201, 204, 205, 207-209, 211, 221
Baron 79, 86, 89
Barth 49, 51, 54, 56, 184, 186, 194, 201
Bassano 57
Bassok 187
Baudet 118
Beale 73
Bean 99
Benoit 54, 100, 102
Bereiter 207, 209
Bergh, Van den 59
Berkowitz 148
Bernard 211
Bernardi, De 88, 127, 128
Bernas 34, 75, 79, 83, 98, 101, 102, 115, 143, 210
Berninger 134
Bielaczyc 208, 209
Billig 77, 92
Biro 56
Blair 47, 48, 56, 82
Blais 185
Blaye 179
Boggs 100
Borel 53

Bouchard 151
Braet 53
Brandt 119
Brassart 117, 118, 121, 123, 124, 126, 128, 129, 132, 138, 144
Brna 190
Broaders 111
Broady 211
Brockriede 54
Bronckart 151, 152, 167
Brossard 139
Brown 98
Bruxelles 52
Bull 211
Bullock 69
Bunt 189, 208
Burleson 54, 56, 57
Burnett 205
Bushey 77, 82, 95

Cacclichia 210
Cacioppo 34, 208, 209
Calicchia 34, 75, 79, 83, 98, 101, 102, 115, 143, 211
Camps 151
C-CHENE 208
Centre des Recherches Sémiologiques of the University of Neuchâtel 53
Chaiken 34
Champaud 57, 118, 119
Chan 209
Chanquoy 123
Charolles 146
Cherry 59
Chi 187
Chittenden 100, 102
Clari 80
Clark 182
Clarke 132
Cognition and Technology Group at Vanderbilt 34
Cohen 199
Coirier 6, 87, 90, 117-119, 126, 128, 129, 132-135, 138-141
Condor 92
Coquin 138, 139
Coquin-Viennot 119
Corgan 56

Costello 132
Couzijn 59, 60
Crawshay-Williams 56

Daiute 130
Damer 56
Damon 150
Dausendschon-Gay 151
Davaud 152
David 150
Dearin 56
Dellerman 90, 134, 135
Denhière 118
Devi 190
Di Paolo 144, 147
Dijk, Van 118
Dillenbourg 179, 191, 229
DiPardo 150
DiSessa 188
Dolz 88, 130, 133, 151
Dorval 144, 147
Doxtader 57
Ducrot 51-53, 57, 141, 153, 187
Duffy 203, 204
Dunn 102

Eckerman 100, 102
Edwards 92
Eemeren, Van 44, 49-51, 56, 57, 60, 61, 66, 73, 85, 90, 94, 182, 185, 186, 201, 204
Ehninger 54
Eisenberg 100, 102, 113, 144, 147
Elbow 69
Erkens 130, 204-207, 209, 211, 218
Espéret 118, 130, 139

Farady 77, 82, 95
Farioli 124, 131
Farrell 52, 57
Fayol 118, 120, 150
Feilke 129
Ferréol 135
Festinger 189
Fincher-Kiefer 75, 143
Fisher 98
Flower 59, 167
Foss 52

Freedman 150
Freeman 56, 212
Fulkerson 100

Gane 92
Gaonac'h 118
Garcia-Debanc 150, 151
Gardenförs 188, 201
Garvey 100, 102, 144
Gaulmyn 151
Gelpe 139
Genishi 144, 147
Gere 150
Gilbert 100
Girardet 34
Giroud 151
Glaser 187
Glaserfeld, Von 203
Glenn 98
Goffman 53
Golden 56
Golder 86, 87, 117-119, 122, 123, 128, 129, 132-134, 138-141, 144-146, 185, 191, 199, 211
Goldman 34
Gombert 88, 117, 119, 120, 123-125, 127, 131, 133, 135, 150
Goodwin 102
Goodyear 199
Göttert 57
Gottman 99, 101
Gouran 54
Govier 56
Greene 35
Greeno 205
Grice 53, 57, 66, 181
Gronbeck 54
Grootendorst 44, 49-51, 56, 57, 60, 66, 73, 90, 182, 185, 186, 201, 204
Gross 34
Guercin 124
Gülich 151
Gundy 144, 147

Habermas 54, 57, 141
Hafner 83, 88
Hamblin 55
Hample 54, 56

Hastie 40
Hayes 59, 121, 134, 167
Healy 56
Henkemans 182, 185, 201, 204
Hightower 210, 212
Hillocks Jr. 73
Hmelo 34
Holmberg 104
Holowchak 185

International Society for the Study of Argumentation 56

Jackson 44, 51, 54
Jacobs 44, 51, 54
Jacobson 101
Janik 208
Jaspers 130, 218
Jermann 216, 222, 223, 225
Johnson 47, 48, 56, 82, 119, 212, 219, 222, 223, 225
Jones 76

Kellogg, 21, 134
Kerbrat-Orecchioni 138, 181
Kienpointer 53, 57
Kintsch 118
Kneupper 54, 99, 100
Kopperschmidt 53, 54, 57
Kowler 69
Krabbe 49, 51, 54, 56, 184, 186, 194, 201
Kraft 151
Kuhn 77, 78, 82, 83, 87-89, 92, 93, 100, 210

Lambelin 139
Lave 179, 181, 200
Learning Research and Development Center 220
Leech 66
Lehn, Van 187
Leinhardt 40
Levine 179
Levinson 66
Levy 121, 134
Lewis 187
Liwag 102

Lorenz 54
Lorenzen 49, 54, 56
Lund 221
Lundquist 57

MacKenzie 213
Maier 53
Mallen 205, 210
Mandl 179
Marchand 90, 126, 134, 135
Mason 206
Maynard 98, 100
McCleary 100
McCutchen 121, 134
McKerrow 52, 54
Means 83, 185, 210
Meyer 54
Middleton 92
Miéville 53
Miller 75, 76, 81, 83, 90, 98, 101, 102, 118, 119, 140, 144, 148, 208
Miyake 180
Moeschler 53, 121, 188, 201
Monteil 118
Moore, D 213, 222
Moore, M.G. 206, 221
Muntigl 201
Murray 73

Naess 73
Nancy 139
Nickerson 100
Nølke 57
Nonnon 187
Norman 118
Nystrand 150

Odoroff 40
Öhlschläger 57
O'Keefe 44, 54, 100, 102
Olbrechts-Tyteca 34, 46, 47, 56, 184
O'Malley 179
Ontario Society for the Study of Argumentation 56
Oser 148
Overeem 130, 218

Pasquier 133, 151, 152

Passerault 118, 119, 138, 139
Pea 206
Pélissier 121, 134
Penner 35
Pennington 40
Perelman 34, 44, 46, 47, 53, 56, 184
Perkins 77, 78, 82, 83, 86-89, 92, 95
Petty 34, 208, 209
Phelps 150
Piaget 139, 148, 203, 205
Pierault-Le Bonniec 138
Pilkington 205, 211
Pilotta 56,
Piolat 88, 117, 119, 121, 123-125, 131, 134, 135, 150
Plantin 119, 182
Pontecorvo 34, 179
Popper 56
Post 35
Pouit 191

Quasthoff 57
Quignard 199

Raccah 52
Radley 92
Ramage 99
Reboul 52, 53
Reimann 187
Reinard 56
Renkl 179
Rescher 99
Resnick 179, 185
Rest 99
Rieke 208
Rijlaarsdam 59, 60
Rogoff 77
Roschelle 204, 207
Ross 99, 102, 104, 113
Rottenberg 99, 100
Roulet 53, 188
Roussey 88, 117, 119, 121, 123-125, 131, 150
Rowland 54
Rubattel 53, 188
Rumelhart 118

Sachs 144, 147

Salmon 185
Salomon 203, 205
Sandak 39
Sandhya 98
Santos, C.M. 77-79, 81, 83, 84, 86, 88, 94
Santos, S.L. 80, 81, 94
Savery 203, 204
Sayeed 210, 212
Scardamalia 207, 209
Schaefer 180, 182
Schank 118
Scheaffer 187
Schelling 53, 188
Schneider 216, 222, 223, 225
Schneuwly 88, 118-120, 129-131, 138, 151, 152
Searle 57, 66, 201
Segal 87
Shantz 100, 102
Siegel 56
Silfies 75, 143
Speech Communication Association 56
Sperber 53
Stainton 40
Stein 34, 75, 79, 81, 83, 98-102, 104, 111, 113, 115, 118, 119, 143, 144, 148, 208, 210, 211
Stevens 150
Steward 69
Stone 199
Suchman 179
Suthers 211
Swanson 134

Teasley 179, 207
Tesla 102
Tiberghien 190, 199
Toulmin 34, 44, 45, 47, 54, 56, 76, 98, 100, 104, 119, 128, 185, 208, 226
Trabasso 98, 100, 102, 144
Trapp 52, 54
Traum 229
Trognon 186
Turnbull 201

Unité de Linguistique Française at the University of Geneva 53
Ury 98

Valette 138
Vasconcelos 88
Veerman 205, 210-212, 222-224, 226
Veevaert 132
Verbiest 57
Vignaux 54, 188
Vigner 145
Virji 40
Völzing 57
Voss 34, 35, 39, 75, 83, 87, 143, 185, 210
Vyc 34

Wallace 54
Walton 48, 49, 56, 184, 186, 188, 201
Wan 219, 222, 223, 225
Wathen 185
Weiner 211
Weiss 144, 147
Wenger 181
Wenzel 52, 54, 57
Wijk, Van 207
Wiley 39, 75, 143
Willard 54, 56
Williams 34
Wilson 53
Witte 59
Woods 48, 49, 56
Wright 34, 75, 98, 101, 102

Zammuner 34, 130, 131, 150
Zarefsky 54
Zeitz 185